THE QUEEN'S KNIGHT

The Queen's Knight Vol. 3

created by Kim Kang Won

Translation - Lauren Na
English Adaptation - Jeannie Anderson
Retouch and Lettering - Keiko Okabe
Production Artist - Vicente Rivera, Jr.
Cover Design - Jennifer Nunn

Editor - Julie Taylor
Digital Imaging Manager - Chris Buford
Pre-Press Manager - Antonio DePietro
Production Managers - Jennifer Miller and Mutsumi Miyazaki
Art Director - Matt Alford
Managing Editor - Jill Freshney
VP of Production - Ron Klamert
Editor-in-Chief - Mike Kiley
President and C.O.O. - John Parker
Publisher and C.E.O. - Stuart Levy

A  Manga

TOKYOPOP Inc.
5900 Wilshire Blvd. Suite 2000
Los Angeles, CA 90036

E-mail: info@TOKYOPOP.com
Come visit us online at www.TOKYOPOP.com

ISBN: 1-59532-259-0

First TOKYOPOP printing: March 2005
10 9 8 7 6 5 4 3 2 1
Printed in the USA

THE QUEEN'S KNIGHT

VOLUME 3

BY KIM KANG WON

HAMBURG // LONDON // LOS ANGELES // TOKYO

LAST TIME IN...

THE QUEEN'S KNIGHT

YUNA MAY BE THE QUEEN OF PHANTASMA, BUT HER HEART IS TORN BETWEEN RETURNING TO GERMANY AND MOVING FORWARD WITH HER NEW LIFE OF ROYALTY. THE DASHING KNIGHT RIENO WANTS HER TO REMAIN HIS QUEEN—WHEN THEY HAD MADE THEIR BLOOD-BINDING CONTRACT, EVIL SPIRITS WERE AWAKENED IN PHANTASMA...AND NOW THOSE DARK FORCES ARE APPROACHING THE CASTLE!

THE QUEEN'S KNIGHT

VOLUME 3

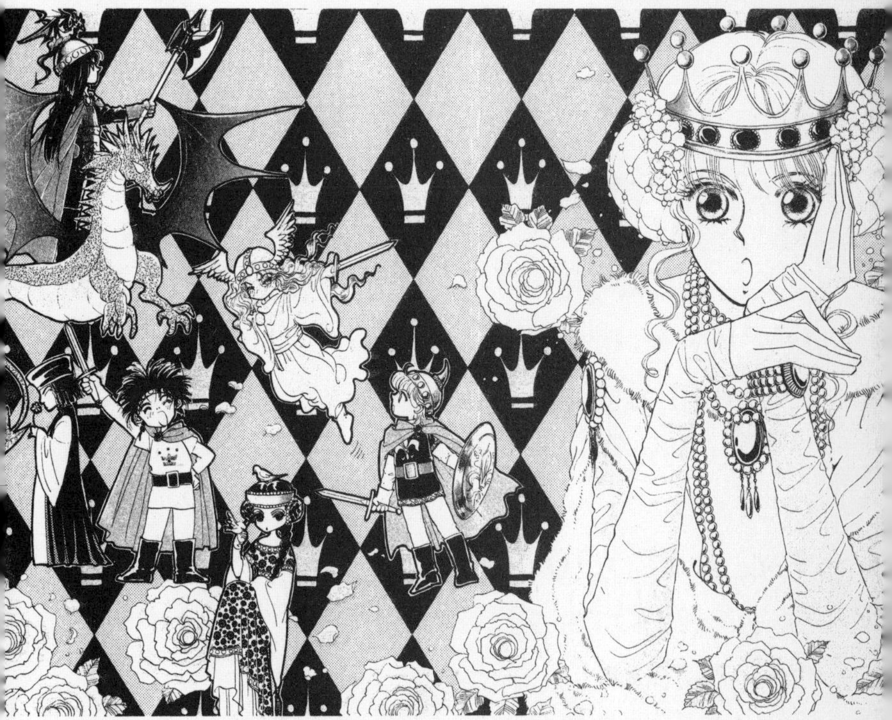

KIM KANG WON

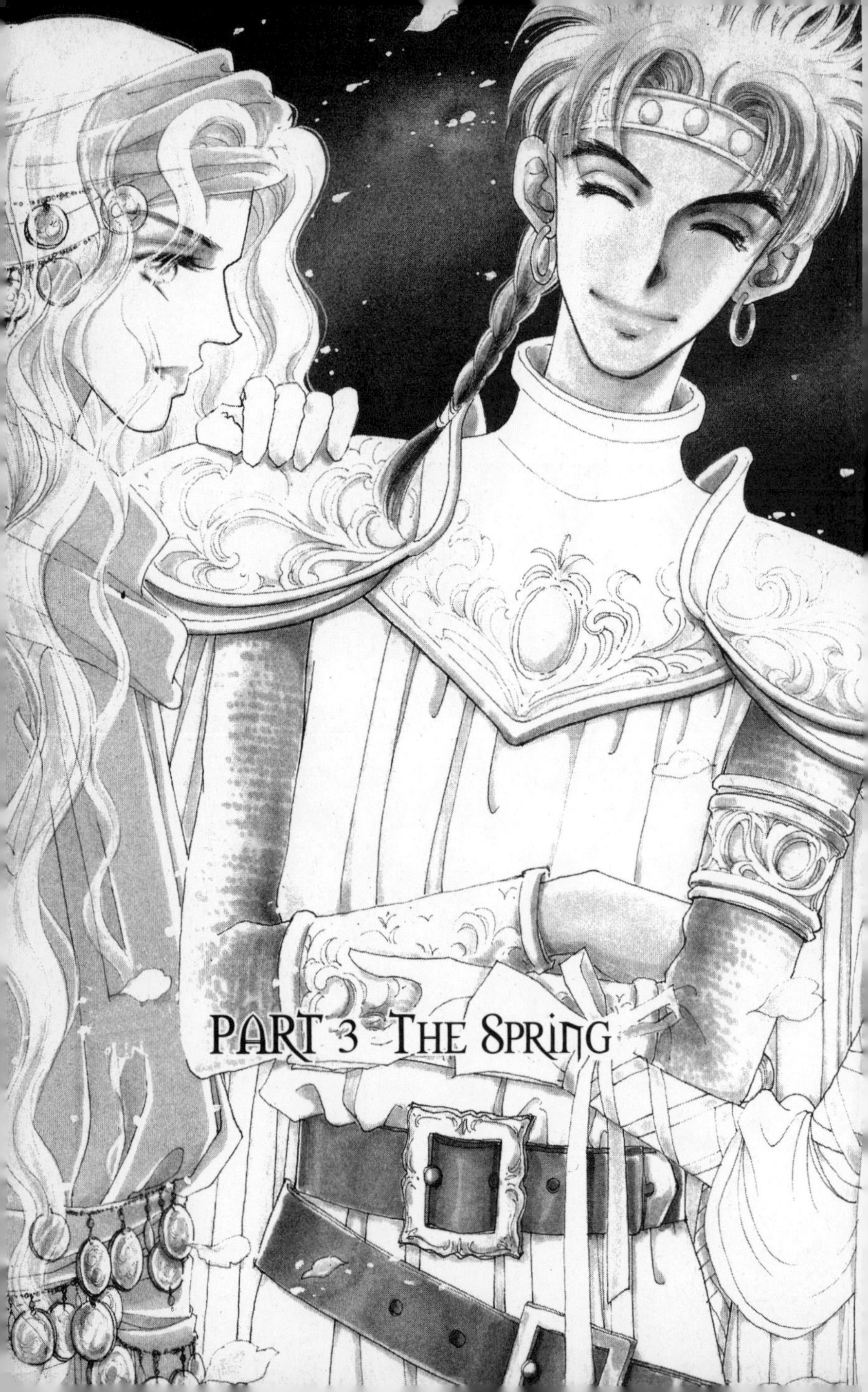
PART 3 THE SPRING

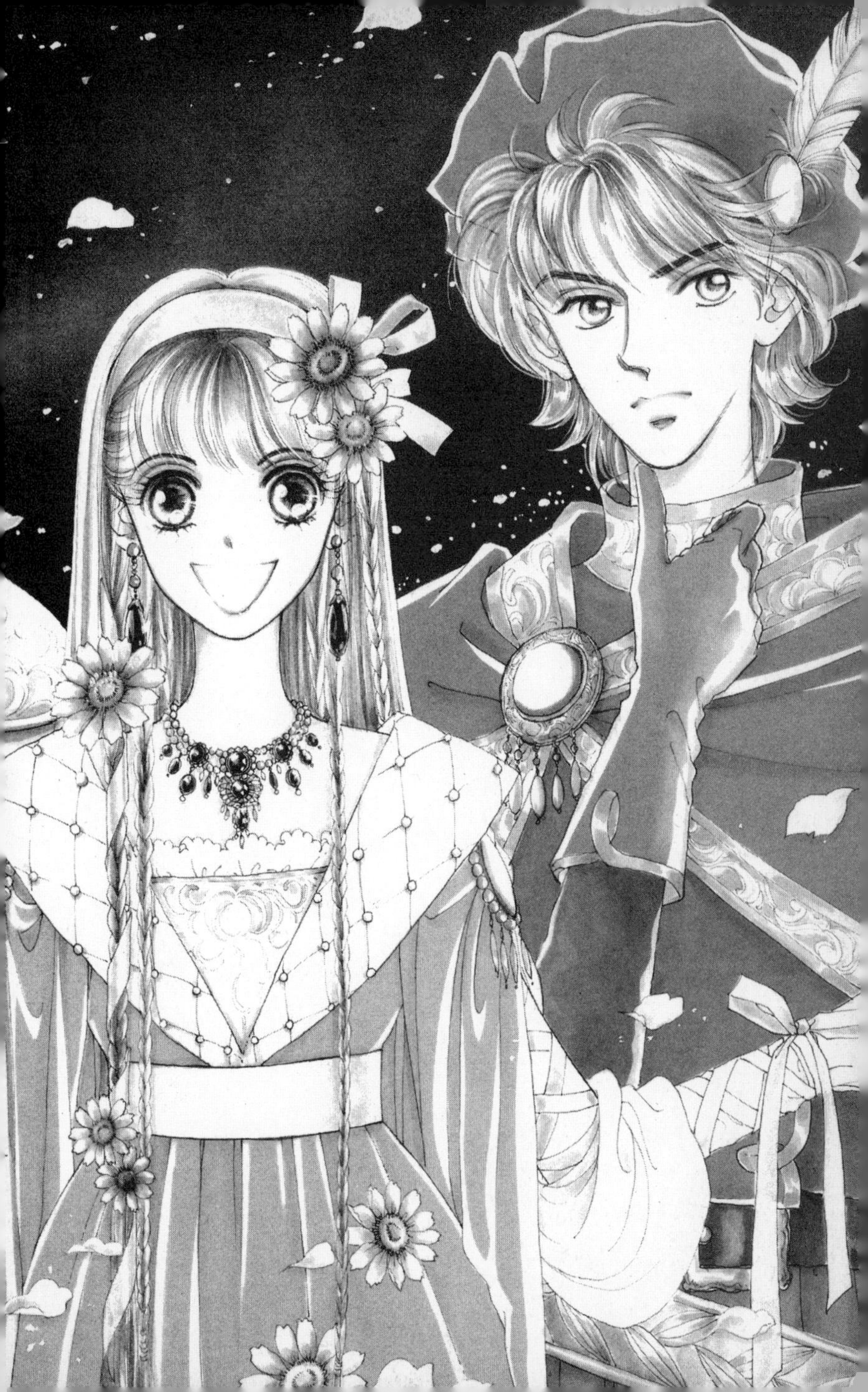

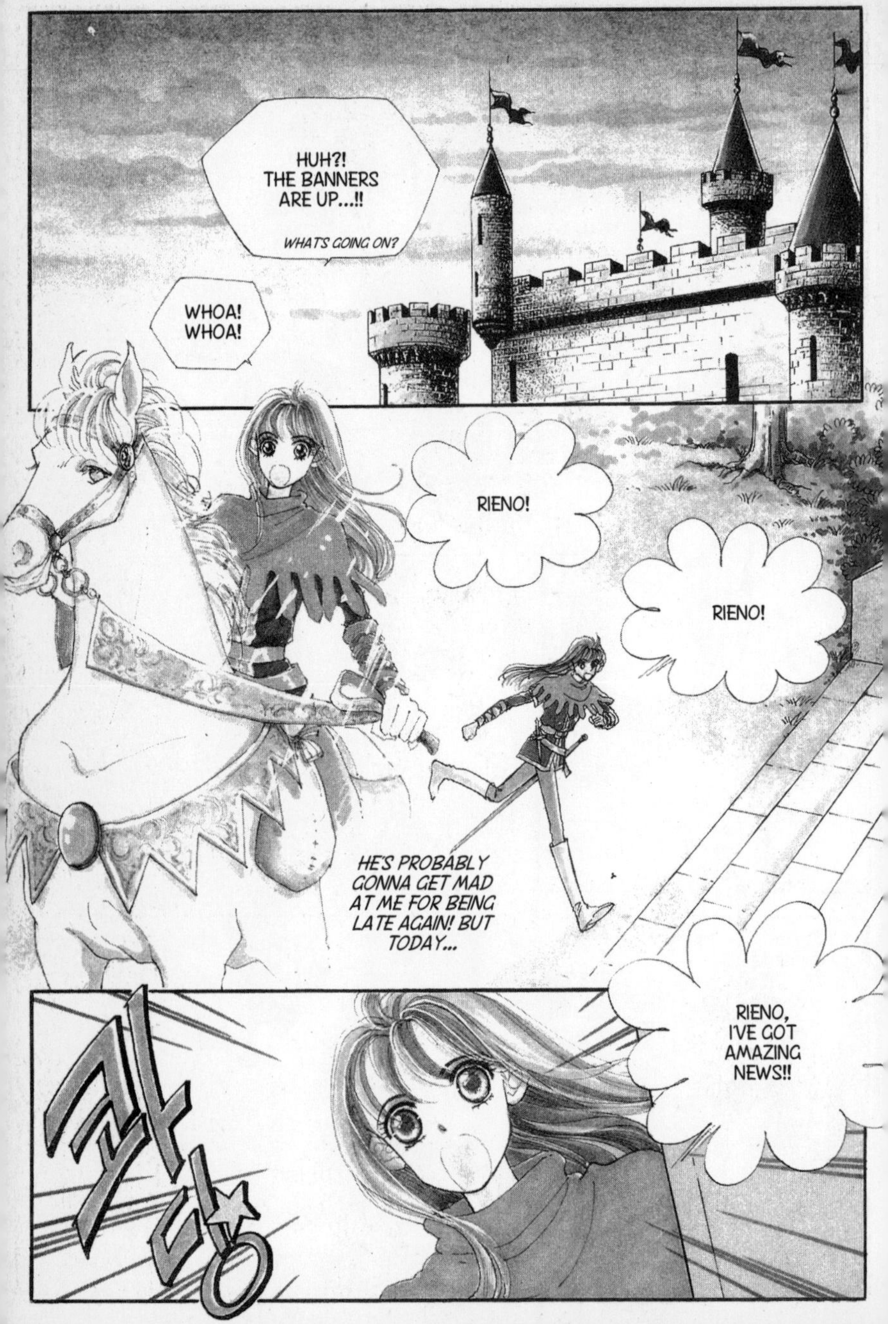
HUH?! THE BANNERS ARE UP...!!
WHAT'S GOING ON?
WHOA! WHOA!
RIENO!
RIENO!
HE'S PROBABLY GONNA GET MAD AT ME FOR BEING LATE AGAIN! BUT TODAY...
RIENO, I'VE GOT AMAZING NEWS!!

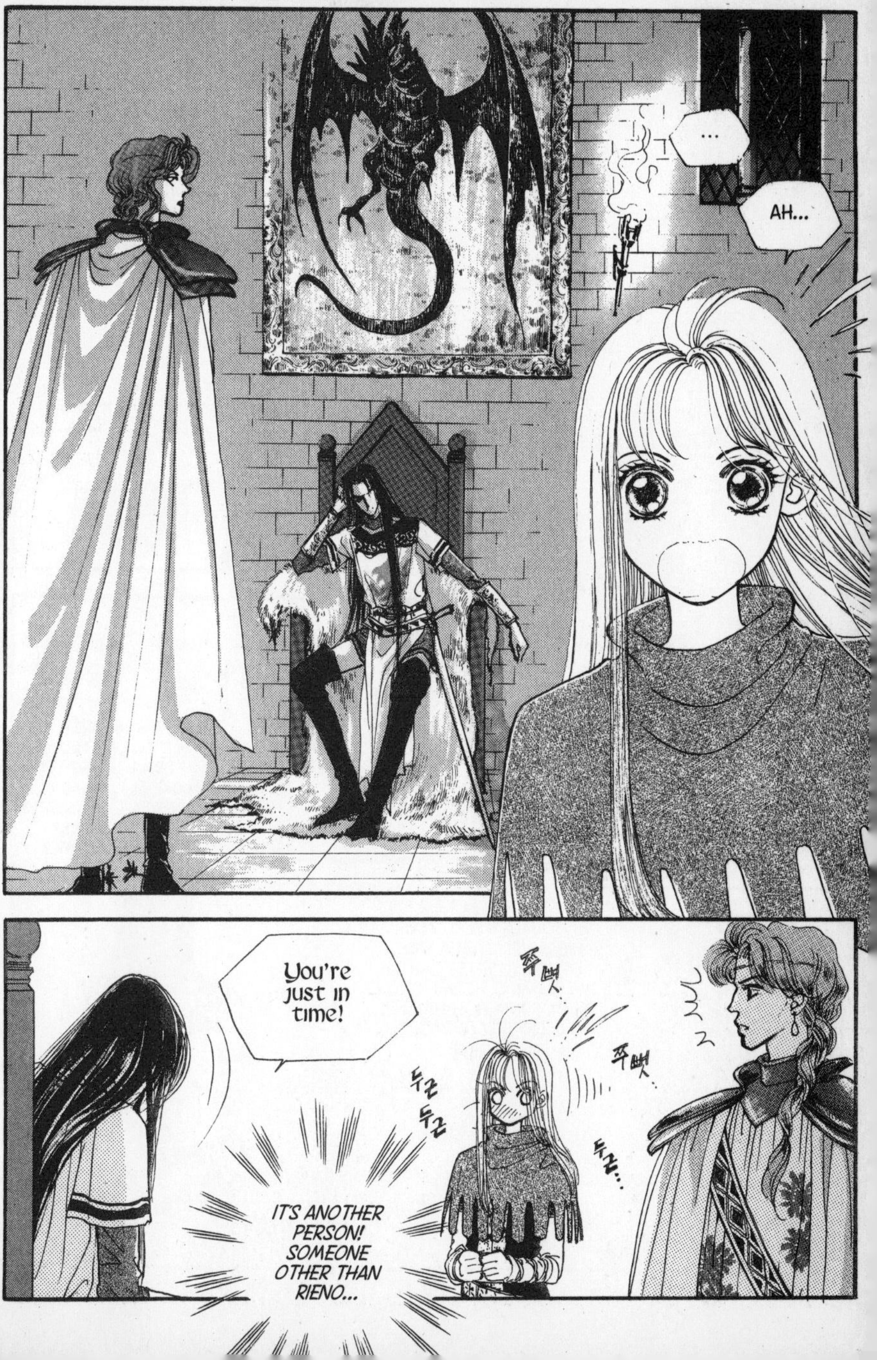
...
AH...
You're just in time!
두근 두근
쭈뼛...
쭈뼛...
두근...
IT'S ANOTHER PERSON! SOMEONE OTHER THAN RIENO...

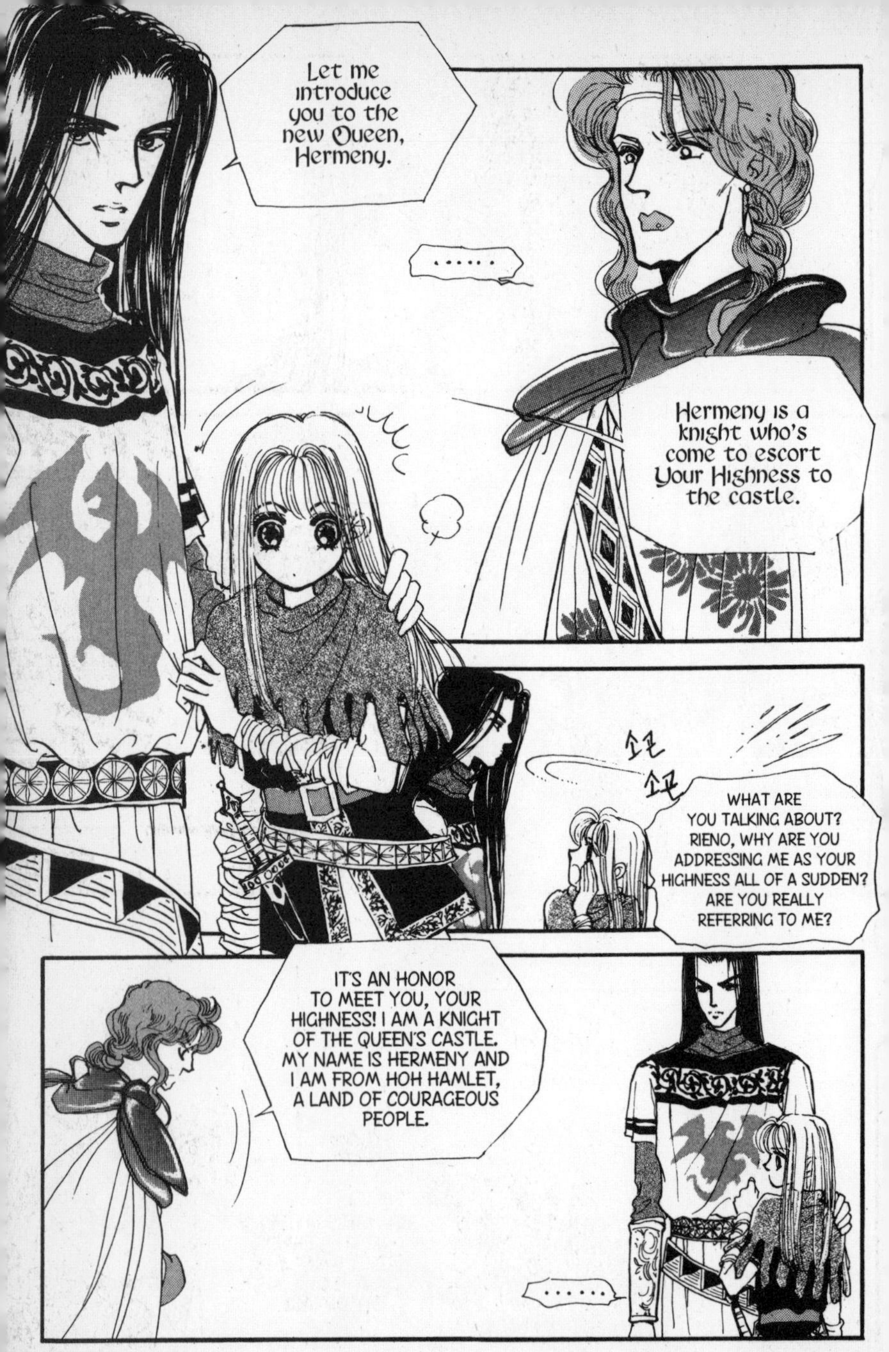
Let me introduce you to the new Queen, Hermeny.
......
Hermeny is a knight who's come to escort Your Highness to the castle.
WHAT ARE YOU TALKING ABOUT? RIENO, WHY ARE YOU ADDRESSING ME AS YOUR HIGHNESS ALL OF A SUDDEN? ARE YOU REALLY REFERRING TO ME?
IT'S AN HONOR TO MEET YOU, YOUR HIGHNESS! I AM A KNIGHT OF THE QUEEN'S CASTLE. MY NAME IS HERMENY AND I AM FROM HOH HAMLET, A LAND OF COURAGEOUS PEOPLE.
......

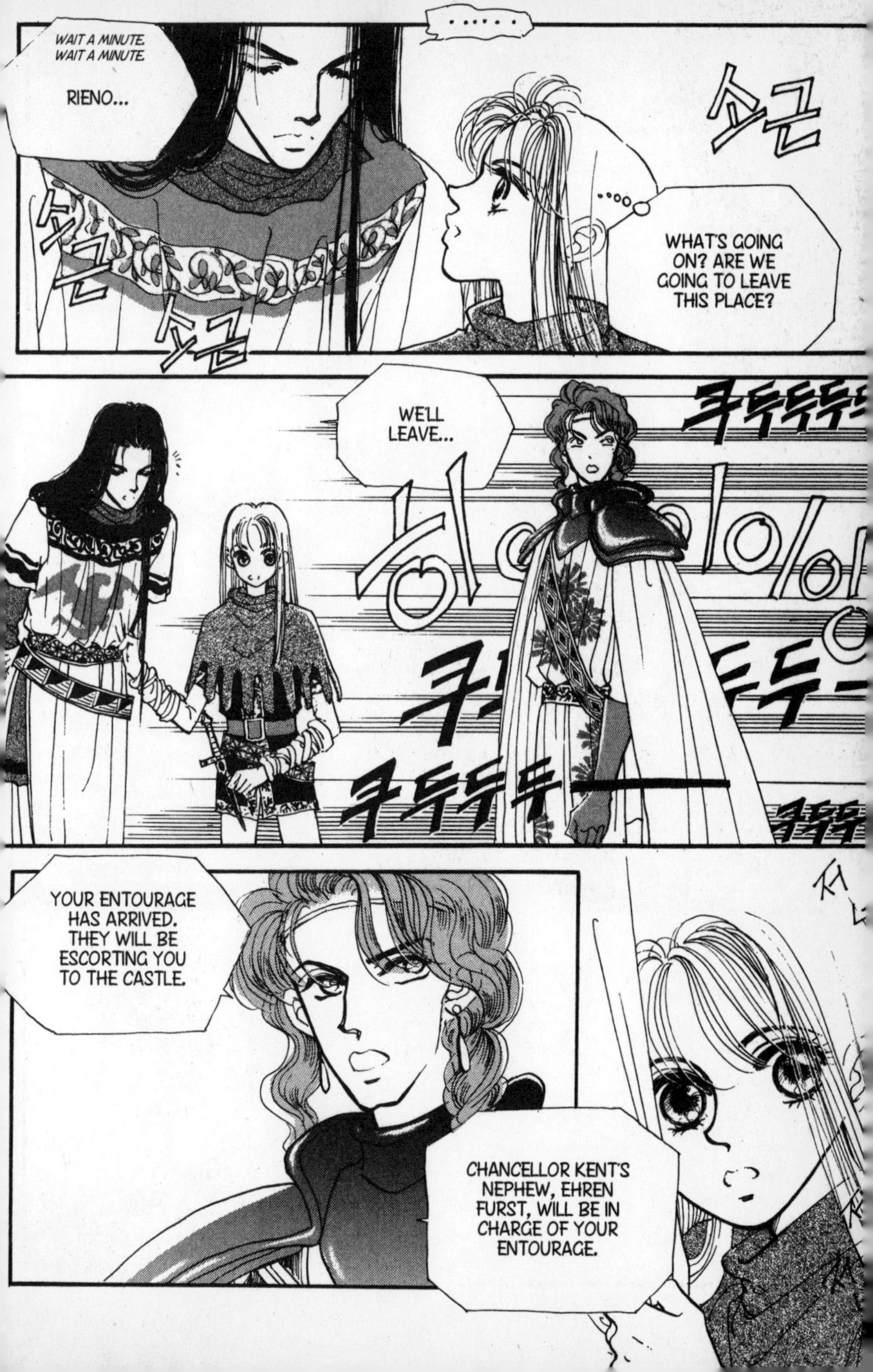

WAIT A MINUTE. WAIT A MINUTE.
RIENO...
......
WHAT'S GOING ON? ARE WE GOING TO LEAVE THIS PLACE?
WE'LL LEAVE...
쿠두두두
YOUR ENTOURAGE HAS ARRIVED. THEY WILL BE ESCORTING YOU TO THE CASTLE.
CHANCELLOR KENT'S NEPHEW, EHREN FURST, WILL BE IN CHARGE OF YOUR ENTOURAGE.

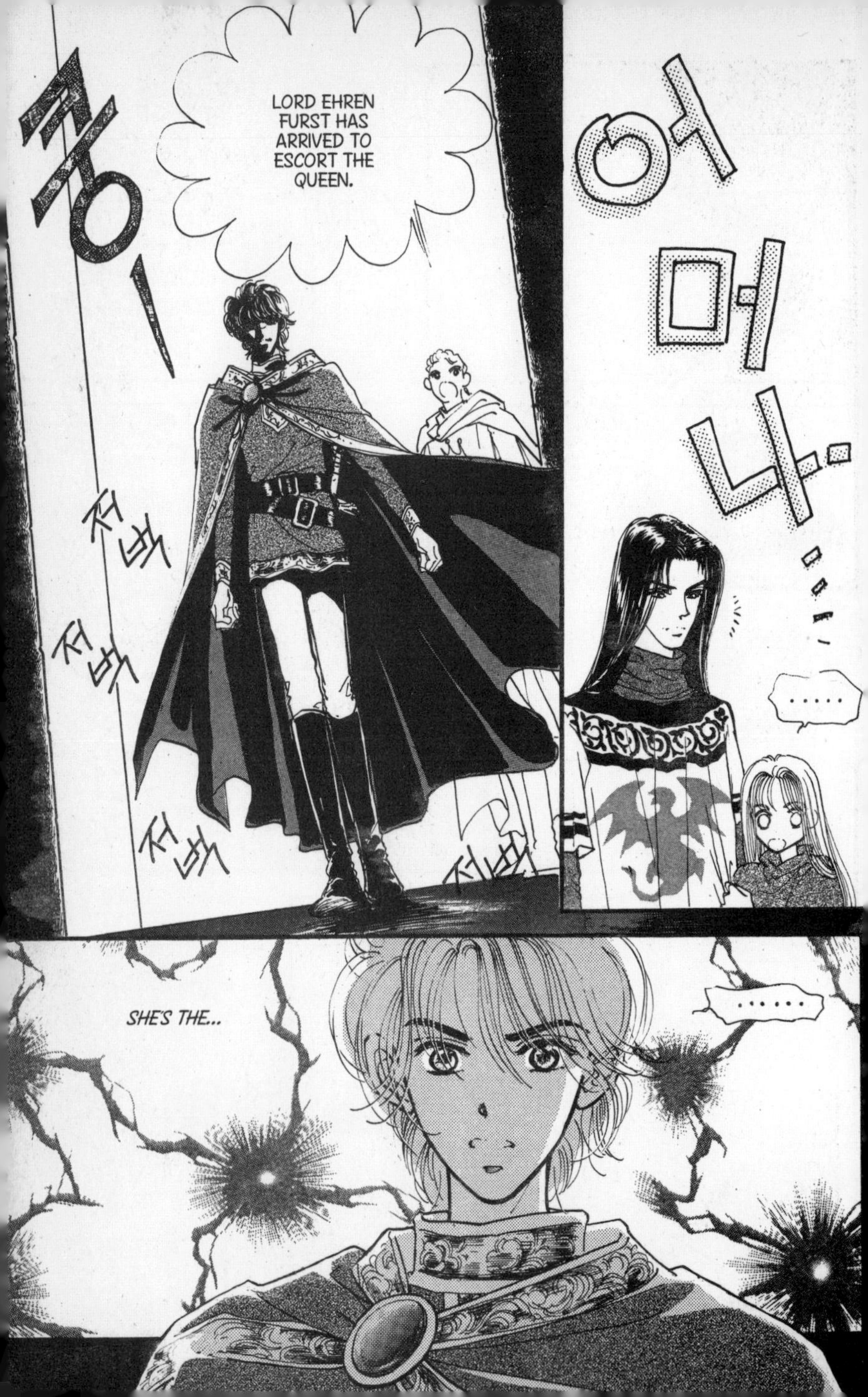
쿵
LORD EHREN FURST HAS ARRIVED TO ESCORT THE QUEEN.
저벅
저벅
저벅
저벅
어머나...
.....
SHE'S THE...
......

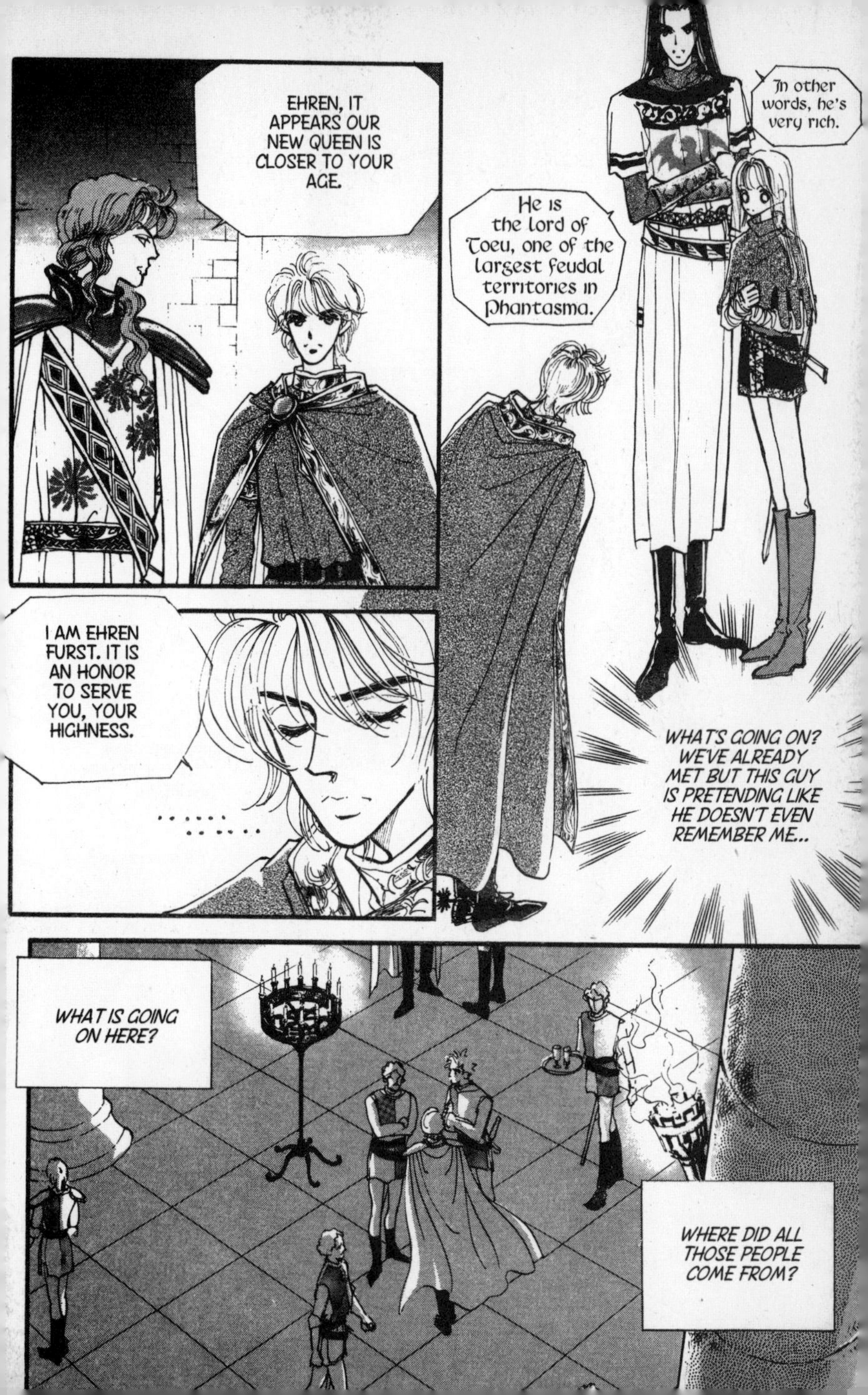
EHREN, IT APPEARS OUR NEW QUEEN IS CLOSER TO YOUR AGE.
I AM EHREN FURST. IT IS AN HONOR TO SERVE YOU, YOUR HIGHNESS.
......
He is the lord of Toeu, one of the largest feudal territories in Phantasma.
In other words, he's very rich.
WHAT'S GOING ON? WE'VE ALREADY MET BUT THIS GUY IS PRETENDING LIKE HE DOESN'T EVEN REMEMBER ME...
WHAT IS GOING ON HERE?
WHERE DID ALL THOSE PEOPLE COME FROM?

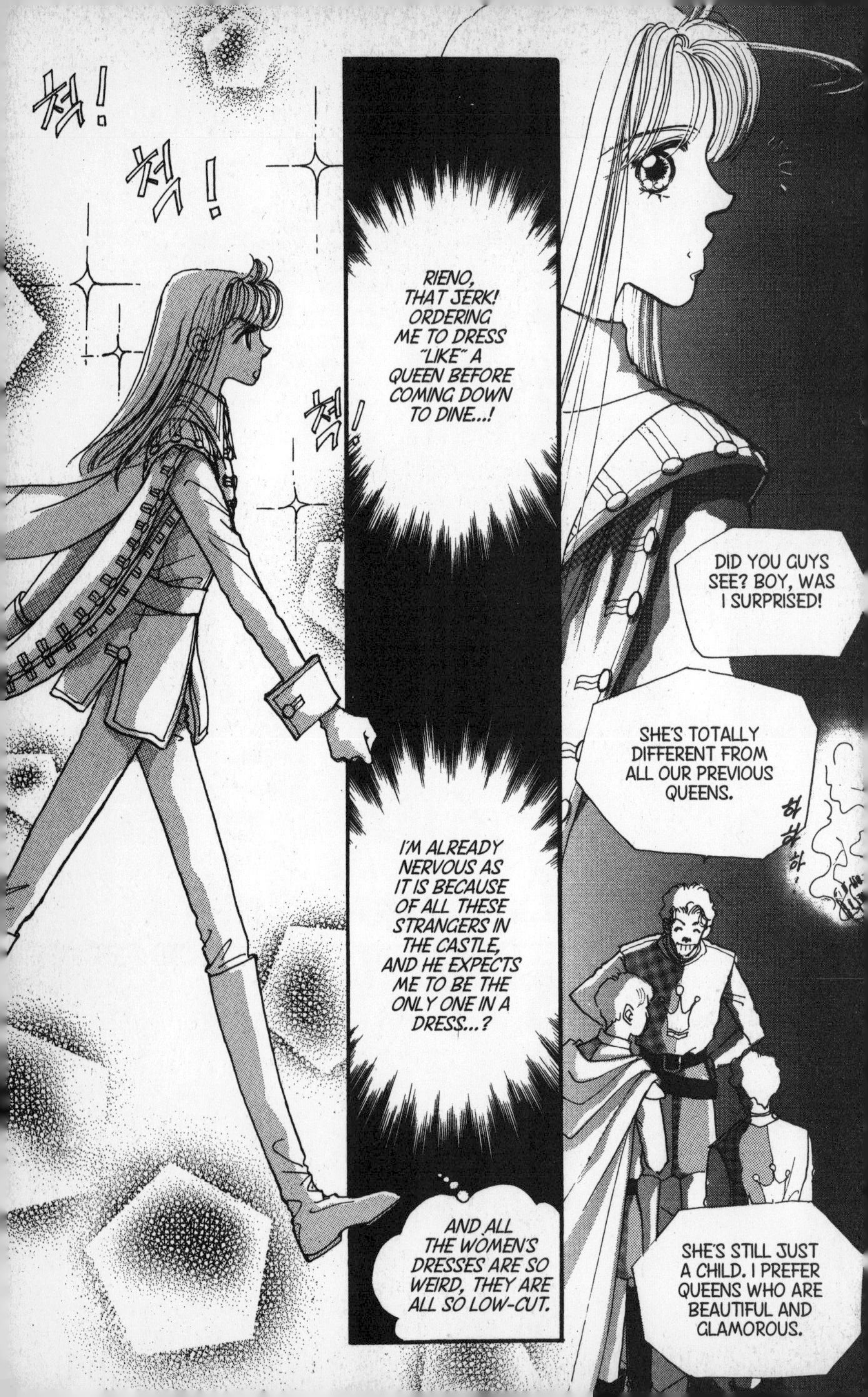
척!
척!
척!
RIENO, THAT JERK! ORDERING ME TO DRESS "LIKE" A QUEEN BEFORE COMING DOWN TO DINE...!
I'M ALREADY NERVOUS AS IT IS BECAUSE OF ALL THESE STRANGERS IN THE CASTLE, AND HE EXPECTS ME TO BE THE ONLY ONE IN A DRESS...?
AND ALL THE WOMEN'S DRESSES ARE SO WEIRD, THEY ARE ALL SO LOW-CUT.
DID YOU GUYS SEE? BOY, WAS I SURPRISED!
SHE'S TOTALLY DIFFERENT FROM ALL OUR PREVIOUS QUEENS.
하하하
SHE'S STILL JUST A CHILD. I PREFER QUEENS WHO ARE BEAUTIFUL AND GLAMOROUS.

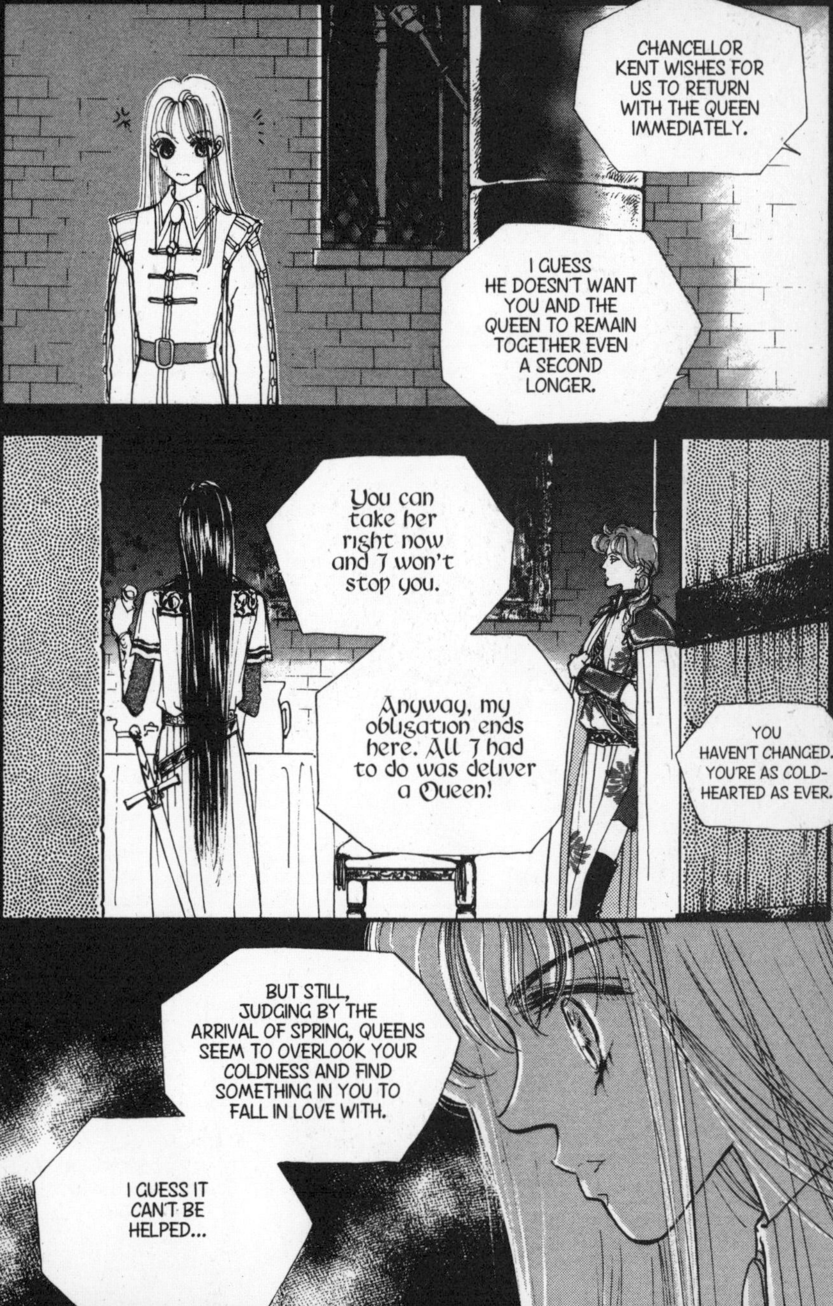
CHANCELLOR KENT WISHES FOR US TO RETURN WITH THE QUEEN IMMEDIATELY.
I GUESS HE DOESN'T WANT YOU AND THE QUEEN TO REMAIN TOGETHER EVEN A SECOND LONGER.
You can take her right now and I won't stop you.
Anyway, my obligation ends here. All I had to do was deliver a Queen!
YOU HAVEN'T CHANGED. YOU'RE AS COLD-HEARTED AS EVER.
BUT STILL, JUDGING BY THE ARRIVAL OF SPRING, QUEENS SEEM TO OVERLOOK YOUR COLDNESS AND FIND SOMETHING IN YOU TO FALL IN LOVE WITH.
I GUESS IT CAN'T BE HELPED...

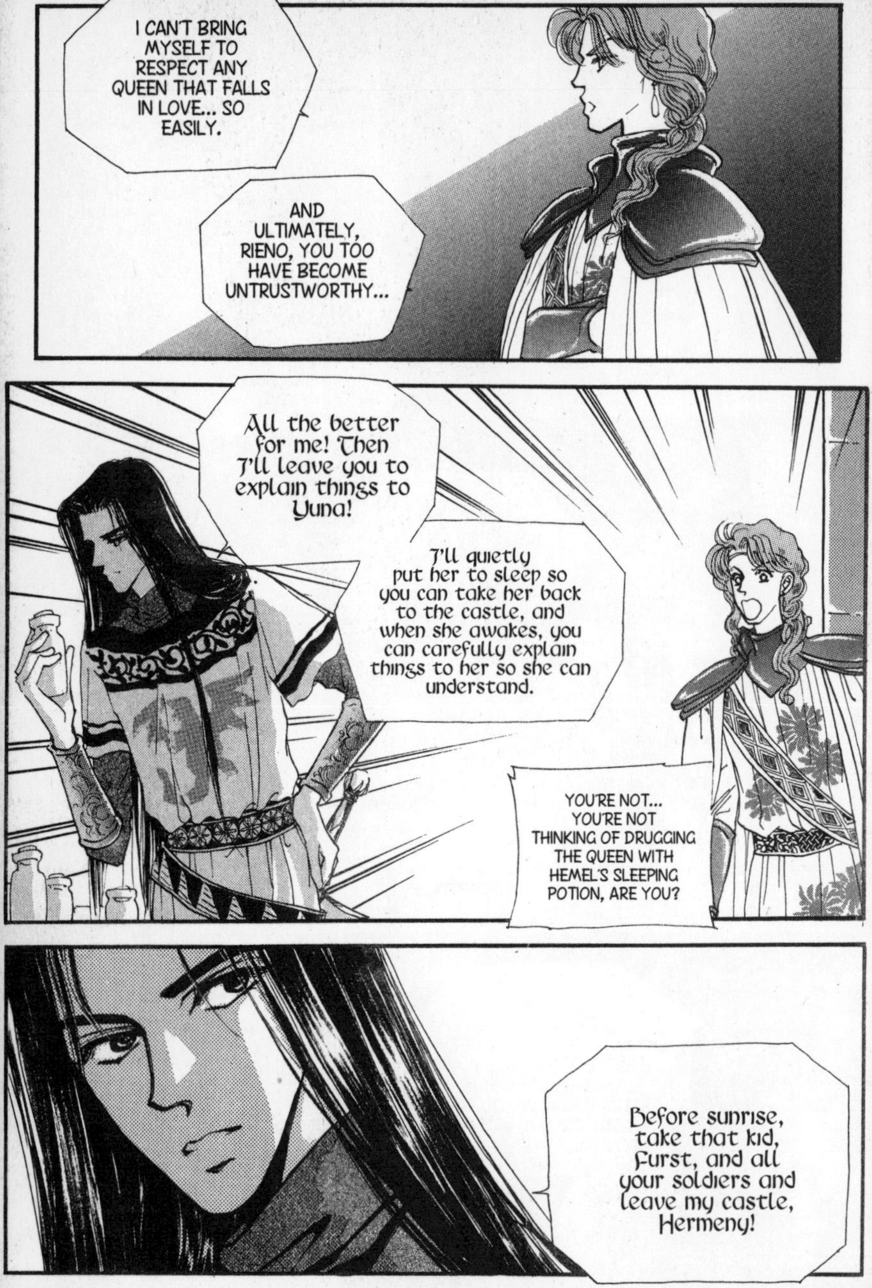
I CAN'T BRING MYSELF TO RESPECT ANY QUEEN THAT FALLS IN LOVE... SO EASILY.
AND ULTIMATELY, RIENO, YOU TOO HAVE BECOME UNTRUSTWORTHY...
All the better for me! Then I'll leave you to explain things to Yuna!
I'll quietly put her to sleep so you can take her back to the castle, and when she awakes, you can carefully explain things to her so she can understand.
YOU'RE NOT... YOU'RE NOT THINKING OF DRUGGING THE QUEEN WITH HEMEL'S SLEEPING POTION, ARE YOU?
Before sunrise, take that kid, Furst, and all your soldiers and leave my castle, Hermeny!

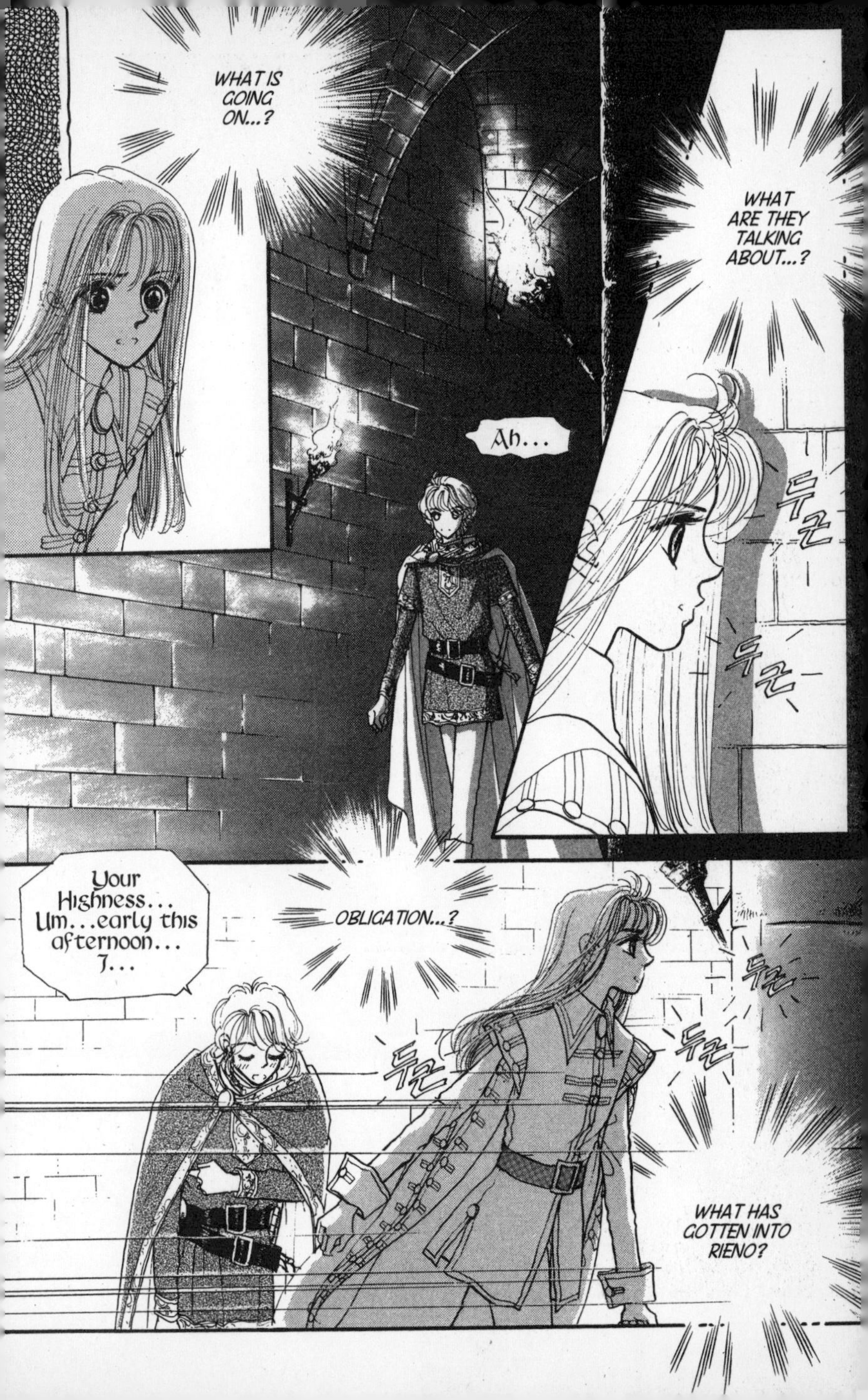
WHAT IS GOING ON...?
Ah...
WHAT ARE THEY TALKING ABOUT...?
두근
두근
Your Highness... Um...early this afternoon... I...
OBLIGATION...?
두근
두근
두근
WHAT HAS GOTTEN INTO RIENO?

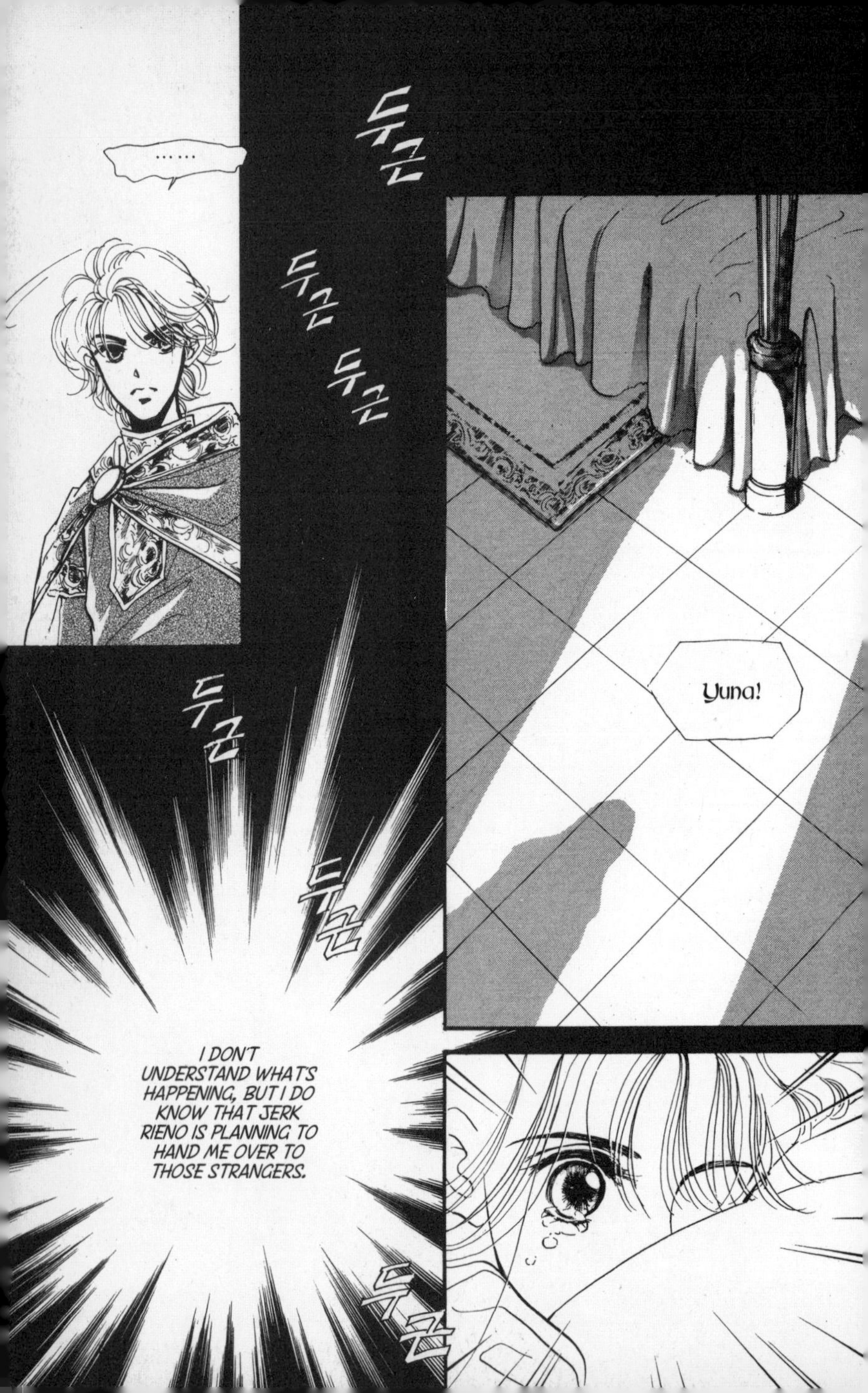
……
두근
두근 두근
Yuna!
두근
두근
I DON'T UNDERSTAND WHAT'S HAPPENING, BUT I DO KNOW THAT JERK RIENO IS PLANNING TO HAND ME OVER TO THOSE STRANGERS.
두근

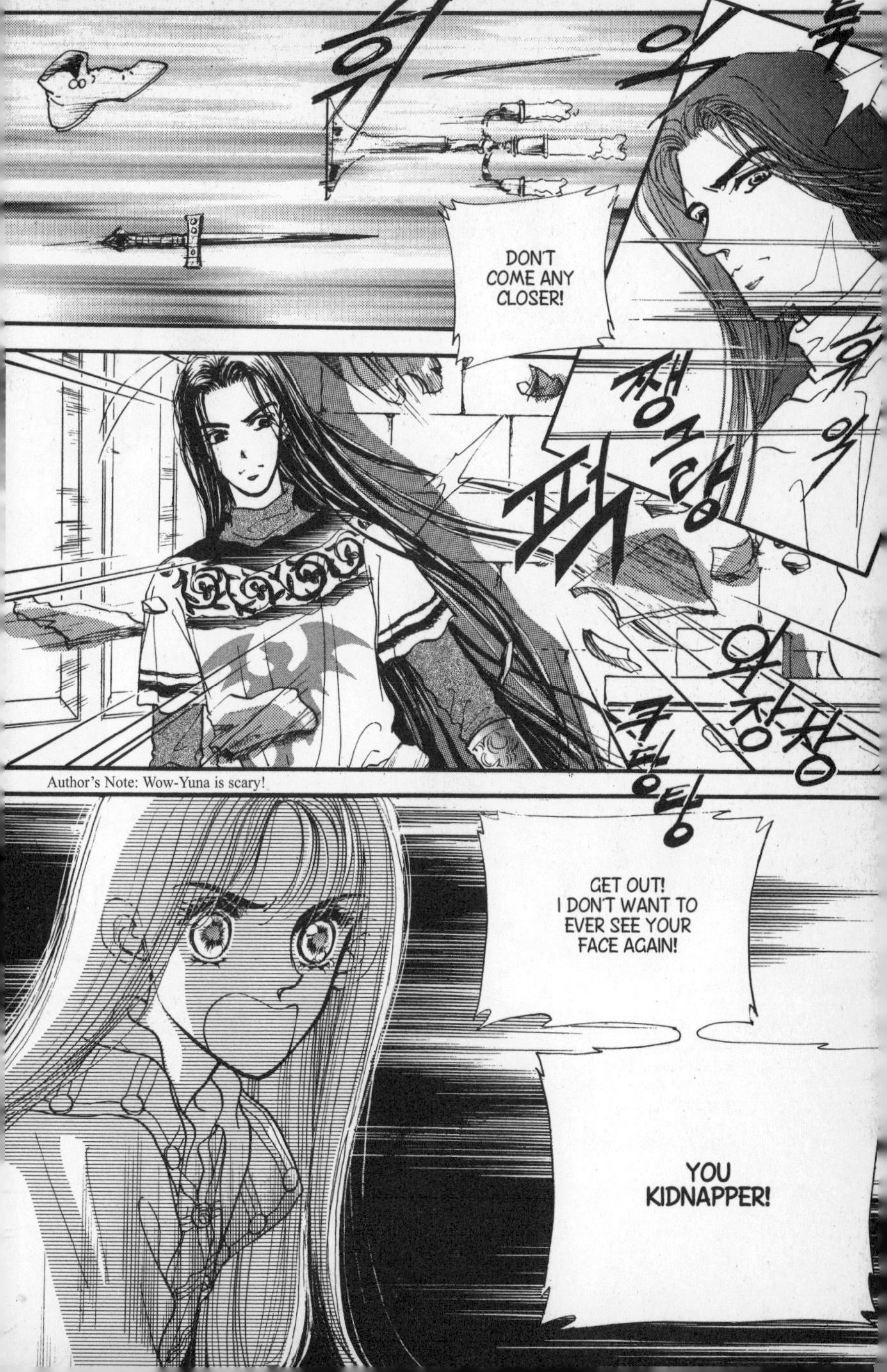
DON'T COME ANY CLOSER!
쨍그랑
퍽
와장창
Author's Note: Wow-Yuna is scary!
GET OUT! I DON'T WANT TO EVER SEE YOUR FACE AGAIN!
YOU KIDNAPPER!

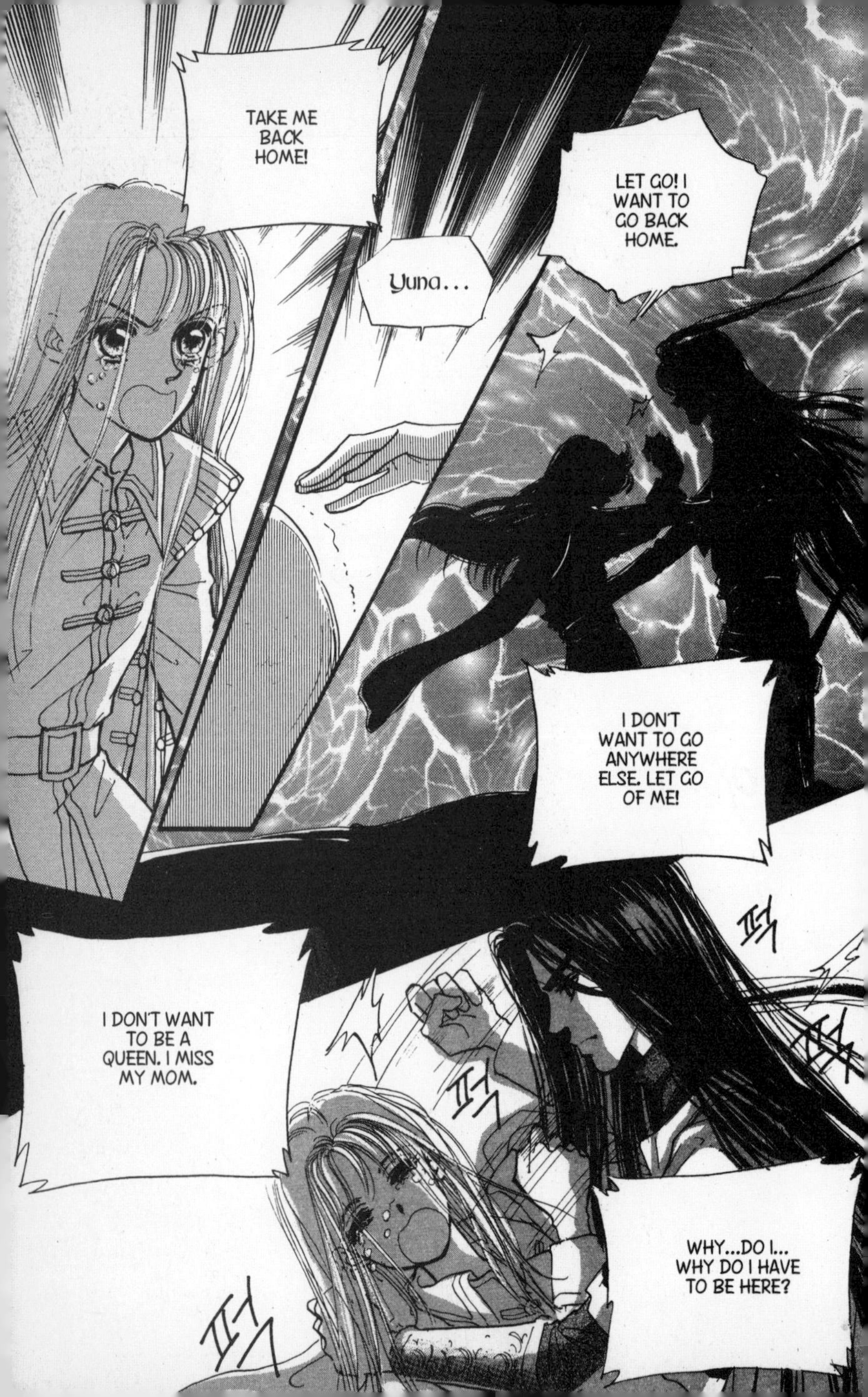
TAKE ME BACK HOME!
Yuna...
LET GO! I WANT TO GO BACK HOME.
I DON'T WANT TO GO ANYWHERE ELSE. LET GO OF ME!
I DON'T WANT TO BE A QUEEN. I MISS MY MOM.
WHY...DO I... WHY DO I HAVE TO BE HERE?

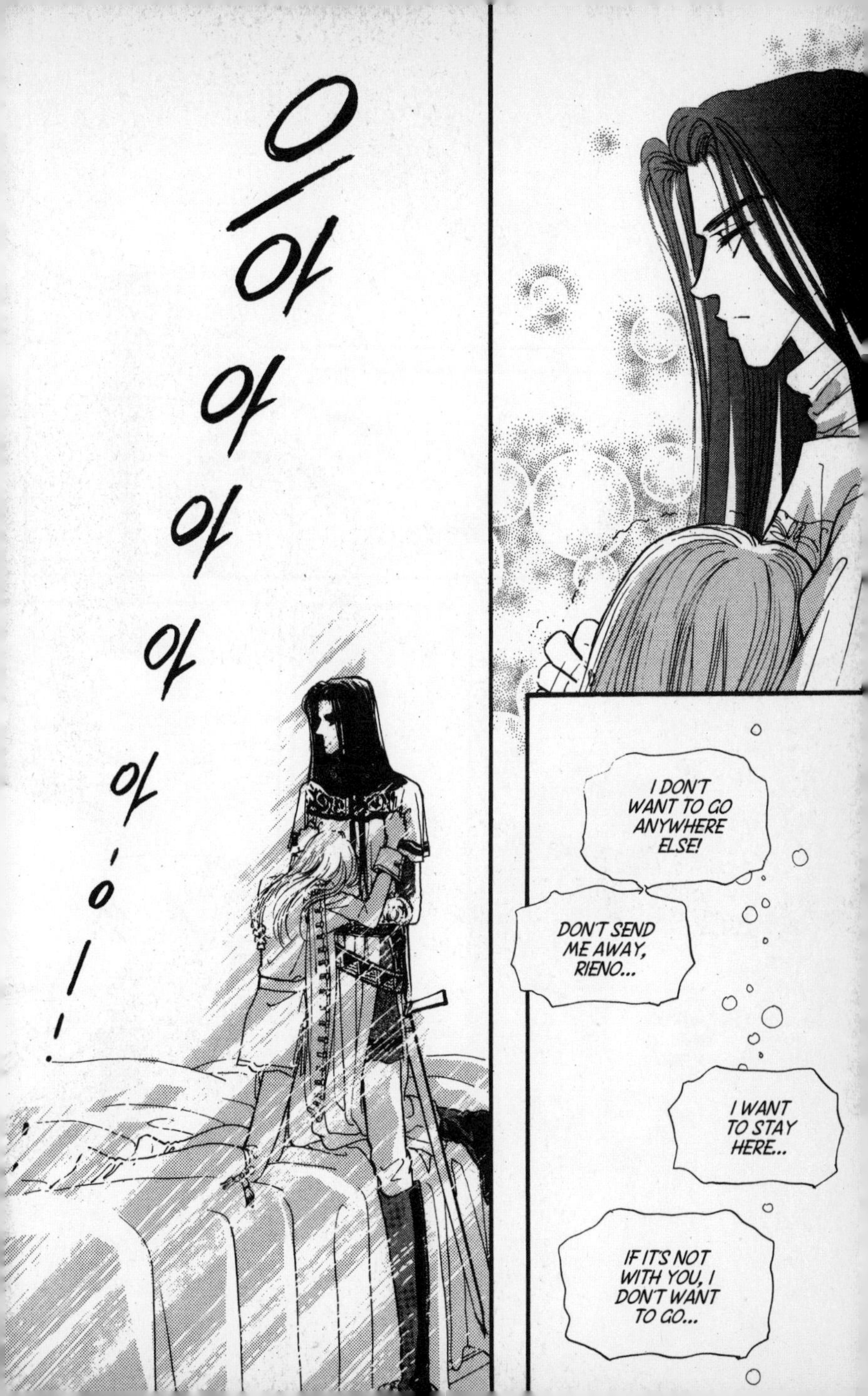
으아아아아아!!
I DON'T WANT TO GO ANYWHERE ELSE!
DON'T SEND ME AWAY, RIENO...
I WANT TO STAY HERE...
IF IT'S NOT WITH YOU, I DON'T WANT TO GO...

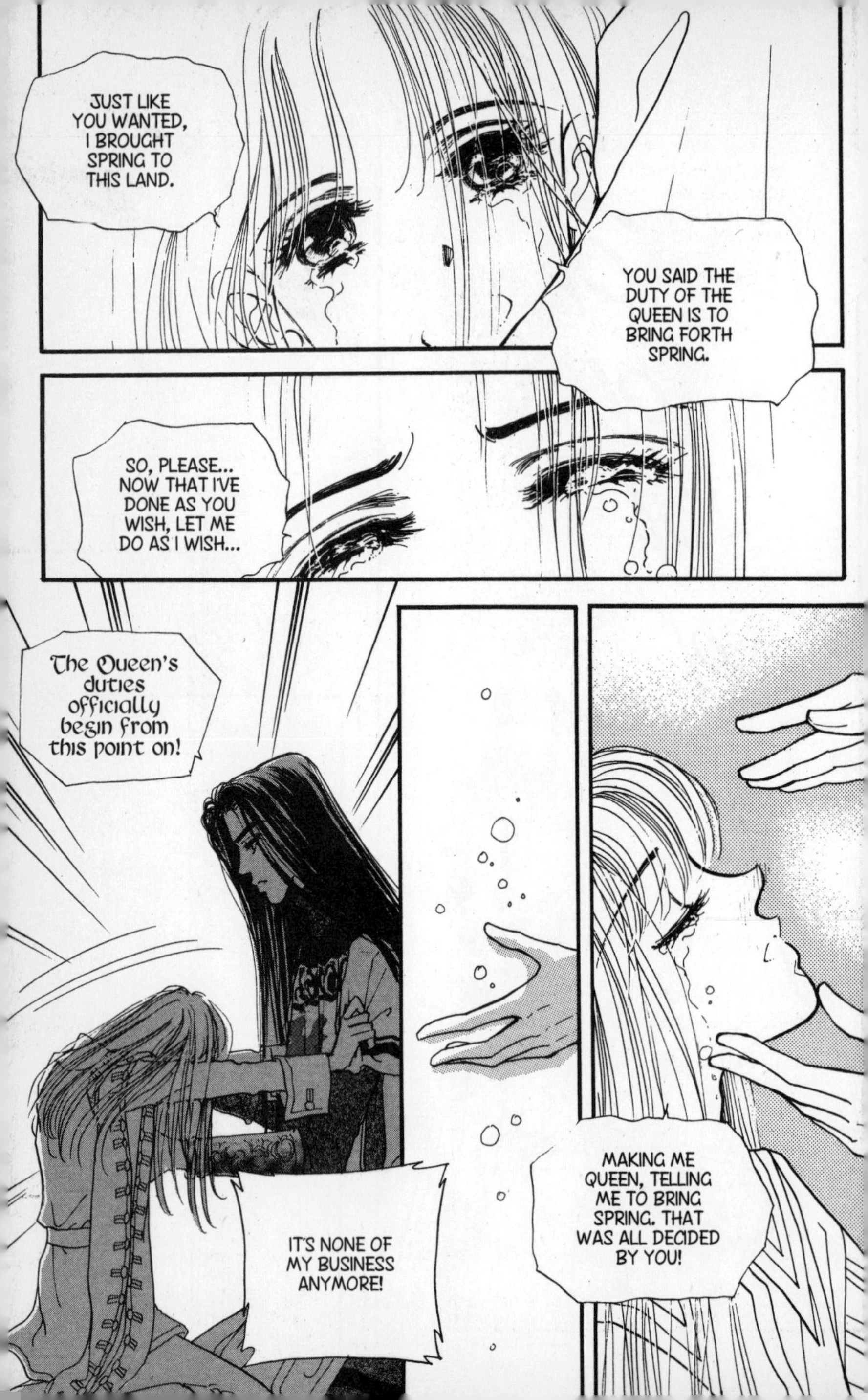
JUST LIKE YOU WANTED, I BROUGHT SPRING TO THIS LAND.
YOU SAID THE DUTY OF THE QUEEN IS TO BRING FORTH SPRING.
SO, PLEASE... NOW THAT I'VE DONE AS YOU WISH, LET ME DO AS I WISH...
The Queen's duties officially begin from this point on!
IT'S NONE OF MY BUSINESS ANYMORE!
MAKING ME QUEEN, TELLING ME TO BRING SPRING. THAT WAS ALL DECIDED BY YOU!

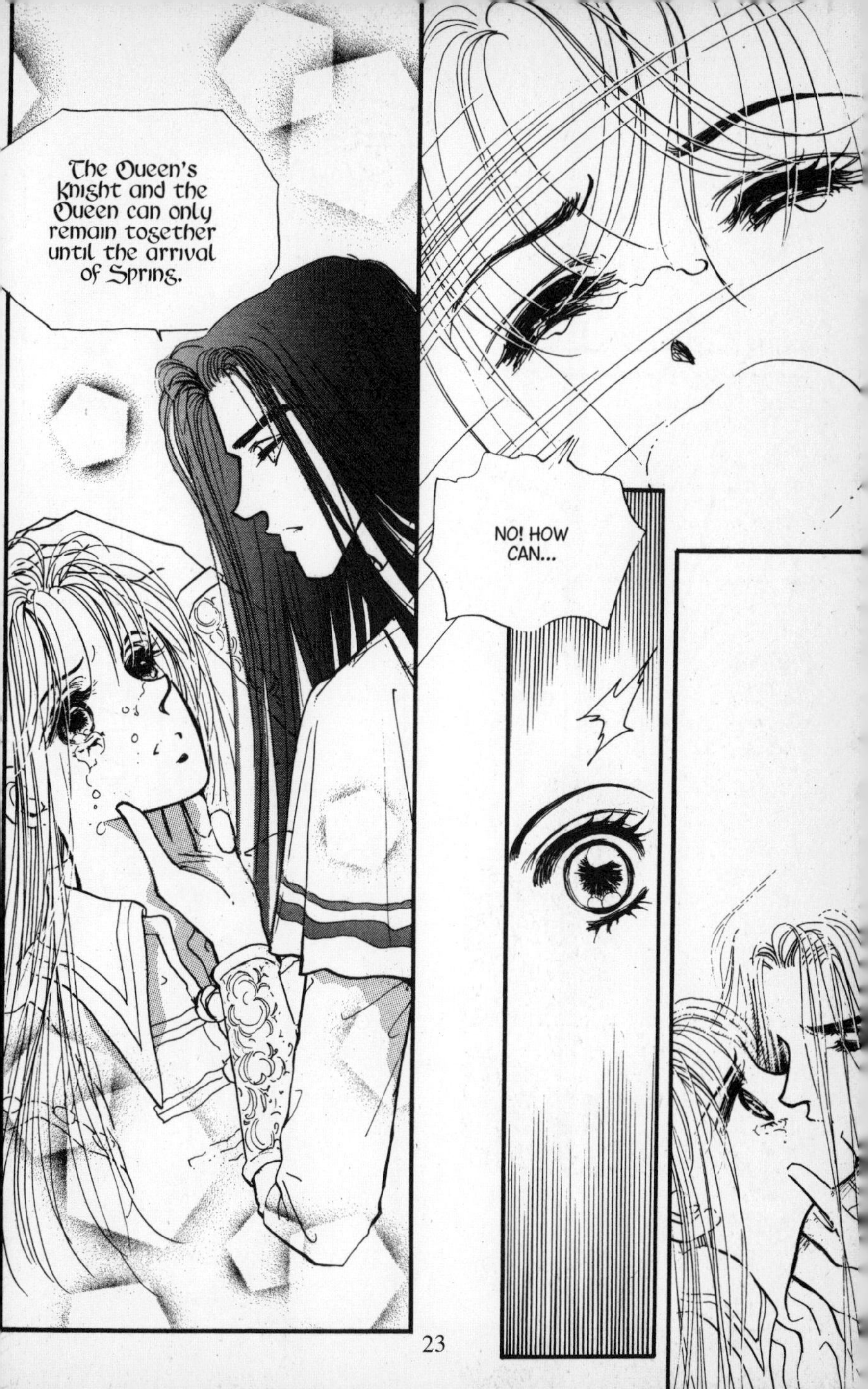
The Queen's Knight and the Queen can only remain together until the arrival of Spring.
NO! HOW CAN...

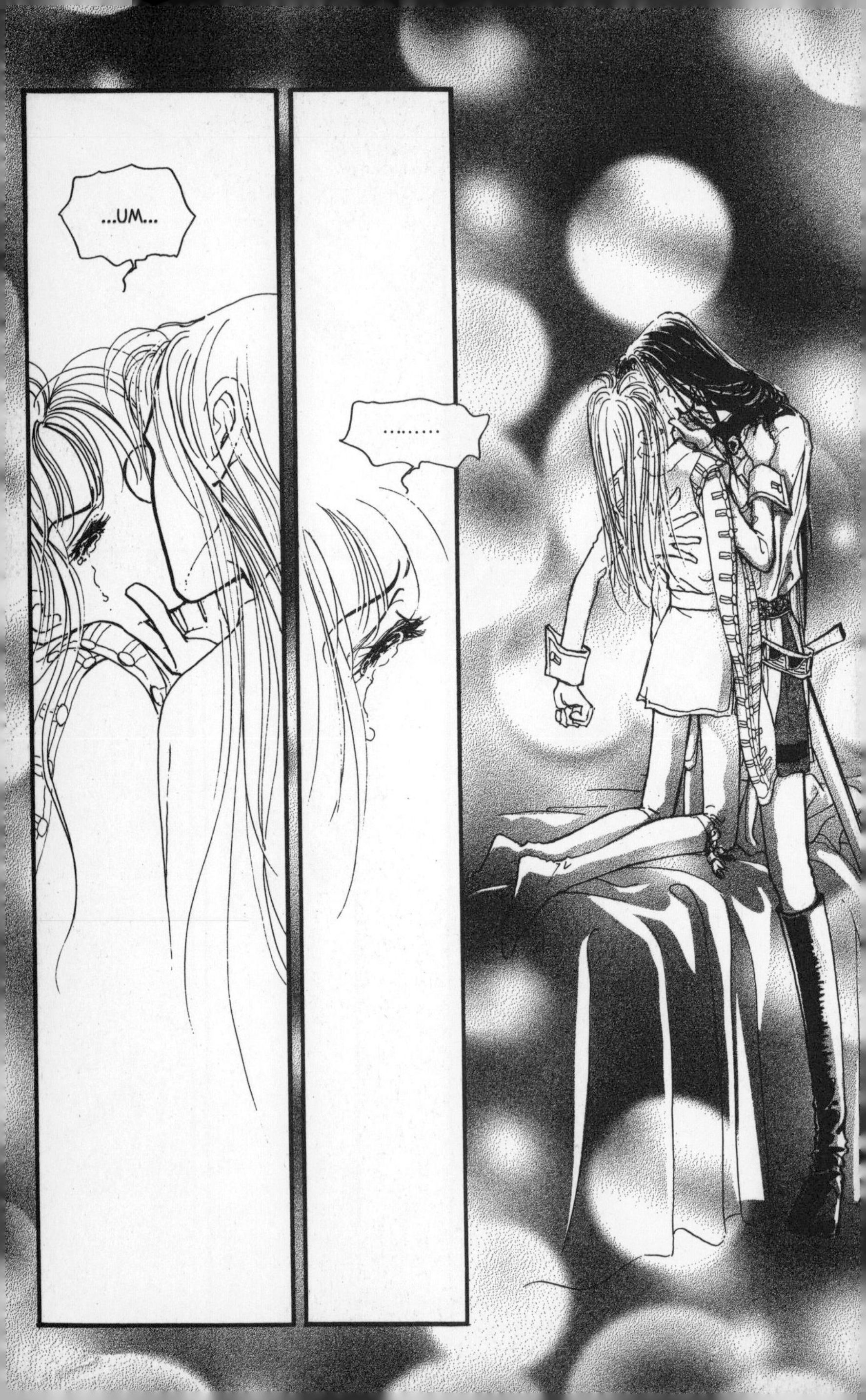
...UM...
....

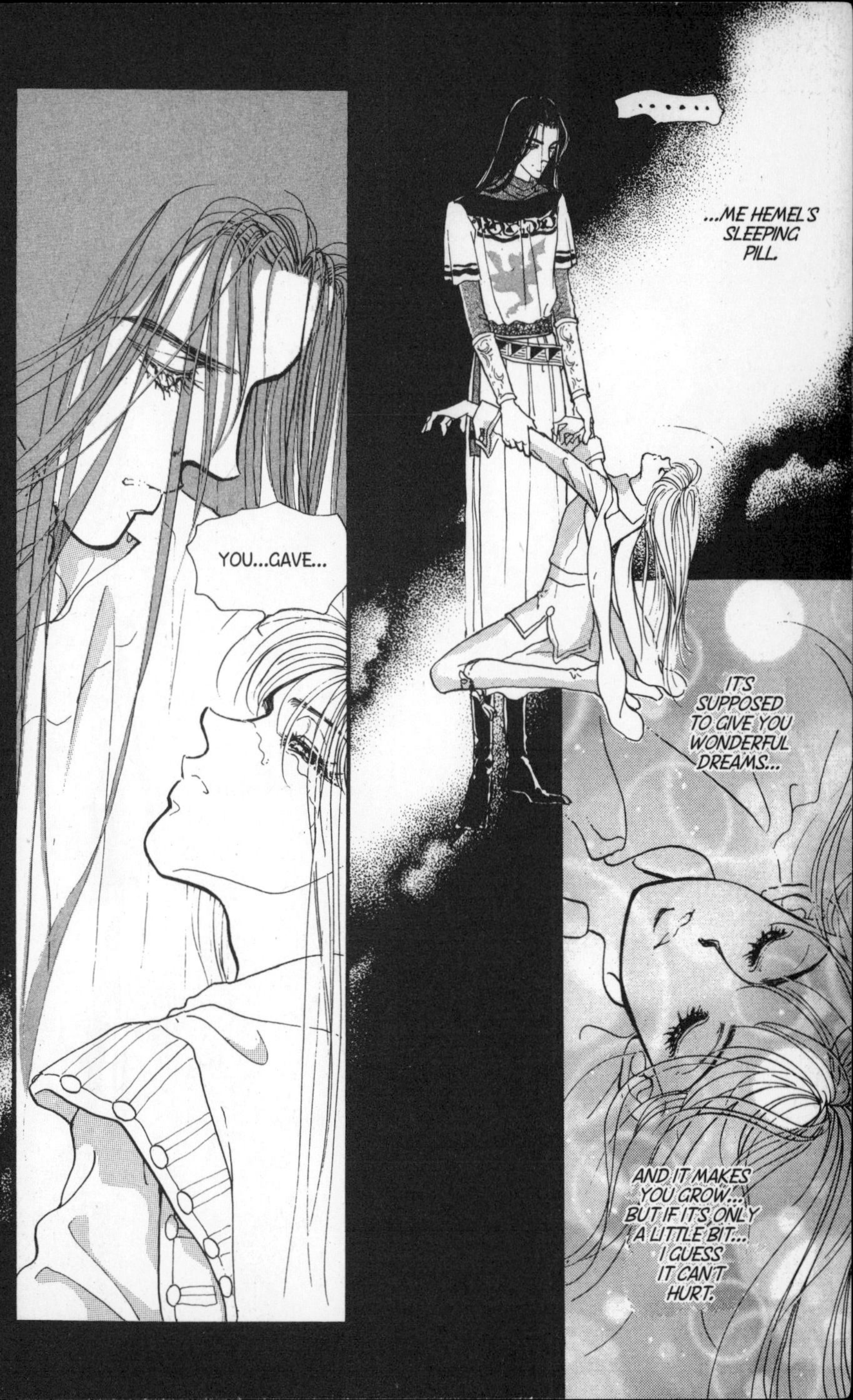
YOU...GAVE...
......
...ME HEMEL'S SLEEPING PILL.
IT'S SUPPOSED TO GIVE YOU WONDERFUL DREAMS...
AND IT MAKES YOU GROW... BUT IF IT'S ONLY A LITTLE BIT... I GUESS IT CAN'T HURT.

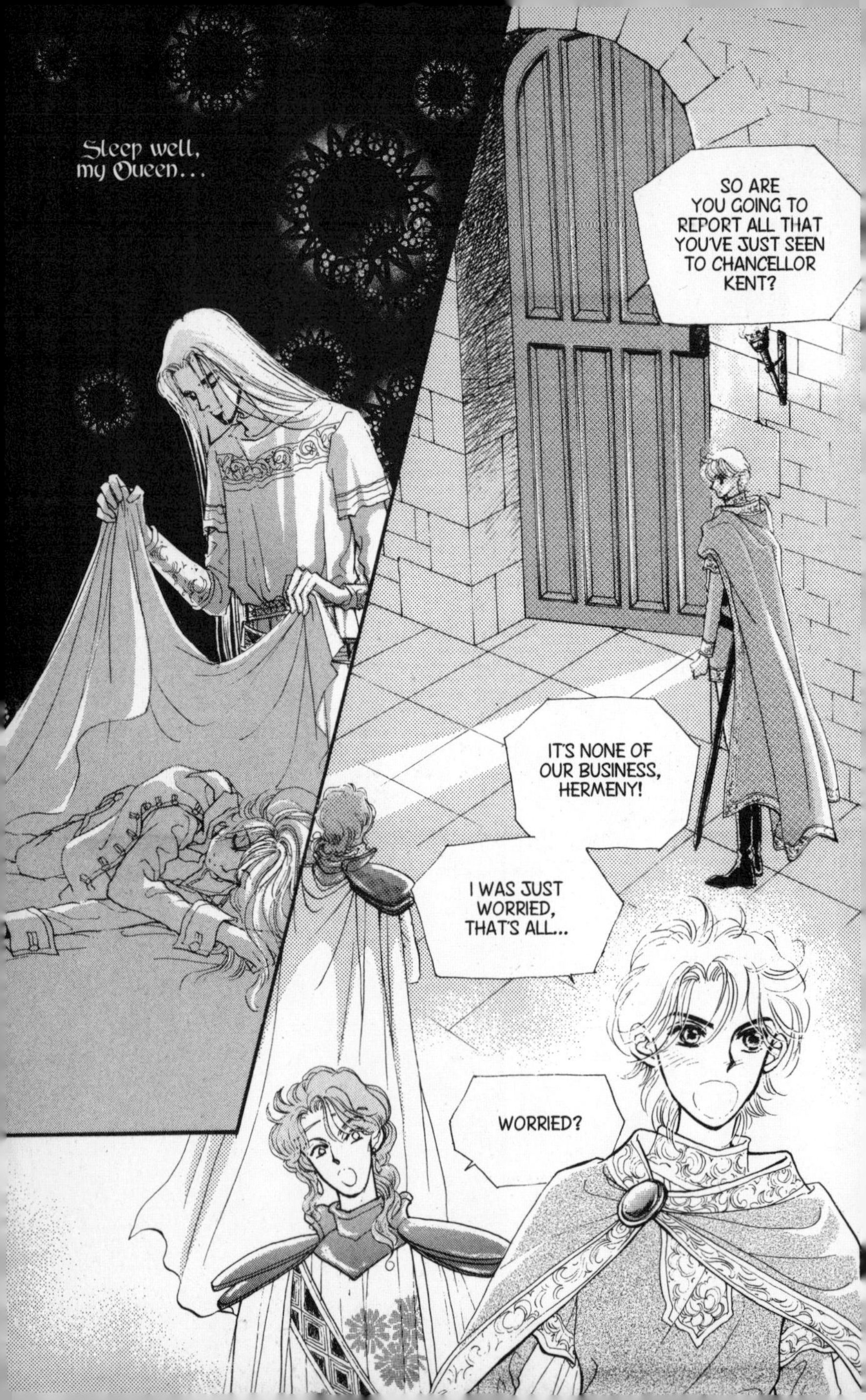
Sleep well, my Queen...
SO ARE YOU GOING TO REPORT ALL THAT YOU'VE JUST SEEN TO CHANCELLOR KENT?
IT'S NONE OF OUR BUSINESS, HERMENY!
I WAS JUST WORRIED, THAT'S ALL...
WORRIED?

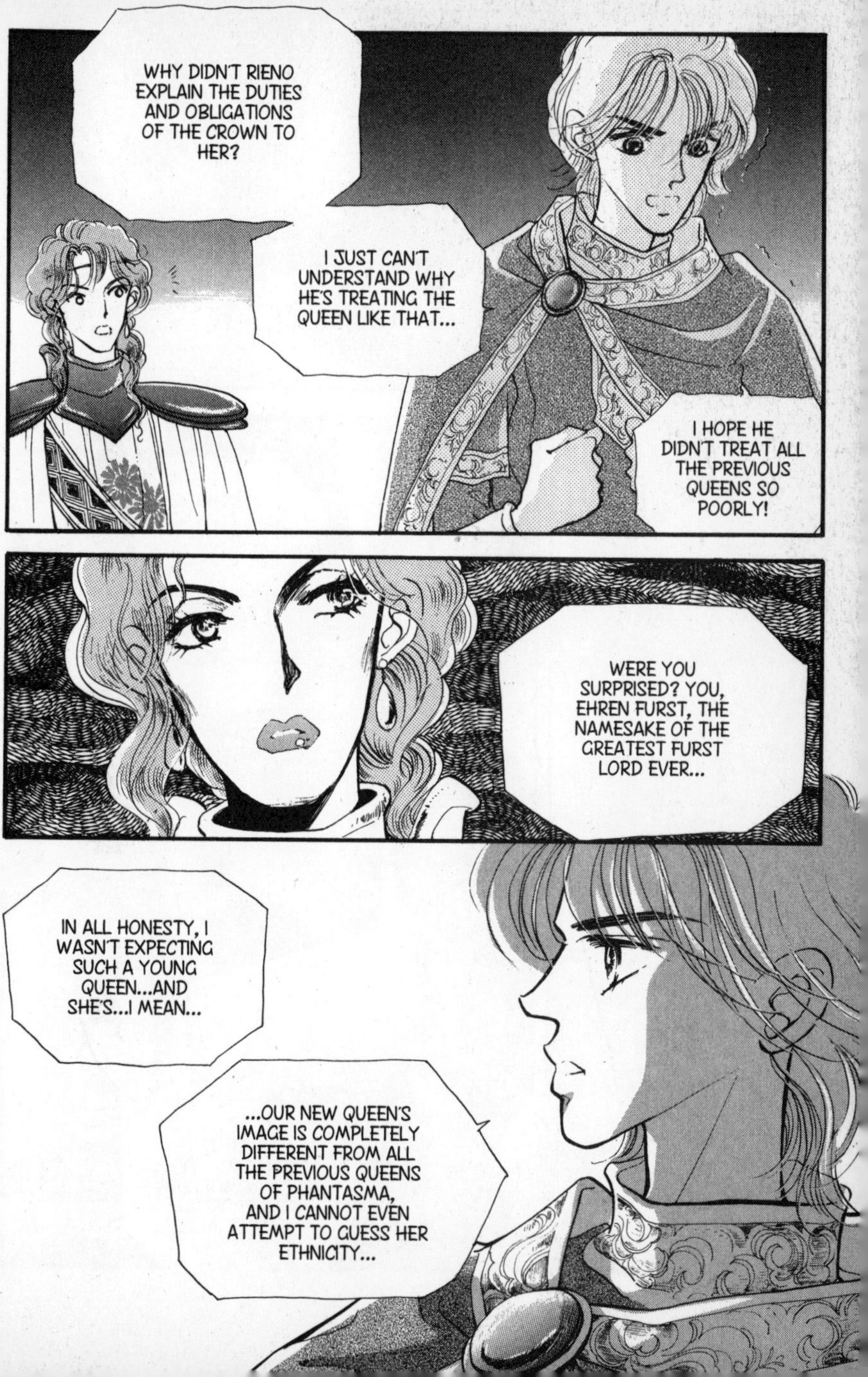
WHY DIDN'T RIENO EXPLAIN THE DUTIES AND OBLIGATIONS OF THE CROWN TO HER?
I JUST CAN'T UNDERSTAND WHY HE'S TREATING THE QUEEN LIKE THAT...
I HOPE HE DIDN'T TREAT ALL THE PREVIOUS QUEENS SO POORLY!
WERE YOU SURPRISED? YOU, EHREN FURST, THE NAMESAKE OF THE GREATEST FURST LORD EVER...
IN ALL HONESTY, I WASN'T EXPECTING SUCH A YOUNG QUEEN...AND SHE'S...I MEAN...
...OUR NEW QUEEN'S IMAGE IS COMPLETELY DIFFERENT FROM ALL THE PREVIOUS QUEENS OF PHANTASMA, AND I CANNOT EVEN ATTEMPT TO GUESS HER ETHNICITY...

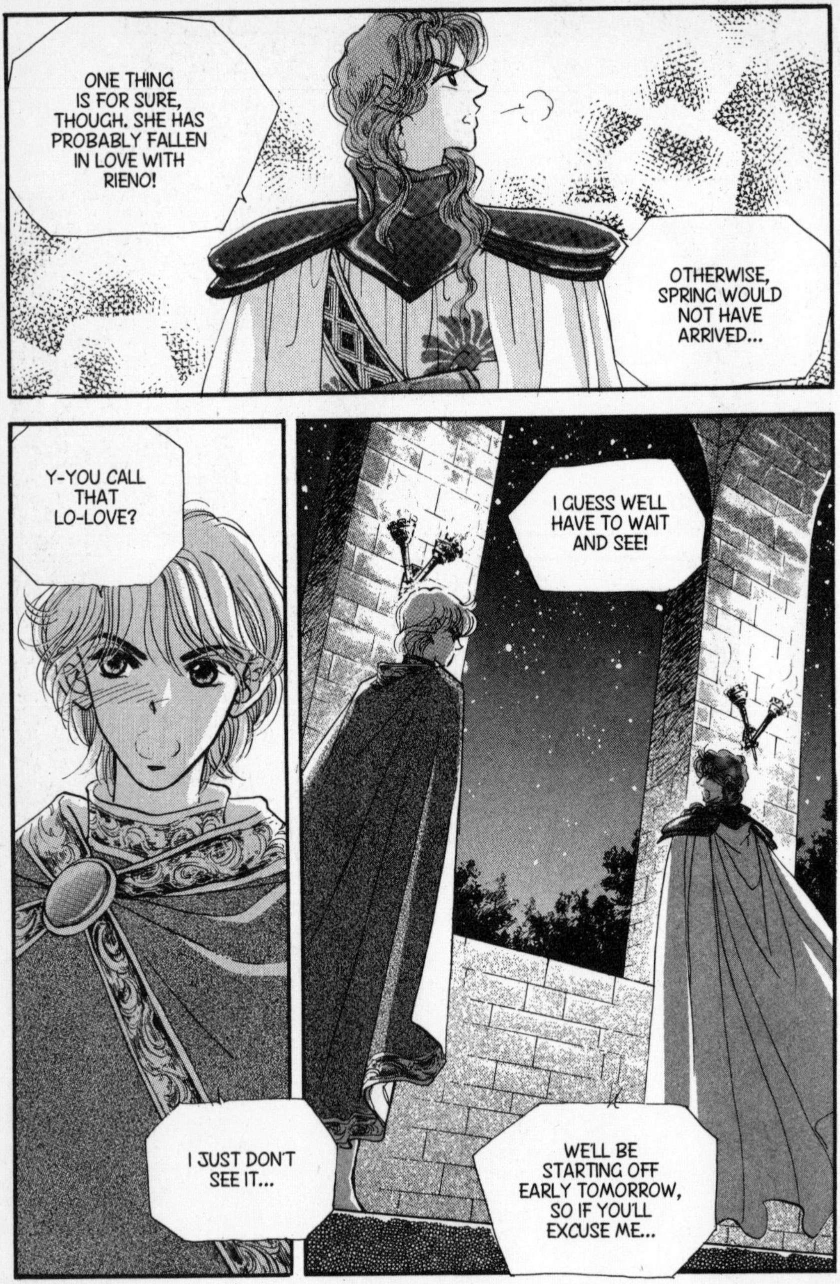
ONE THING IS FOR SURE, THOUGH. SHE HAS PROBABLY FALLEN IN LOVE WITH RIENO!
OTHERWISE, SPRING WOULD NOT HAVE ARRIVED...
Y-YOU CALL THAT LO-LOVE?
I JUST DON'T SEE IT...
I GUESS WE'LL HAVE TO WAIT AND SEE!
WE'LL BE STARTING OFF EARLY TOMORROW, SO IF YOU'LL EXCUSE ME...

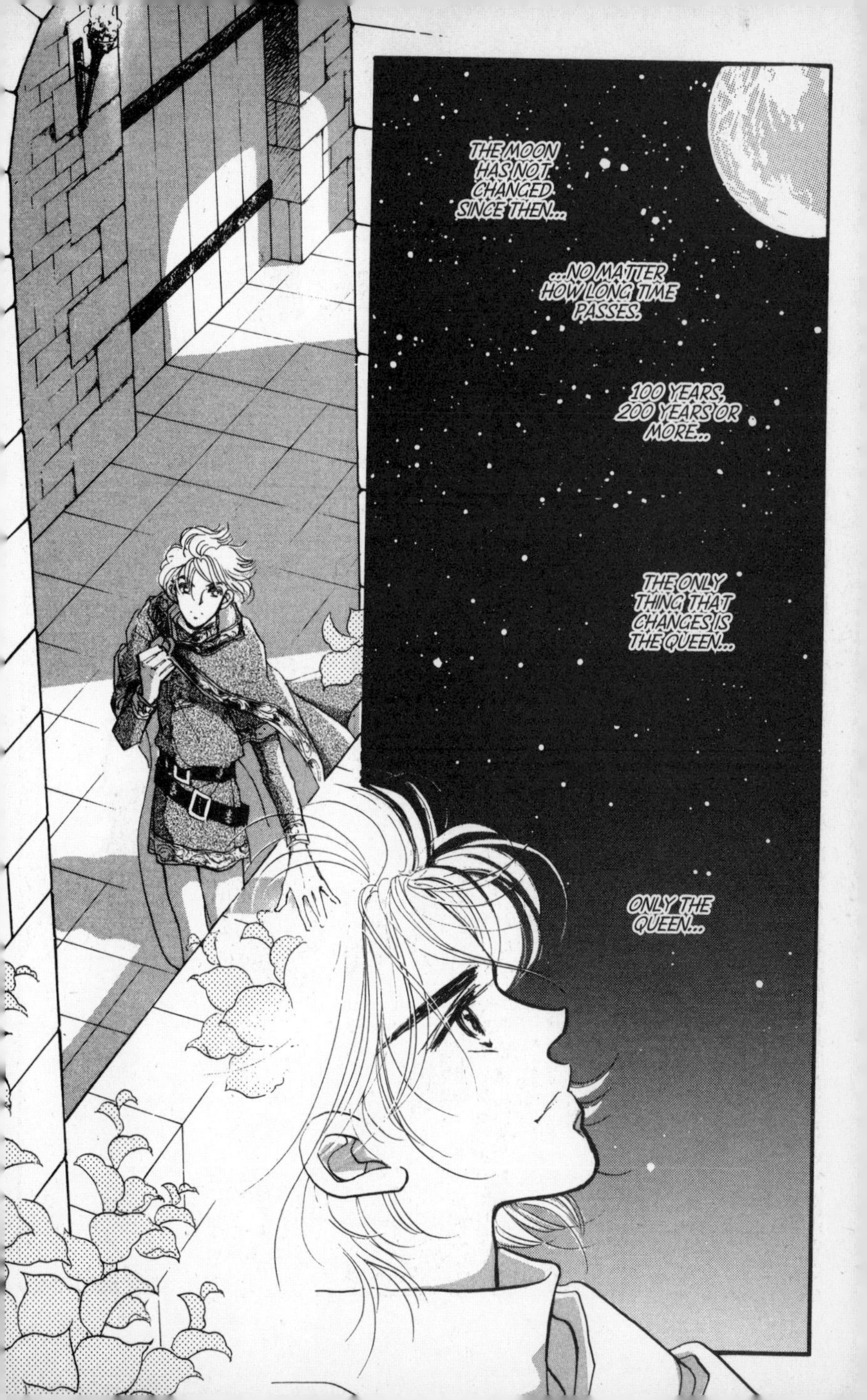
THE MOON HAS NOT CHANGED SINCE THEN...
...NO MATTER HOW LONG TIME PASSES.
100 YEARS, 200 YEARS OR MORE...
THE ONLY THING THAT CHANGES IS THE QUEEN...
ONLY THE QUEEN...

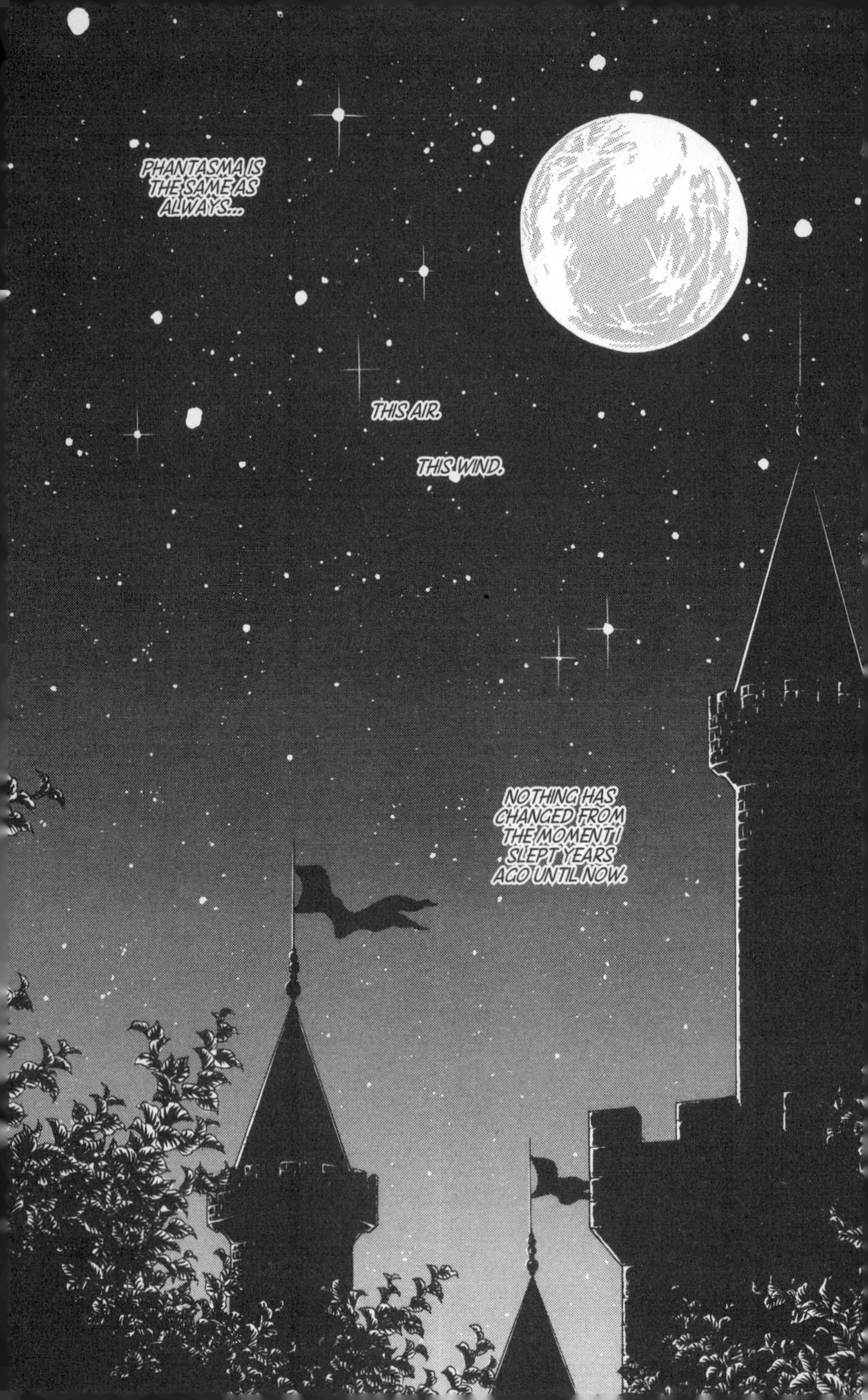
PHANTASMA IS THE SAME AS ALWAYS...
THIS AIR.
THIS WIND.
NOTHING HAS CHANGED FROM THE MOMENT I SLEPT YEARS AGO UNTIL NOW.

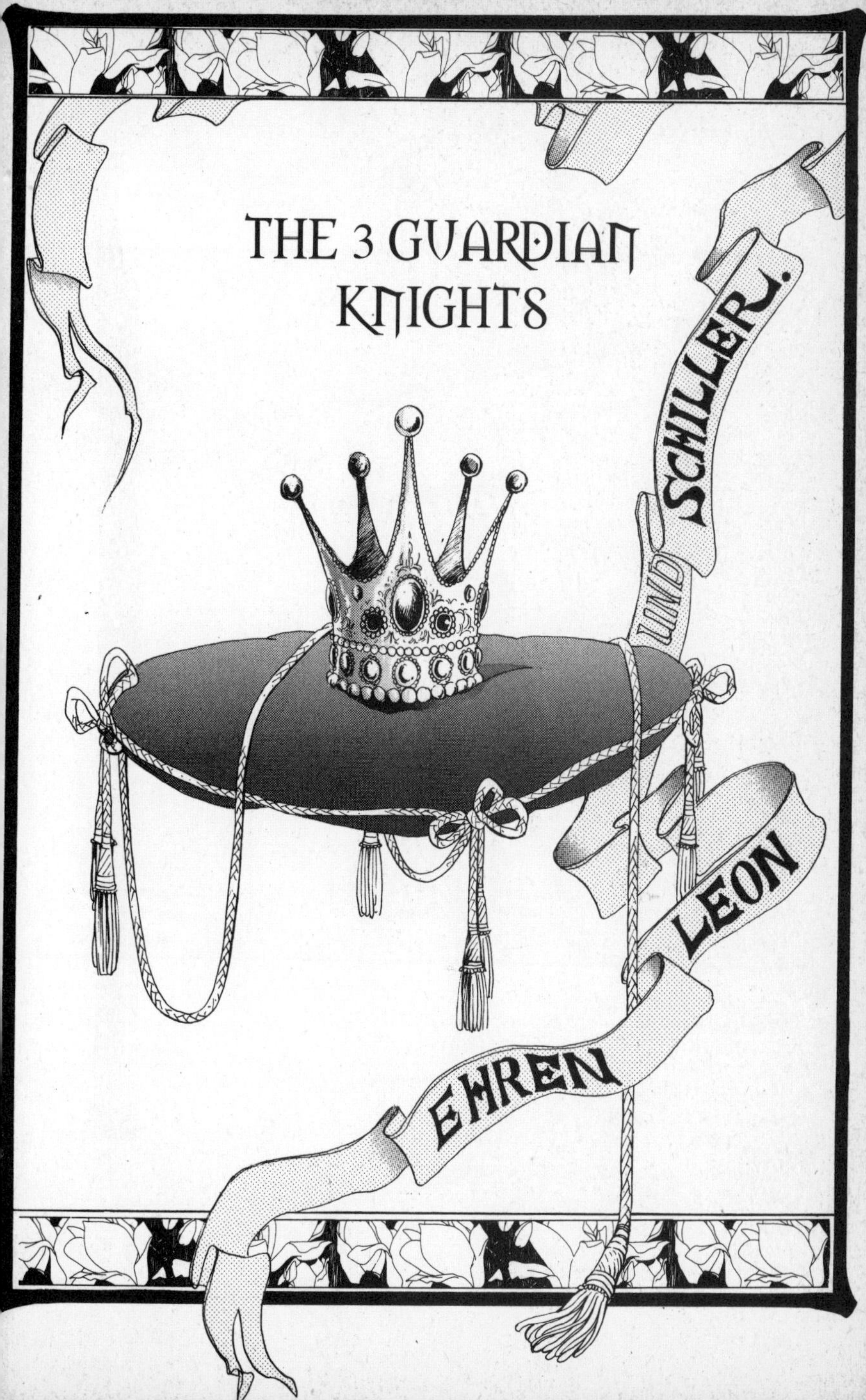
THE 3 GUARDIAN KNIGHTS
EHREN LEON UND SCHILLER.

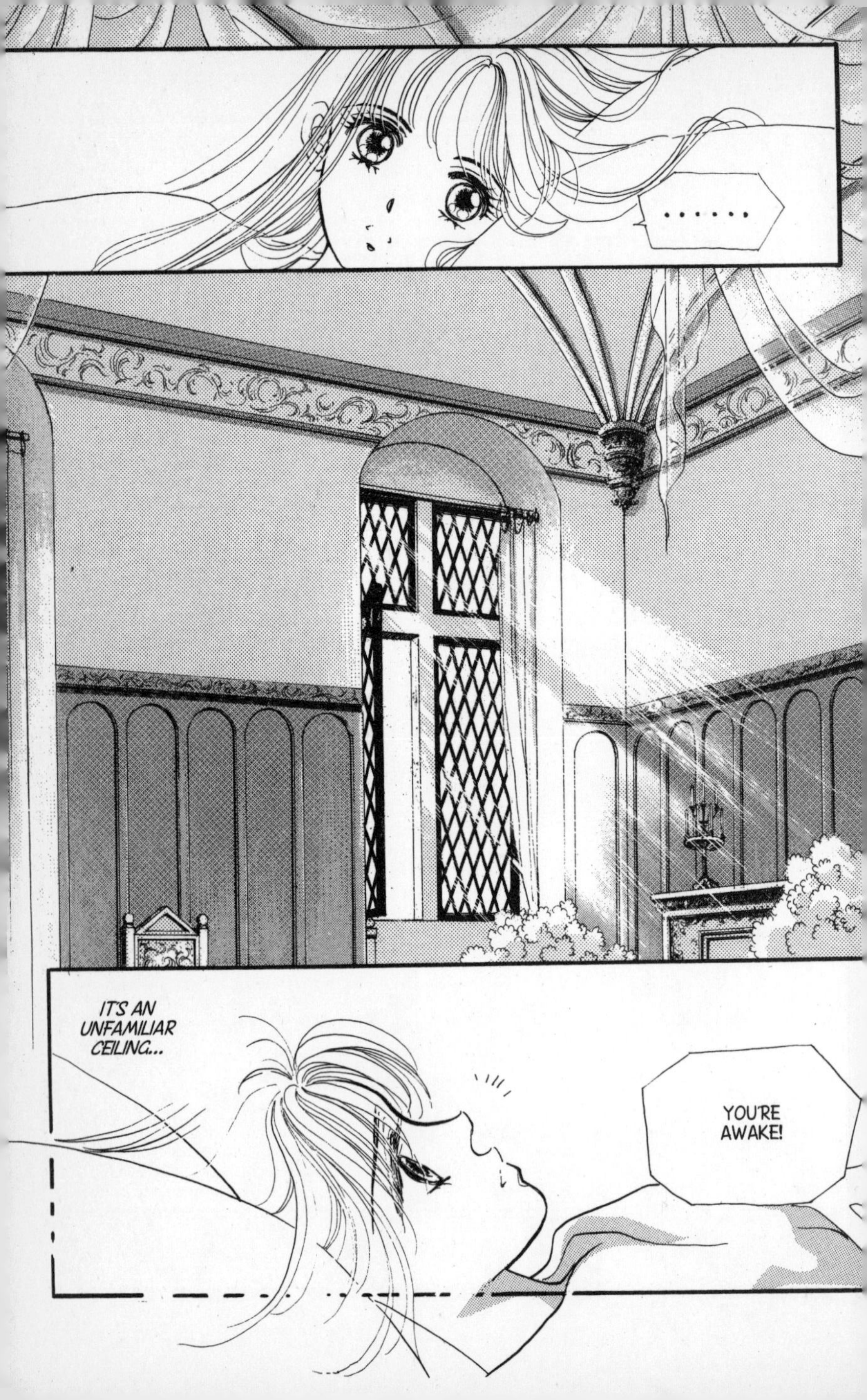
......
IT'S AN UNFAMILIAR CEILING...
YOU'RE AWAKE!

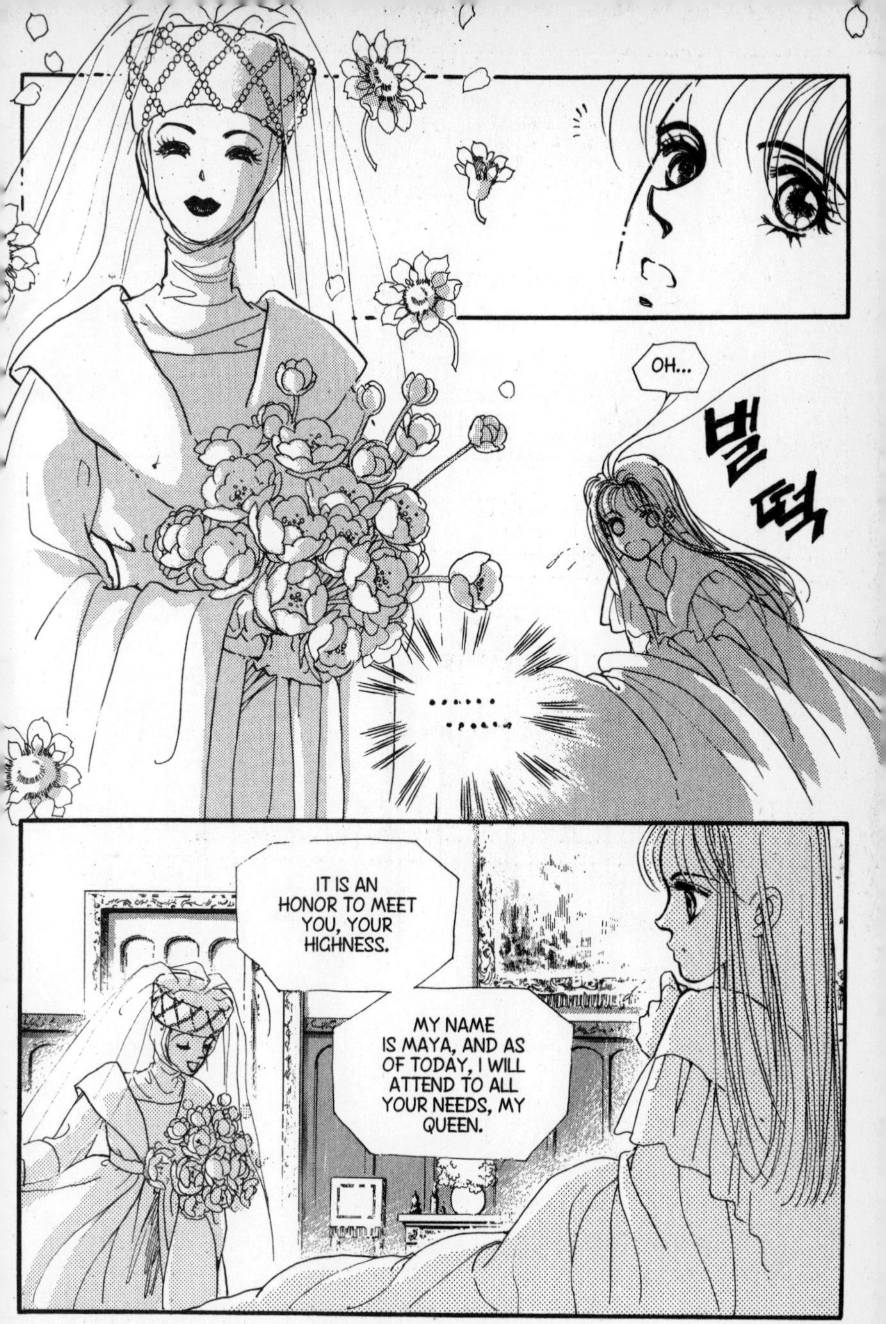
OH...
벌떡
......
......
IT IS AN HONOR TO MEET YOU, YOUR HIGHNESS.
MY NAME IS MAYA, AND AS OF TODAY, I WILL ATTEND TO ALL YOUR NEEDS, MY QUEEN.

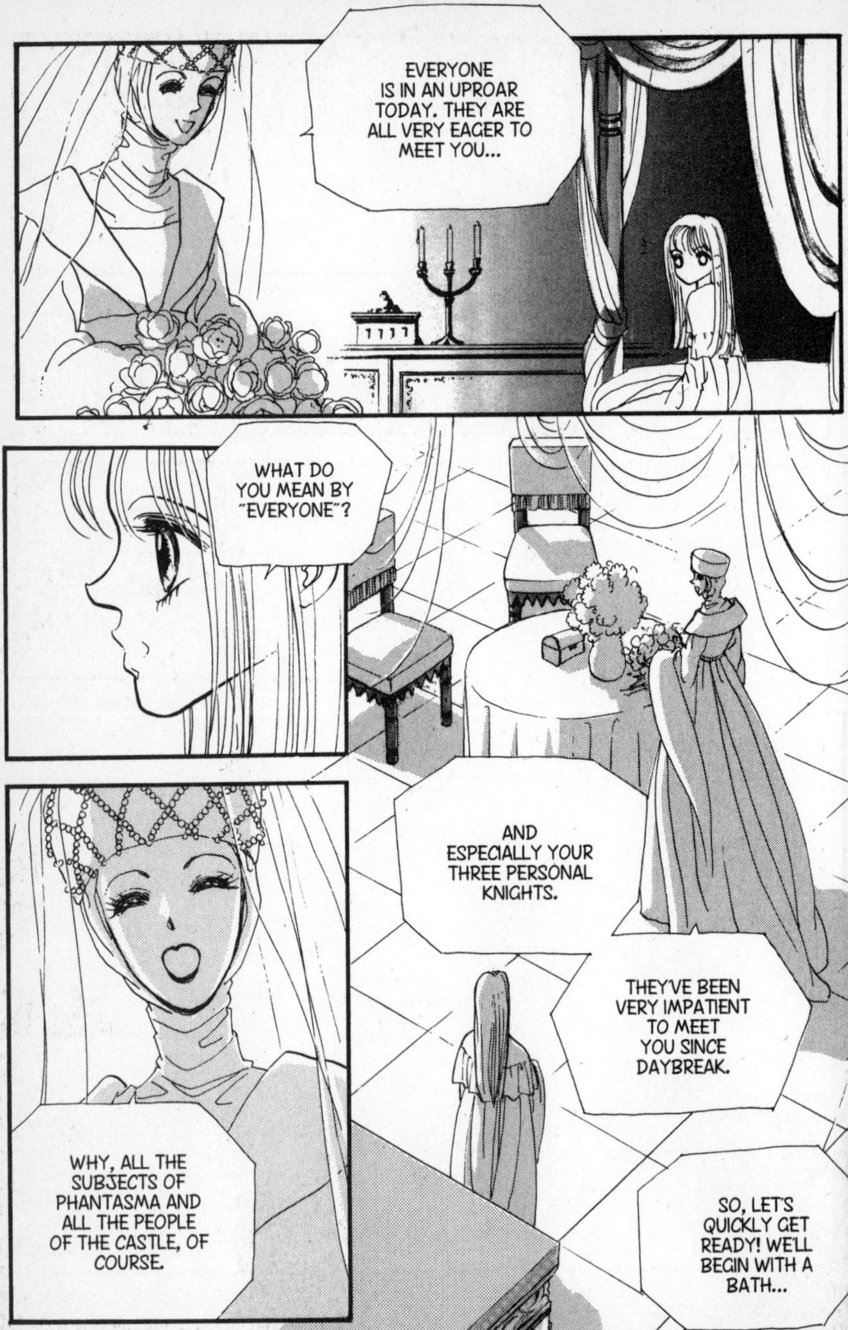
EVERYONE IS IN AN UPROAR TODAY. THEY ARE ALL VERY EAGER TO MEET YOU...
WHAT DO YOU MEAN BY "EVERYONE"?
WHY, ALL THE SUBJECTS OF PHANTASMA AND ALL THE PEOPLE OF THE CASTLE, OF COURSE.
AND ESPECIALLY YOUR THREE PERSONAL KNIGHTS.
THEY'VE BEEN VERY IMPATIENT TO MEET YOU SINCE DAYBREAK.
SO, LET'S QUICKLY GET READY! WE'LL BEGIN WITH A BATH...

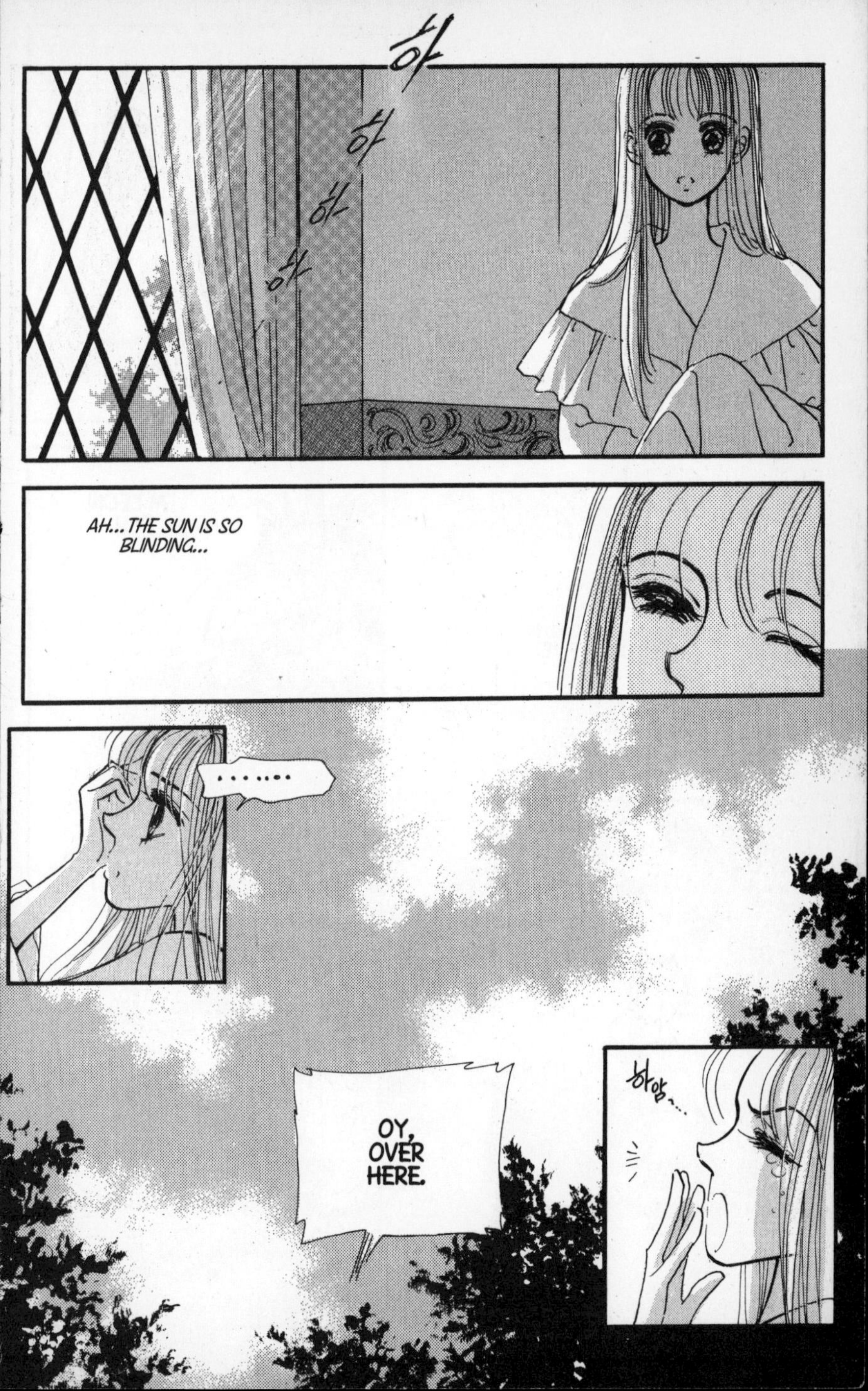
하
하
하
앙
AH...THE SUN IS SO BLINDING...
......
OY, OVER HERE.
하암...

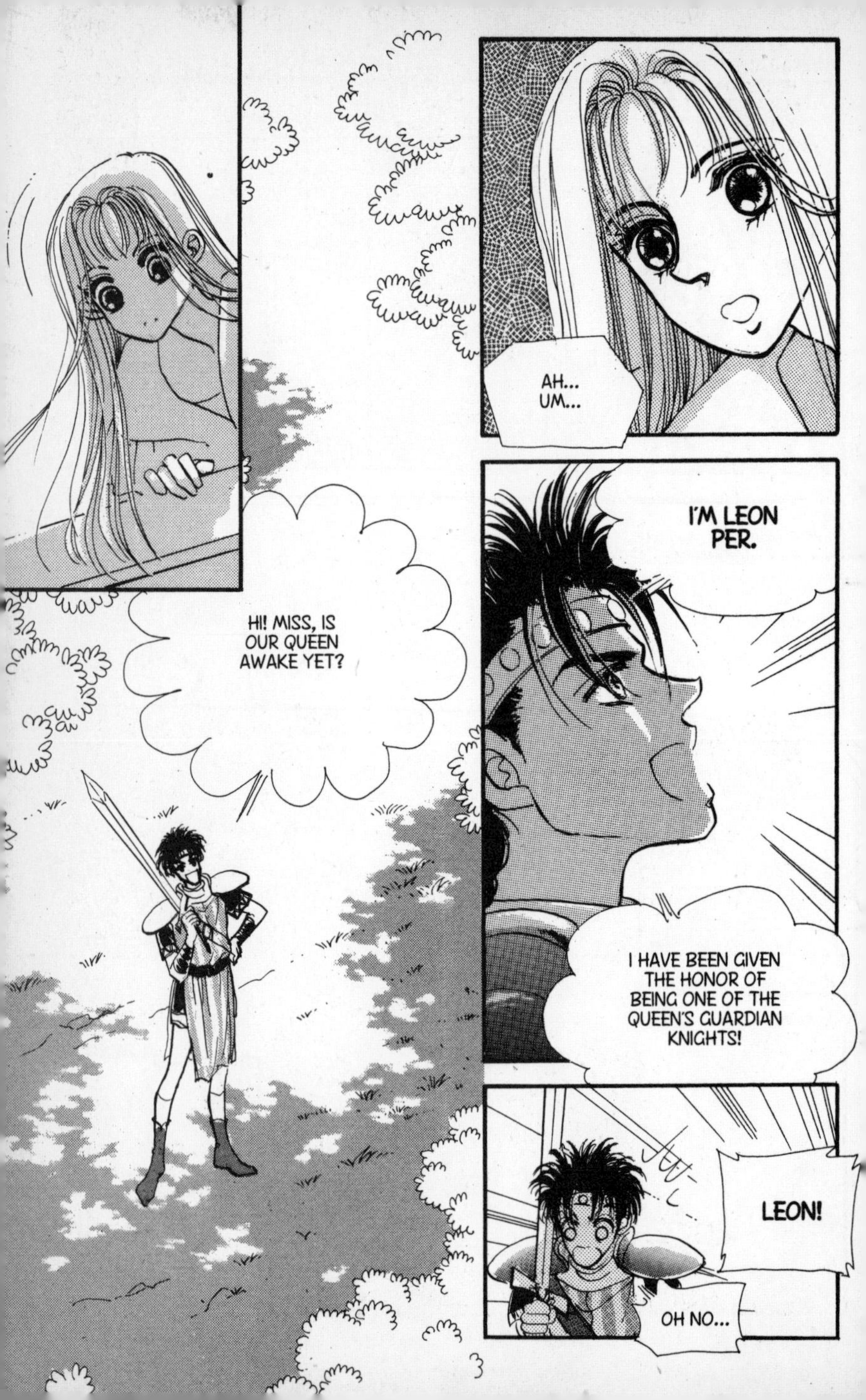
AH... UM...
HI! MISS, IS OUR QUEEN AWAKE YET?
I'M LEON PER.
I HAVE BEEN GIVEN THE HONOR OF BEING ONE OF THE QUEEN'S GUARDIAN KNIGHTS!
LEON!
OH NO...

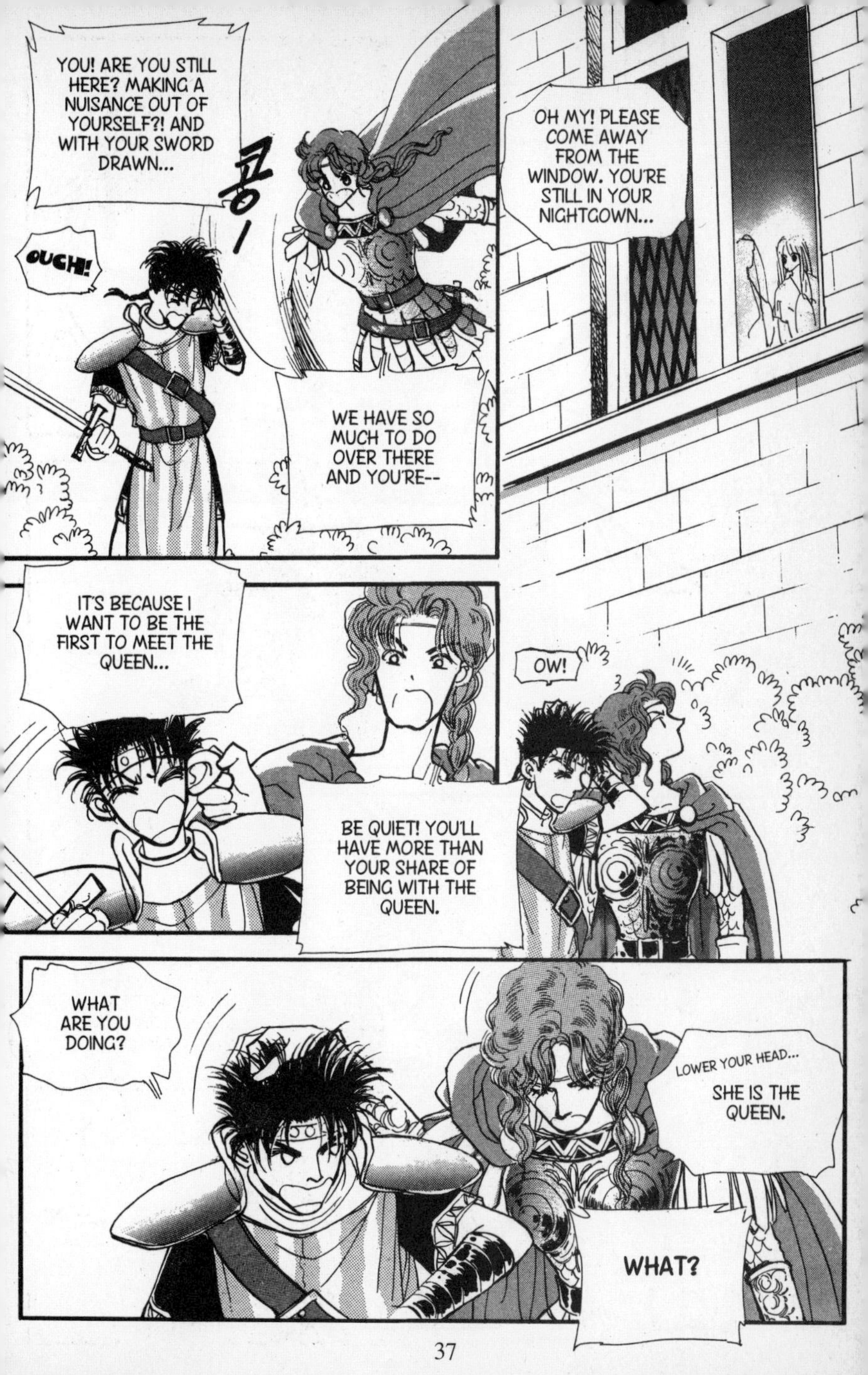
YOU! ARE YOU STILL HERE? MAKING A NUISANCE OUT OF YOURSELF?! AND WITH YOUR SWORD DRAWN...
콩!
OUCH!
WE HAVE SO MUCH TO DO OVER THERE AND YOU'RE--
OH MY! PLEASE COME AWAY FROM THE WINDOW. YOU'RE STILL IN YOUR NIGHTGOWN...
IT'S BECAUSE I WANT TO BE THE FIRST TO MEET THE QUEEN...
BE QUIET! YOU'LL HAVE MORE THAN YOUR SHARE OF BEING WITH THE QUEEN.
OW!
WHAT ARE YOU DOING?
LOWER YOUR HEAD...
SHE IS THE QUEEN.
WHAT?

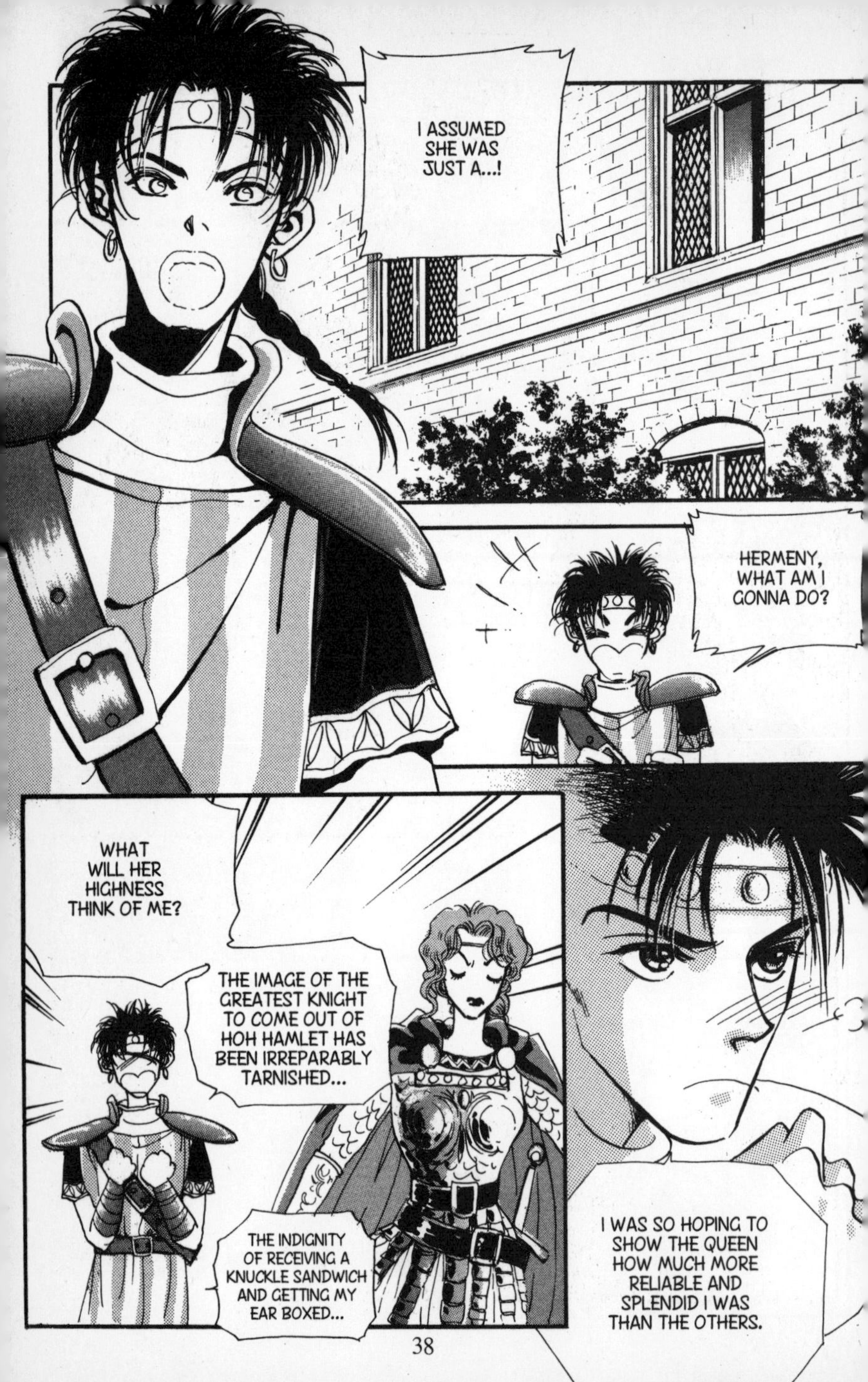
I ASSUMED SHE WAS JUST A...!
HERMENY, WHAT AM I GONNA DO?
WHAT WILL HER HIGHNESS THINK OF ME?
THE IMAGE OF THE GREATEST KNIGHT TO COME OUT OF HOH HAMLET HAS BEEN IRREPARABLY TARNISHED...
THE INDIGNITY OF RECEIVING A KNUCKLE SANDWICH AND GETTING MY EAR BOXED...
I WAS SO HOPING TO SHOW THE QUEEN HOW MUCH MORE RELIABLE AND SPLENDID I WAS THAN THE OTHERS.

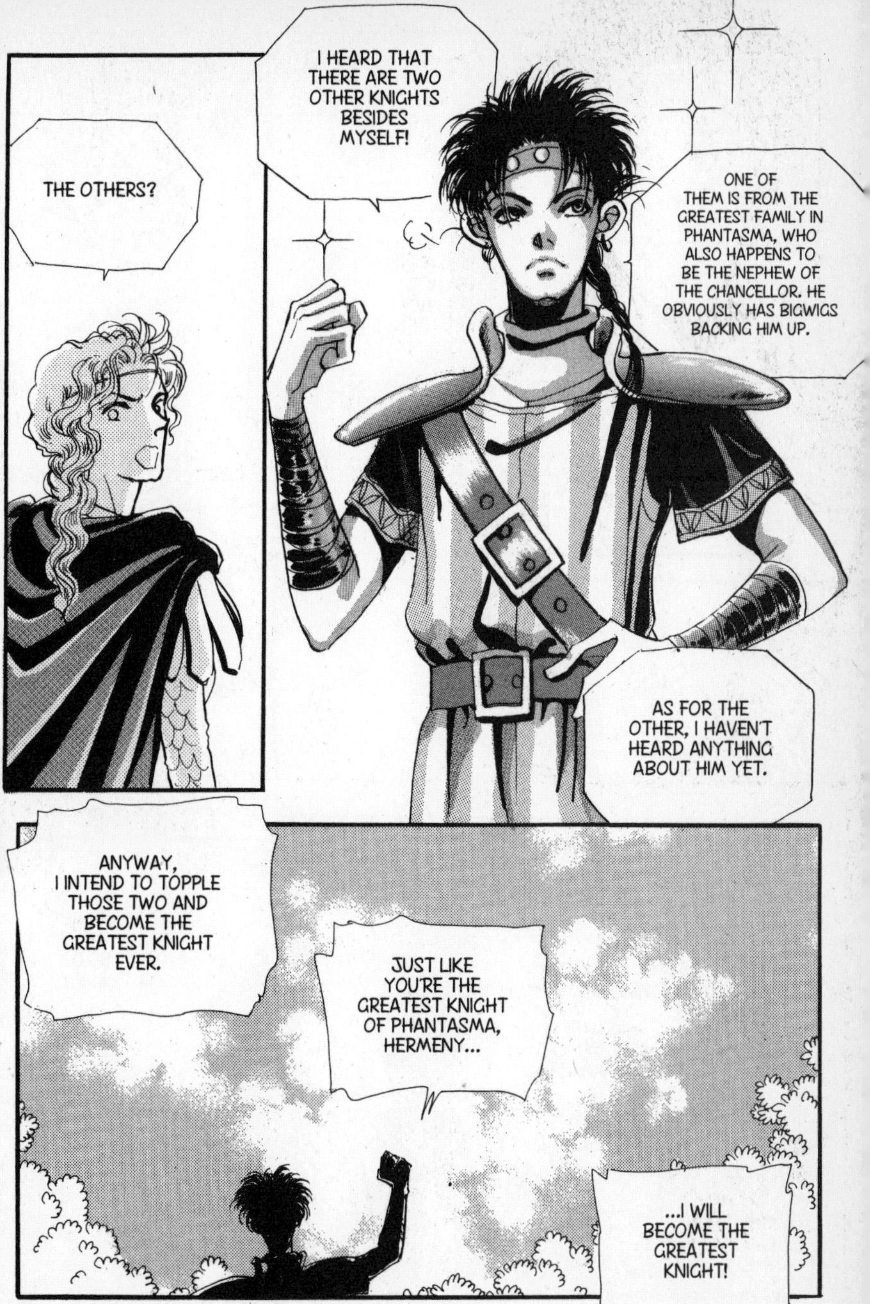
THE OTHERS?
I HEARD THAT THERE ARE TWO OTHER KNIGHTS BESIDES MYSELF!
ONE OF THEM IS FROM THE GREATEST FAMILY IN PHANTASMA, WHO ALSO HAPPENS TO BE THE NEPHEW OF THE CHANCELLOR. HE OBVIOUSLY HAS BIGWIGS BACKING HIM UP.
AS FOR THE OTHER, I HAVEN'T HEARD ANYTHING ABOUT HIM YET.
ANYWAY, I INTEND TO TOPPLE THOSE TWO AND BECOME THE GREATEST KNIGHT EVER.
JUST LIKE YOU'RE THE GREATEST KNIGHT OF PHANTASMA, HERMENY...
...I WILL BECOME THE GREATEST KNIGHT!

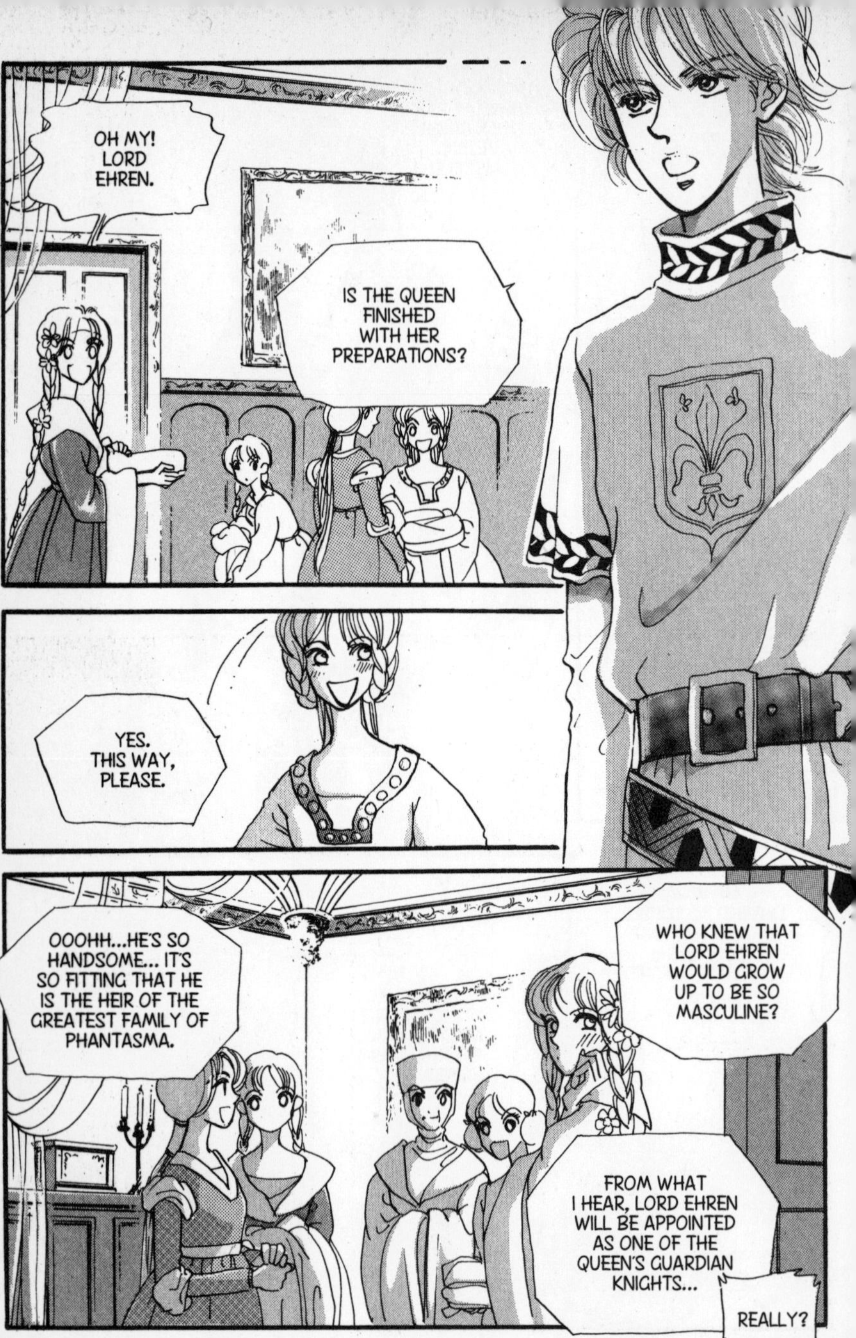
OH MY! LORD EHREN.
IS THE QUEEN FINISHED WITH HER PREPARATIONS?
YES. THIS WAY, PLEASE.
OOOHH...HE'S SO HANDSOME... IT'S SO FITTING THAT HE IS THE HEIR OF THE GREATEST FAMILY OF PHANTASMA.
WHO KNEW THAT LORD EHREN WOULD GROW UP TO BE SO MASCULINE?
FROM WHAT I HEAR, LORD EHREN WILL BE APPOINTED AS ONE OF THE QUEEN'S GUARDIAN KNIGHTS...
REALLY?

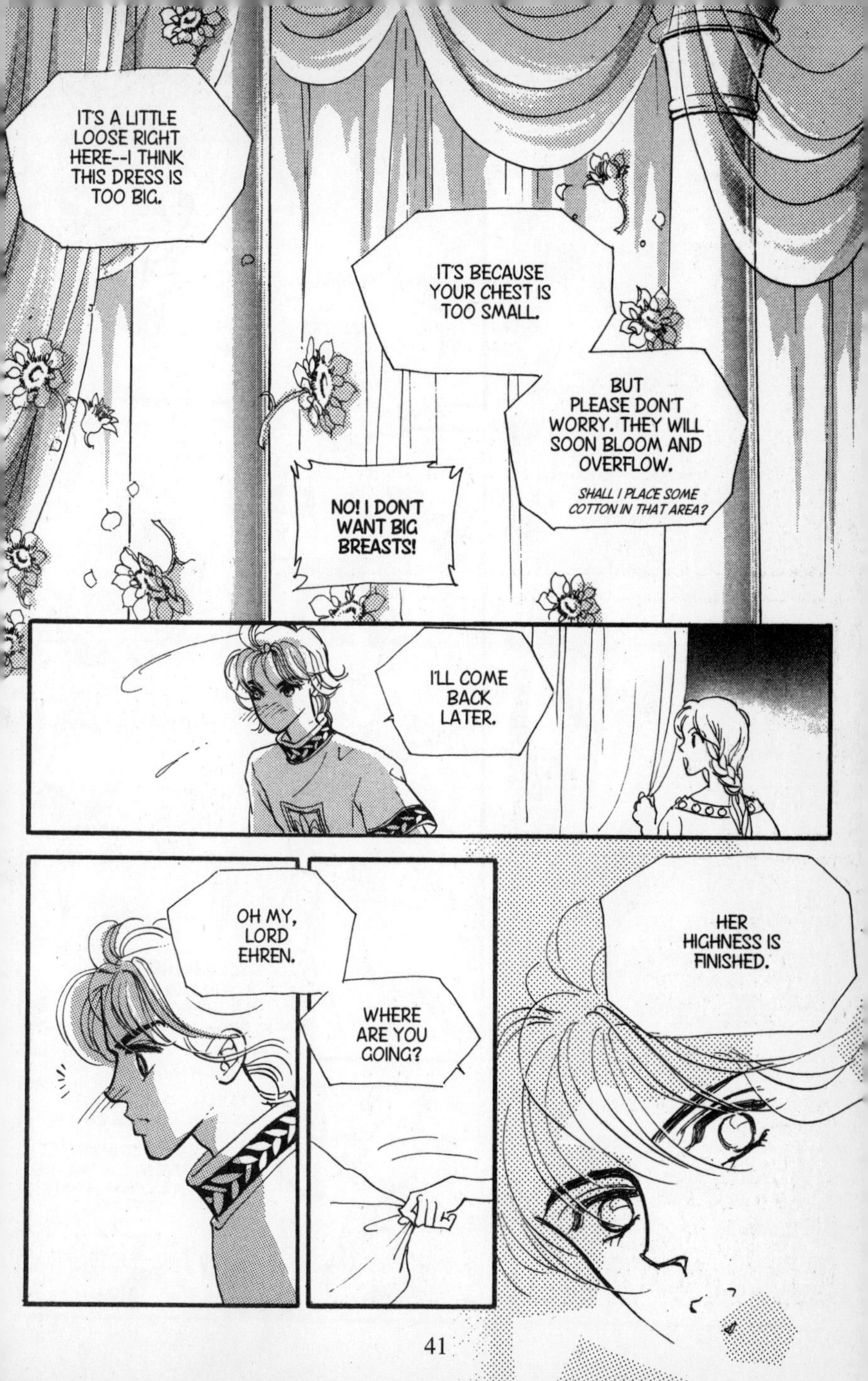
IT'S A LITTLE LOOSE RIGHT HERE--I THINK THIS DRESS IS TOO BIG.
IT'S BECAUSE YOUR CHEST IS TOO SMALL.
BUT PLEASE DON'T WORRY. THEY WILL SOON BLOOM AND OVERFLOW.
SHALL I PLACE SOME COTTON IN THAT AREA?
NO! I DON'T WANT BIG BREASTS!
I'LL COME BACK LATER.
OH MY, LORD EHREN.
WHERE ARE YOU GOING?
HER HIGHNESS IS FINISHED.

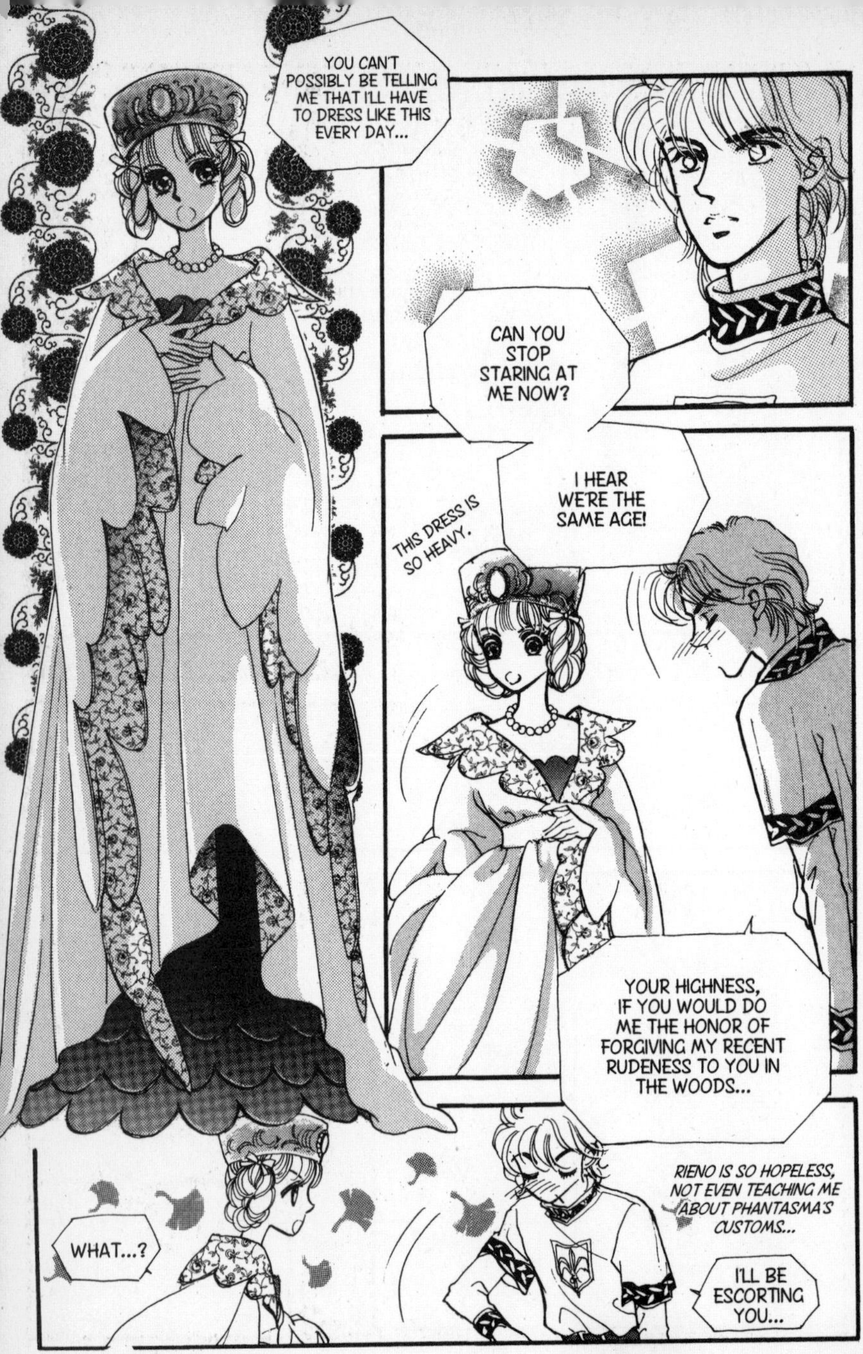
YOU CAN'T POSSIBLY BE TELLING ME THAT I'LL HAVE TO DRESS LIKE THIS EVERY DAY...
CAN YOU STOP STARING AT ME NOW?
I HEAR WE'RE THE SAME AGE!
THIS DRESS IS SO HEAVY.
YOUR HIGHNESS, IF YOU WOULD DO ME THE HONOR OF FORGIVING MY RECENT RUDENESS TO YOU IN THE WOODS...
WHAT...?
RIENO IS SO HOPELESS, NOT EVEN TEACHING ME ABOUT PHANTASMA'S CUSTOMS...
I'LL BE ESCORTING YOU...

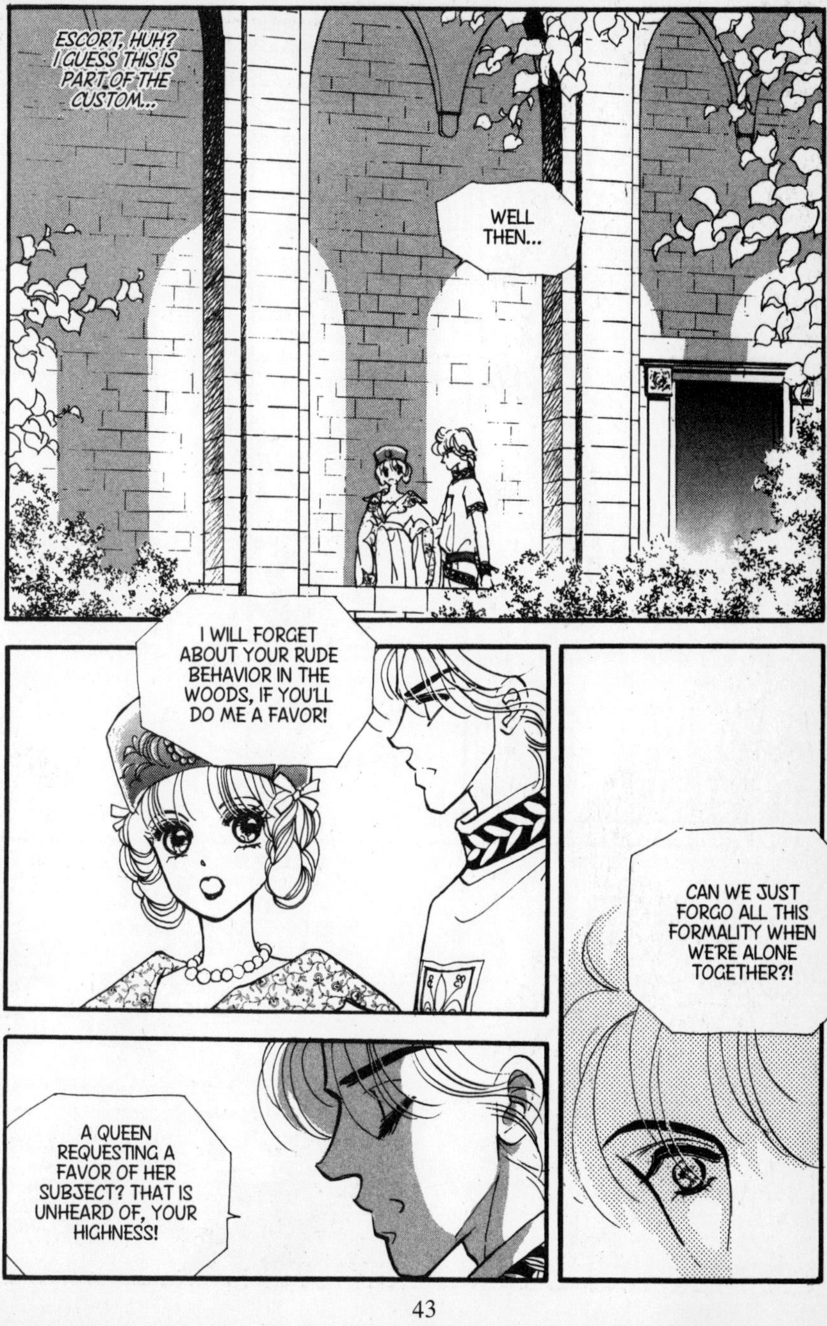
ESCORT, HUH? I GUESS THIS IS PART OF THE CUSTOM...
WELL THEN...
I WILL FORGET ABOUT YOUR RUDE BEHAVIOR IN THE WOODS, IF YOU'LL DO ME A FAVOR!
A QUEEN REQUESTING A FAVOR OF HER SUBJECT? THAT IS UNHEARD OF, YOUR HIGHNESS!
CAN WE JUST FORGO ALL THIS FORMALITY WHEN WE'RE ALONE TOGETHER?!

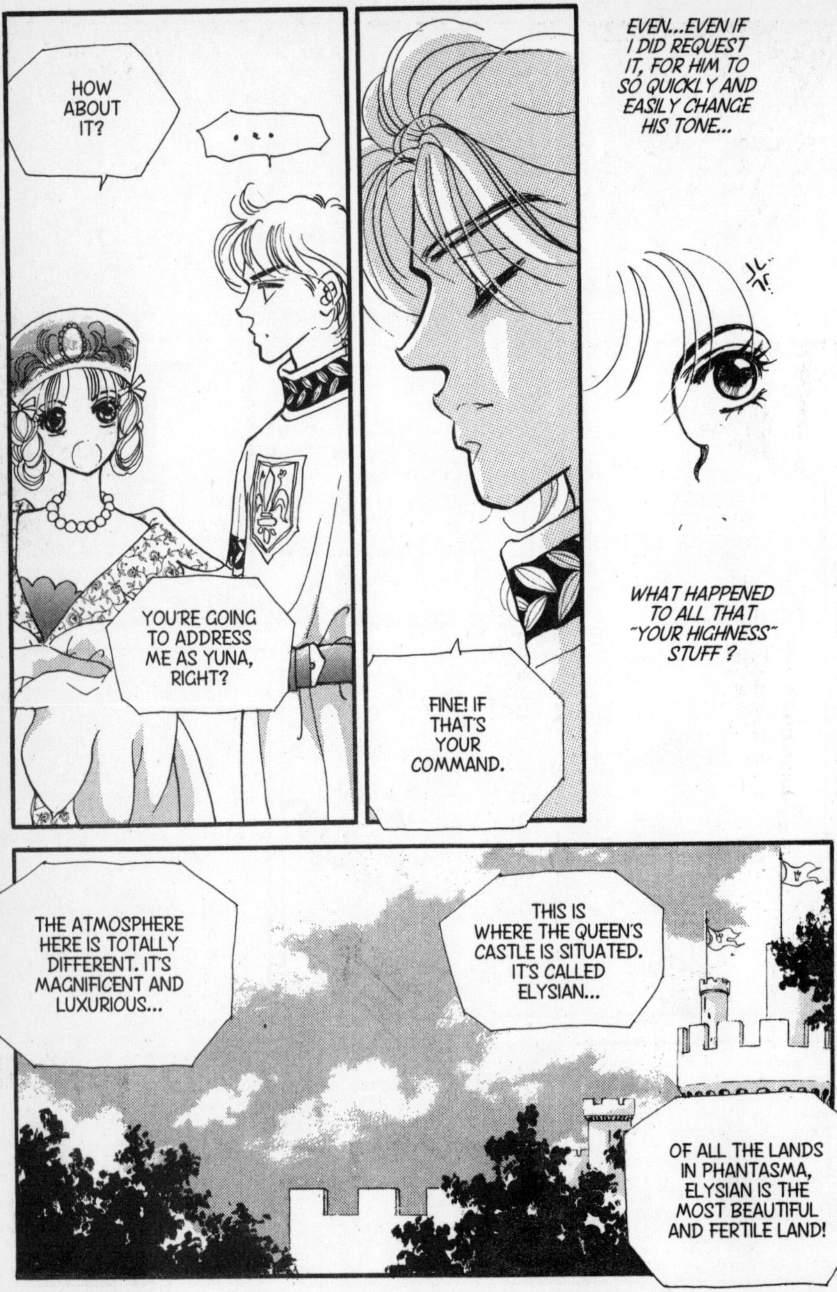
HOW ABOUT IT?
...
YOU'RE GOING TO ADDRESS ME AS YUNA, RIGHT?
FINE! IF THAT'S YOUR COMMAND.
EVEN...EVEN IF I DID REQUEST IT, FOR HIM TO SO QUICKLY AND EASILY CHANGE HIS TONE...
WHAT HAPPENED TO ALL THAT "YOUR HIGHNESS" STUFF ?
THE ATMOSPHERE HERE IS TOTALLY DIFFERENT. IT'S MAGNIFICENT AND LUXURIOUS...
THIS IS WHERE THE QUEEN'S CASTLE IS SITUATED. IT'S CALLED ELYSIAN...
OF ALL THE LANDS IN PHANTASMA, ELYSIAN IS THE MOST BEAUTIFUL AND FERTILE LAND!

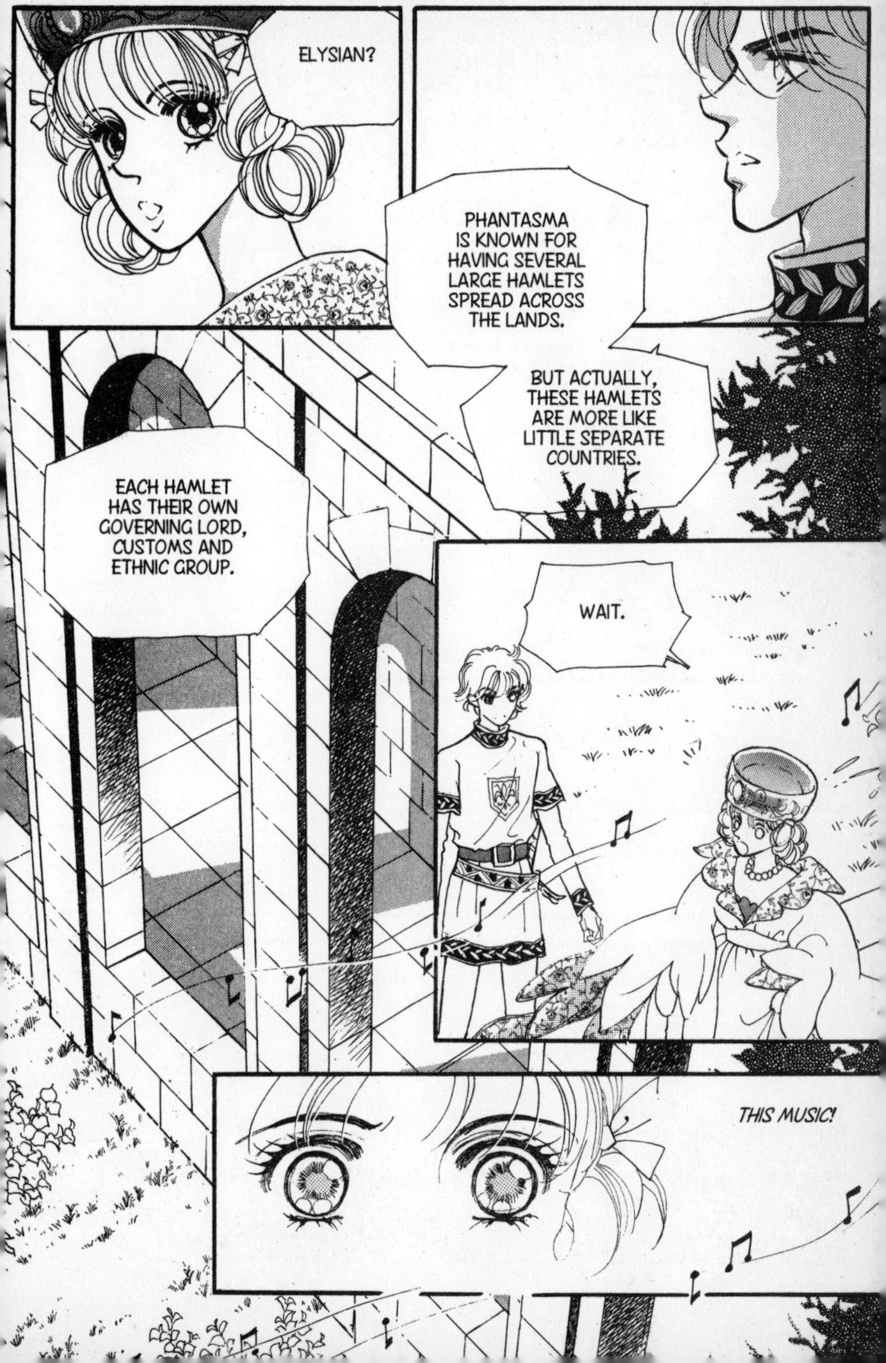
ELYSIAN?
PHANTASMA IS KNOWN FOR HAVING SEVERAL LARGE HAMLETS SPREAD ACROSS THE LANDS.
EACH HAMLET HAS THEIR OWN GOVERNING LORD, CUSTOMS AND ETHNIC GROUP.
BUT ACTUALLY, THESE HAMLETS ARE MORE LIKE LITTLE SEPARATE COUNTRIES.
WAIT.
THIS MUSIC!

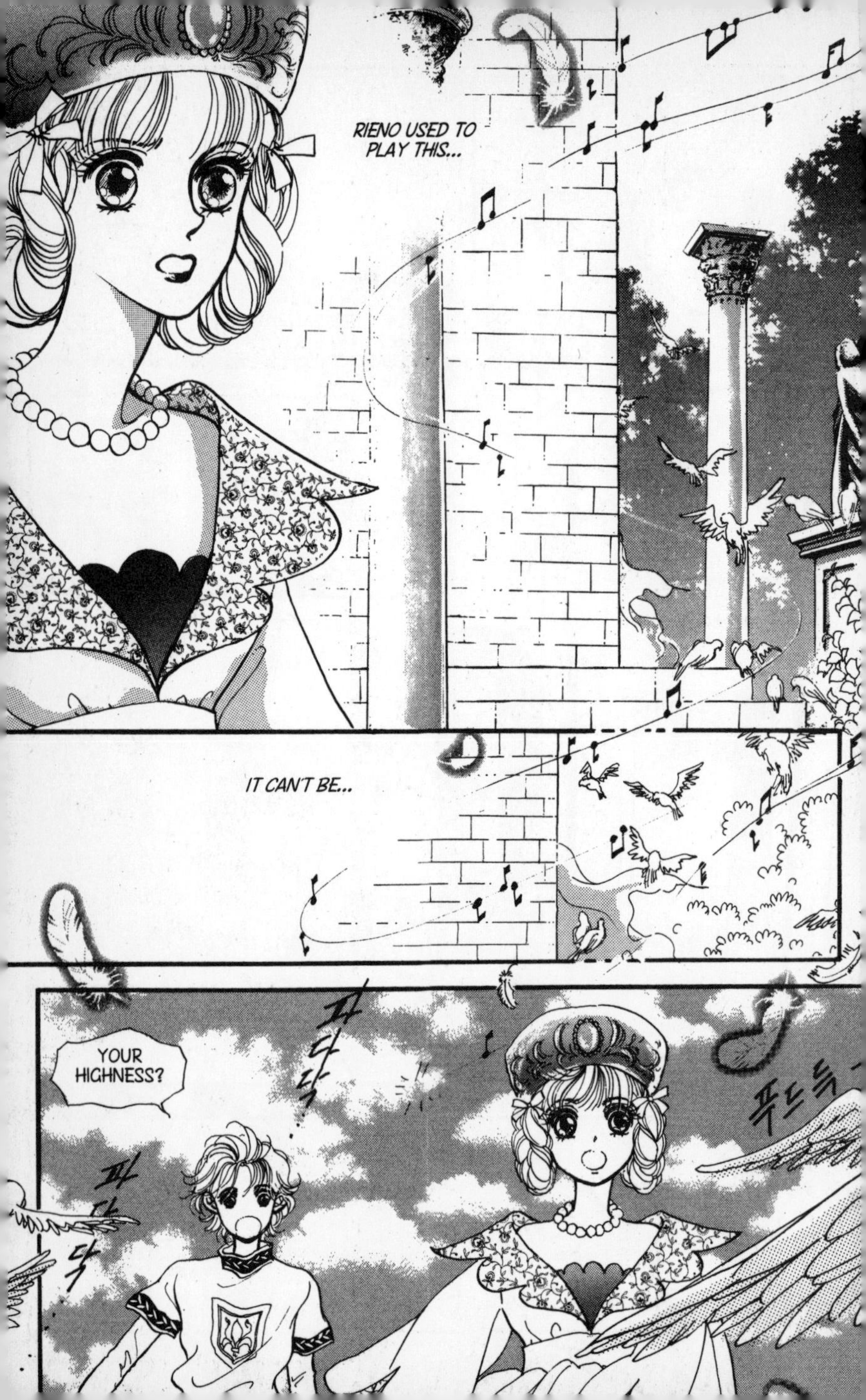
RIENO USED TO PLAY THIS...
IT CAN'T BE...
YOUR HIGHNESS?

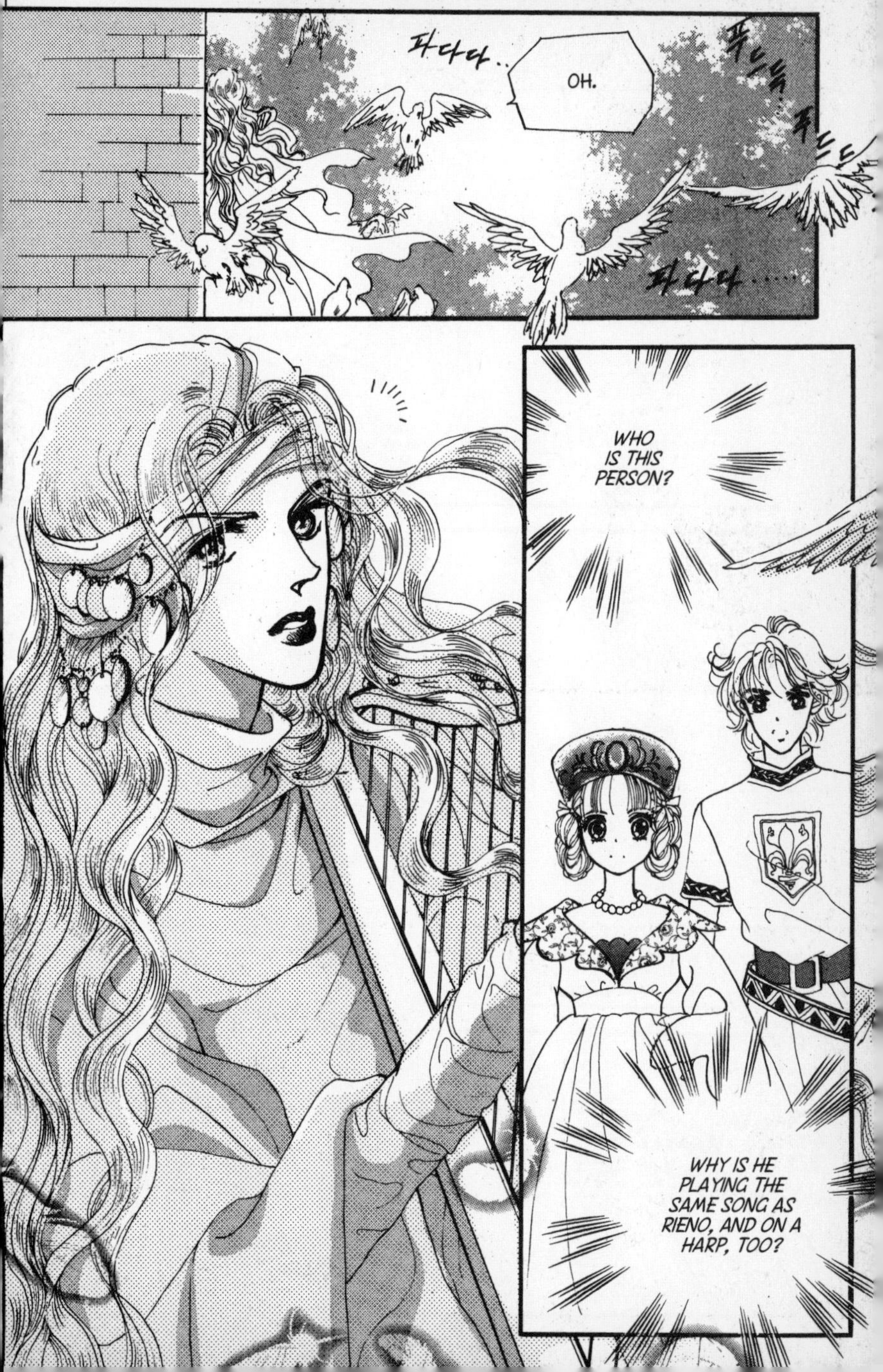
파다다..
OH.
푸드득..
푸드득
파다다......
WHO IS THIS PERSON?
WHY IS HE PLAYING THE SAME SONG AS RIENO, AND ON A HARP, TOO?

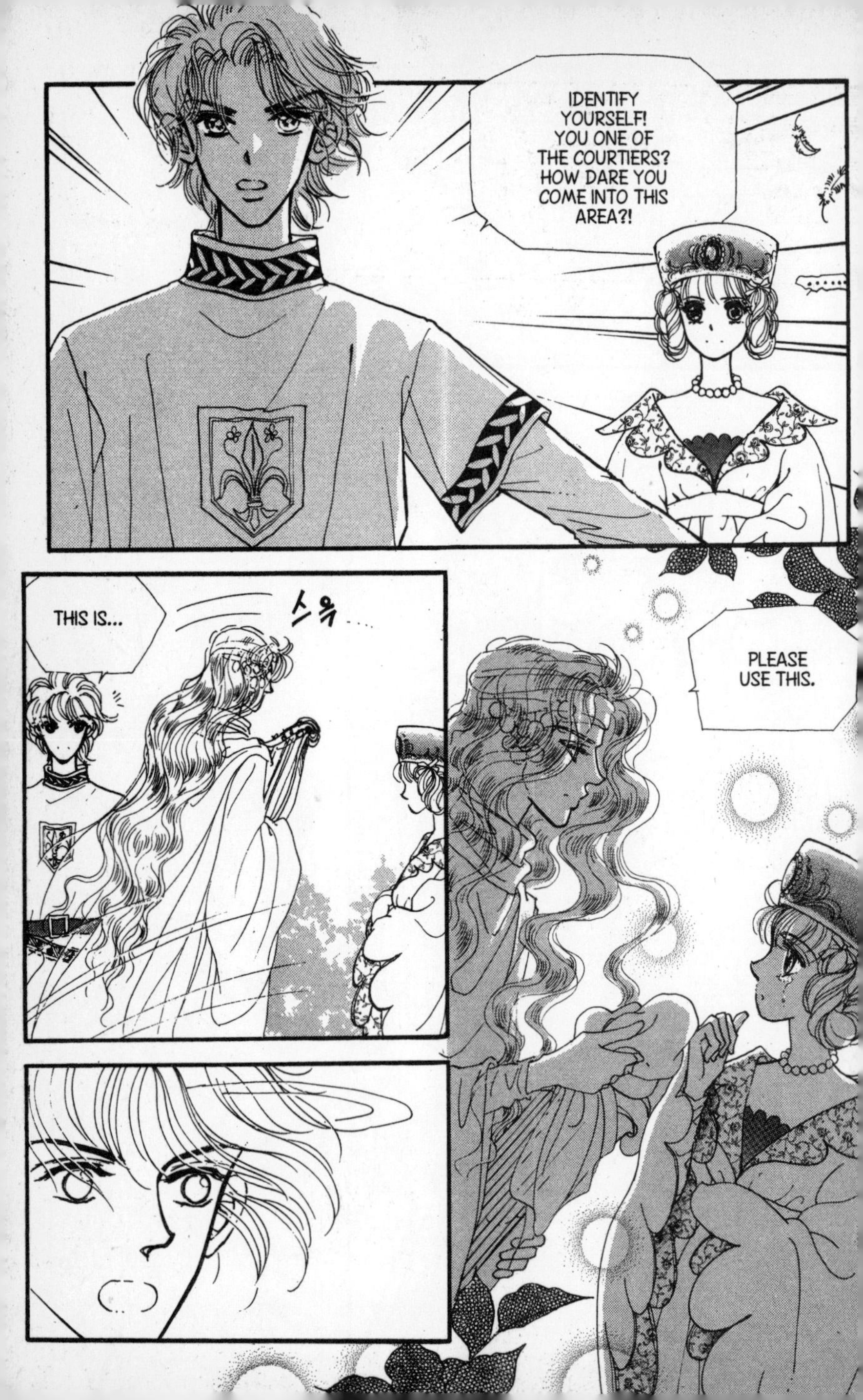
IDENTIFY YOURSELF! YOU ONE OF THE COURTIERS? HOW DARE YOU COME INTO THIS AREA?!
THIS IS...
스윽
PLEASE USE THIS.

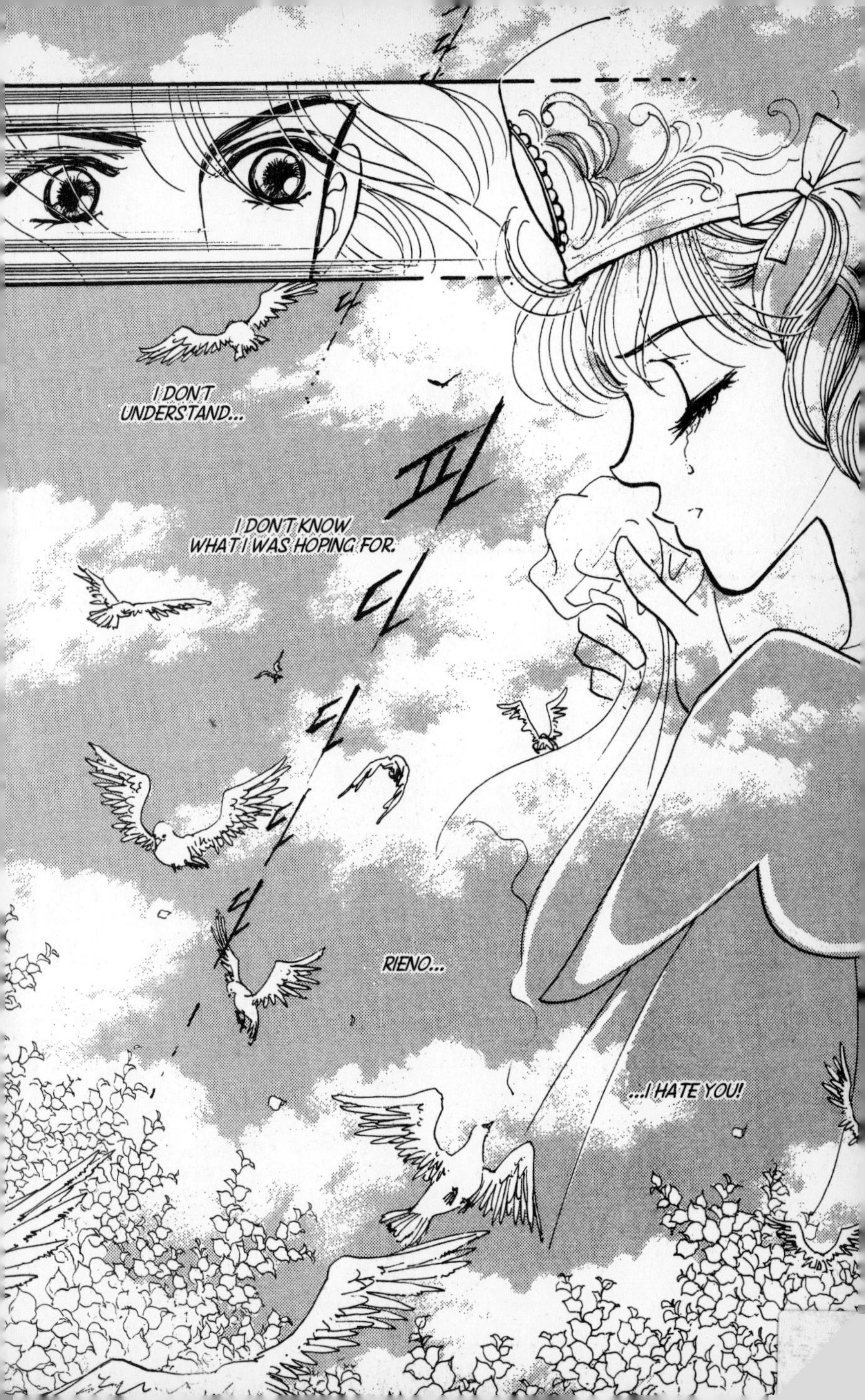

I DON'T UNDERSTAND...
I DON'T KNOW WHAT I WAS HOPING FOR.
RIENO...
...I HATE YOU!

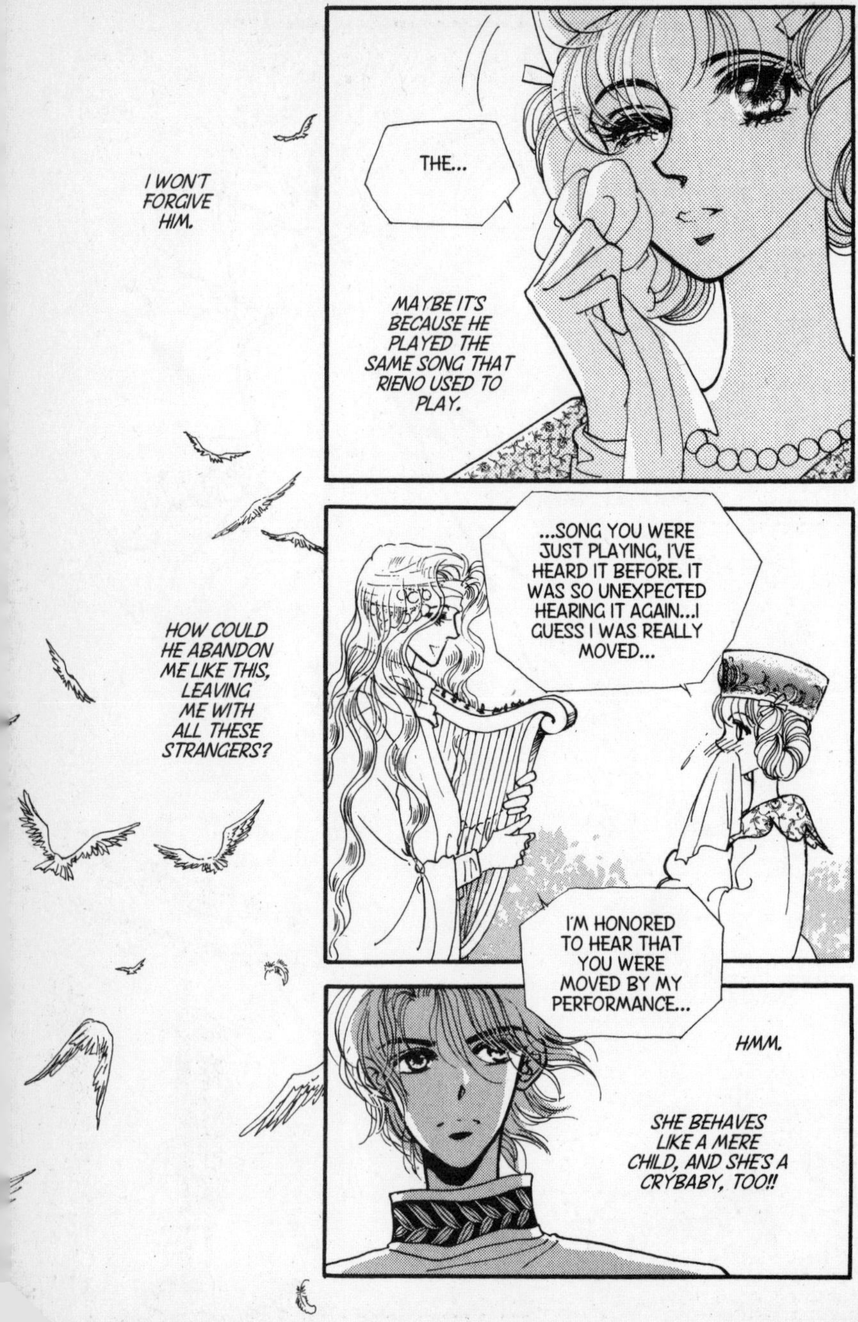
I WON'T FORGIVE HIM.
THE...
MAYBE IT'S BECAUSE HE PLAYED THE SAME SONG THAT RIENO USED TO PLAY.
HOW COULD HE ABANDON ME LIKE THIS, LEAVING ME WITH ALL THESE STRANGERS?
...SONG YOU WERE JUST PLAYING, I'VE HEARD IT BEFORE. IT WAS SO UNEXPECTED HEARING IT AGAIN...I GUESS I WAS REALLY MOVED...
I'M HONORED TO HEAR THAT YOU WERE MOVED BY MY PERFORMANCE...
HMM.
SHE BEHAVES LIKE A MERE CHILD, AND SHE'S A CRYBABY, TOO!!

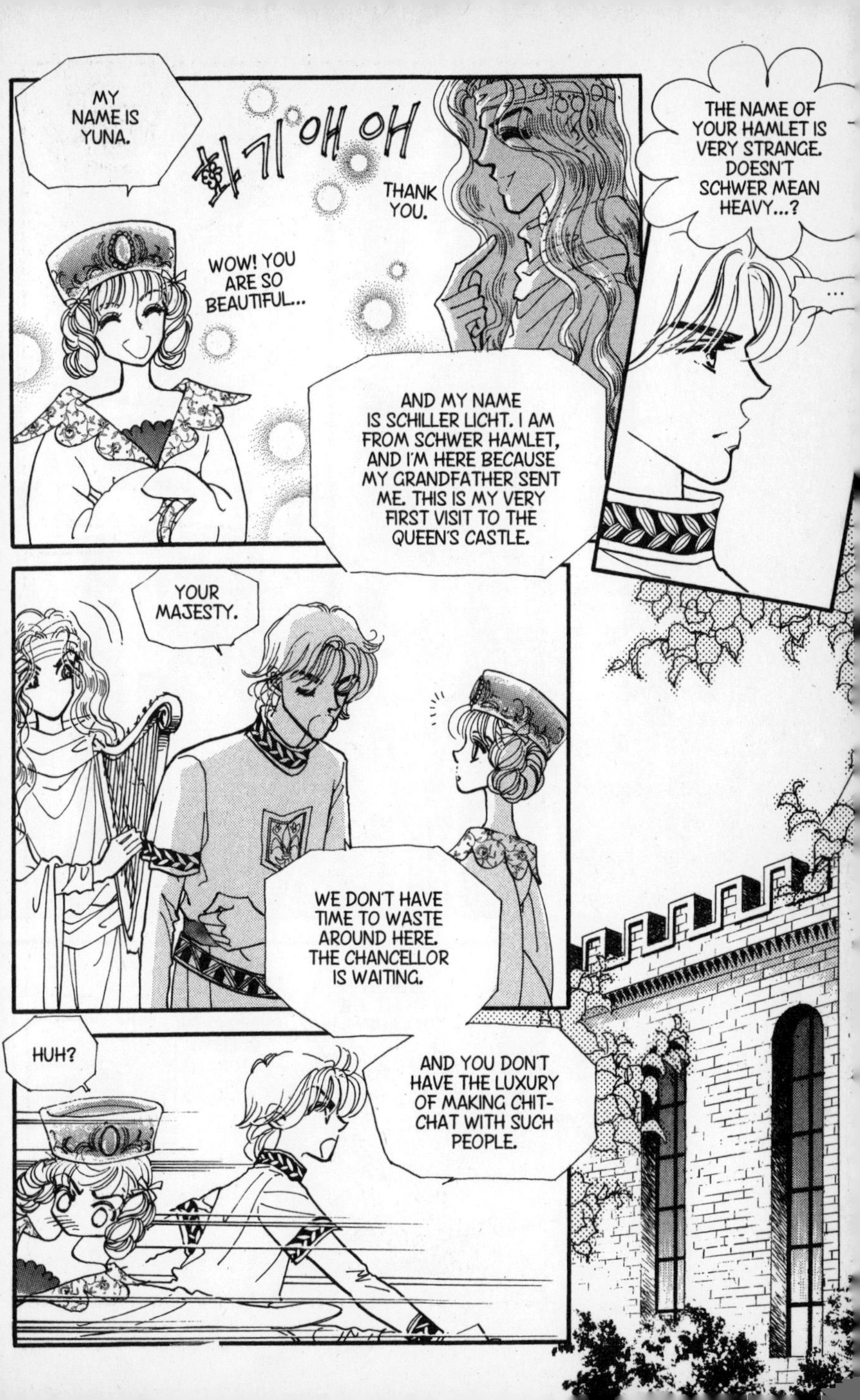
MY NAME IS YUNA.
화기애애
THANK YOU.
WOW! YOU ARE SO BEAUTIFUL...
AND MY NAME IS SCHILLER LICHT. I AM FROM SCHWER HAMLET, AND I'M HERE BECAUSE MY GRANDFATHER SENT ME. THIS IS MY VERY FIRST VISIT TO THE QUEEN'S CASTLE.
THE NAME OF YOUR HAMLET IS VERY STRANGE. DOESN'T SCHWER MEAN HEAVY...?
...
YOUR MAJESTY.
WE DON'T HAVE TIME TO WASTE AROUND HERE. THE CHANCELLOR IS WAITING.
HUH?
AND YOU DON'T HAVE THE LUXURY OF MAKING CHIT-CHAT WITH SUCH PEOPLE.

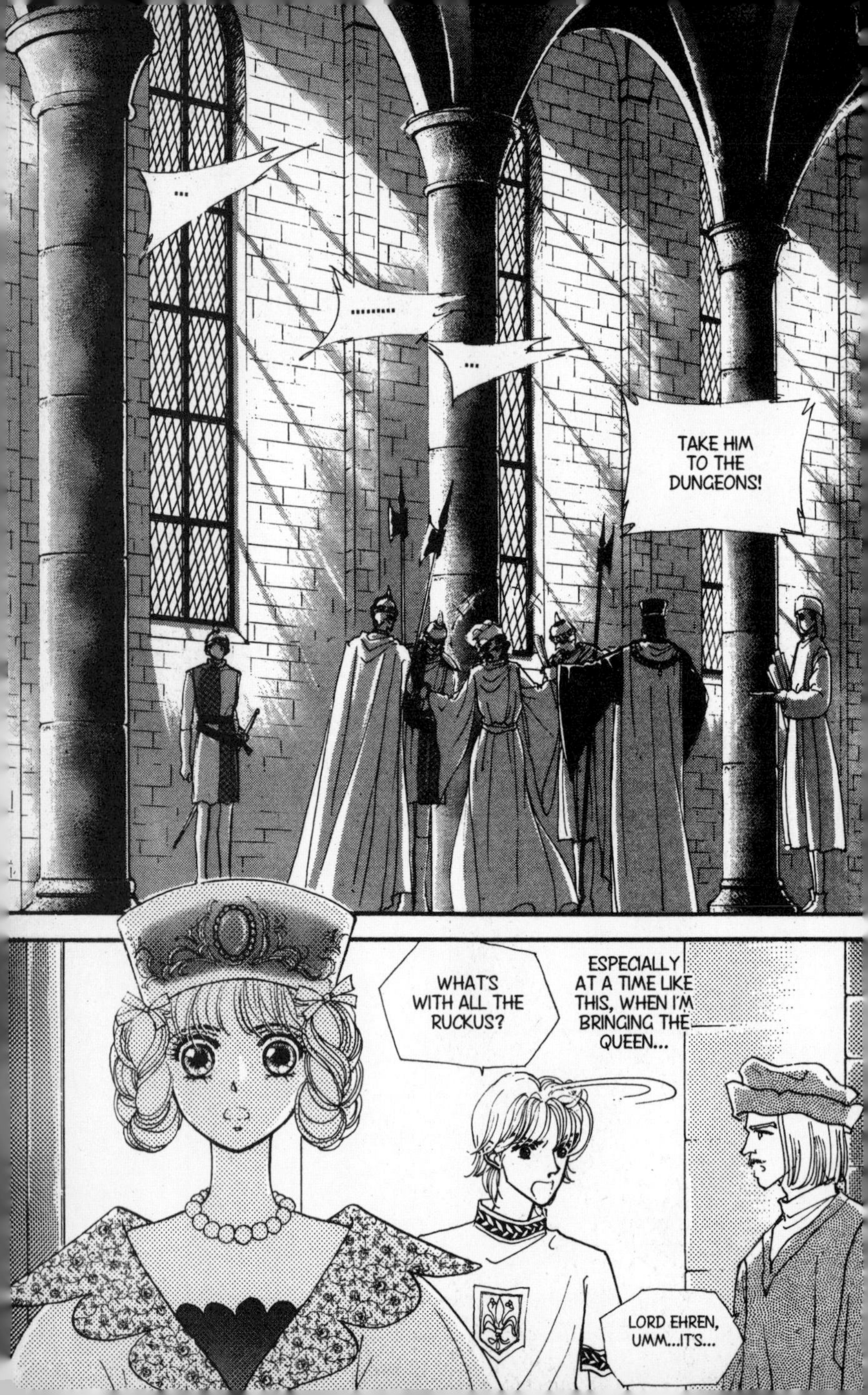
...
....
...
TAKE HIM TO THE DUNGEONS!
WHAT'S WITH ALL THE RUCKUS?
ESPECIALLY AT A TIME LIKE THIS, WHEN I'M BRINGING THE QUEEN...
LORD EHREN, UMM...ITS...

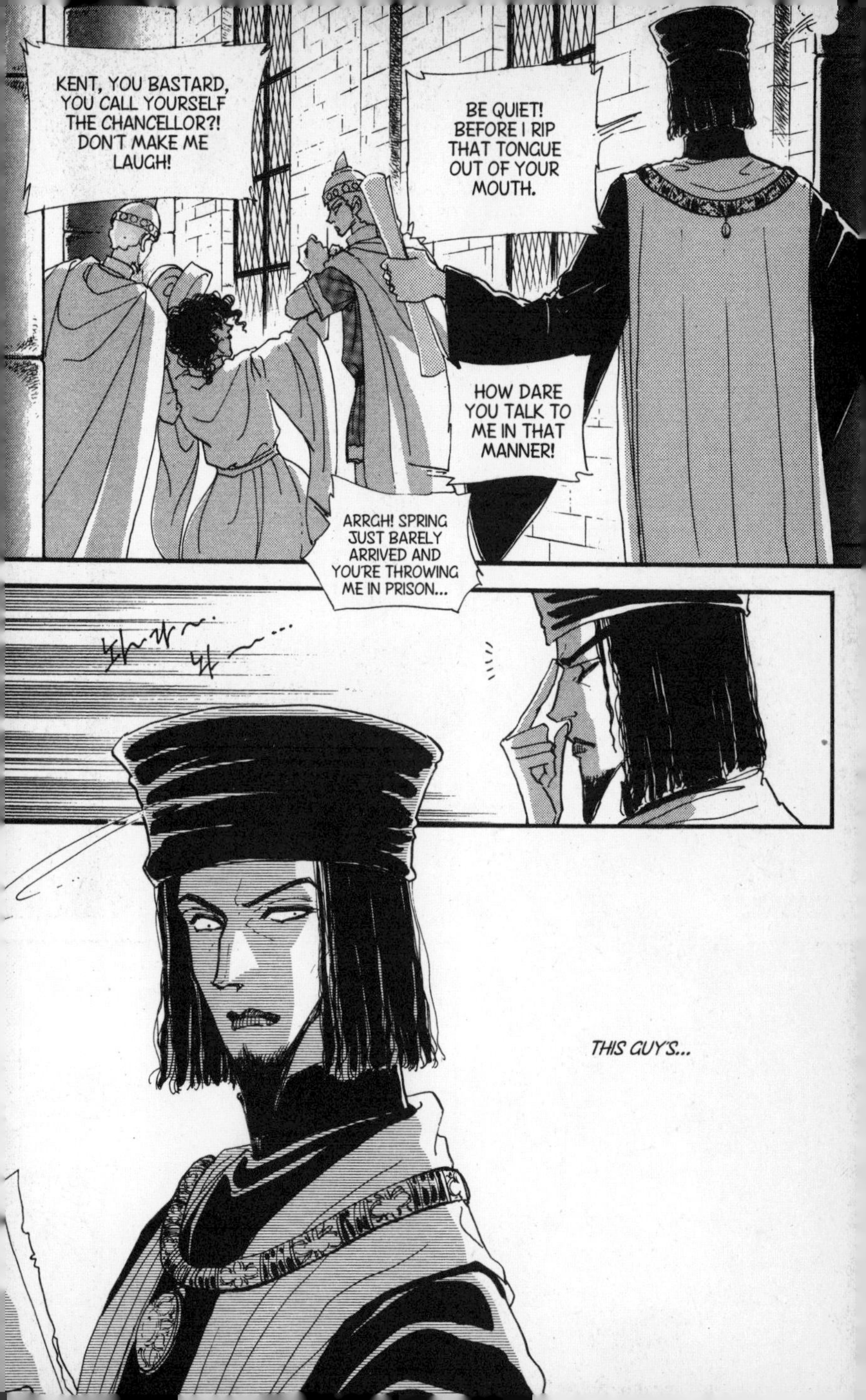
KENT, YOU BASTARD, YOU CALL YOURSELF THE CHANCELLOR?! DON'T MAKE ME LAUGH!
BE QUIET! BEFORE I RIP THAT TONGUE OUT OF YOUR MOUTH.
HOW DARE YOU TALK TO ME IN THAT MANNER!
ARRGH! SPRING JUST BARELY ARRIVED AND YOU'RE THROWING ME IN PRISON...
THIS GUY'S...

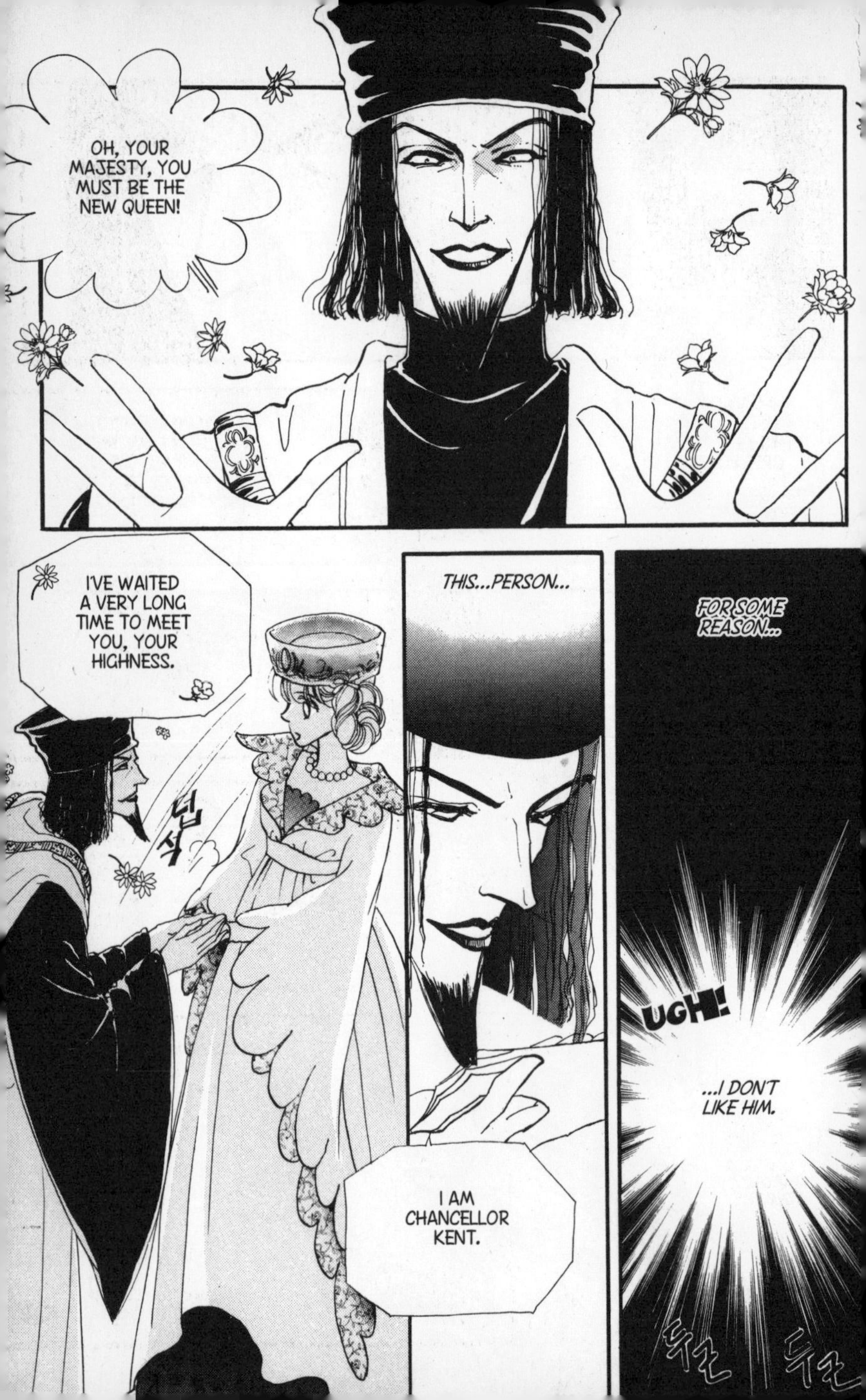
OH, YOUR MAJESTY, YOU MUST BE THE NEW QUEEN!
I'VE WAITED A VERY LONG TIME TO MEET YOU, YOUR HIGHNESS.
덥석
THIS...PERSON...
I AM CHANCELLOR KENT.
FOR SOME REASON...
UGH!
...I DON'T LIKE HIM.
두근 두근

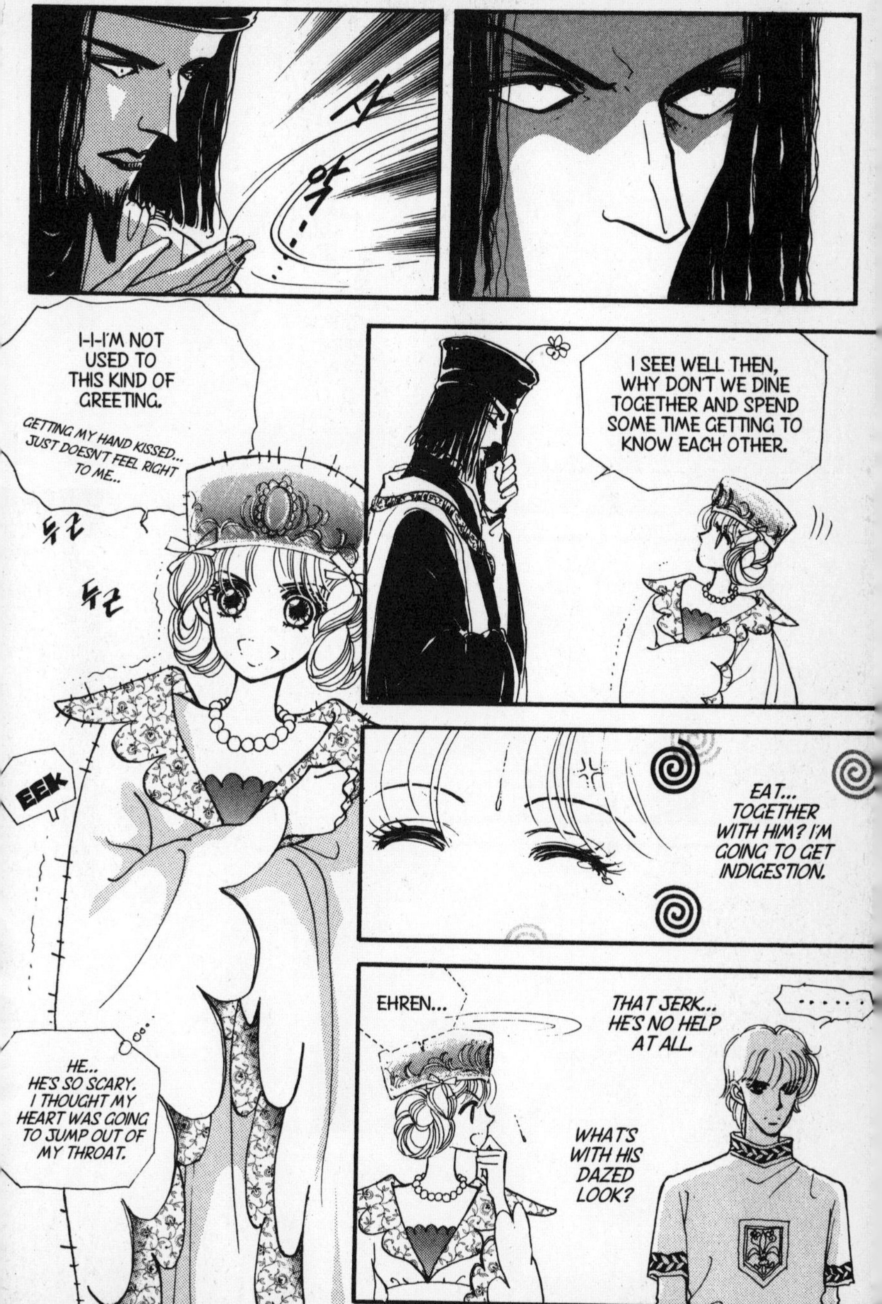
사악...
I-I-I'M NOT USED TO THIS KIND OF GREETING.
GETTING MY HAND KISSED... JUST DOESN'T FEEL RIGHT TO ME..
두근
두근
EEK
HE... HE'S SO SCARY. I THOUGHT MY HEART WAS GOING TO JUMP OUT OF MY THROAT.
I SEE! WELL THEN, WHY DON'T WE DINE TOGETHER AND SPEND SOME TIME GETTING TO KNOW EACH OTHER.
EAT... TOGETHER WITH HIM? I'M GOING TO GET INDIGESTION.
EHREN...
THAT JERK... HE'S NO HELP AT ALL.
......
WHAT'S WITH HIS DAZED LOOK?

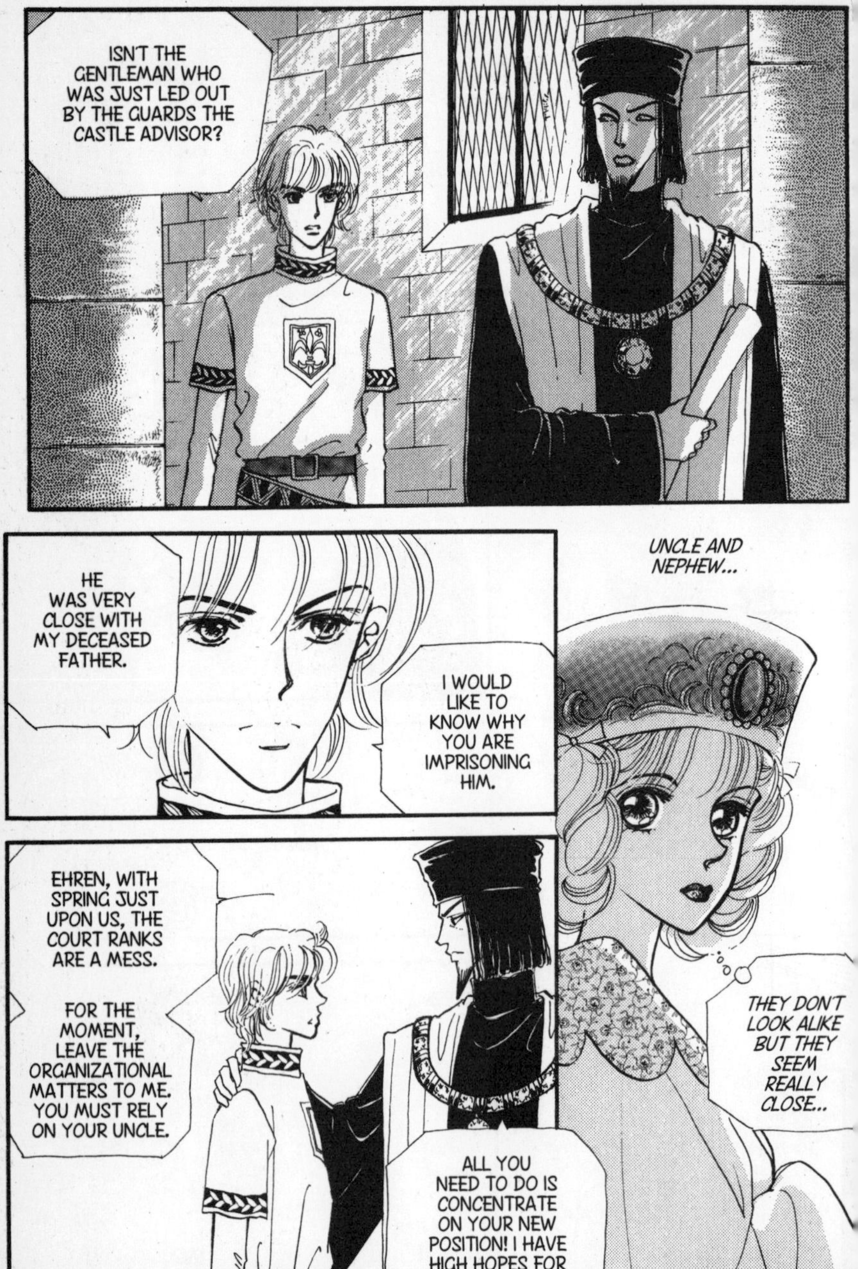
ISN'T THE GENTLEMAN WHO WAS JUST LED OUT BY THE GUARDS THE CASTLE ADVISOR?
HE WAS VERY CLOSE WITH MY DECEASED FATHER.
I WOULD LIKE TO KNOW WHY YOU ARE IMPRISONING HIM.
UNCLE AND NEPHEW...
EHREN, WITH SPRING JUST UPON US, THE COURT RANKS ARE A MESS.
FOR THE MOMENT, LEAVE THE ORGANIZATIONAL MATTERS TO ME. YOU MUST RELY ON YOUR UNCLE.
ALL YOU NEED TO DO IS CONCENTRATE ON YOUR NEW POSITION! I HAVE HIGH HOPES FOR YOU.
THEY DON'T LOOK ALIKE BUT THEY SEEM REALLY CLOSE...

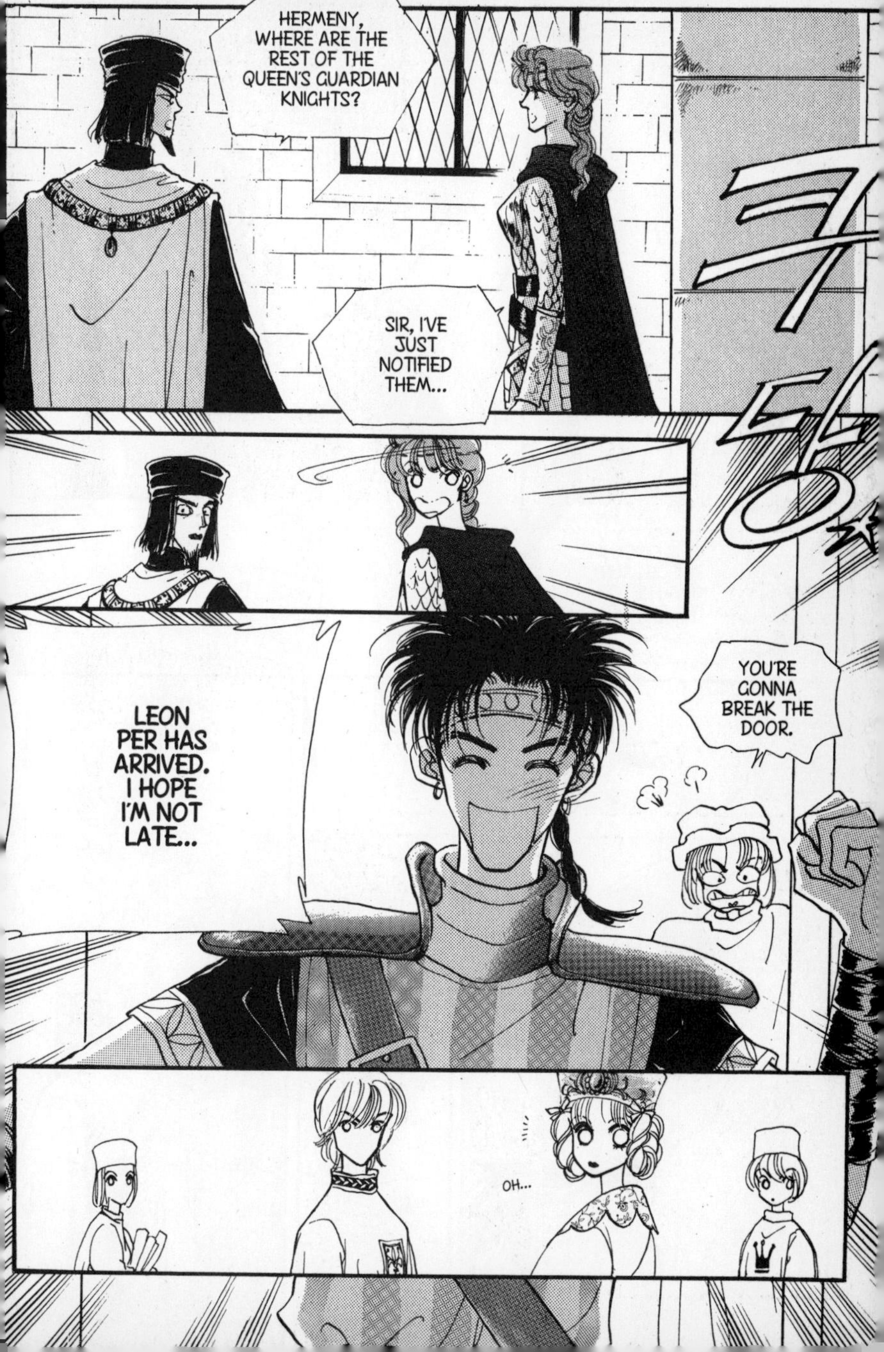
HERMENY, WHERE ARE THE REST OF THE QUEEN'S GUARDIAN KNIGHTS?
SIR, I'VE JUST NOTIFIED THEM...
LEON PER HAS ARRIVED. I HOPE I'M NOT LATE...
YOU'RE GONNA BREAK THE DOOR.
OH...

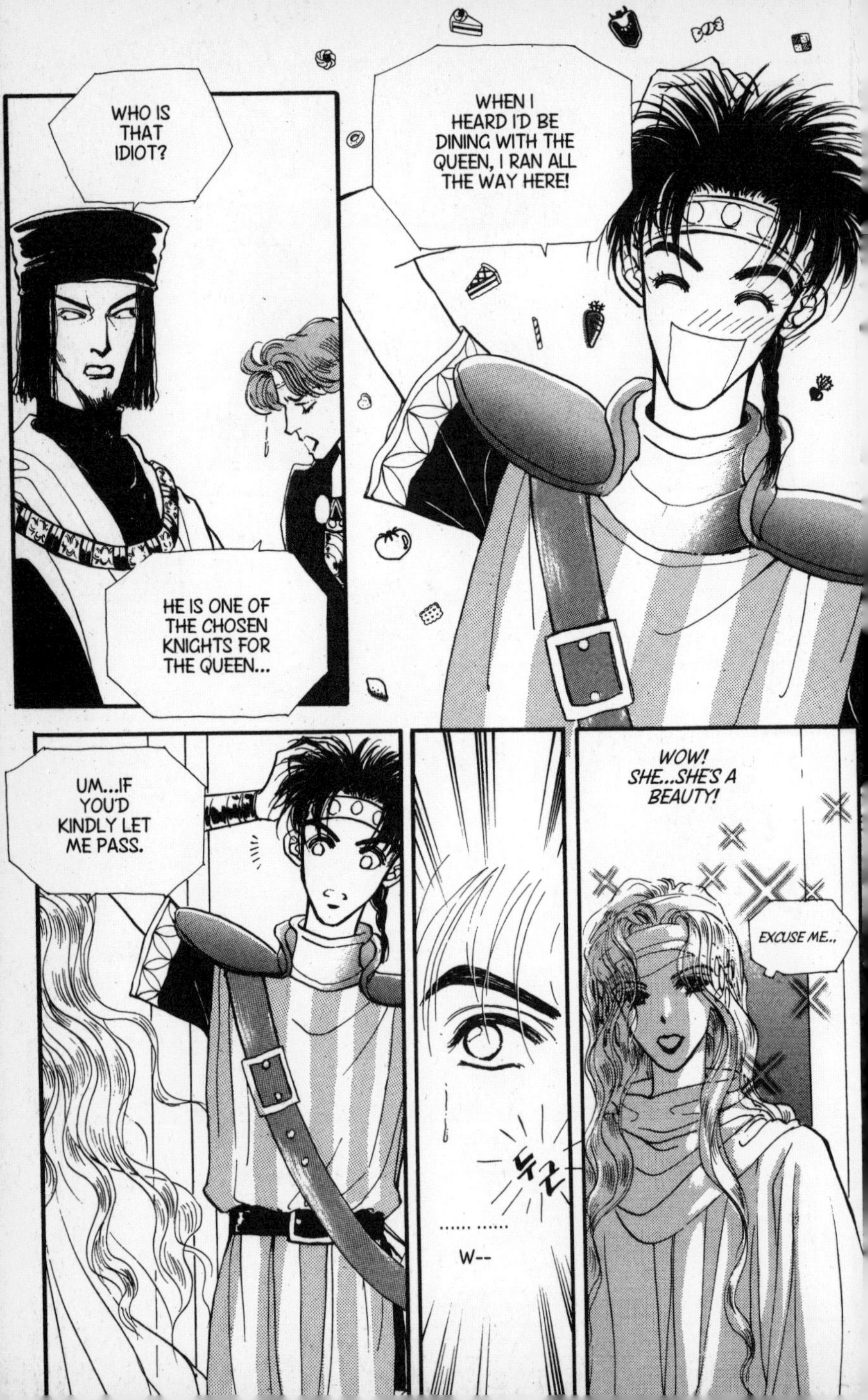
WHO IS THAT IDIOT?
HE IS ONE OF THE CHOSEN KNIGHTS FOR THE QUEEN...
WHEN I HEARD I'D BE DINING WITH THE QUEEN, I RAN ALL THE WAY HERE!
UM...IF YOU'D KINDLY LET ME PASS.
....
W--
WOW! SHE...SHE'S A BEAUTY!
EXCUSE ME...

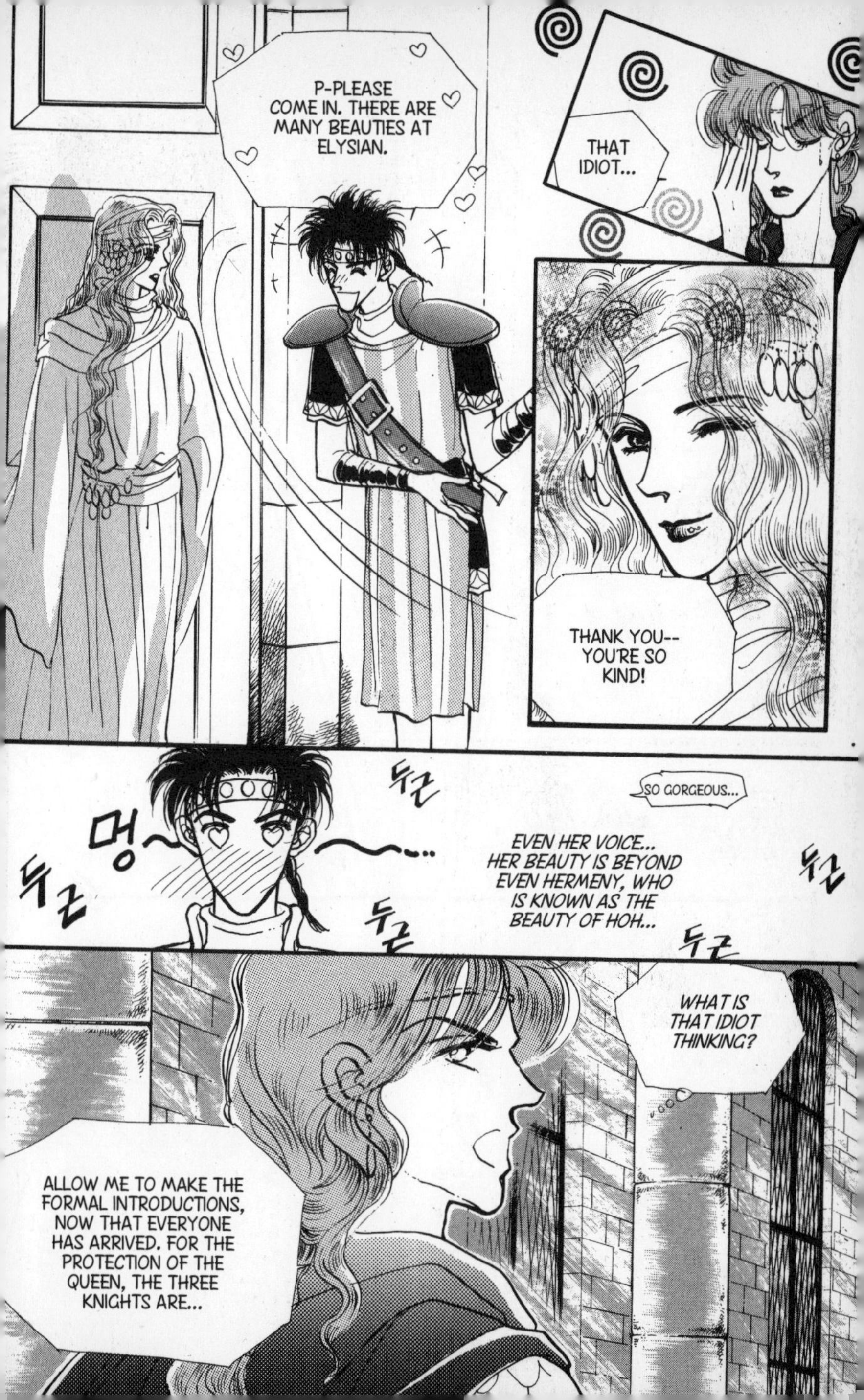
P-PLEASE COME IN. THERE ARE MANY BEAUTIES AT ELYSIAN.
THAT IDIOT...
THANK YOU-- YOU'RE SO KIND!
두근
멍~
두근
SO GORGEOUS...
EVEN HER VOICE... HER BEAUTY IS BEYOND EVEN HERMENY, WHO IS KNOWN AS THE BEAUTY OF HOH...
두근
두근
두근
WHAT IS THAT IDIOT THINKING?
ALLOW ME TO MAKE THE FORMAL INTRODUCTIONS, NOW THAT EVERYONE HAS ARRIVED. FOR THE PROTECTION OF THE QUEEN, THE THREE KNIGHTS ARE...

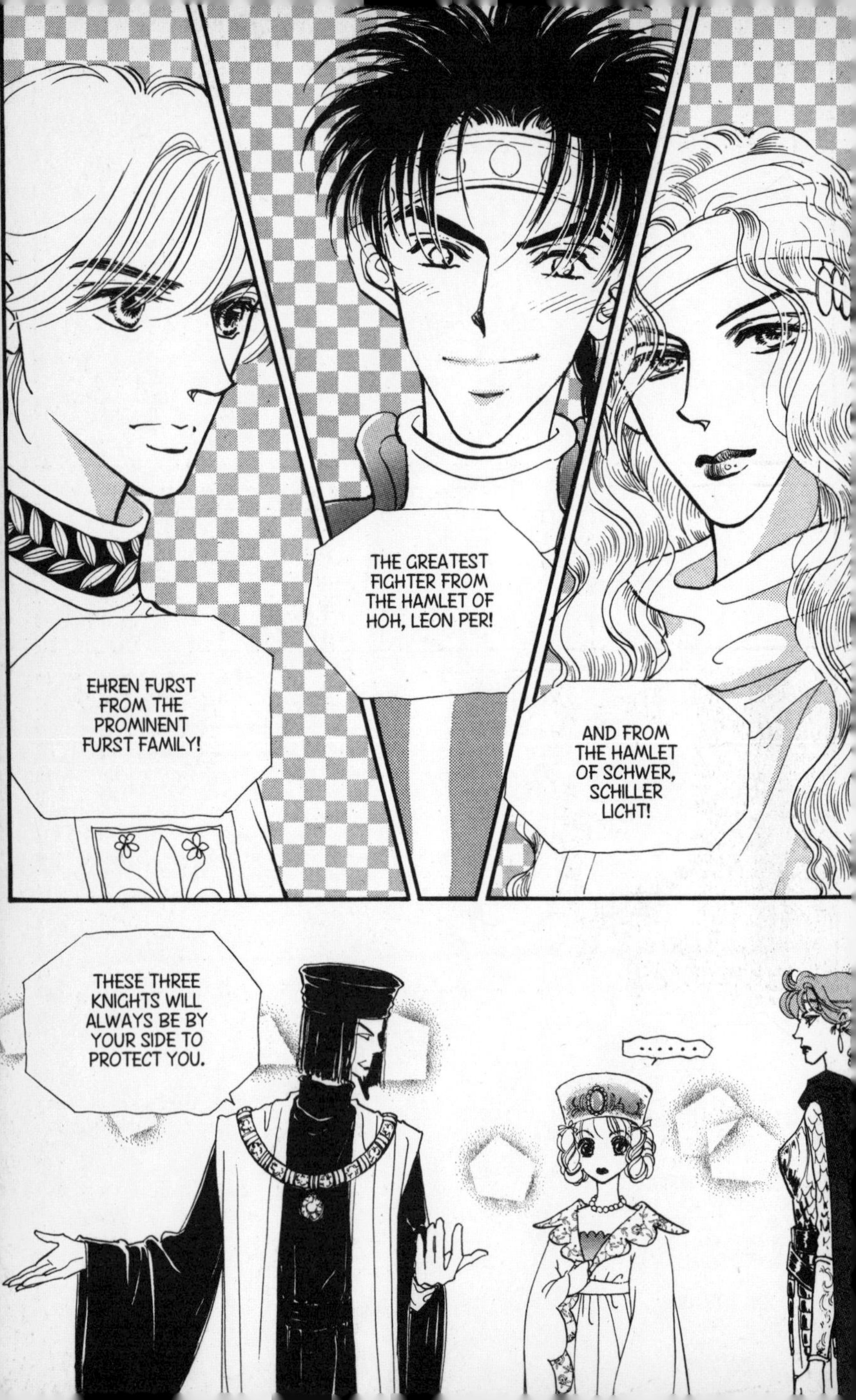
EHREN FURST FROM THE PROMINENT FURST FAMILY!
THE GREATEST FIGHTER FROM THE HAMLET OF HOH, LEON PER!
AND FROM THE HAMLET OF SCHWER, SCHILLER LICHT!
THESE THREE KNIGHTS WILL ALWAYS BE BY YOUR SIDE TO PROTECT YOU.
......

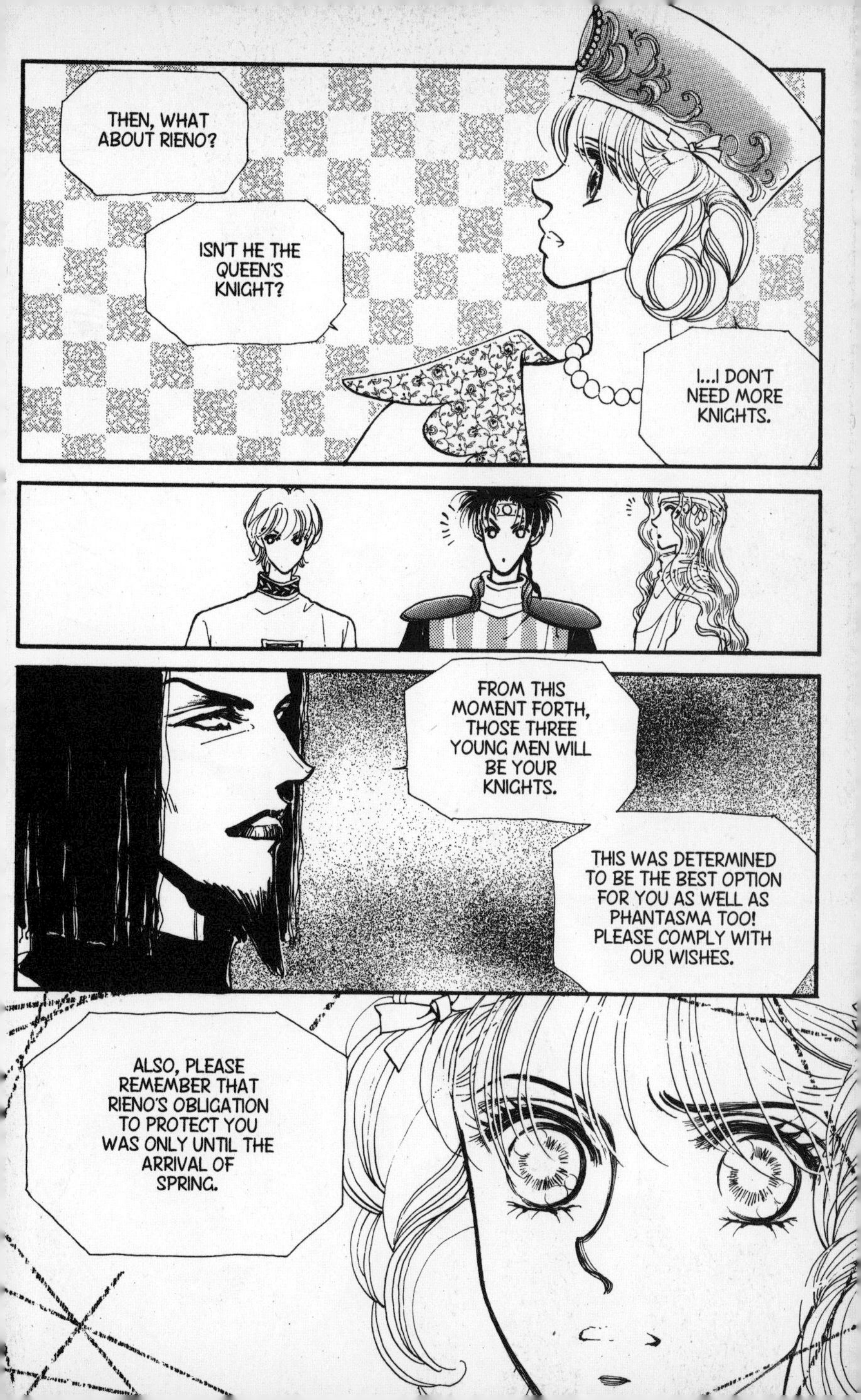
THEN, WHAT ABOUT RIENO?
ISN'T HE THE QUEEN'S KNIGHT?
I...I DON'T NEED MORE KNIGHTS.
FROM THIS MOMENT FORTH, THOSE THREE YOUNG MEN WILL BE YOUR KNIGHTS.
THIS WAS DETERMINED TO BE THE BEST OPTION FOR YOU AS WELL AS PHANTASMA TOO! PLEASE COMPLY WITH OUR WISHES.
ALSO, PLEASE REMEMBER THAT RIENO'S OBLIGATION TO PROTECT YOU WAS ONLY UNTIL THE ARRIVAL OF SPRING.

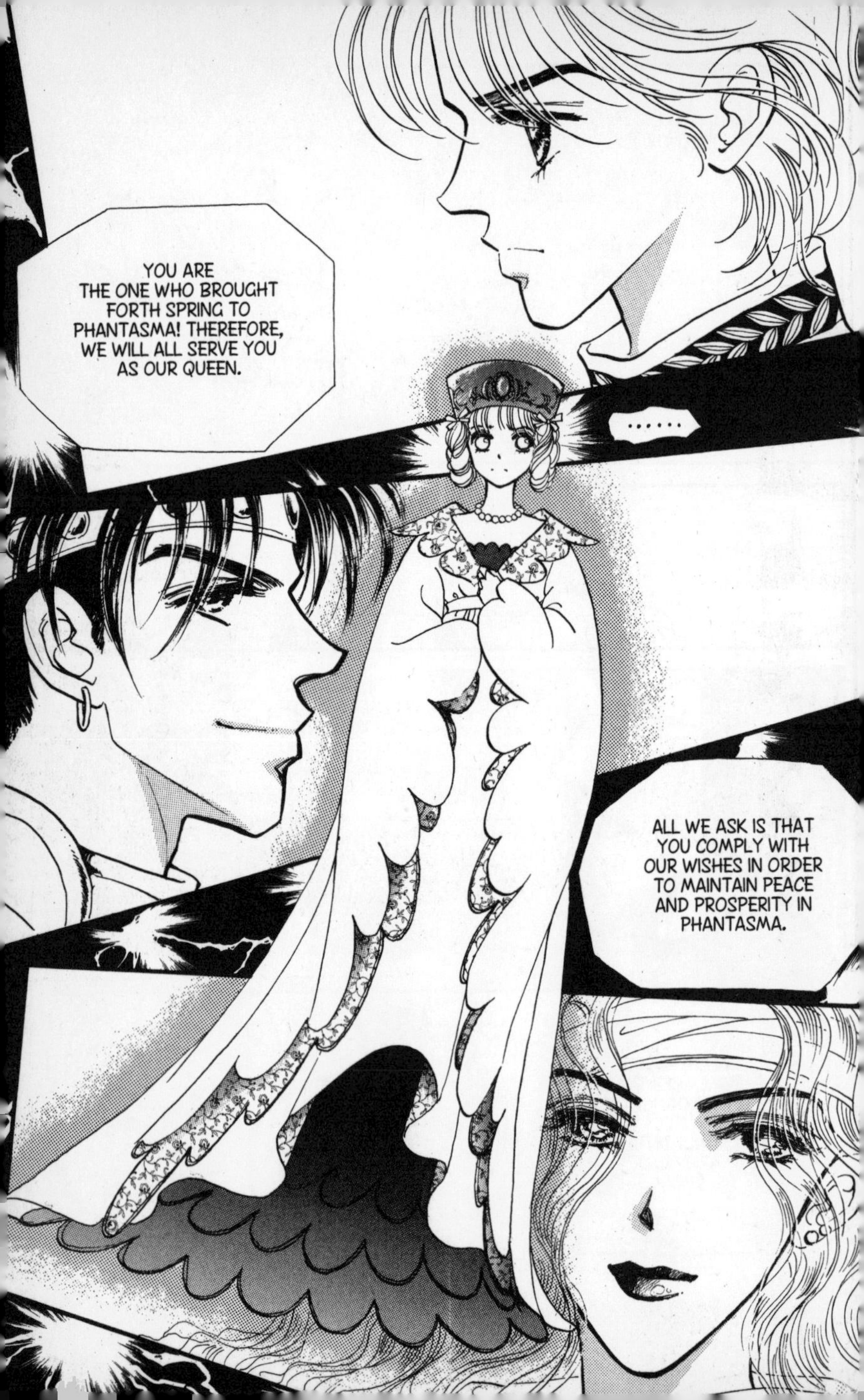
YOU ARE THE ONE WHO BROUGHT FORTH SPRING TO PHANTASMA! THEREFORE, WE WILL ALL SERVE YOU AS OUR QUEEN.
......
ALL WE ASK IS THAT YOU COMPLY WITH OUR WISHES IN ORDER TO MAINTAIN PEACE AND PROSPERITY IN PHANTASMA.

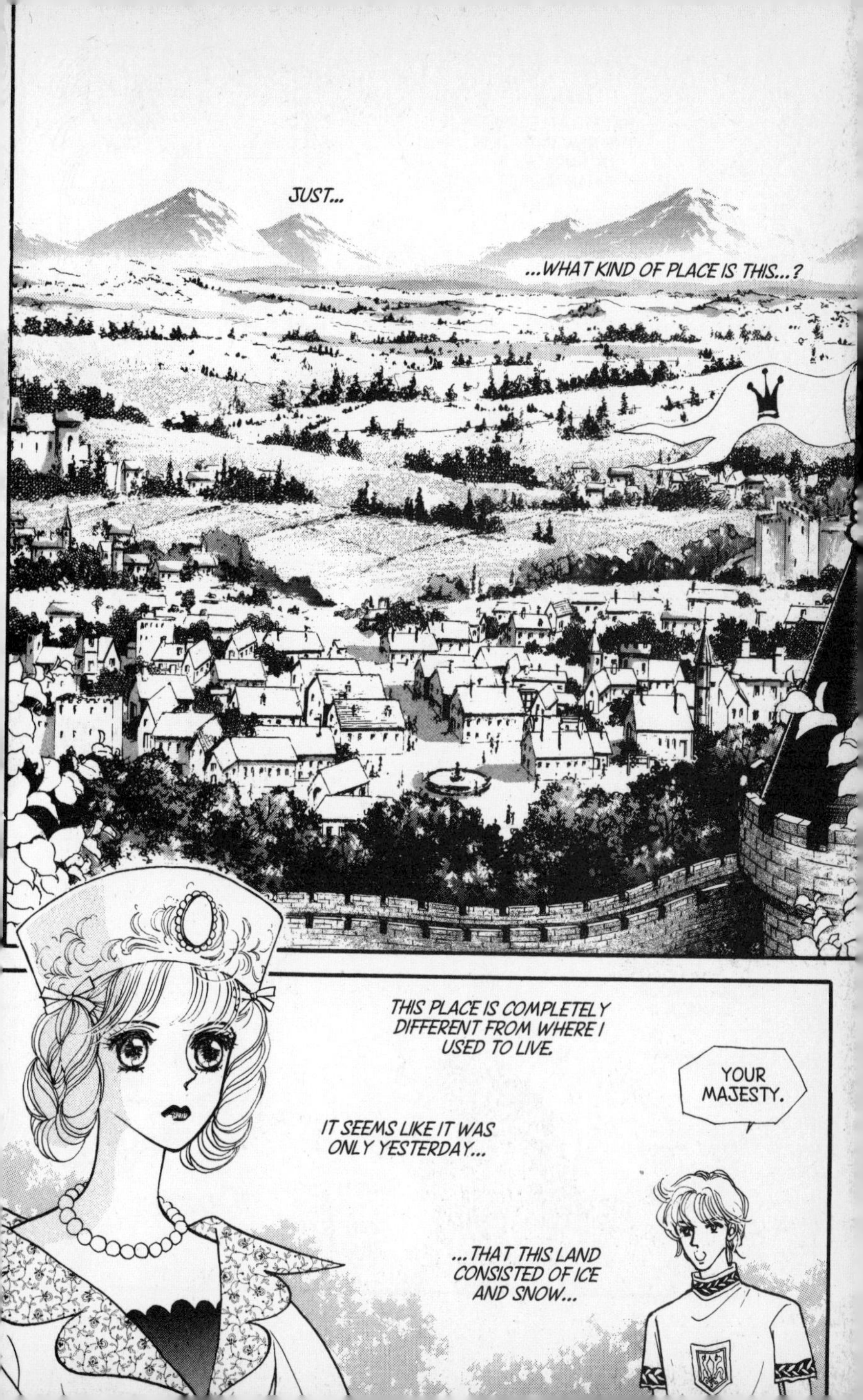
JUST...
...WHAT KIND OF PLACE IS THIS...?
THIS PLACE IS COMPLETELY DIFFERENT FROM WHERE I USED TO LIVE.
YOUR MAJESTY.
IT SEEMS LIKE IT WAS ONLY YESTERDAY...
...THAT THIS LAND CONSISTED OF ICE AND SNOW...

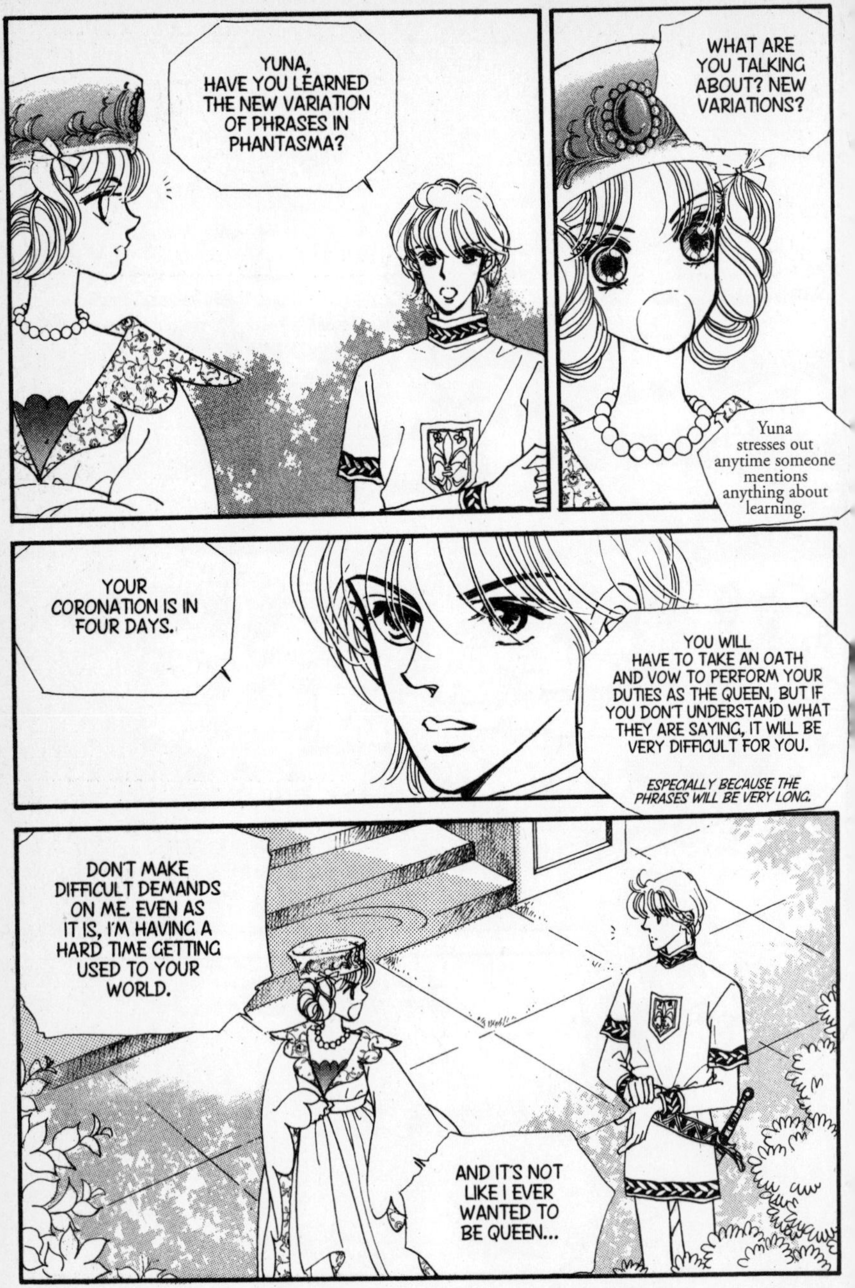
YUNA, HAVE YOU LEARNED THE NEW VARIATION OF PHRASES IN PHANTASMA?
WHAT ARE YOU TALKING ABOUT? NEW VARIATIONS?
Yuna stresses out anytime someone mentions anything about learning.
YOUR CORONATION IS IN FOUR DAYS.
YOU WILL HAVE TO TAKE AN OATH AND VOW TO PERFORM YOUR DUTIES AS THE QUEEN, BUT IF YOU DON'T UNDERSTAND WHAT THEY ARE SAYING, IT WILL BE VERY DIFFICULT FOR YOU.
ESPECIALLY BECAUSE THE PHRASES WILL BE VERY LONG.
DON'T MAKE DIFFICULT DEMANDS ON ME. EVEN AS IT IS, I'M HAVING A HARD TIME GETTING USED TO YOUR WORLD.
AND IT'S NOT LIKE I EVER WANTED TO BE QUEEN...

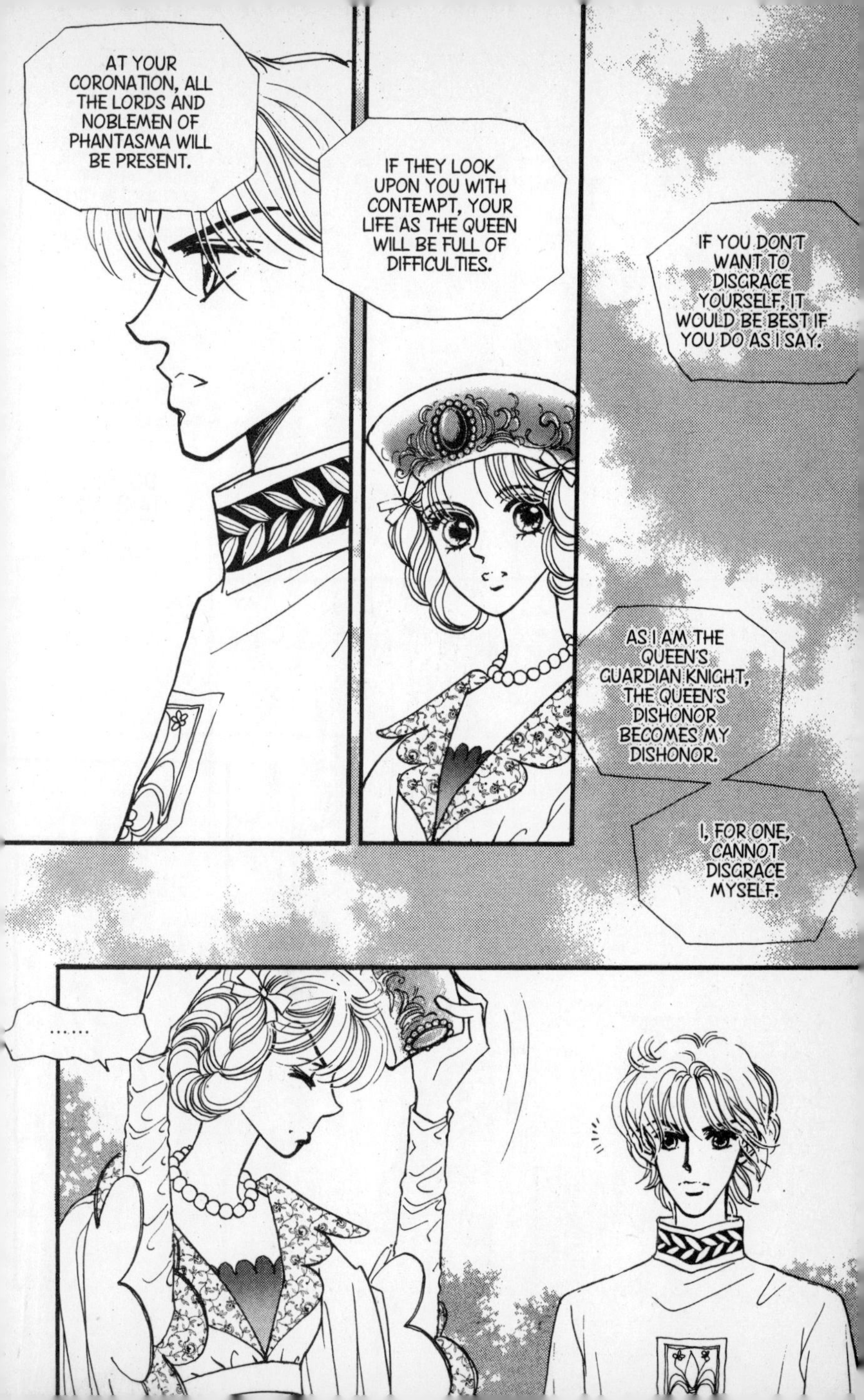
AT YOUR CORONATION, ALL THE LORDS AND NOBLEMEN OF PHANTASMA WILL BE PRESENT.
IF THEY LOOK UPON YOU WITH CONTEMPT, YOUR LIFE AS THE QUEEN WILL BE FULL OF DIFFICULTIES.
IF YOU DON'T WANT TO DISGRACE YOURSELF, IT WOULD BE BEST IF YOU DO AS I SAY.
AS I AM THE QUEEN'S GUARDIAN KNIGHT, THE QUEEN'S DISHONOR BECOMES MY DISHONOR.
I, FOR ONE, CANNOT DISGRACE MYSELF.
......

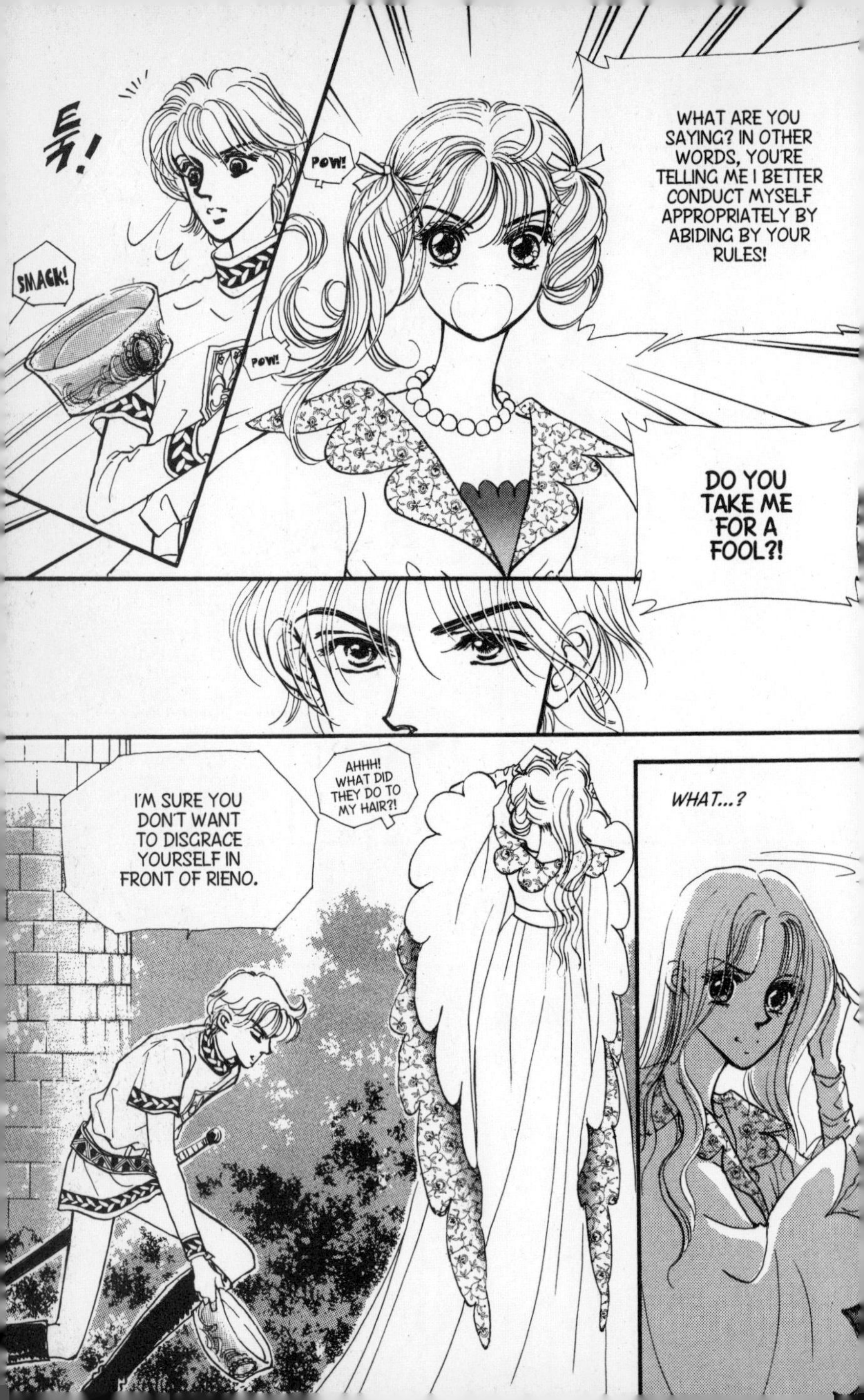
툭!
SMACK!
POW!
POW!
WHAT ARE YOU SAYING? IN OTHER WORDS, YOU'RE TELLING ME I BETTER CONDUCT MYSELF APPROPRIATELY BY ABIDING BY YOUR RULES!
DO YOU TAKE ME FOR A FOOL?!
I'M SURE YOU DON'T WANT TO DISGRACE YOURSELF IN FRONT OF RIENO.
AHHH! WHAT DID THEY DO TO MY HAIR?!
WHAT...?

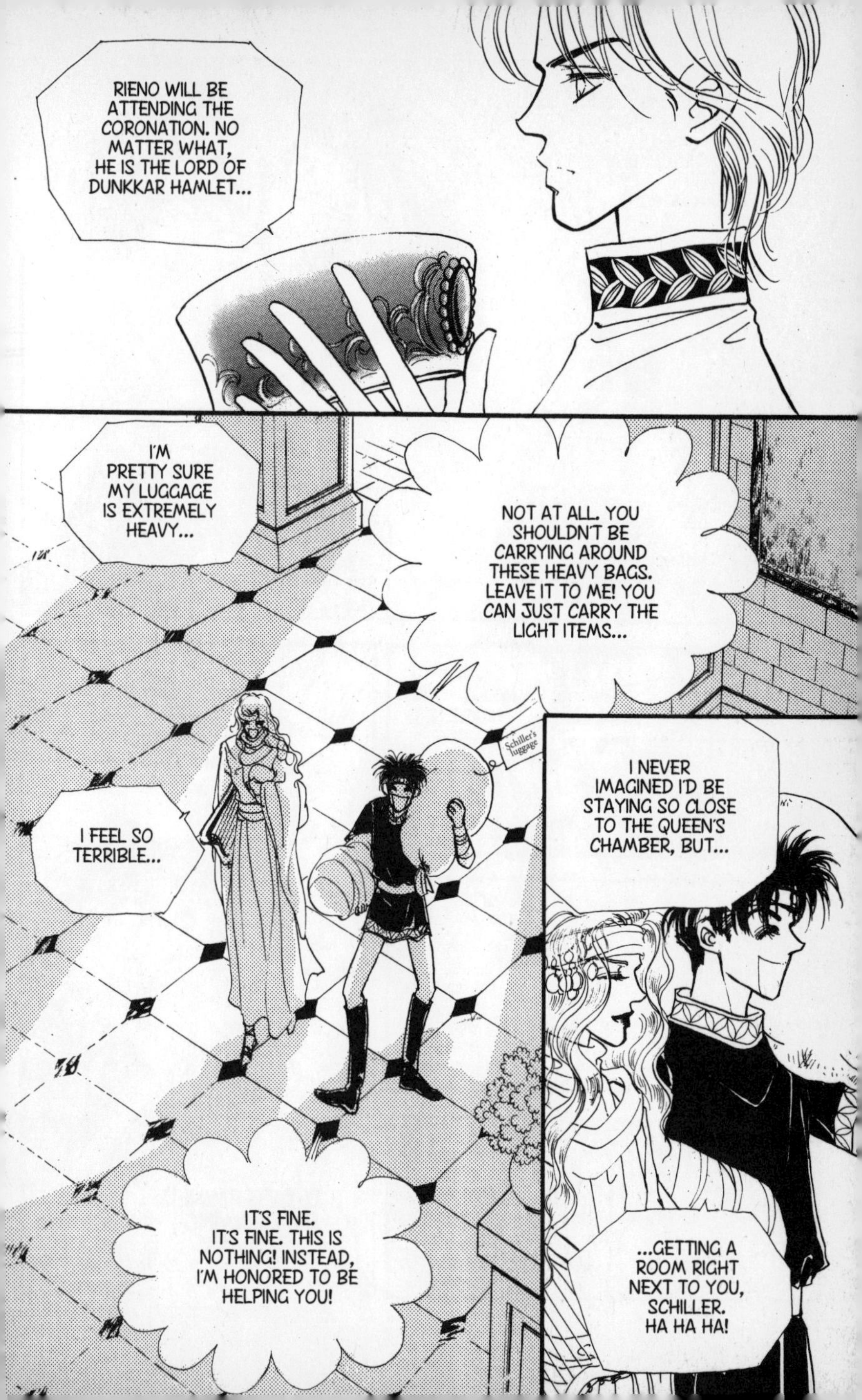
RIENO WILL BE ATTENDING THE CORONATION. NO MATTER WHAT, HE IS THE LORD OF DUNKKAR HAMLET...
I'M PRETTY SURE MY LUGGAGE IS EXTREMELY HEAVY...
NOT AT ALL. YOU SHOULDN'T BE CARRYING AROUND THESE HEAVY BAGS. LEAVE IT TO ME! YOU CAN JUST CARRY THE LIGHT ITEMS...
Schiller's luggage
I FEEL SO TERRIBLE...
IT'S FINE. IT'S FINE. THIS IS NOTHING! INSTEAD, I'M HONORED TO BE HELPING YOU!
I NEVER IMAGINED I'D BE STAYING SO CLOSE TO THE QUEEN'S CHAMBER, BUT...
...GETTING A ROOM RIGHT NEXT TO YOU, SCHILLER. HA HA HA!

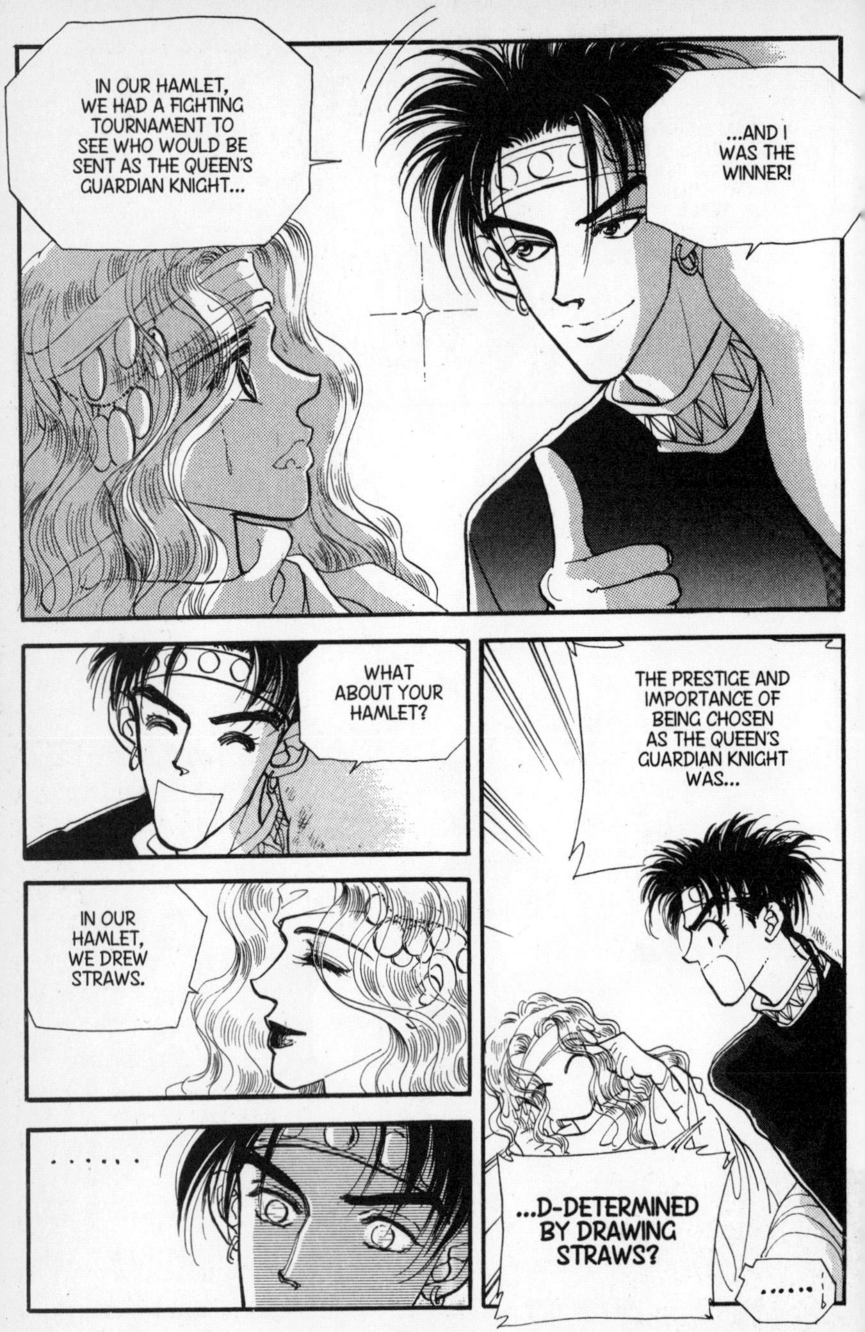
IN OUR HAMLET, WE HAD A FIGHTING TOURNAMENT TO SEE WHO WOULD BE SENT AS THE QUEEN'S GUARDIAN KNIGHT...
...AND I WAS THE WINNER!
WHAT ABOUT YOUR HAMLET?
IN OUR HAMLET, WE DREW STRAWS.
......
THE PRESTIGE AND IMPORTANCE OF BEING CHOSEN AS THE QUEEN'S GUARDIAN KNIGHT WAS...
...D-DETERMINED BY DRAWING STRAWS?
......!

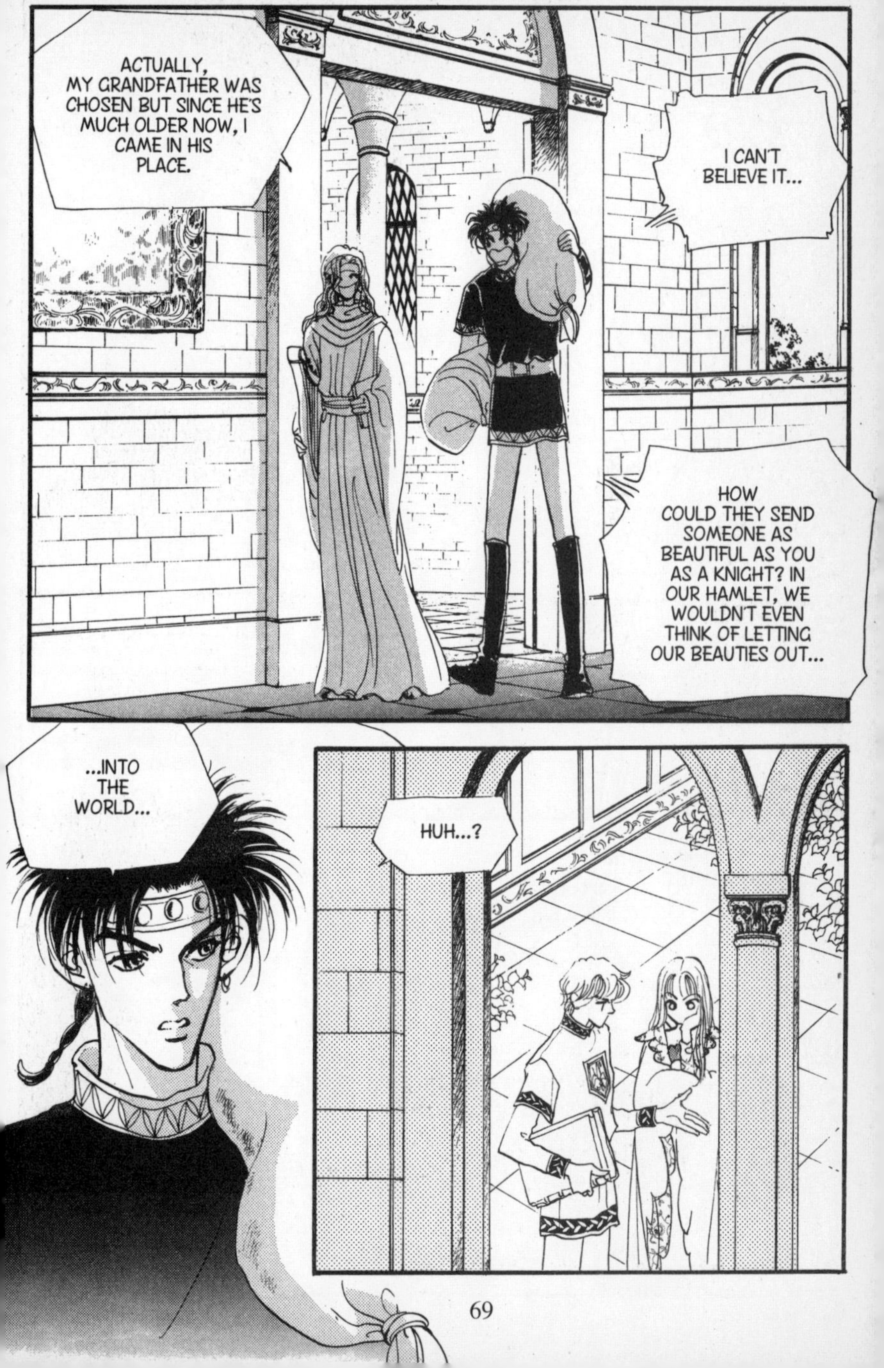
ACTUALLY, MY GRANDFATHER WAS CHOSEN BUT SINCE HE'S MUCH OLDER NOW, I CAME IN HIS PLACE.
I CAN'T BELIEVE IT...
HOW COULD THEY SEND SOMEONE AS BEAUTIFUL AS YOU AS A KNIGHT? IN OUR HAMLET, WE WOULDN'T EVEN THINK OF LETTING OUR BEAUTIES OUT...
...INTO THE WORLD...
HUH...?

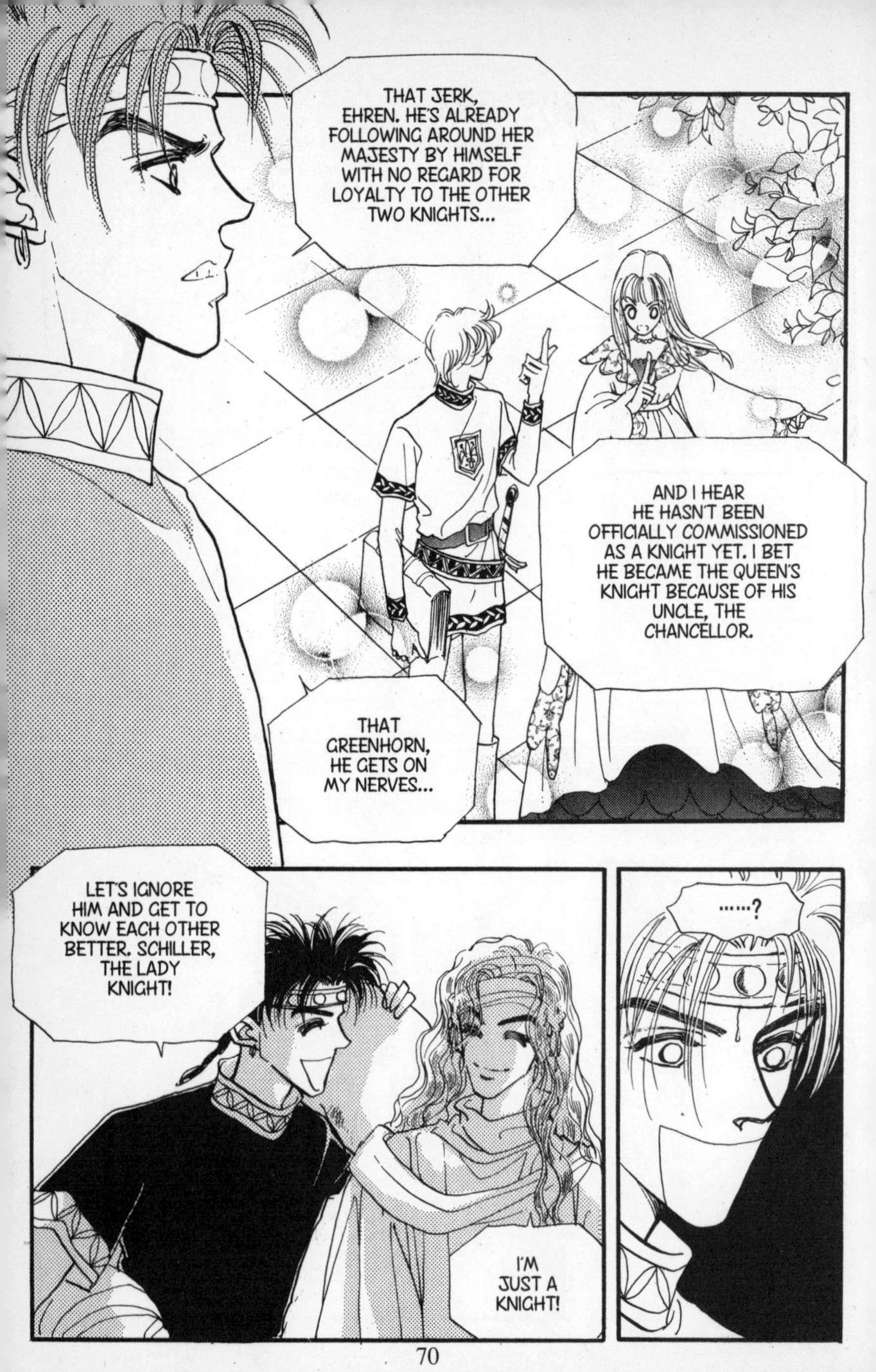
THAT JERK, EHREN. HE'S ALREADY FOLLOWING AROUND HER MAJESTY BY HIMSELF WITH NO REGARD FOR LOYALTY TO THE OTHER TWO KNIGHTS...
AND I HEAR HE HASN'T BEEN OFFICIALLY COMMISSIONED AS A KNIGHT YET. I BET HE BECAME THE QUEEN'S KNIGHT BECAUSE OF HIS UNCLE, THE CHANCELLOR.
THAT GREENHORN, HE GETS ON MY NERVES...
LET'S IGNORE HIM AND GET TO KNOW EACH OTHER BETTER. SCHILLER, THE LADY KNIGHT!
I'M JUST A KNIGHT!
......?

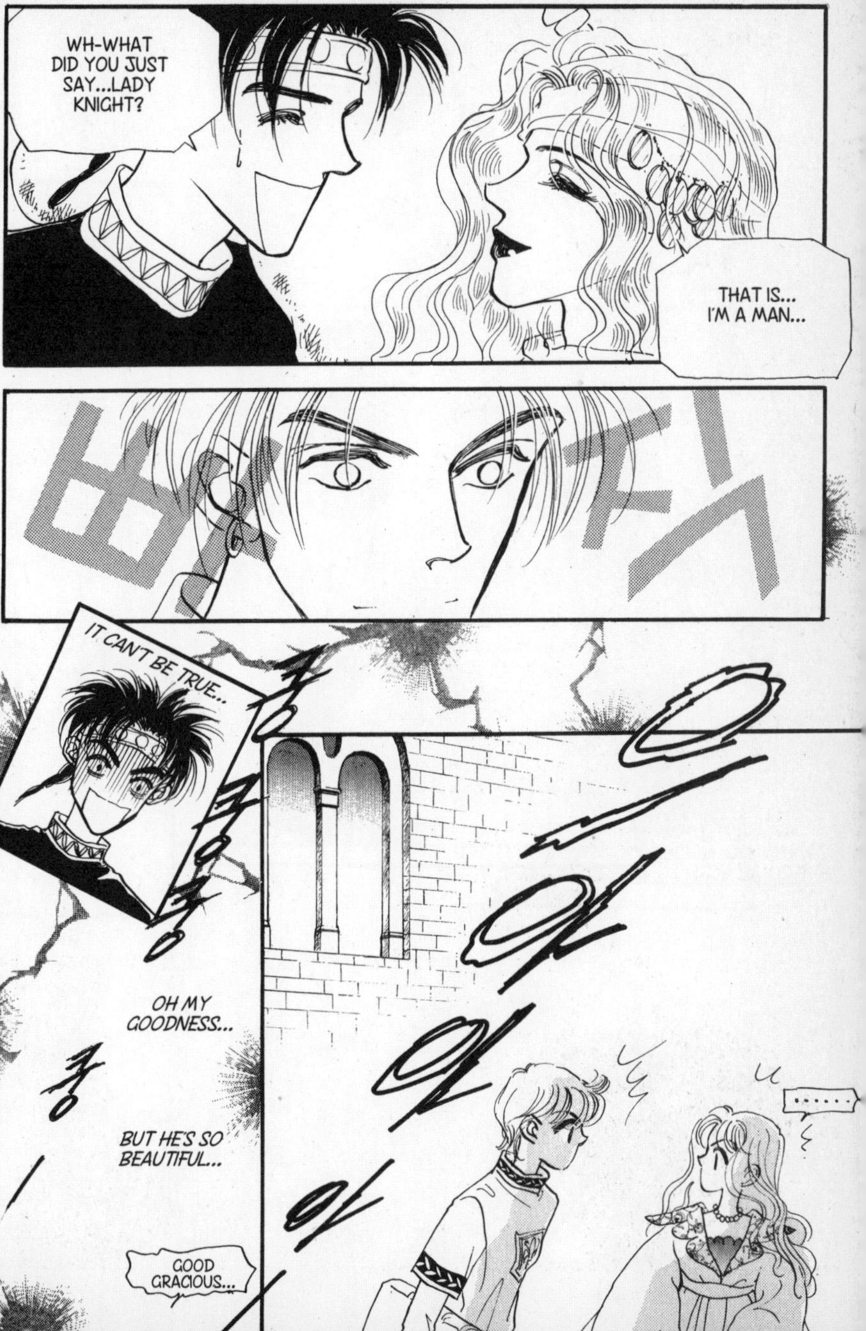
WH-WHAT DID YOU JUST SAY...LADY KNIGHT?
THAT IS... I'M A MAN...
IT CAN'T BE TRUE...
OH MY GOODNESS...
BUT HE'S SO BEAUTIFUL...
GOOD GRACIOUS...
......

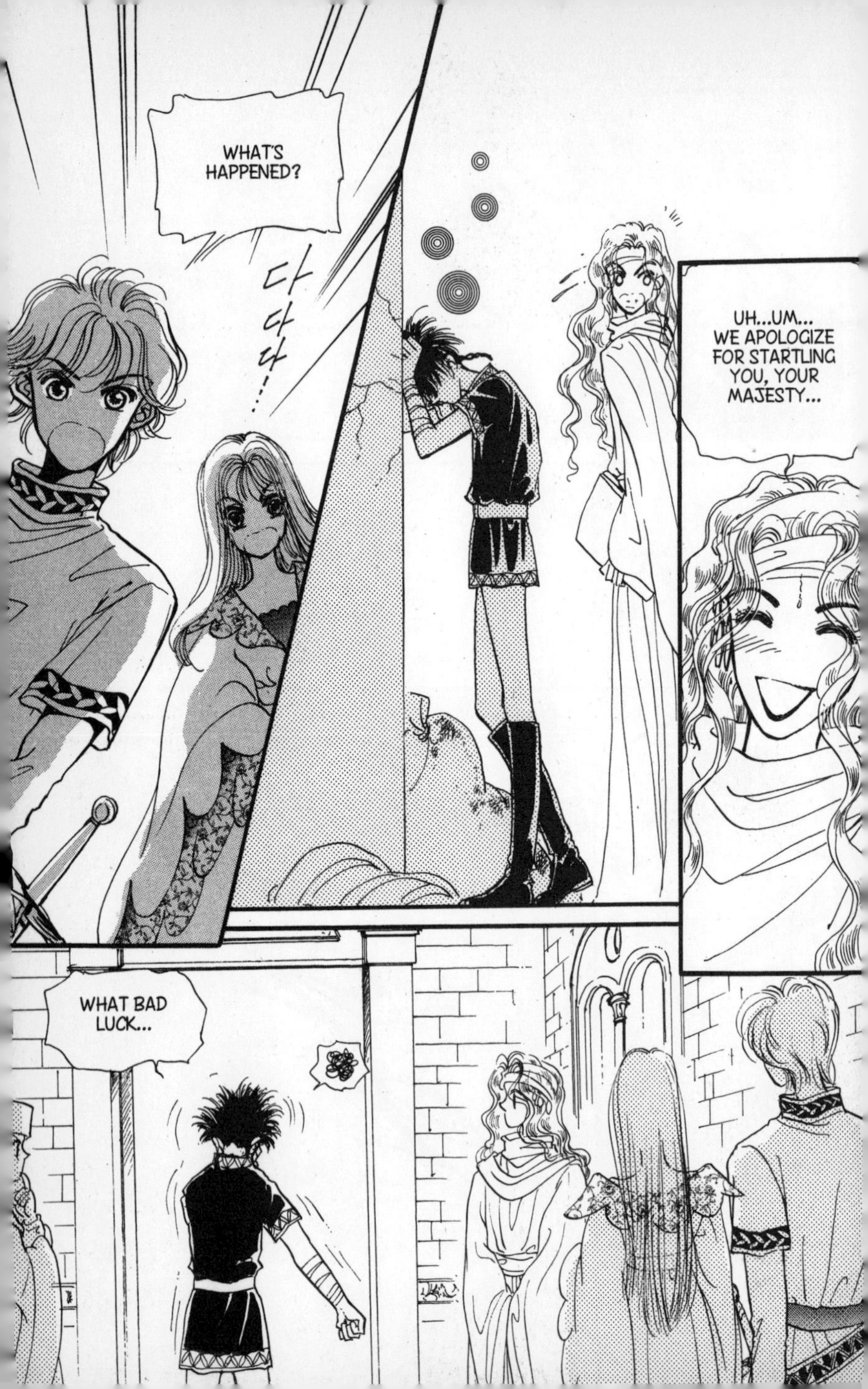
WHAT'S HAPPENED?
다다다...!
UH...UM... WE APOLOGIZE FOR STARTLING YOU, YOUR MAJESTY...
WHAT BAD LUCK...

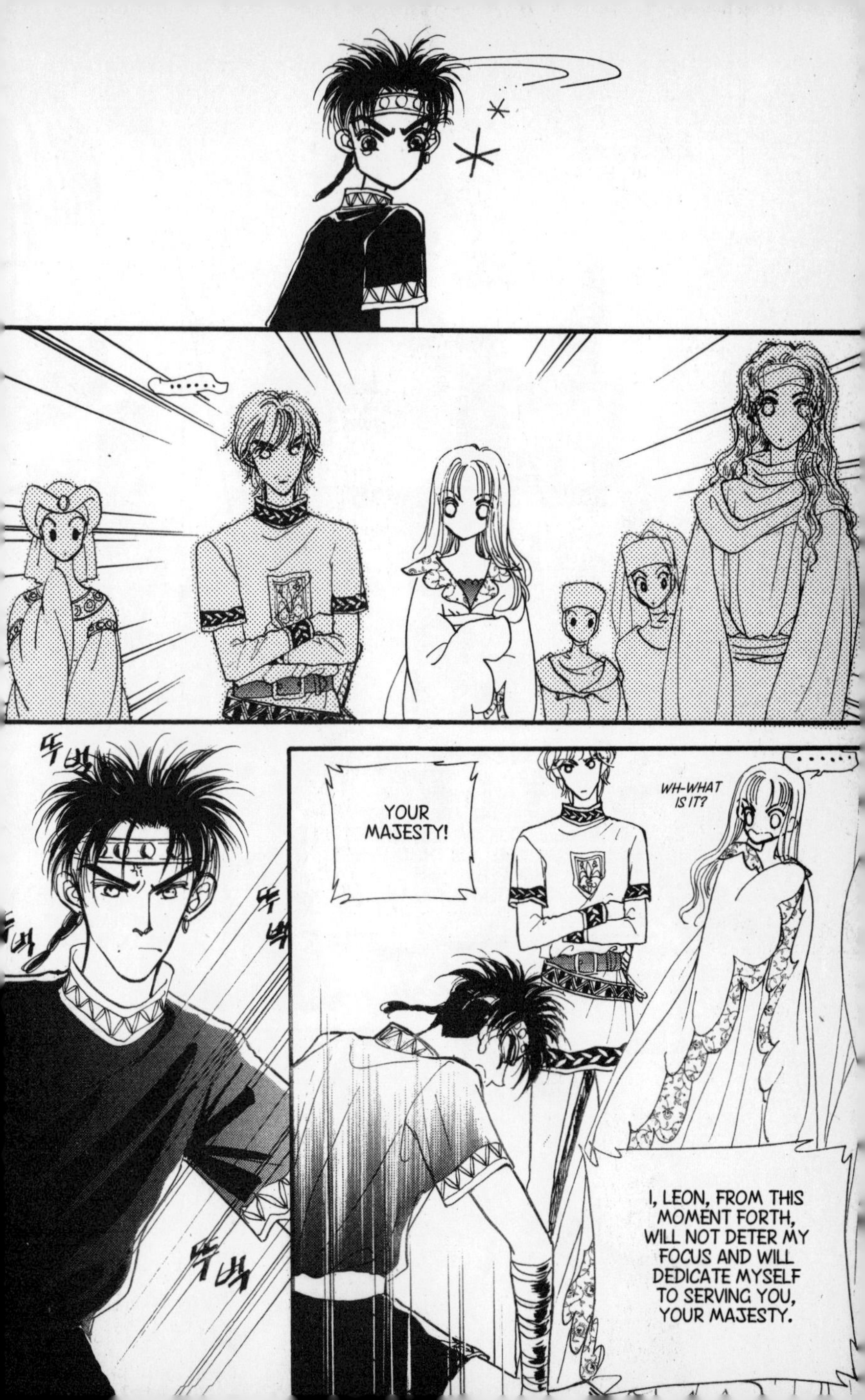
.....
뚜벅
뚜벅
뚜벅
뚜벅
YOUR MAJESTY!
WH-WHAT IS IT?
......
I, LEON, FROM THIS MOMENT FORTH, WILL NOT DETER MY FOCUS AND WILL DEDICATE MYSELF TO SERVING YOU, YOUR MAJESTY.

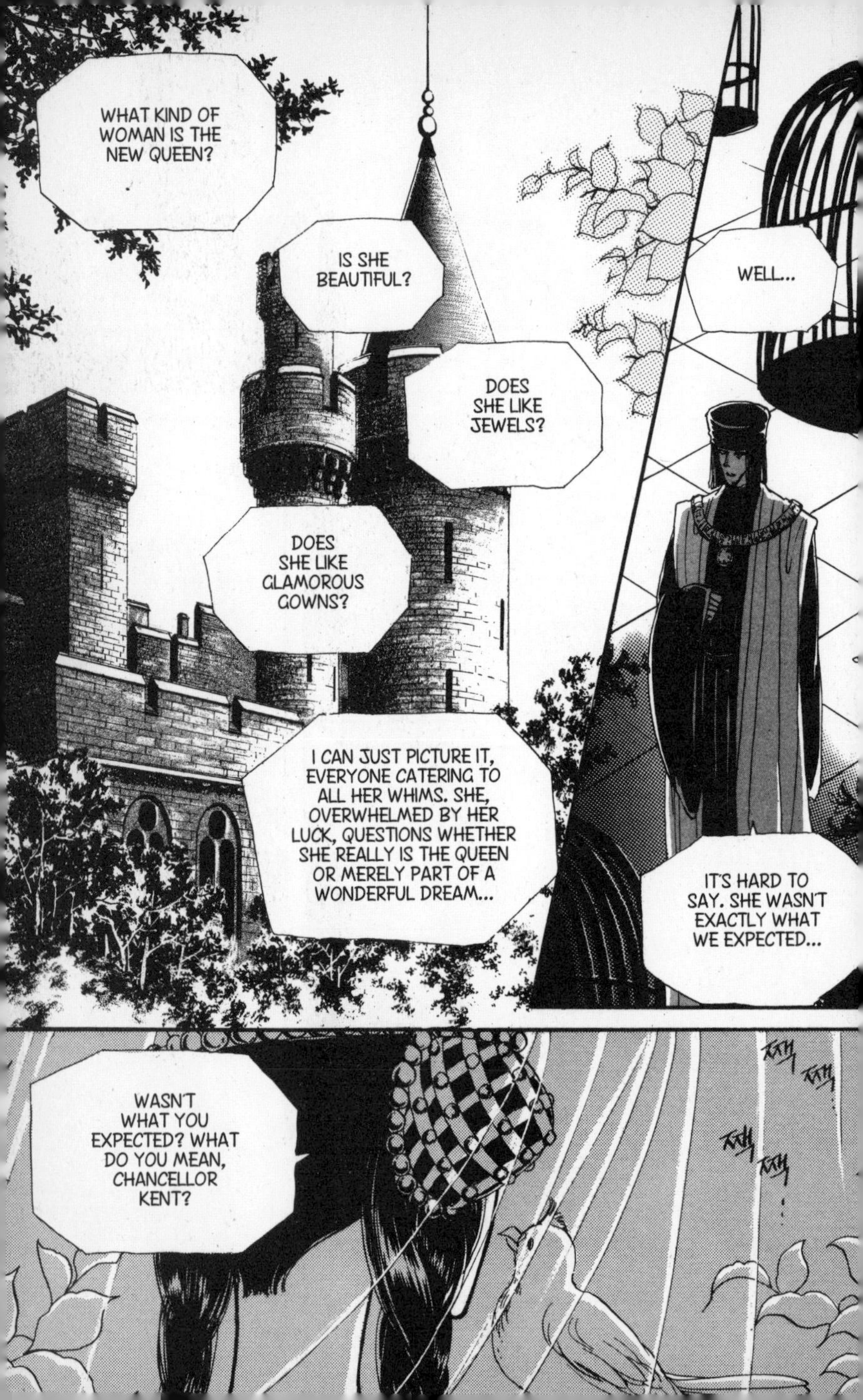
WHAT KIND OF WOMAN IS THE NEW QUEEN?
IS SHE BEAUTIFUL?
DOES SHE LIKE JEWELS?
DOES SHE LIKE GLAMOROUS GOWNS?
I CAN JUST PICTURE IT, EVERYONE CATERING TO ALL HER WHIMS. SHE, OVERWHELMED BY HER LUCK, QUESTIONS WHETHER SHE REALLY IS THE QUEEN OR MERELY PART OF A WONDERFUL DREAM...
WELL...
IT'S HARD TO SAY. SHE WASN'T EXACTLY WHAT WE EXPECTED...
WASN'T WHAT YOU EXPECTED? WHAT DO YOU MEAN, CHANCELLOR KENT?

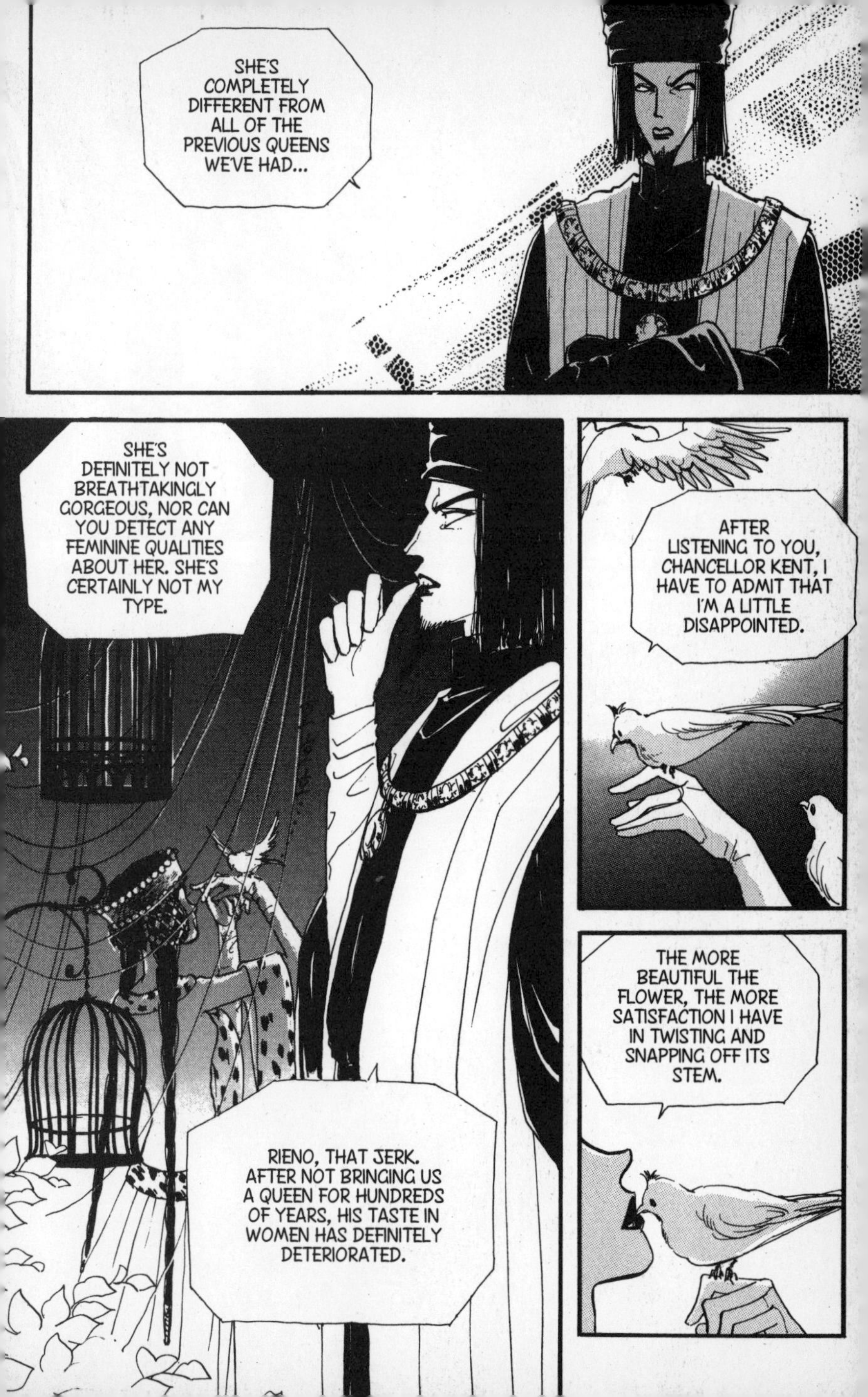
SHE'S COMPLETELY DIFFERENT FROM ALL OF THE PREVIOUS QUEENS WE'VE HAD...
SHE'S DEFINITELY NOT BREATHTAKINGLY GORGEOUS, NOR CAN YOU DETECT ANY FEMININE QUALITIES ABOUT HER. SHE'S CERTAINLY NOT MY TYPE.
RIENO, THAT JERK. AFTER NOT BRINGING US A QUEEN FOR HUNDREDS OF YEARS, HIS TASTE IN WOMEN HAS DEFINITELY DETERIORATED.
AFTER LISTENING TO YOU, CHANCELLOR KENT, I HAVE TO ADMIT THAT I'M A LITTLE DISAPPOINTED.
THE MORE BEAUTIFUL THE FLOWER, THE MORE SATISFACTION I HAVE IN TWISTING AND SNAPPING OFF ITS STEM.

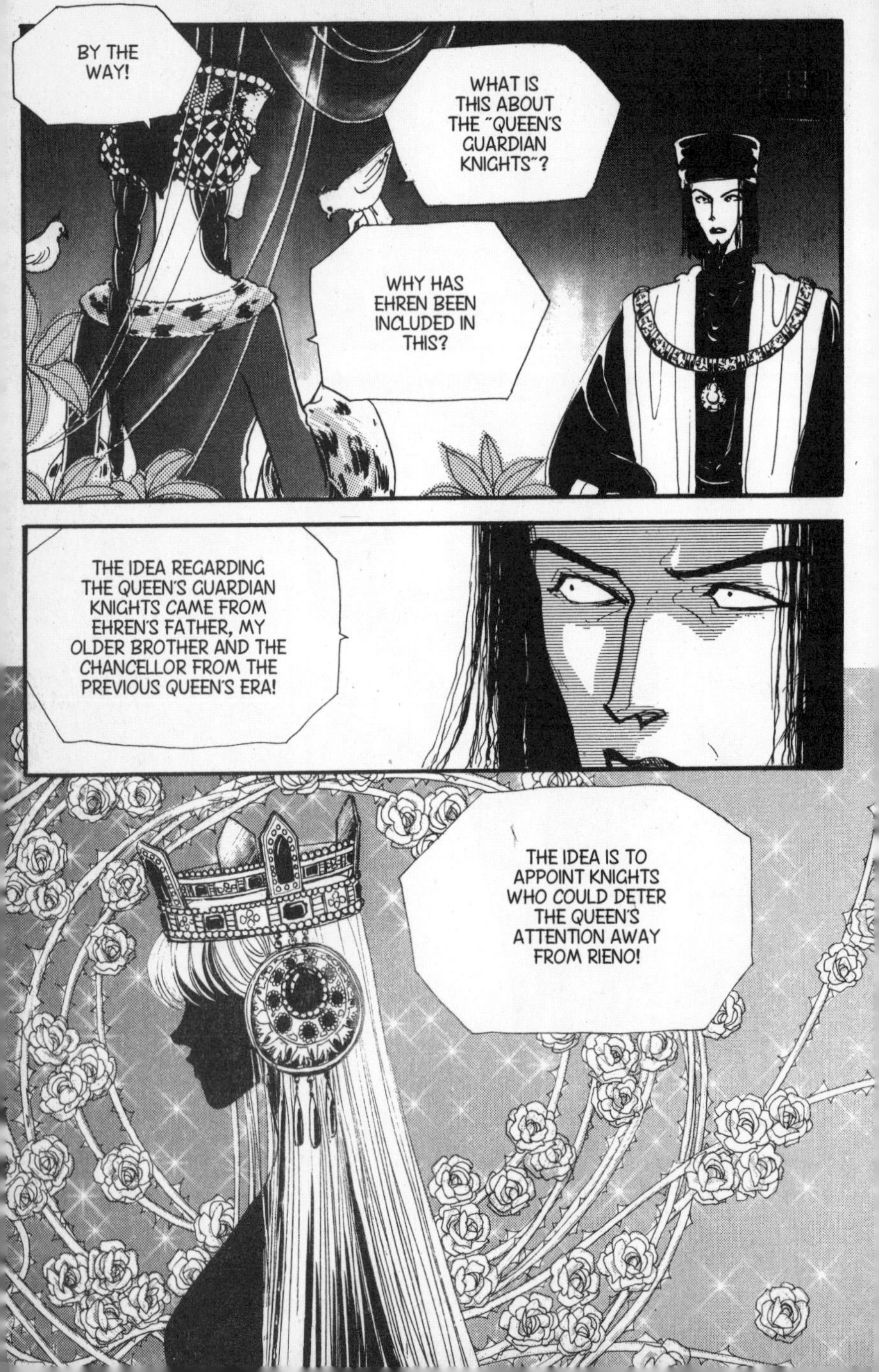
BY THE WAY!
WHAT IS THIS ABOUT THE "QUEEN'S GUARDIAN KNIGHTS"?
WHY HAS EHREN BEEN INCLUDED IN THIS?
THE IDEA REGARDING THE QUEEN'S GUARDIAN KNIGHTS CAME FROM EHREN'S FATHER, MY OLDER BROTHER AND THE CHANCELLOR FROM THE PREVIOUS QUEEN'S ERA!
THE IDEA IS TO APPOINT KNIGHTS WHO COULD DETER THE QUEEN'S ATTENTION AWAY FROM RIENO!

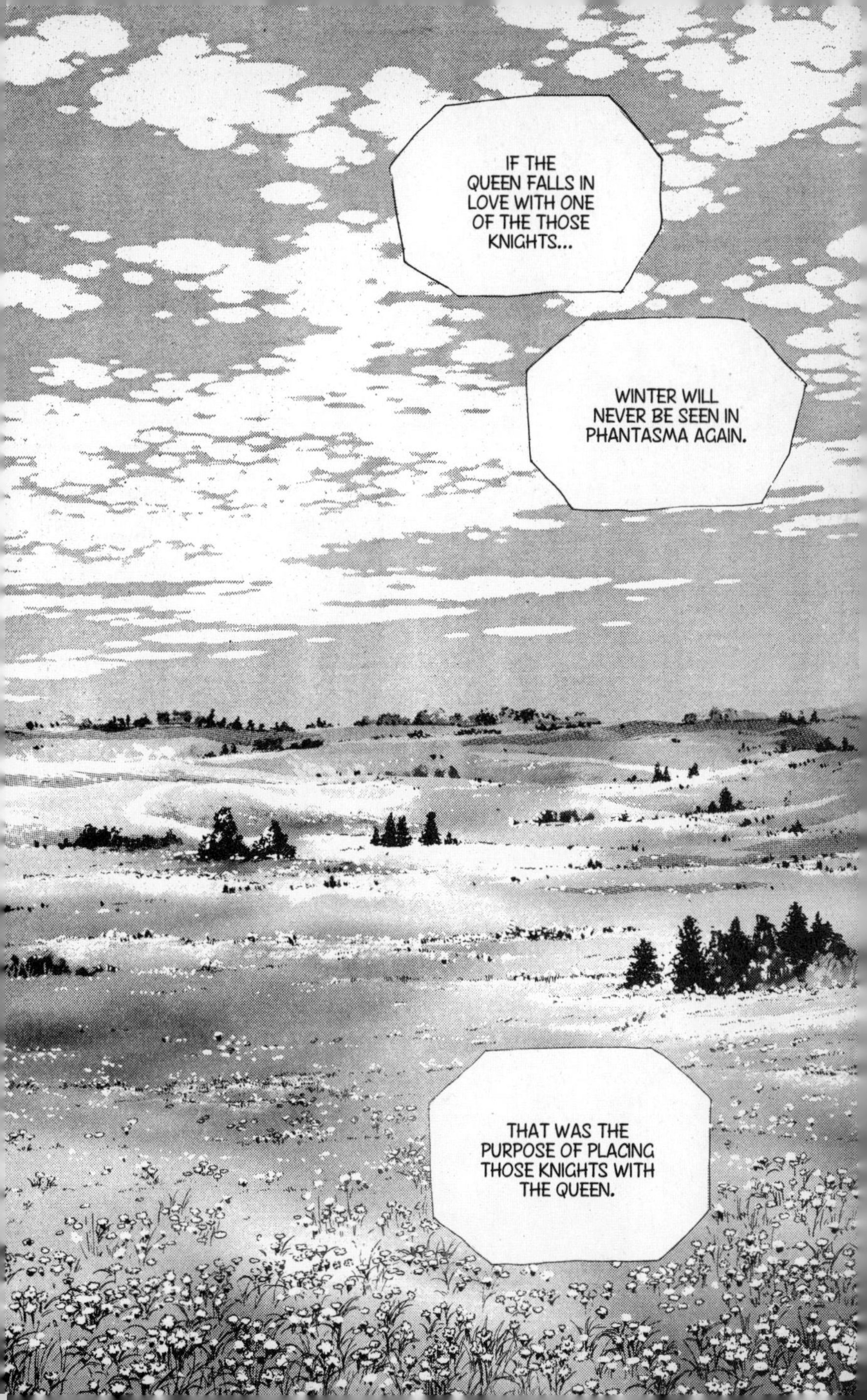
IF THE QUEEN FALLS IN LOVE WITH ONE OF THE THOSE KNIGHTS...
WINTER WILL NEVER BE SEEN IN PHANTASMA AGAIN.
THAT WAS THE PURPOSE OF PLACING THOSE KNIGHTS WITH THE QUEEN.

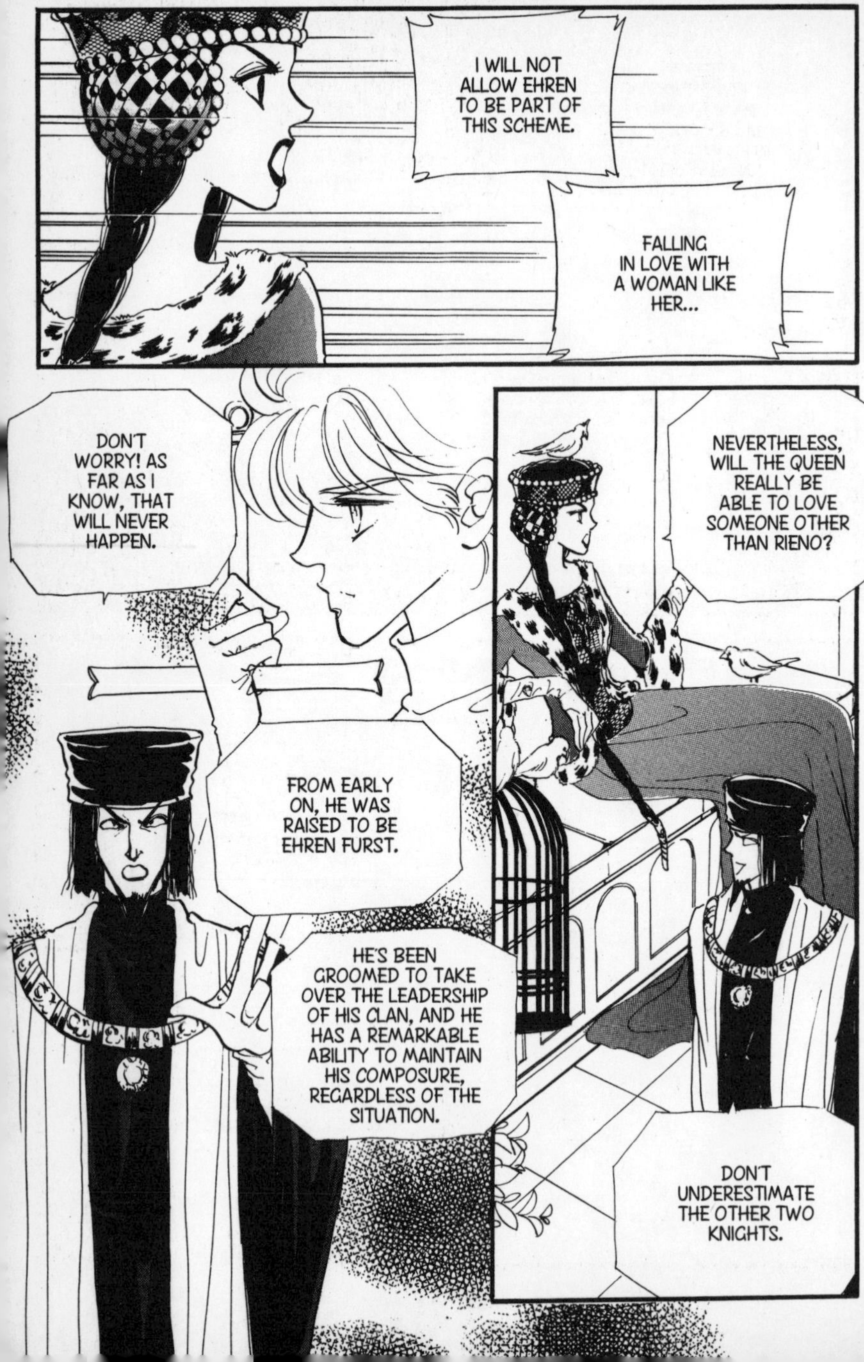
I WILL NOT ALLOW EHREN TO BE PART OF THIS SCHEME.
FALLING IN LOVE WITH A WOMAN LIKE HER...
DON'T WORRY! AS FAR AS I KNOW, THAT WILL NEVER HAPPEN.
FROM EARLY ON, HE WAS RAISED TO BE EHREN FURST.
HE'S BEEN GROOMED TO TAKE OVER THE LEADERSHIP OF HIS CLAN, AND HE HAS A REMARKABLE ABILITY TO MAINTAIN HIS COMPOSURE, REGARDLESS OF THE SITUATION.
NEVERTHELESS, WILL THE QUEEN REALLY BE ABLE TO LOVE SOMEONE OTHER THAN RIENO?
DON'T UNDERESTIMATE THE OTHER TWO KNIGHTS.

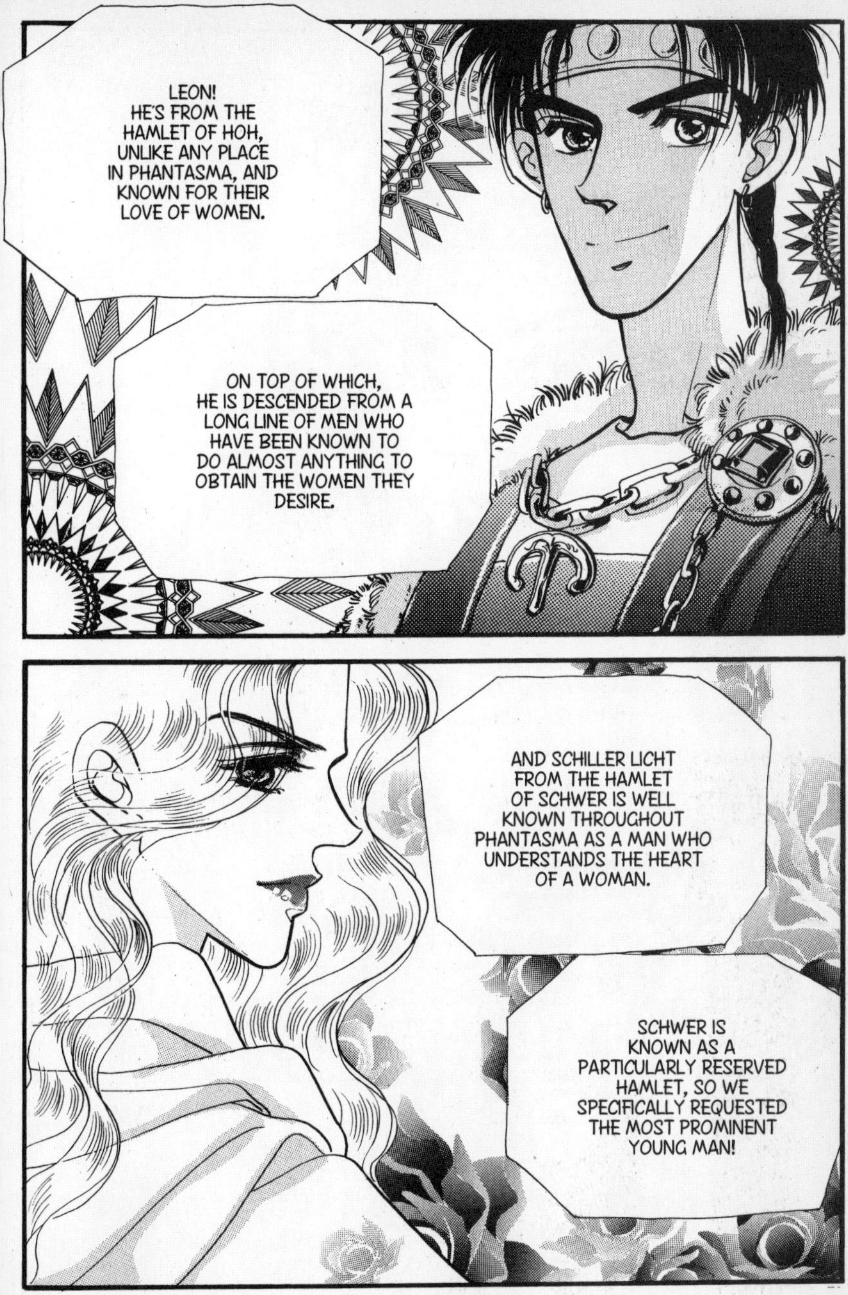
LEON! HE'S FROM THE HAMLET OF HOH, UNLIKE ANY PLACE IN PHANTASMA, AND KNOWN FOR THEIR LOVE OF WOMEN.
ON TOP OF WHICH, HE IS DESCENDED FROM A LONG LINE OF MEN WHO HAVE BEEN KNOWN TO DO ALMOST ANYTHING TO OBTAIN THE WOMEN THEY DESIRE.
AND SCHILLER LICHT FROM THE HAMLET OF SCHWER IS WELL KNOWN THROUGHOUT PHANTASMA AS A MAN WHO UNDERSTANDS THE HEART OF A WOMAN.
SCHWER IS KNOWN AS A PARTICULARLY RESERVED HAMLET, SO WE SPECIFICALLY REQUESTED THE MOST PROMINENT YOUNG MAN!

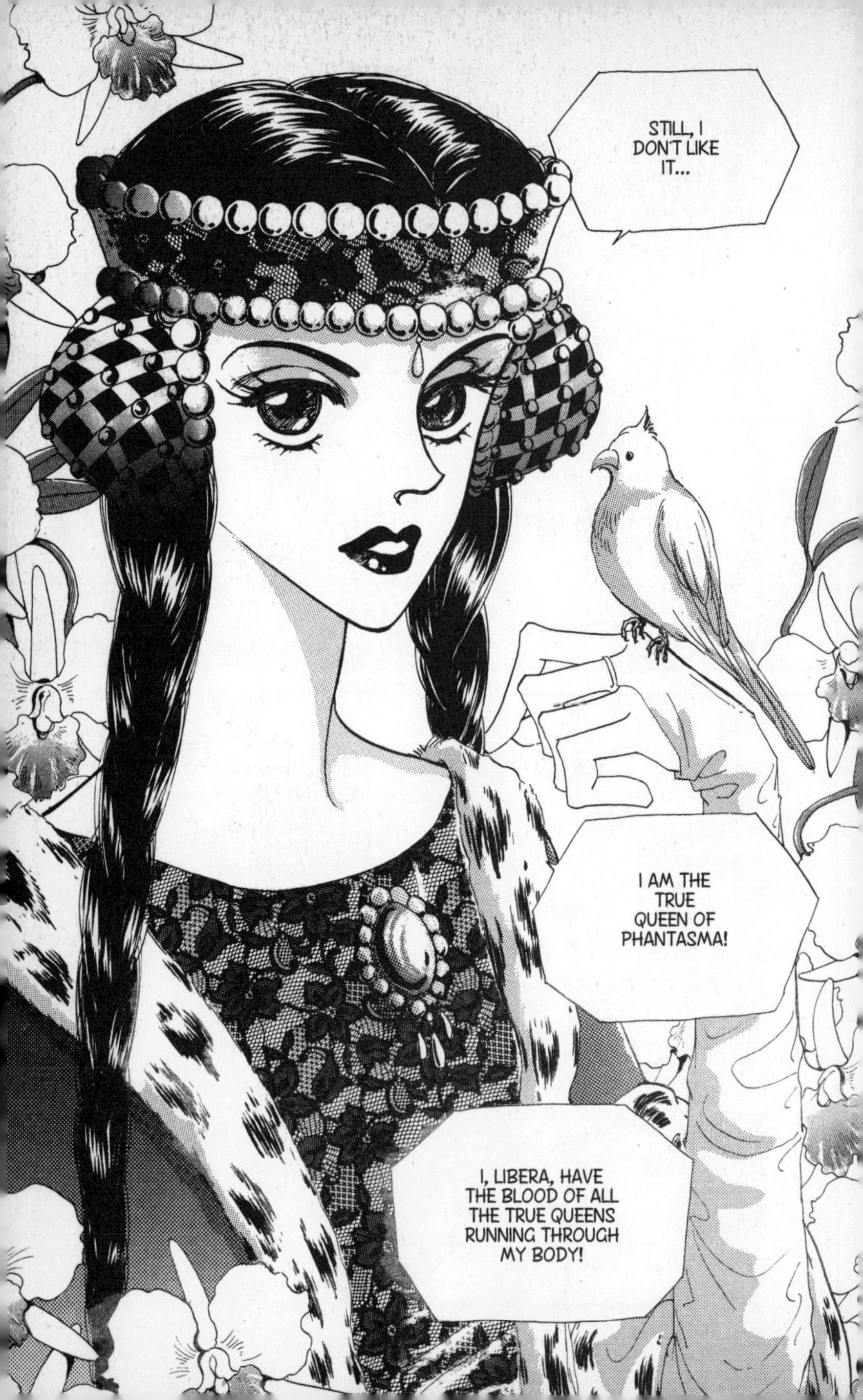
STILL, I DON'T LIKE IT...
I AM THE TRUE QUEEN OF PHANTASMA!
I, LIBERA, HAVE THE BLOOD OF ALL THE TRUE QUEENS RUNNING THROUGH MY BODY!

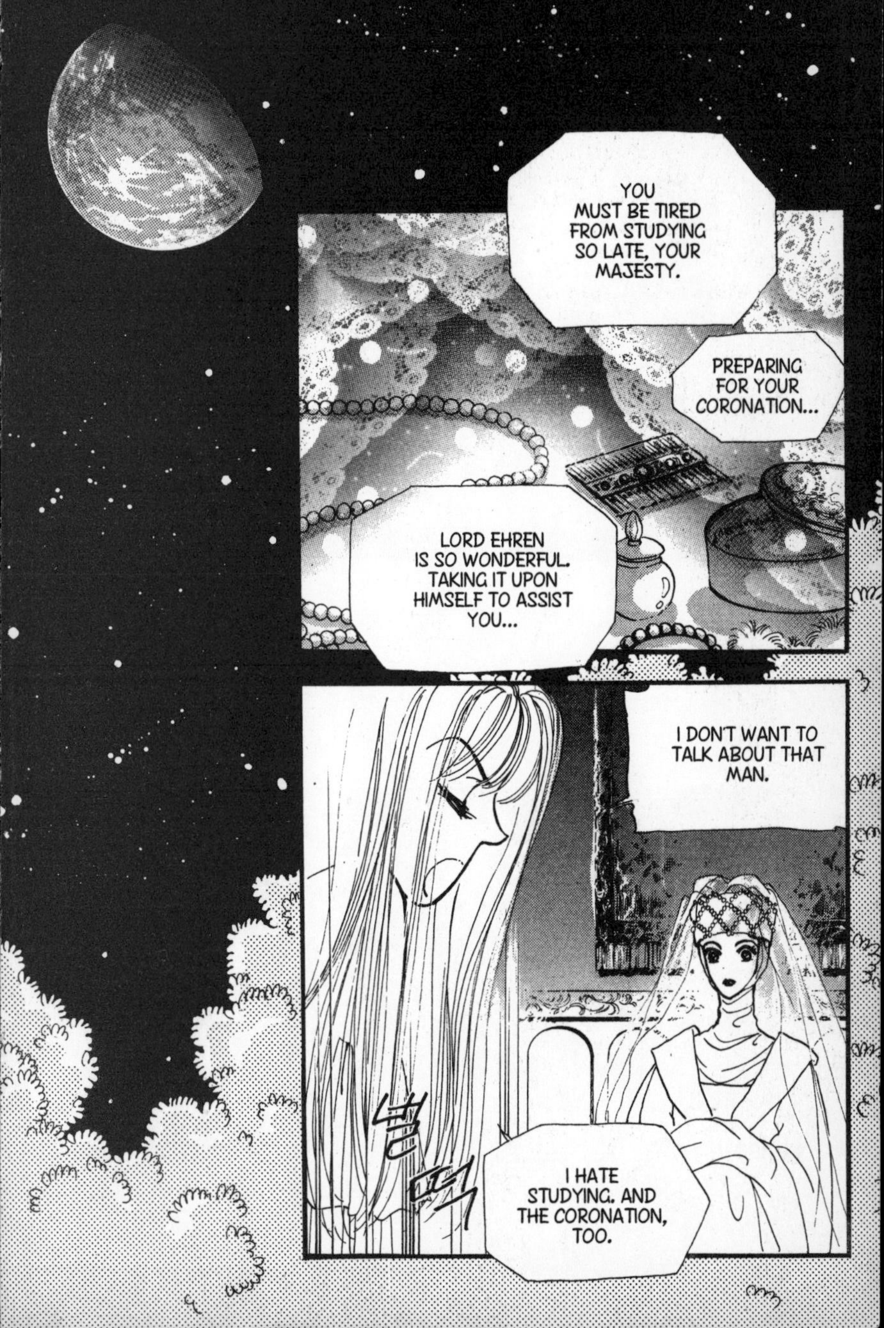
YOU MUST BE TIRED FROM STUDYING SO LATE, YOUR MAJESTY.
PREPARING FOR YOUR CORONATION...
LORD EHREN IS SO WONDERFUL. TAKING IT UPON HIMSELF TO ASSIST YOU...
I DON'T WANT TO TALK ABOUT THAT MAN.
I HATE STUDYING. AND THE CORONATION, TOO.

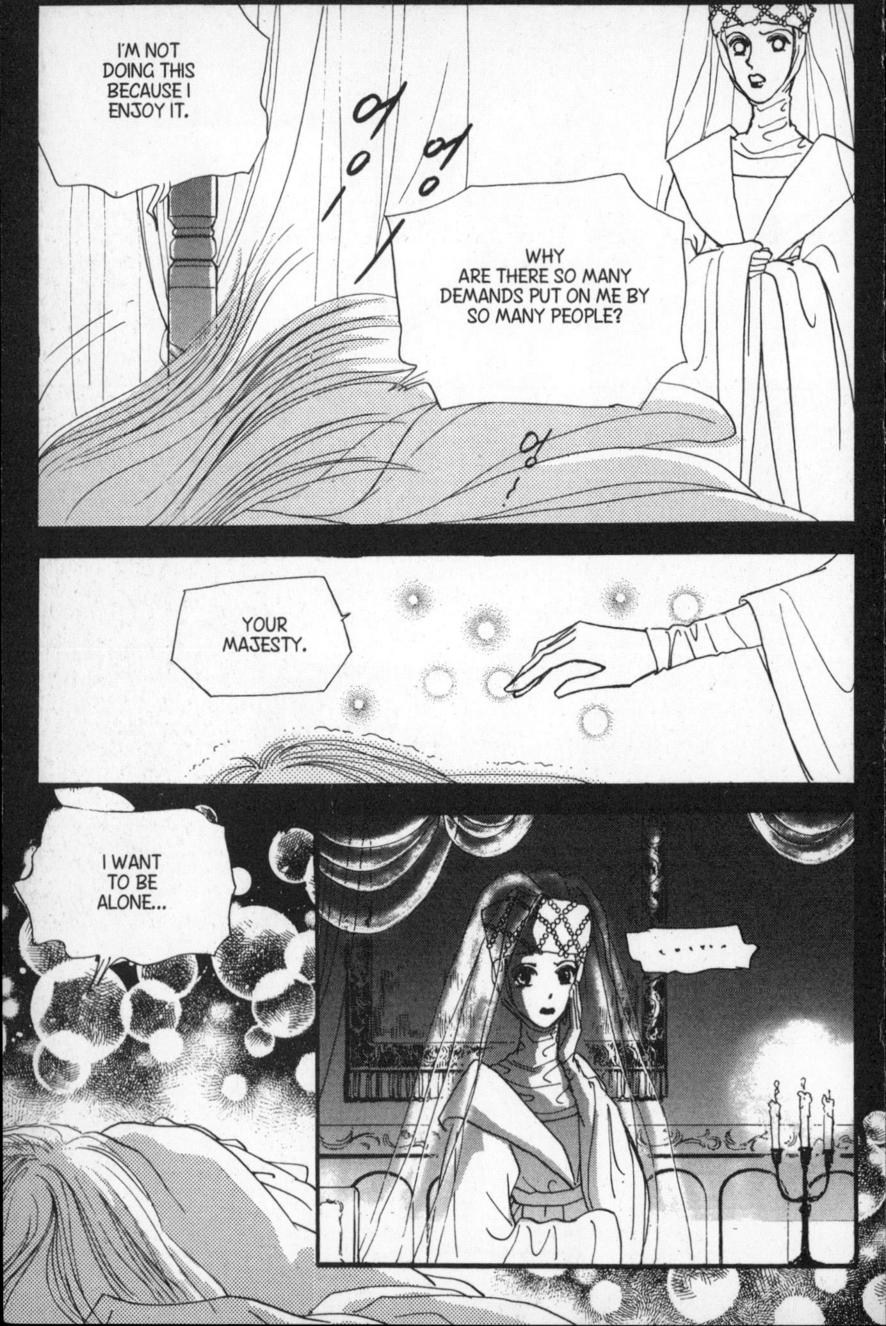
I'M NOT DOING THIS BECAUSE I ENJOY IT.
WHY ARE THERE SO MANY DEMANDS PUT ON ME BY SO MANY PEOPLE?
YOUR MAJESTY.
I WANT TO BE ALONE...
......

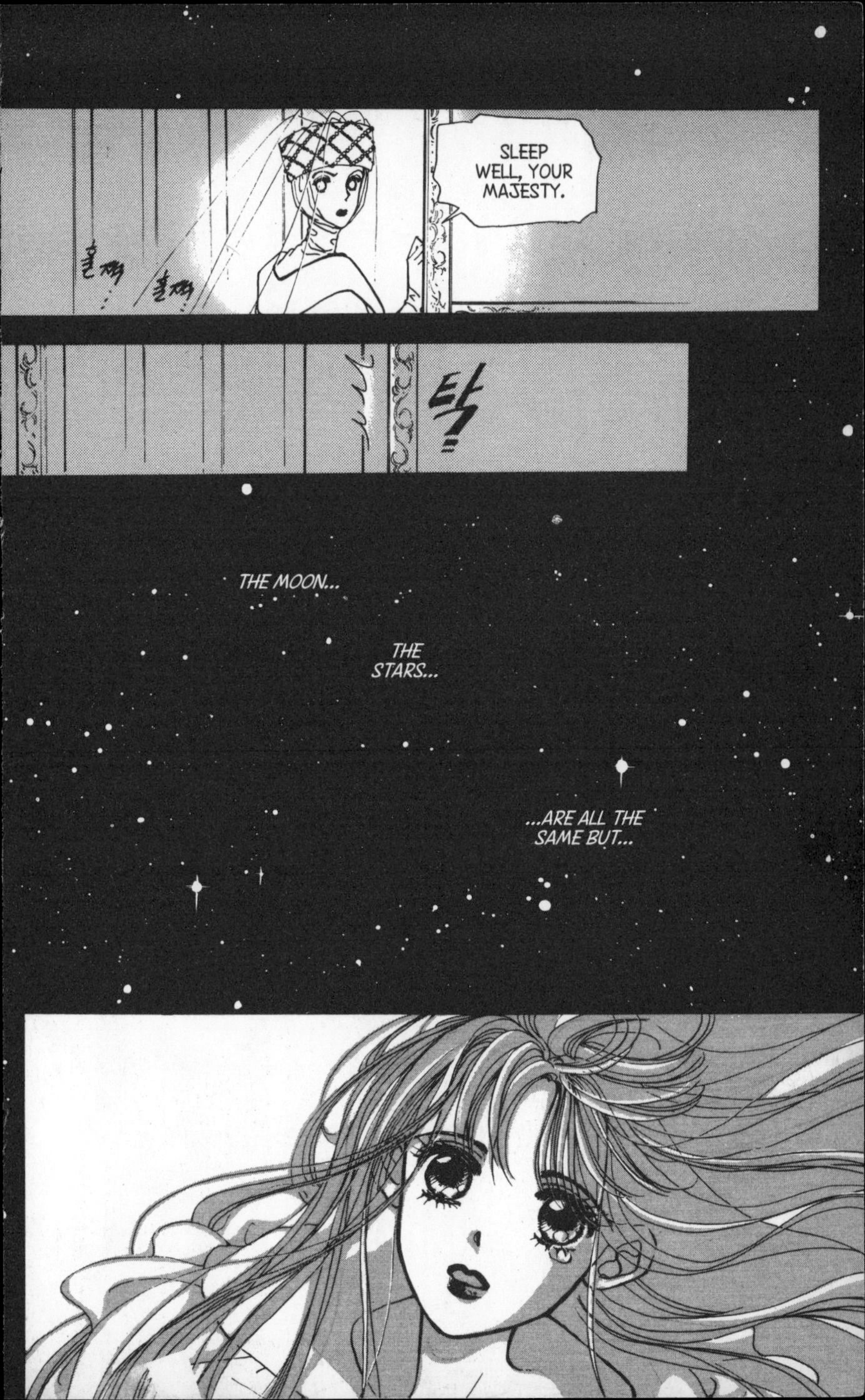
훌쩍
훌쩍
SLEEP WELL, YOUR MAJESTY.
탁!
THE MOON...
THE STARS...
...ARE ALL THE SAME BUT...

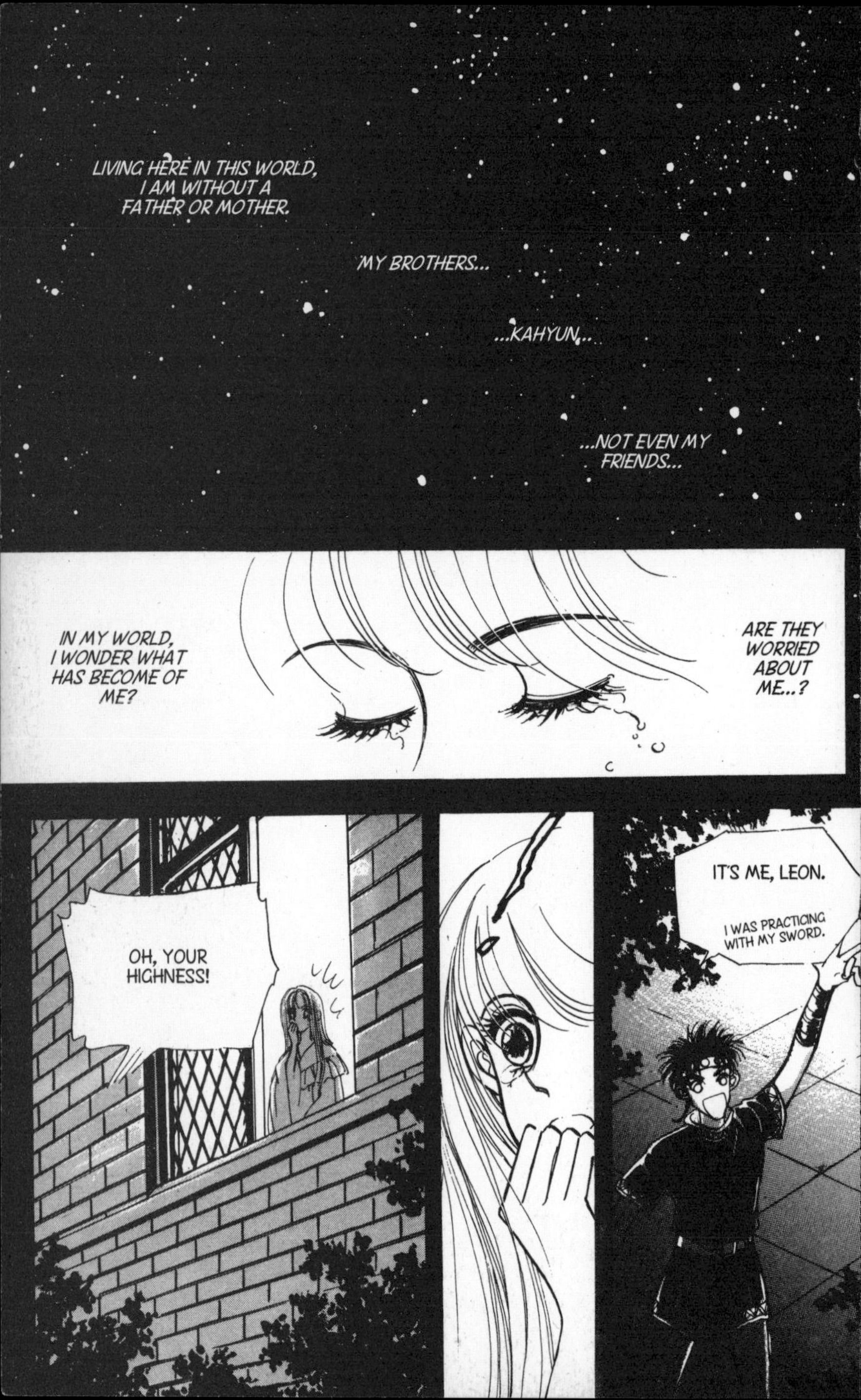
LIVING HERE IN THIS WORLD, I AM WITHOUT A FATHER OR MOTHER.
MY BROTHERS...
...KAHYUN...
...NOT EVEN MY FRIENDS...
IN MY WORLD, I WONDER WHAT HAS BECOME OF ME?
ARE THEY WORRIED ABOUT ME...?
OH, YOUR HIGHNESS!
IT'S ME, LEON.
I WAS PRACTICING WITH MY SWORD.

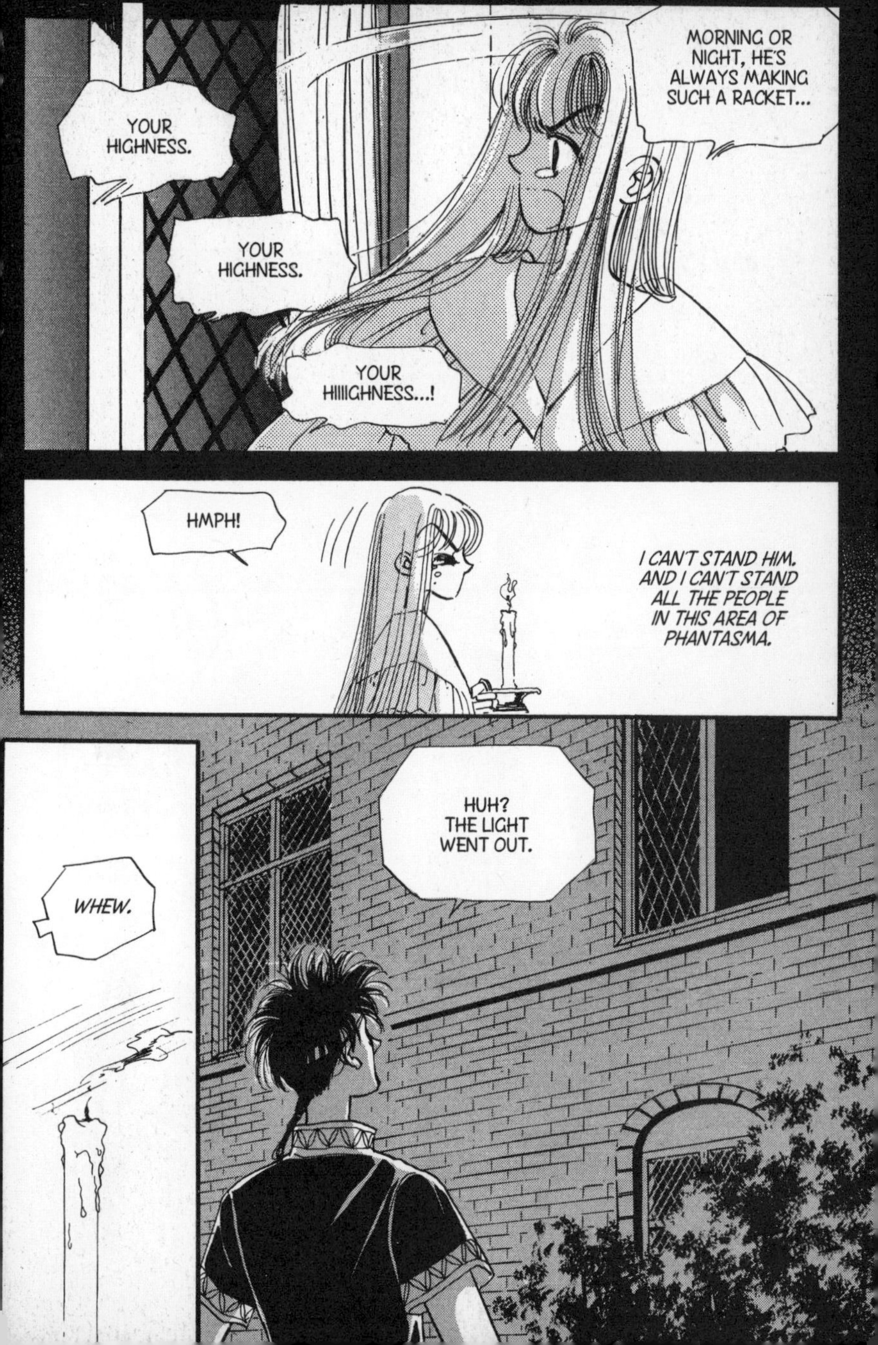
YOUR HIGHNESS.
YOUR HIGHNESS.
YOUR HIIIIGHNESS...!
MORNING OR NIGHT, HE'S ALWAYS MAKING SUCH A RACKET...
HMPH!
I CAN'T STAND HIM. AND I CAN'T STAND ALL THE PEOPLE IN THIS AREA OF PHANTASMA.
WHEW.
HUH? THE LIGHT WENT OUT.

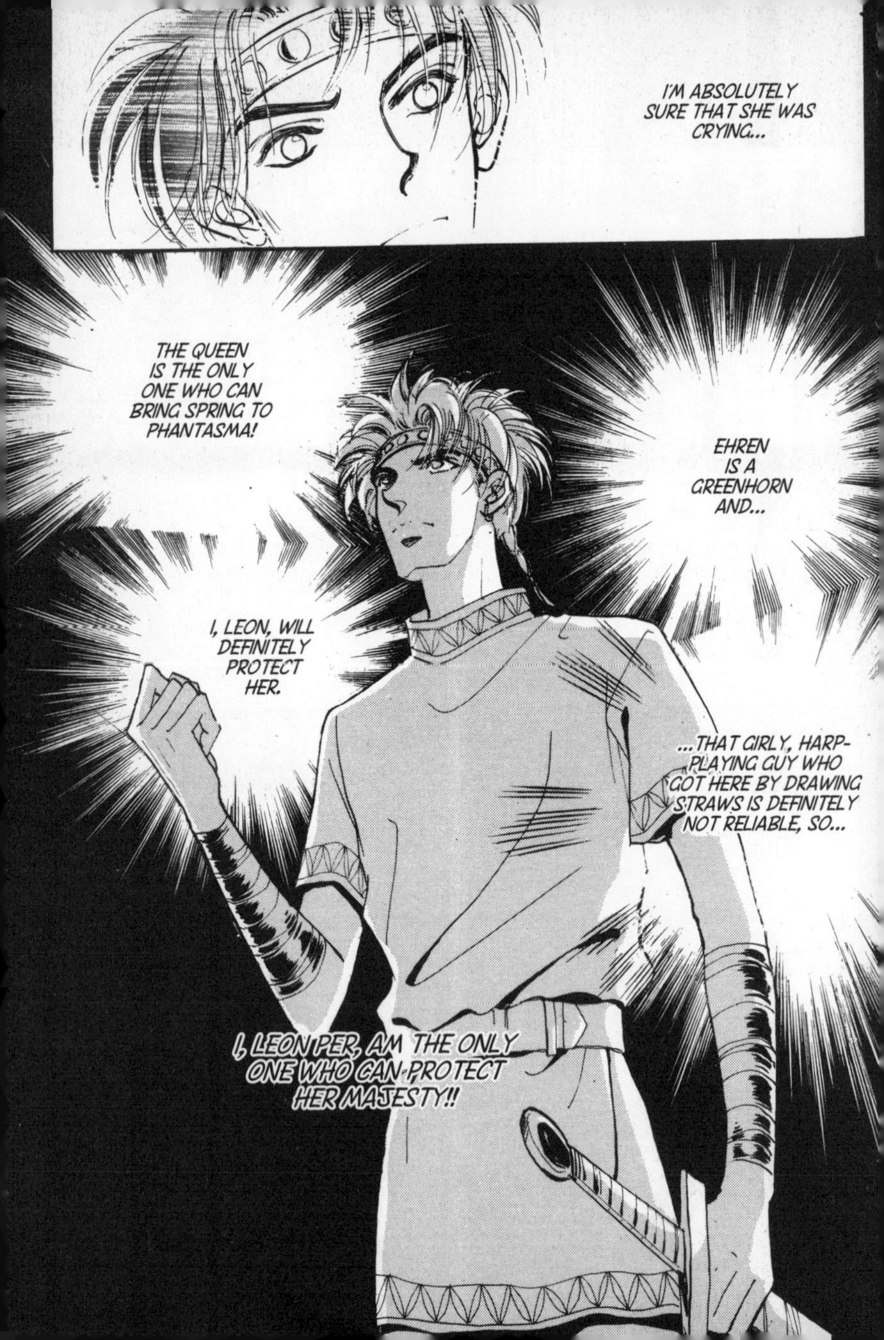

I'M ABSOLUTELY SURE THAT SHE WAS CRYING...
THE QUEEN IS THE ONLY ONE WHO CAN BRING SPRING TO PHANTASMA!
EHREN IS A GREENHORN AND...
I, LEON, WILL DEFINITELY PROTECT HER.
...THAT GIRLY, HARP-PLAYING GUY WHO GOT HERE BY DRAWING STRAWS IS DEFINITELY NOT RELIABLE, SO...
I, LEON PER, AM THE ONLY ONE WHO CAN PROTECT HER MAJESTY!!

Ehren Fürst

Leon Per

Schiller Licht

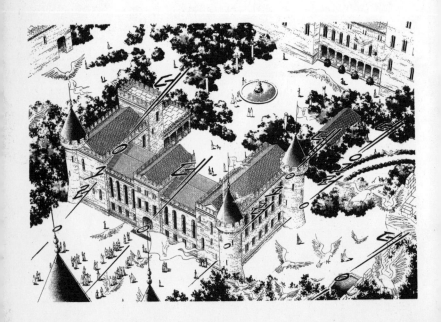

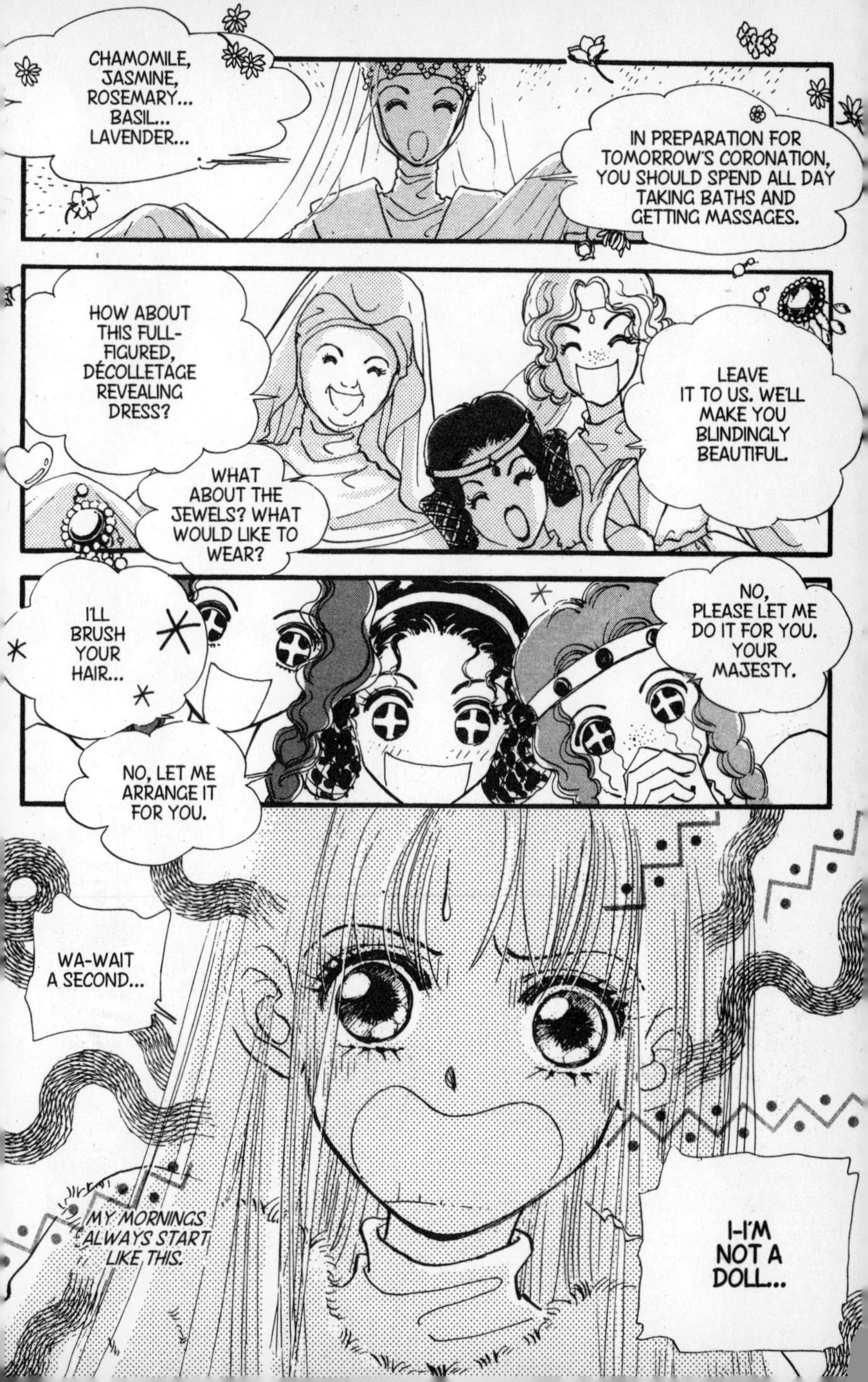
CHAMOMILE, JASMINE, ROSEMARY... BASIL... LAVENDER...
IN PREPARATION FOR TOMORROW'S CORONATION, YOU SHOULD SPEND ALL DAY TAKING BATHS AND GETTING MASSAGES.
HOW ABOUT THIS FULL-FIGURED, DÉCOLLETAGE REVEALING DRESS?
WHAT ABOUT THE JEWELS? WHAT WOULD LIKE TO WEAR?
LEAVE IT TO US. WE'LL MAKE YOU BLINDINGLY BEAUTIFUL.
I'LL BRUSH YOUR HAIR...
NO, LET ME ARRANGE IT FOR YOU.
NO, PLEASE LET ME DO IT FOR YOU. YOUR MAJESTY.
WA-WAIT A SECOND...
MY MORNINGS ALWAYS START LIKE THIS.
I-I'M NOT A DOLL...

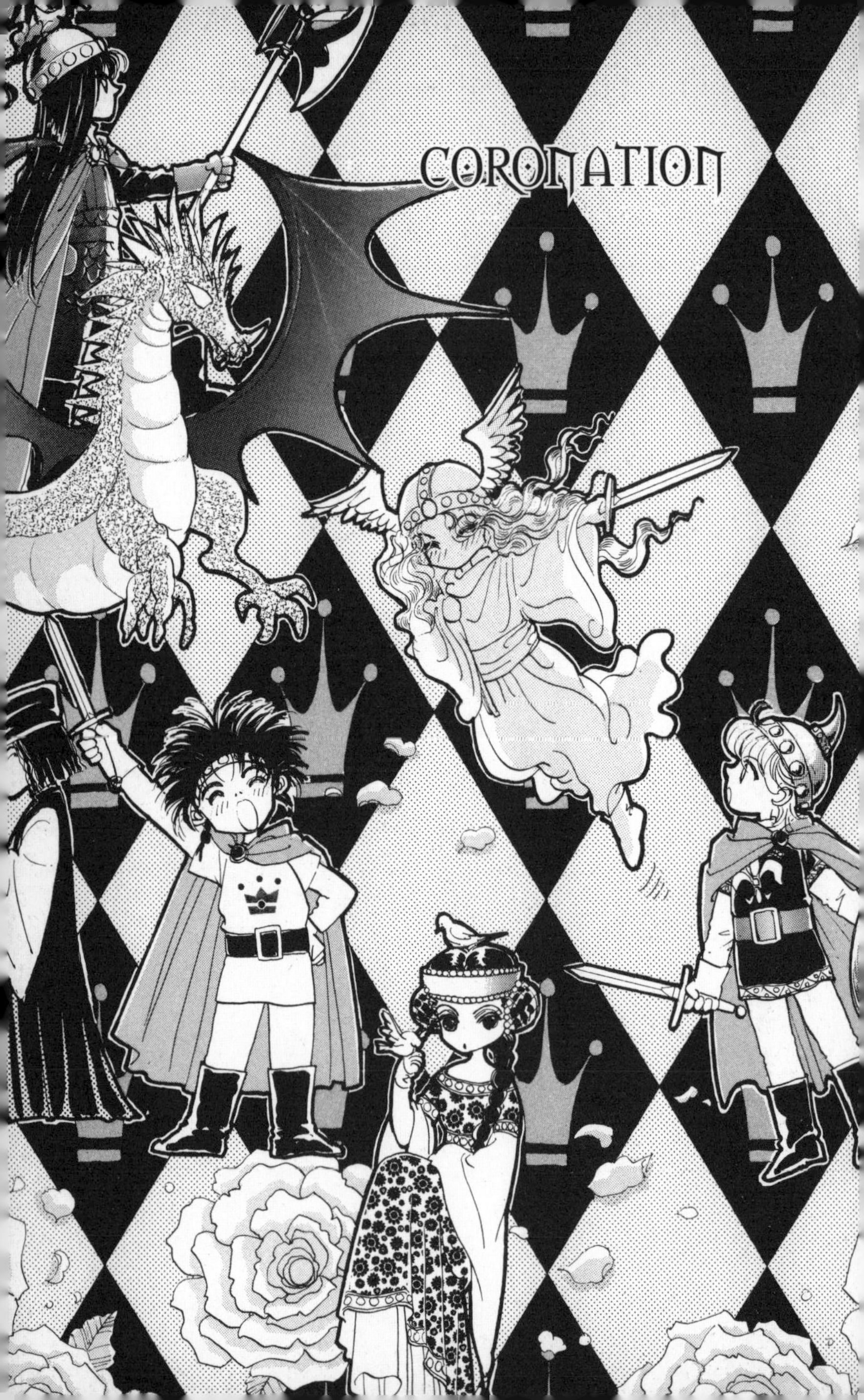
CORONATION

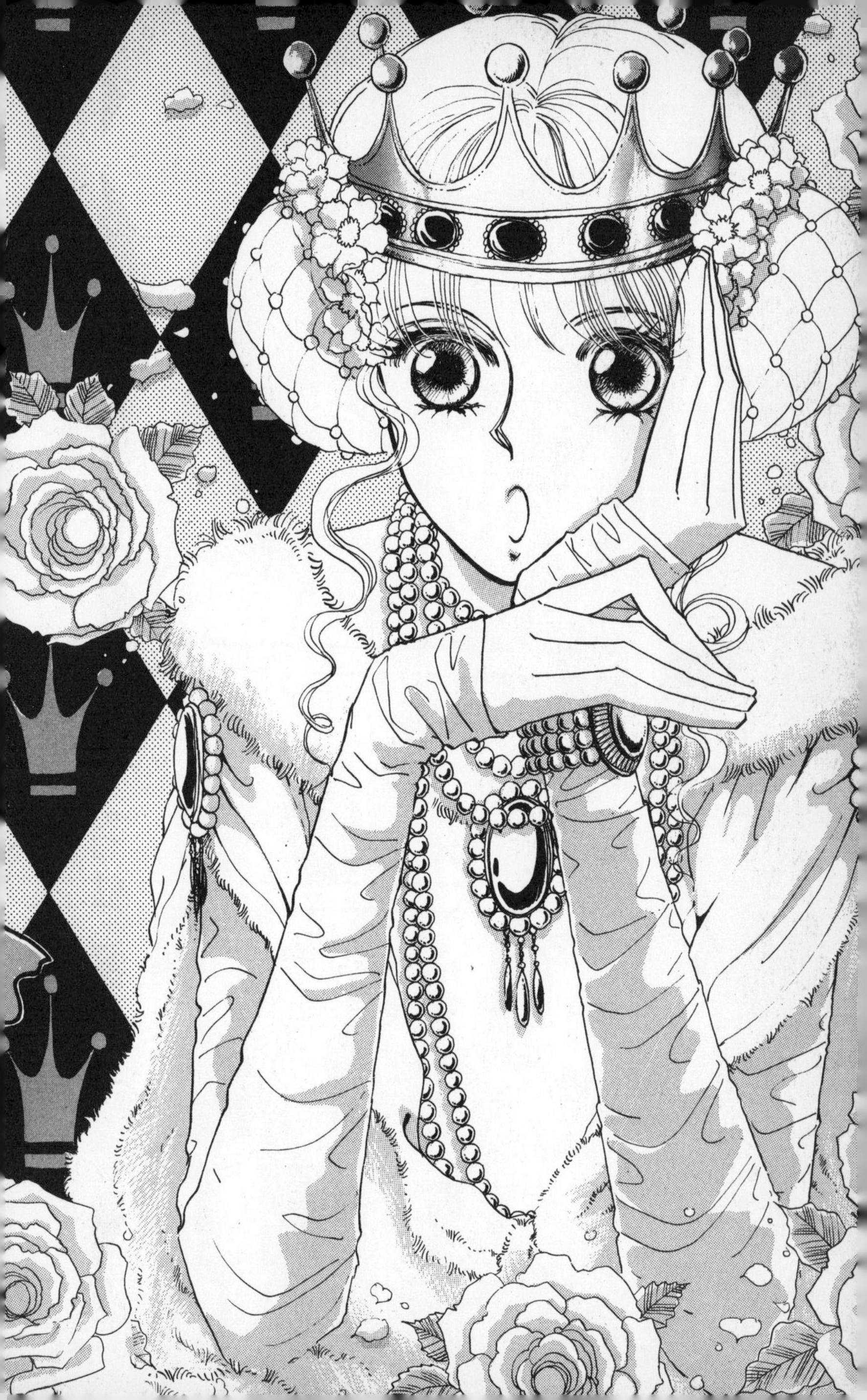

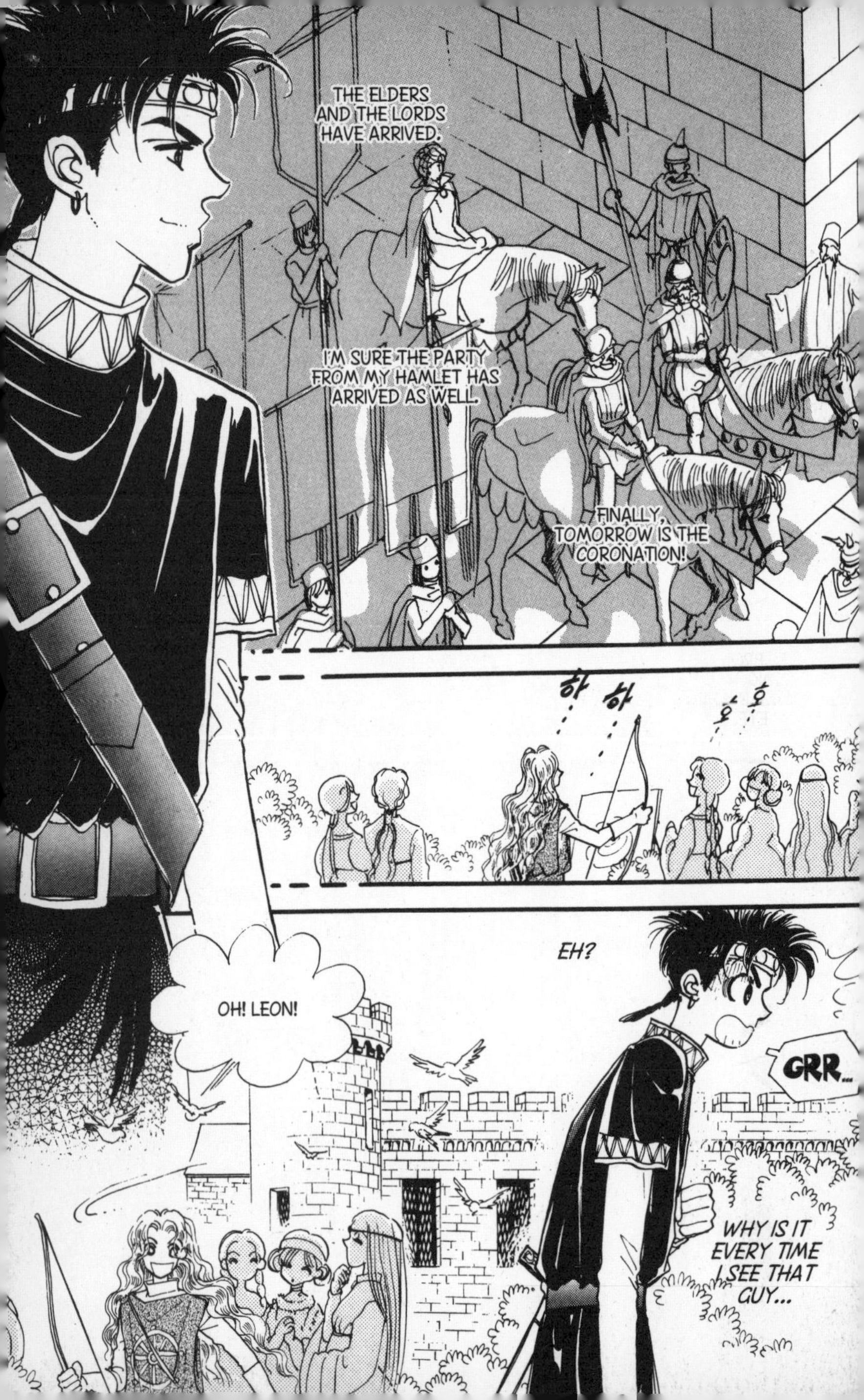
THE ELDERS AND THE LORDS HAVE ARRIVED.
I'M SURE THE PARTY FROM MY HAMLET HAS ARRIVED AS WELL.
FINALLY, TOMORROW IS THE CORONATION!
하 하
호 호
OH! LEON!
EH?
GRR...
WHY IS IT EVERY TIME I SEE THAT GUY...

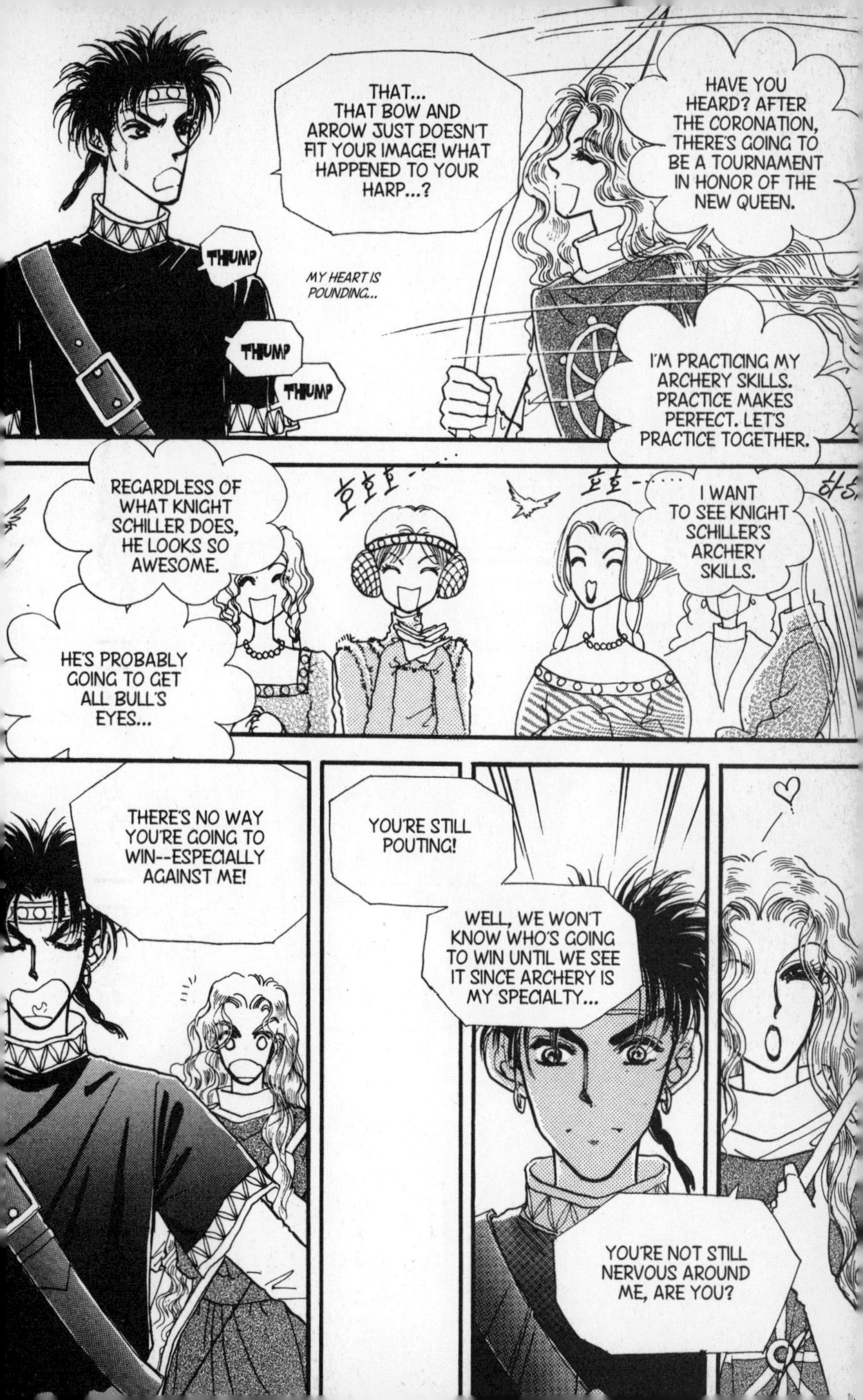
THAT... THAT BOW AND ARROW JUST DOESN'T FIT YOUR IMAGE! WHAT HAPPENED TO YOUR HARP...?
HAVE YOU HEARD? AFTER THE CORONATION, THERE'S GOING TO BE A TOURNAMENT IN HONOR OF THE NEW QUEEN.
THUMP
MY HEART IS POUNDING...
THUMP
THUMP
I'M PRACTICING MY ARCHERY SKILLS. PRACTICE MAKES PERFECT. LET'S PRACTICE TOGETHER.
REGARDLESS OF WHAT KNIGHT SCHILLER DOES, HE LOOKS SO AWESOME.
HE'S PROBABLY GOING TO GET ALL BULL'S EYES...
호호호......
호호......
I WANT TO SEE KNIGHT SCHILLER'S ARCHERY SKILLS.
THERE'S NO WAY YOU'RE GOING TO WIN--ESPECIALLY AGAINST ME!
YOU'RE STILL POUTING!
WELL, WE WON'T KNOW WHO'S GOING TO WIN UNTIL WE SEE IT SINCE ARCHERY IS MY SPECIALTY...
YOU'RE NOT STILL NERVOUS AROUND ME, ARE YOU?

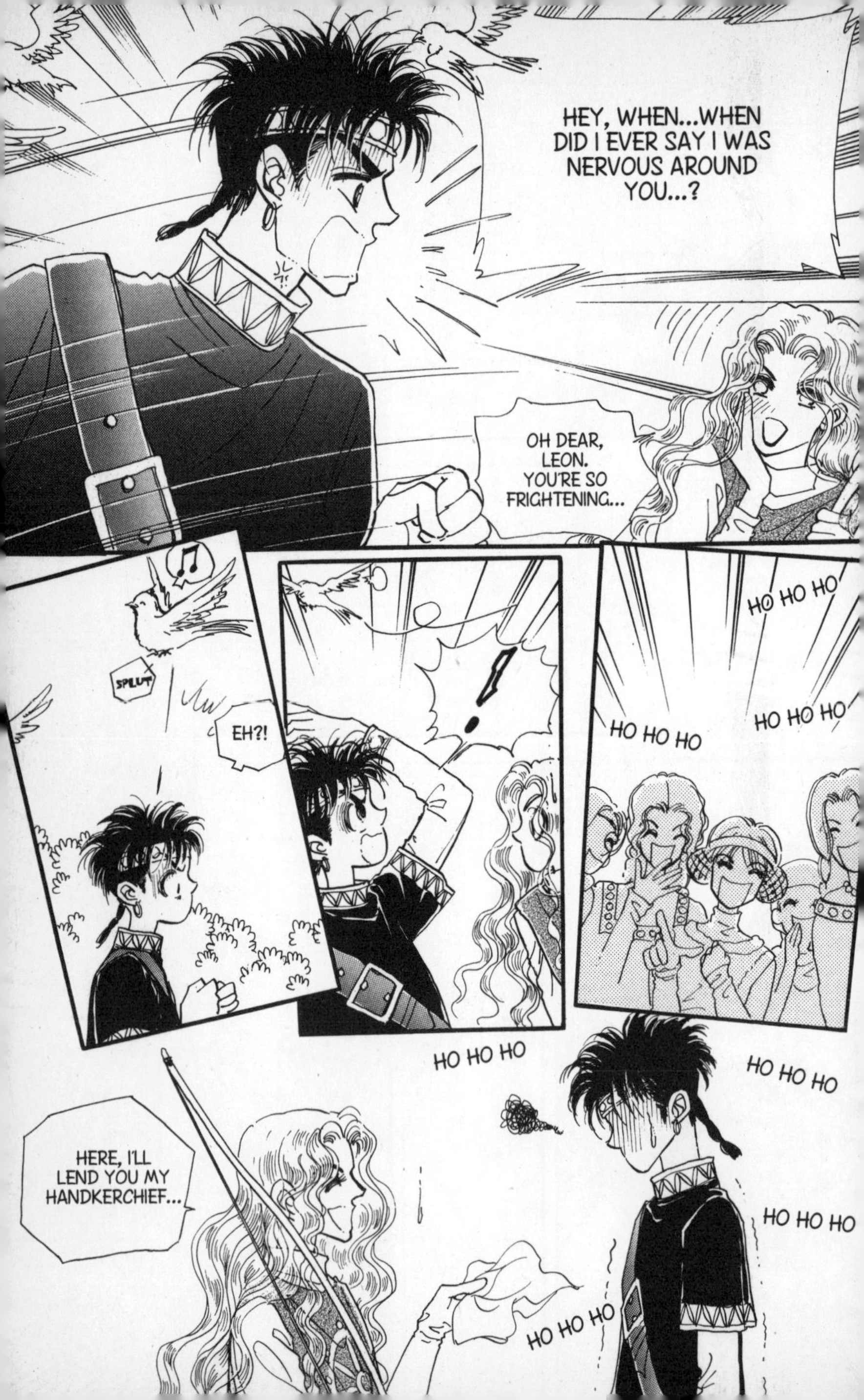
HEY, WHEN...WHEN DID I EVER SAY I WAS NERVOUS AROUND YOU...?
OH DEAR, LEON. YOU'RE SO FRIGHTENING...
SPLUT
EH?!
HO HO HO
HO HO HO
HO HO HO
HO HO HO
HO HO HO
HERE, I'LL LEND YOU MY HANDKERCHIEF...
HO HO HO
HO HO HO

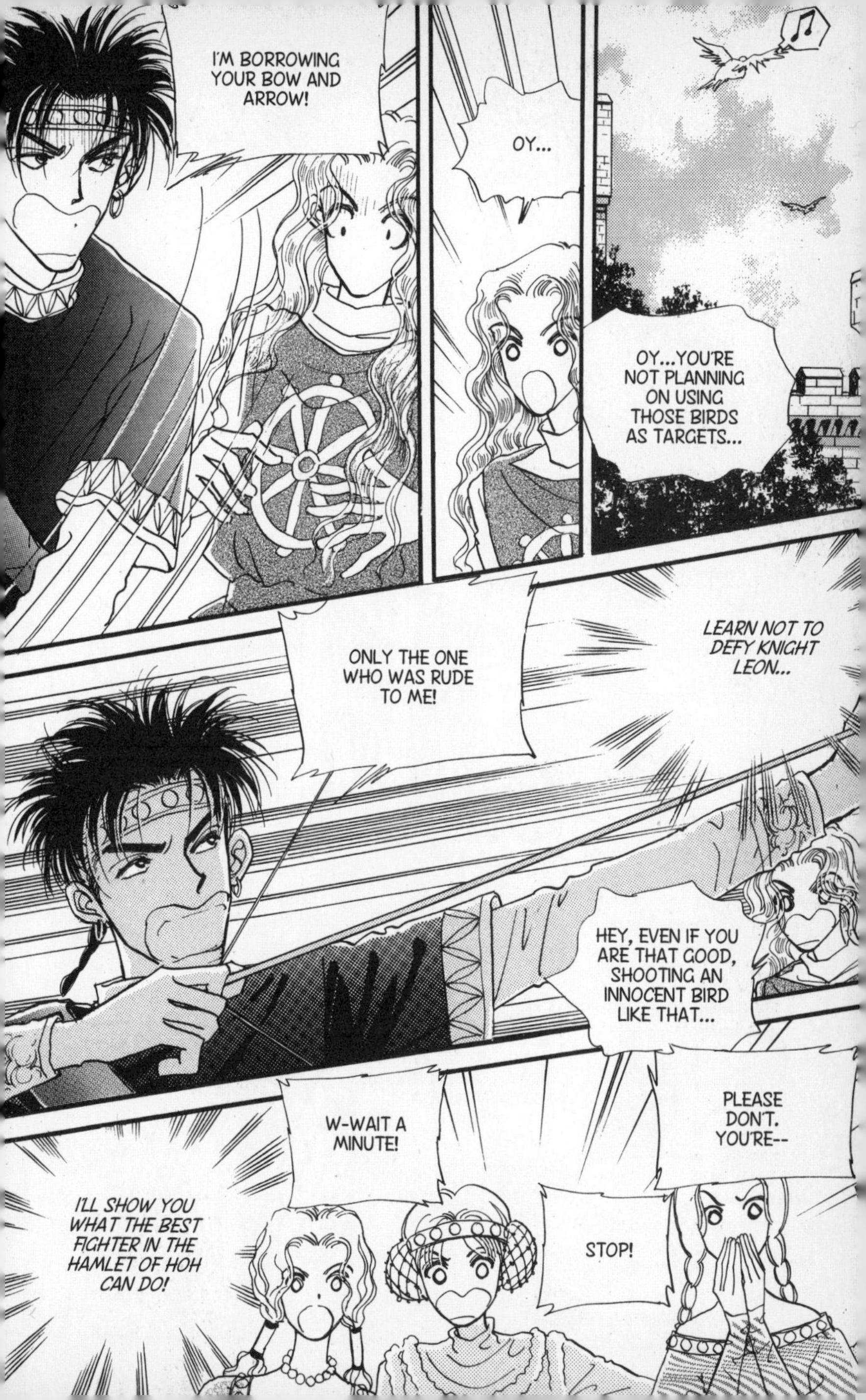
I'M BORROWING YOUR BOW AND ARROW!
OY...
OY...YOU'RE NOT PLANNING ON USING THOSE BIRDS AS TARGETS...
ONLY THE ONE WHO WAS RUDE TO ME!
LEARN NOT TO DEFY KNIGHT LEON...
HEY, EVEN IF YOU ARE THAT GOOD, SHOOTING AN INNOCENT BIRD LIKE THAT...
I'LL SHOW YOU WHAT THE BEST FIGHTER IN THE HAMLET OF HOH CAN DO!
W-WAIT A MINUTE!
PLEASE DON'T. YOU'RE--
STOP!

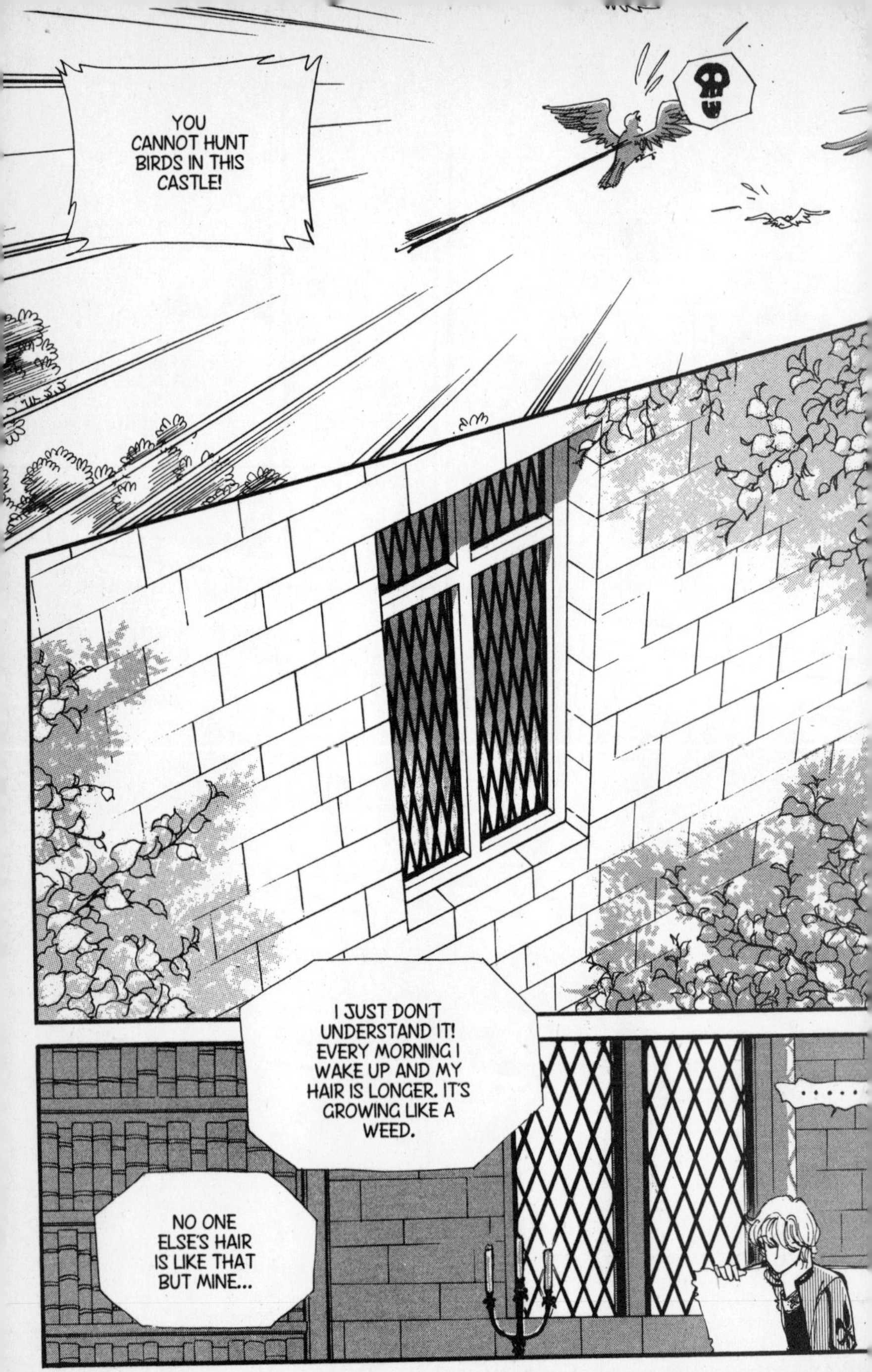
YOU CANNOT HUNT BIRDS IN THIS CASTLE!
I JUST DON'T UNDERSTAND IT! EVERY MORNING I WAKE UP AND MY HAIR IS LONGER. IT'S GROWING LIKE A WEED.
NO ONE ELSE'S HAIR IS LIKE THAT BUT MINE...

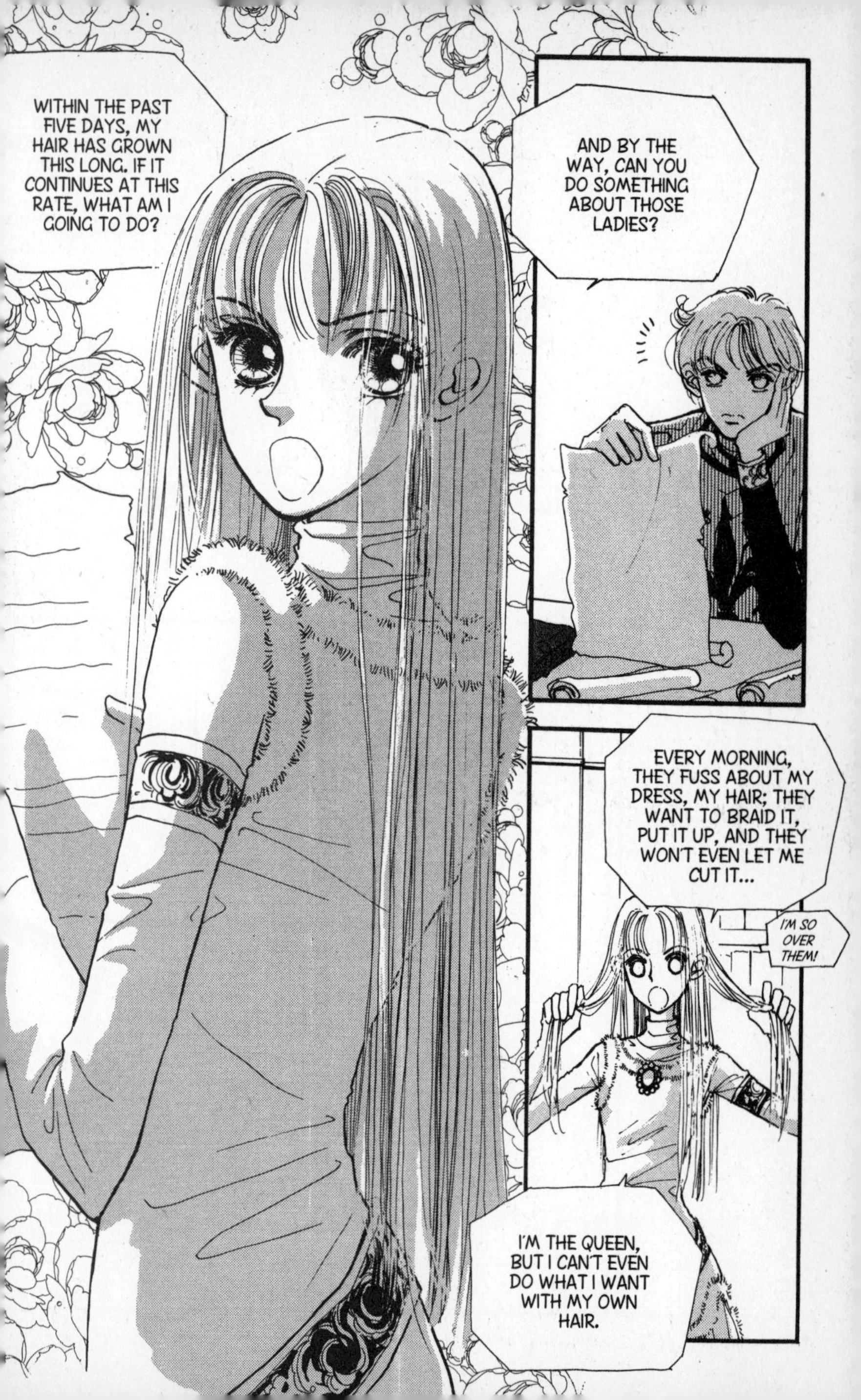

WITHIN THE PAST FIVE DAYS, MY HAIR HAS GROWN THIS LONG. IF IT CONTINUES AT THIS RATE, WHAT AM I GOING TO DO?
AND BY THE WAY, CAN YOU DO SOMETHING ABOUT THOSE LADIES?
EVERY MORNING, THEY FUSS ABOUT MY DRESS, MY HAIR; THEY WANT TO BRAID IT, PUT IT UP, AND THEY WON'T EVEN LET ME CUT IT...
I'M SO OVER THEM!
I'M THE QUEEN, BUT I CAN'T EVEN DO WHAT I WANT WITH MY OWN HAIR.

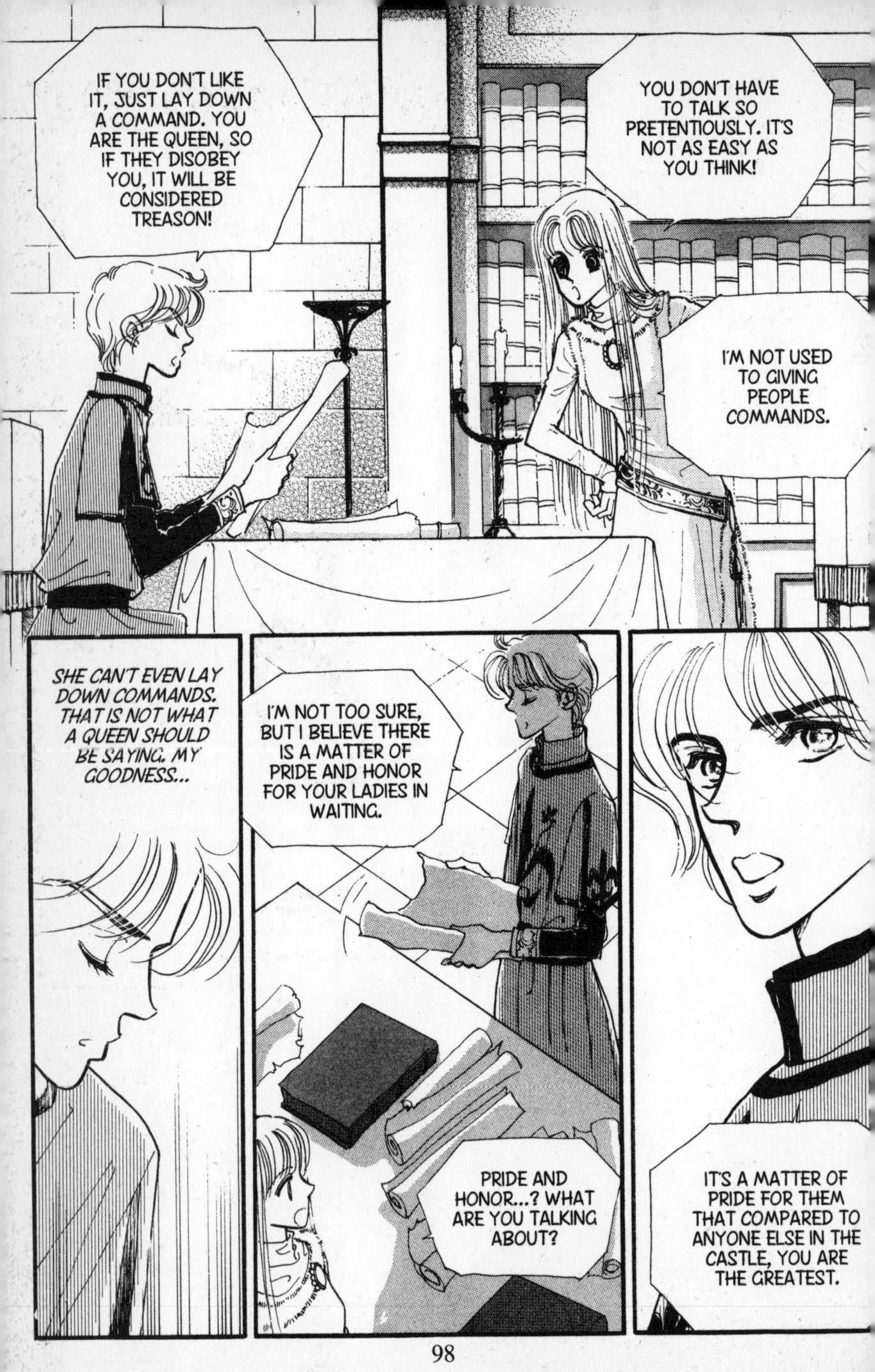
IF YOU DON'T LIKE IT, JUST LAY DOWN A COMMAND. YOU ARE THE QUEEN, SO IF THEY DISOBEY YOU, IT WILL BE CONSIDERED TREASON!
YOU DON'T HAVE TO TALK SO PRETENTIOUSLY. IT'S NOT AS EASY AS YOU THINK!
I'M NOT USED TO GIVING PEOPLE COMMANDS.
SHE CAN'T EVEN LAY DOWN COMMANDS. THAT IS NOT WHAT A QUEEN SHOULD BE SAYING. MY GOODNESS...
I'M NOT TOO SURE, BUT I BELIEVE THERE IS A MATTER OF PRIDE AND HONOR FOR YOUR LADIES IN WAITING.
PRIDE AND HONOR...? WHAT ARE YOU TALKING ABOUT?
IT'S A MATTER OF PRIDE FOR THEM THAT COMPARED TO ANYONE ELSE IN THE CASTLE, YOU ARE THE GREATEST.

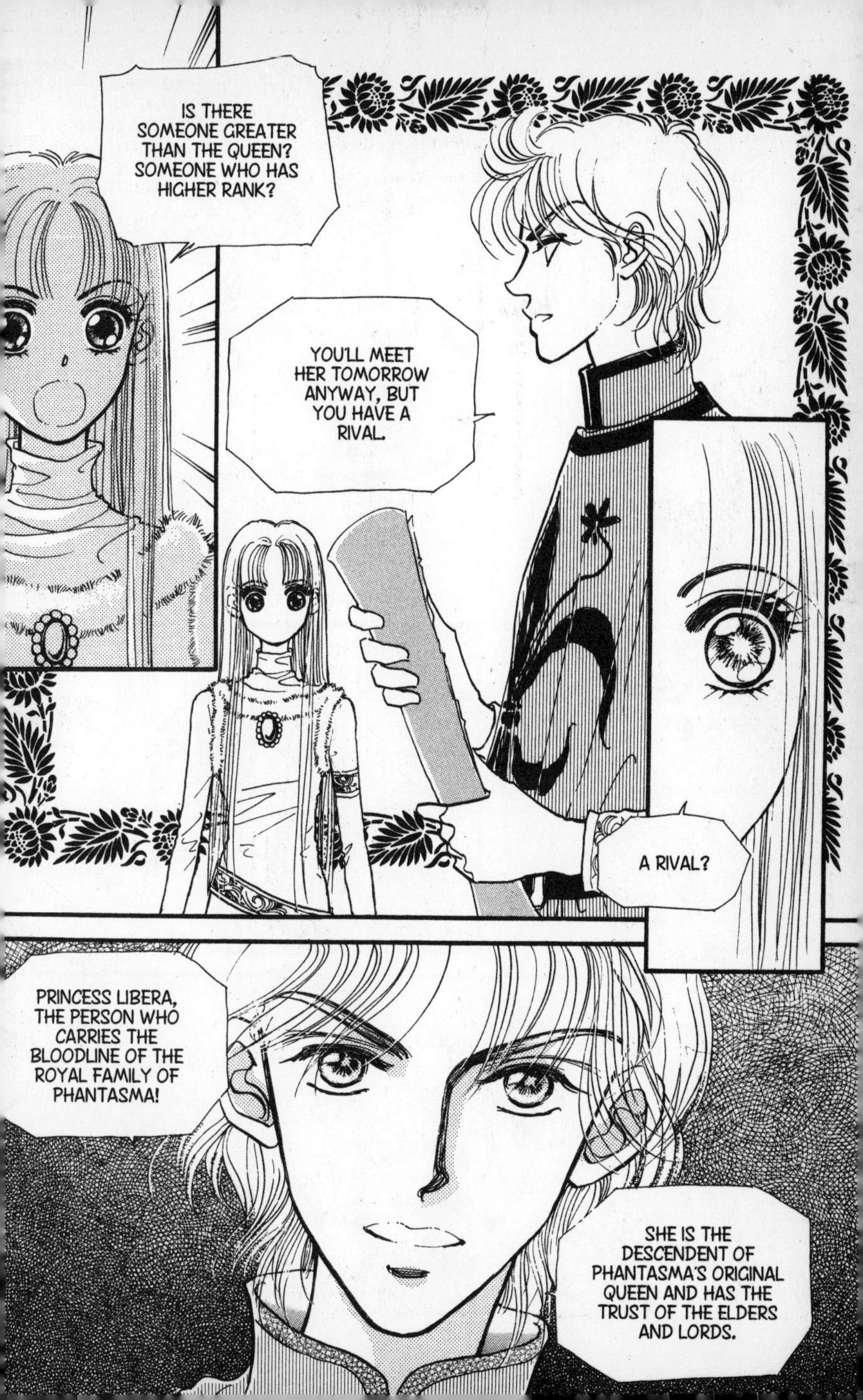
IS THERE SOMEONE GREATER THAN THE QUEEN? SOMEONE WHO HAS HIGHER RANK?
YOU'LL MEET HER TOMORROW ANYWAY, BUT YOU HAVE A RIVAL.
A RIVAL?
PRINCESS LIBERA, THE PERSON WHO CARRIES THE BLOODLINE OF THE ROYAL FAMILY OF PHANTASMA!
SHE IS THE DESCENDENT OF PHANTASMA'S ORIGINAL QUEEN AND HAS THE TRUST OF THE ELDERS AND LORDS.

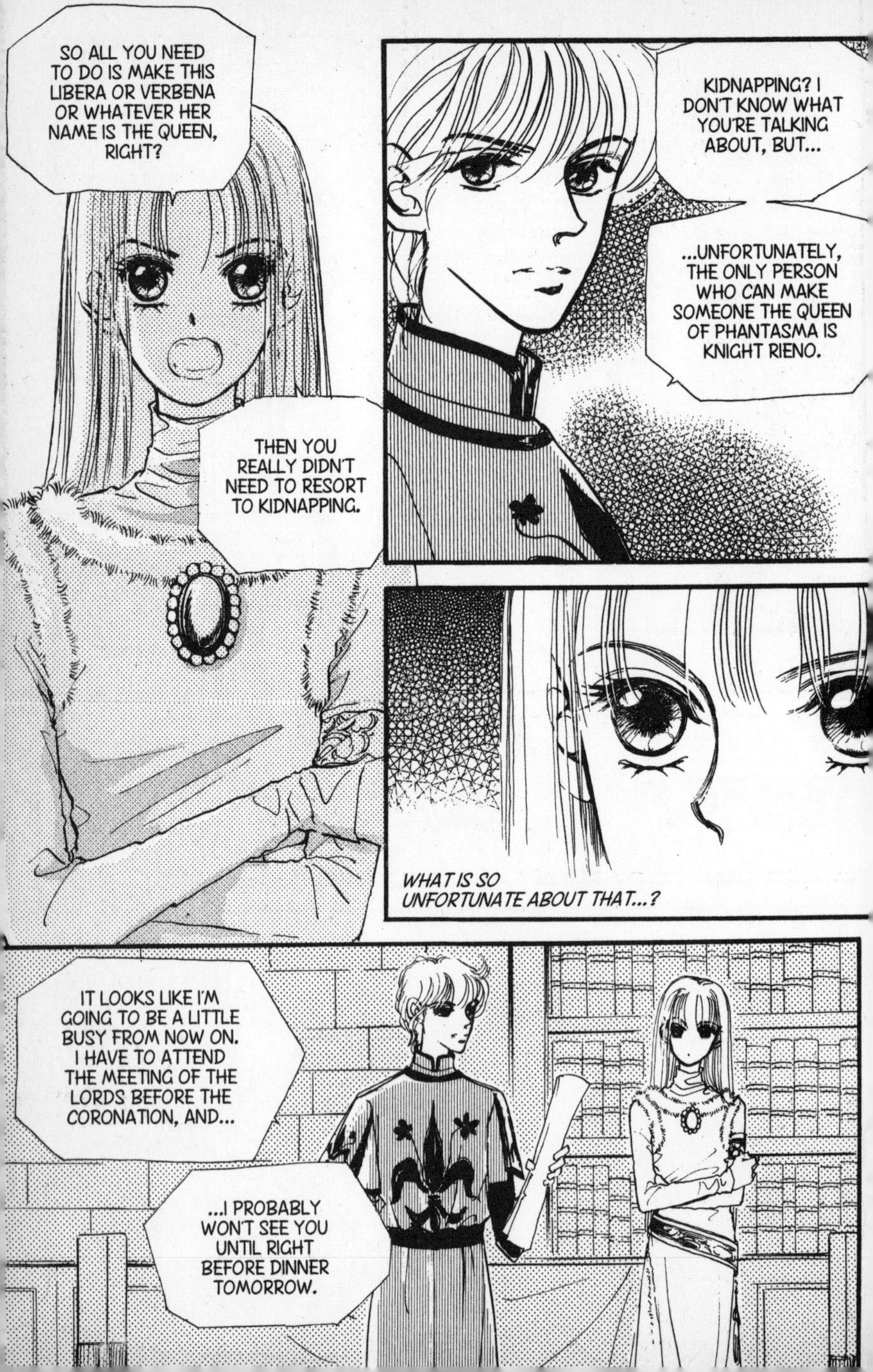
SO ALL YOU NEED TO DO IS MAKE THIS LIBERA OR VERBENA OR WHATEVER HER NAME IS THE QUEEN, RIGHT?
THEN YOU REALLY DIDN'T NEED TO RESORT TO KIDNAPPING.
KIDNAPPING? I DON'T KNOW WHAT YOU'RE TALKING ABOUT, BUT...
...UNFORTUNATELY, THE ONLY PERSON WHO CAN MAKE SOMEONE THE QUEEN OF PHANTASMA IS KNIGHT RIENO.
WHAT IS SO UNFORTUNATE ABOUT THAT...?
IT LOOKS LIKE I'M GOING TO BE A LITTLE BUSY FROM NOW ON. I HAVE TO ATTEND THE MEETING OF THE LORDS BEFORE THE CORONATION, AND...
...I PROBABLY WON'T SEE YOU UNTIL RIGHT BEFORE DINNER TOMORROW.

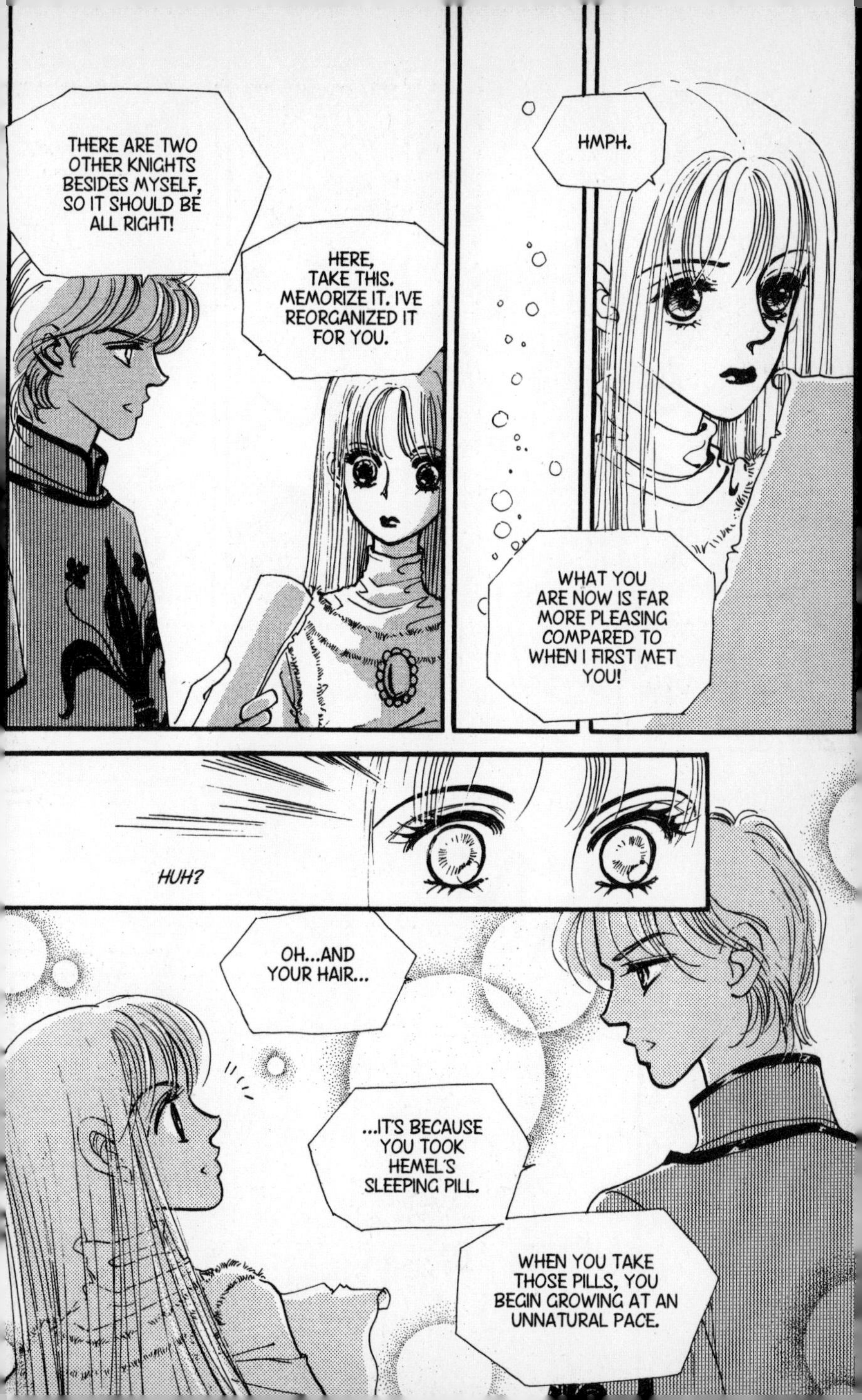
THERE ARE TWO OTHER KNIGHTS BESIDES MYSELF, SO IT SHOULD BE ALL RIGHT!
HERE, TAKE THIS. MEMORIZE IT. I'VE REORGANIZED IT FOR YOU.
HMPH.
WHAT YOU ARE NOW IS FAR MORE PLEASING COMPARED TO WHEN I FIRST MET YOU!
HUH?
OH...AND YOUR HAIR...
...IT'S BECAUSE YOU TOOK HEMEL'S SLEEPING PILL.
WHEN YOU TAKE THOSE PILLS, YOU BEGIN GROWING AT AN UNNATURAL PACE.

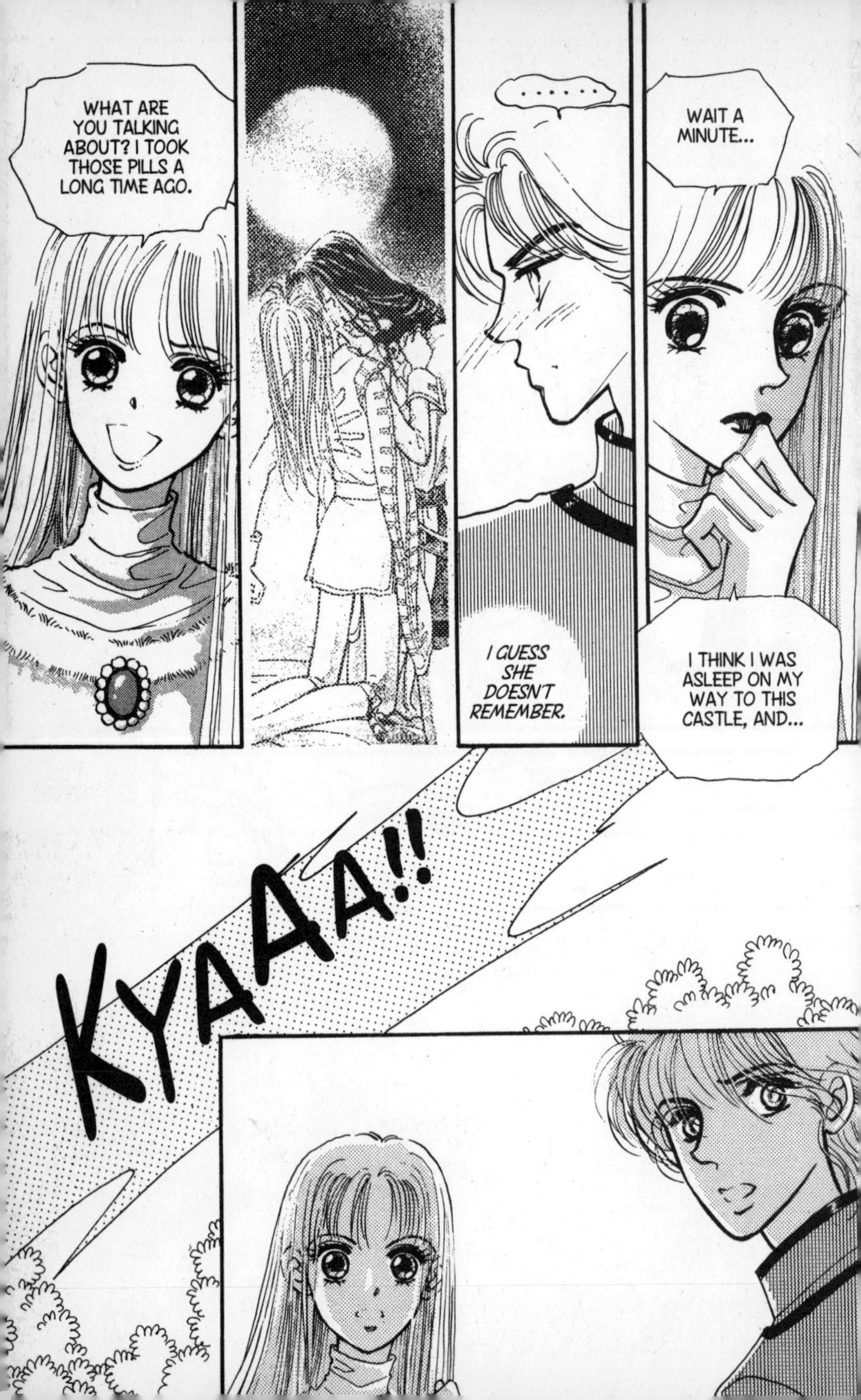
WHAT ARE YOU TALKING ABOUT? I TOOK THOSE PILLS A LONG TIME AGO.
......
I GUESS SHE DOESN'T REMEMBER.
WAIT A MINUTE...
I THINK I WAS ASLEEP ON MY WAY TO THIS CASTLE, AND...
KYAAA!!

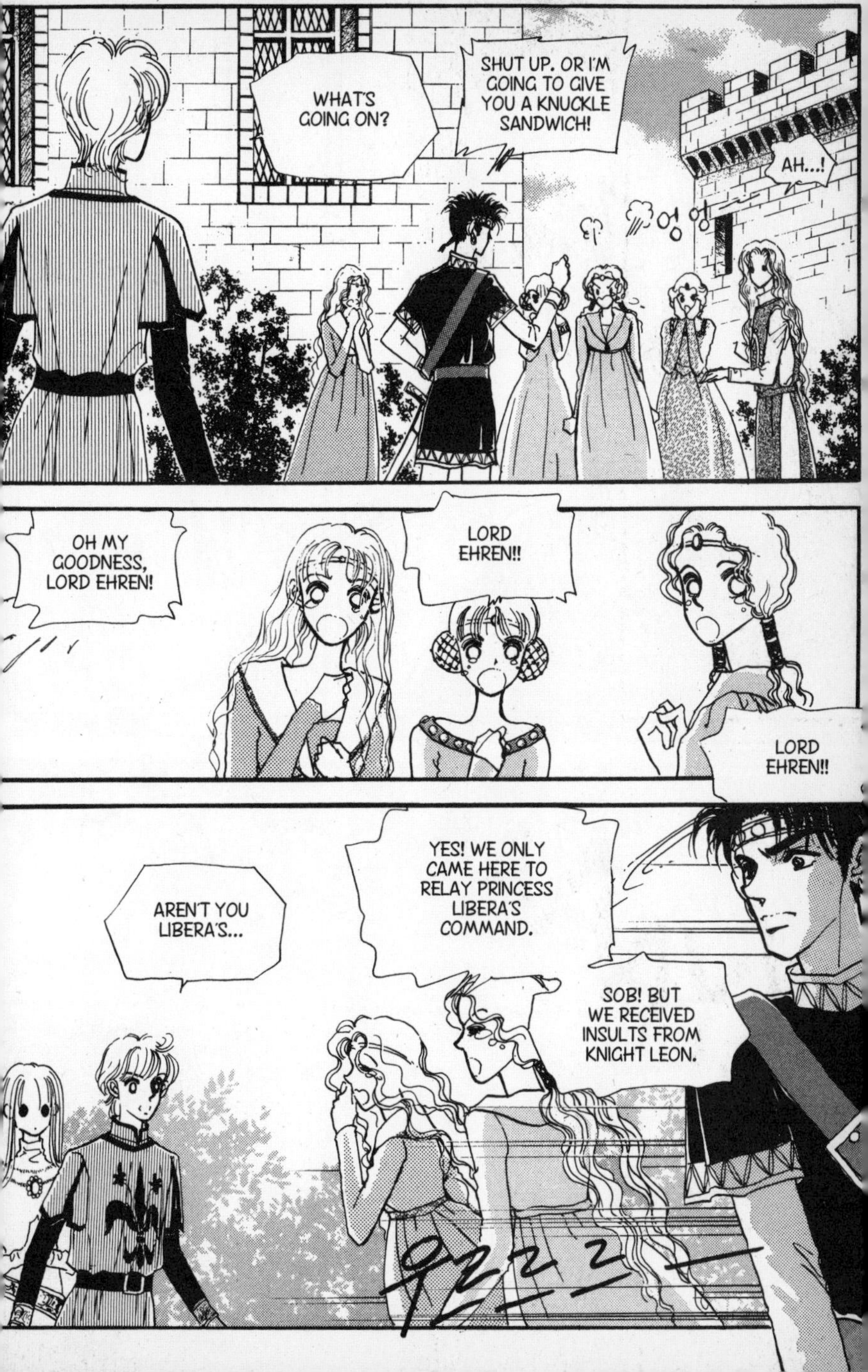
WHAT'S GOING ON?
SHUT UP. OR I'M GOING TO GIVE YOU A KNUCKLE SANDWICH!
AH...!
OH MY GOODNESS, LORD EHREN!
LORD EHREN!!
LORD EHREN!!
AREN'T YOU LIBERA'S...
YES! WE ONLY CAME HERE TO RELAY PRINCESS LIBERA'S COMMAND.
SOB! BUT WE RECEIVED INSULTS FROM KNIGHT LEON.

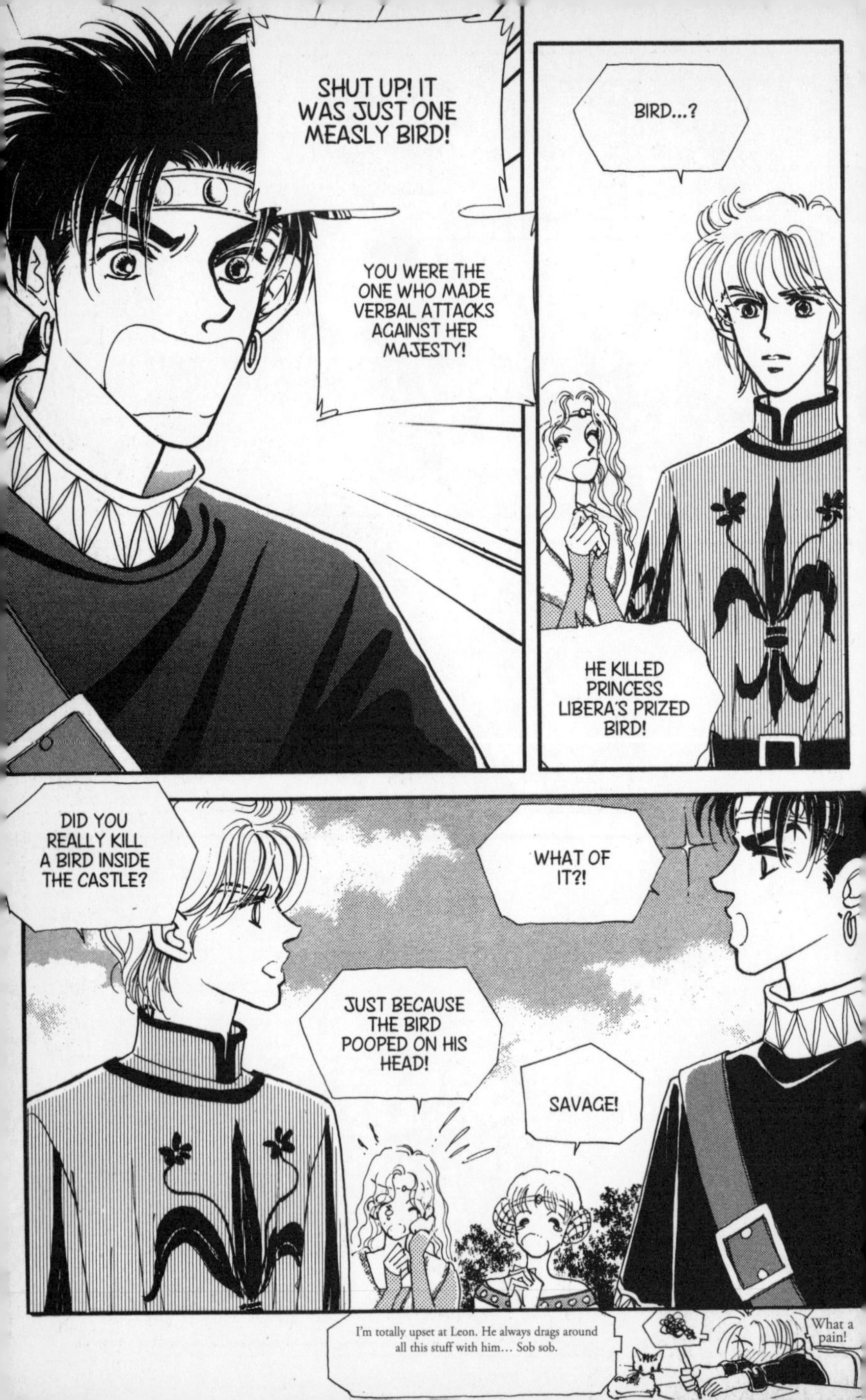
SHUT UP! IT WAS JUST ONE MEASLY BIRD!
YOU WERE THE ONE WHO MADE VERBAL ATTACKS AGAINST HER MAJESTY!
BIRD...?
HE KILLED PRINCESS LIBERA'S PRIZED BIRD!
DID YOU REALLY KILL A BIRD INSIDE THE CASTLE?
WHAT OF IT?!
JUST BECAUSE THE BIRD POOPED ON HIS HEAD!
SAVAGE!
I'm totally upset at Leon. He always drags around all this stuff with him… Sob sob.
What a pain!

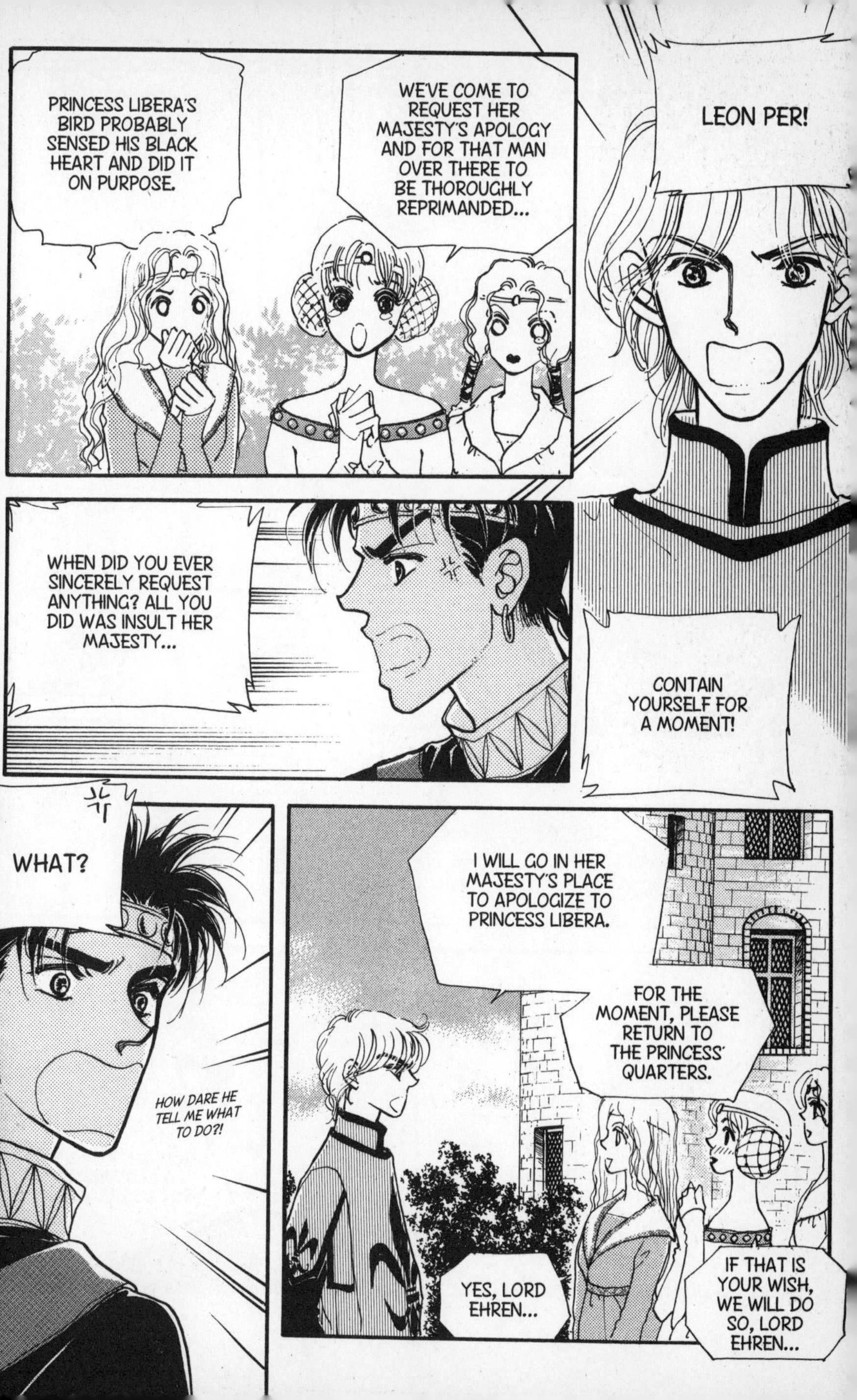
PRINCESS LIBERA'S BIRD PROBABLY SENSED HIS BLACK HEART AND DID IT ON PURPOSE.
WE'VE COME TO REQUEST HER MAJESTY'S APOLOGY AND FOR THAT MAN OVER THERE TO BE THOROUGHLY REPRIMANDED...
WHEN DID YOU EVER SINCERELY REQUEST ANYTHING? ALL YOU DID WAS INSULT HER MAJESTY...
LEON PER!
CONTAIN YOURSELF FOR A MOMENT!
WHAT?
HOW DARE HE TELL ME WHAT TO DO?!
I WILL GO IN HER MAJESTY'S PLACE TO APOLOGIZE TO PRINCESS LIBERA.
FOR THE MOMENT, PLEASE RETURN TO THE PRINCESS' QUARTERS.
YES, LORD EHREN...
IF THAT IS YOUR WISH, WE WILL DO SO, LORD EHREN...

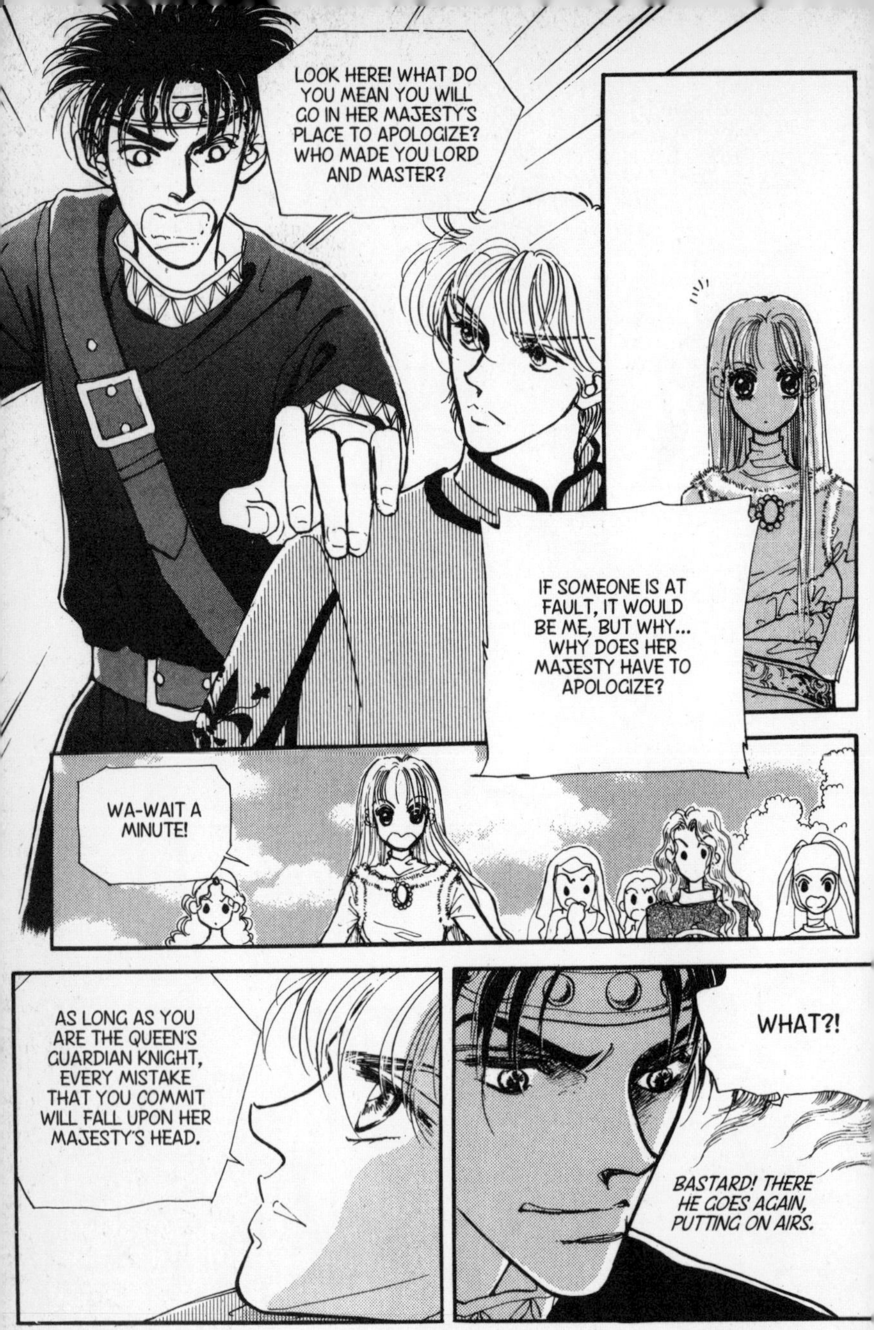
LOOK HERE! WHAT DO YOU MEAN YOU WILL GO IN HER MAJESTY'S PLACE TO APOLOGIZE? WHO MADE YOU LORD AND MASTER?
IF SOMEONE IS AT FAULT, IT WOULD BE ME, BUT WHY... WHY DOES HER MAJESTY HAVE TO APOLOGIZE?
WA-WAIT A MINUTE!
AS LONG AS YOU ARE THE QUEEN'S GUARDIAN KNIGHT, EVERY MISTAKE THAT YOU COMMIT WILL FALL UPON HER MAJESTY'S HEAD.
WHAT?!
BASTARD! THERE HE GOES AGAIN, PUTTING ON AIRS.

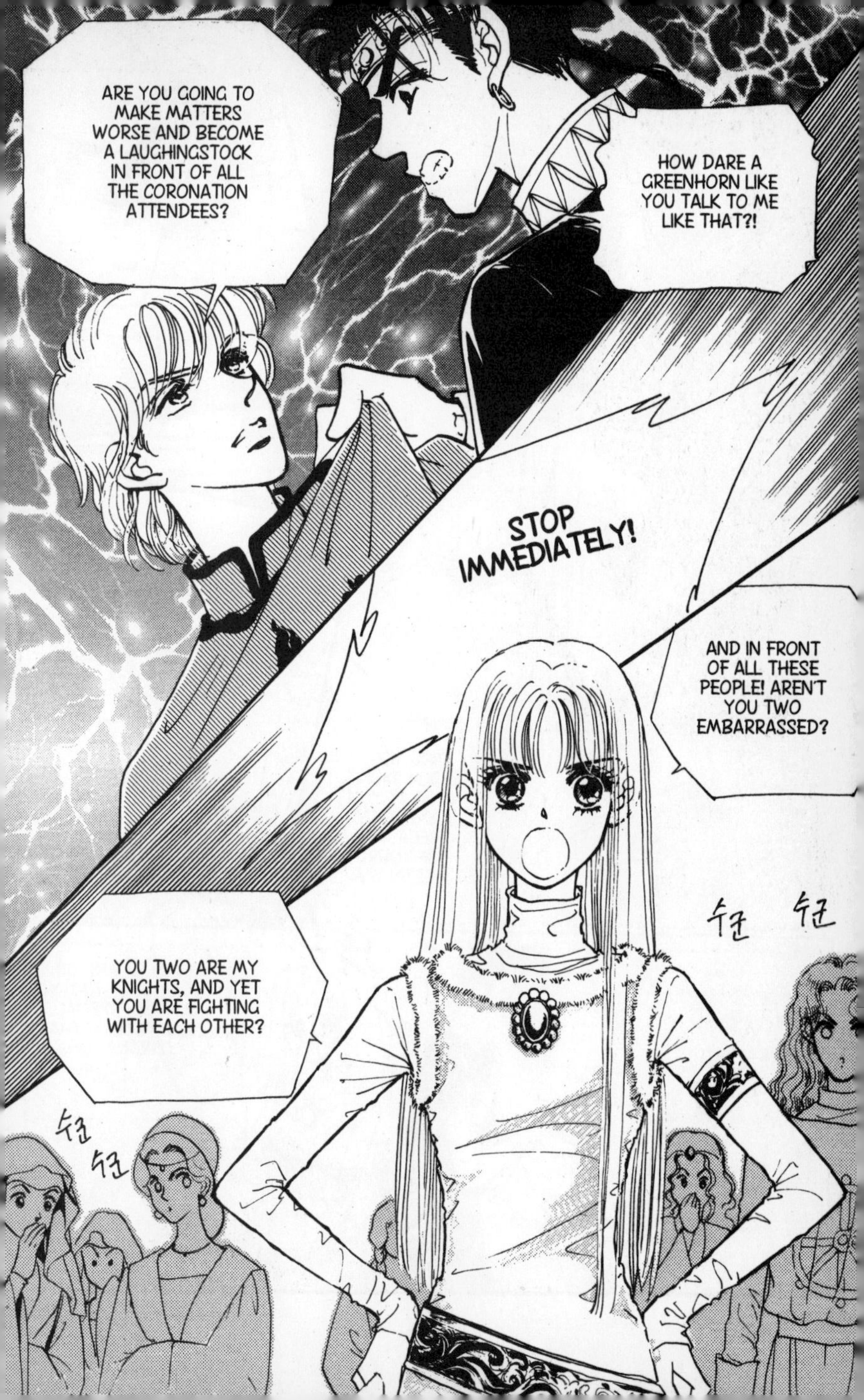
ARE YOU GOING TO MAKE MATTERS WORSE AND BECOME A LAUGHINGSTOCK IN FRONT OF ALL THE CORONATION ATTENDEES?
HOW DARE A GREENHORN LIKE YOU TALK TO ME LIKE THAT?!
STOP IMMEDIATELY!
YOU TWO ARE MY KNIGHTS, AND YET YOU ARE FIGHTING WITH EACH OTHER?
AND IN FRONT OF ALL THESE PEOPLE! AREN'T YOU TWO EMBARRASSED?
수군 수군
수군 수군

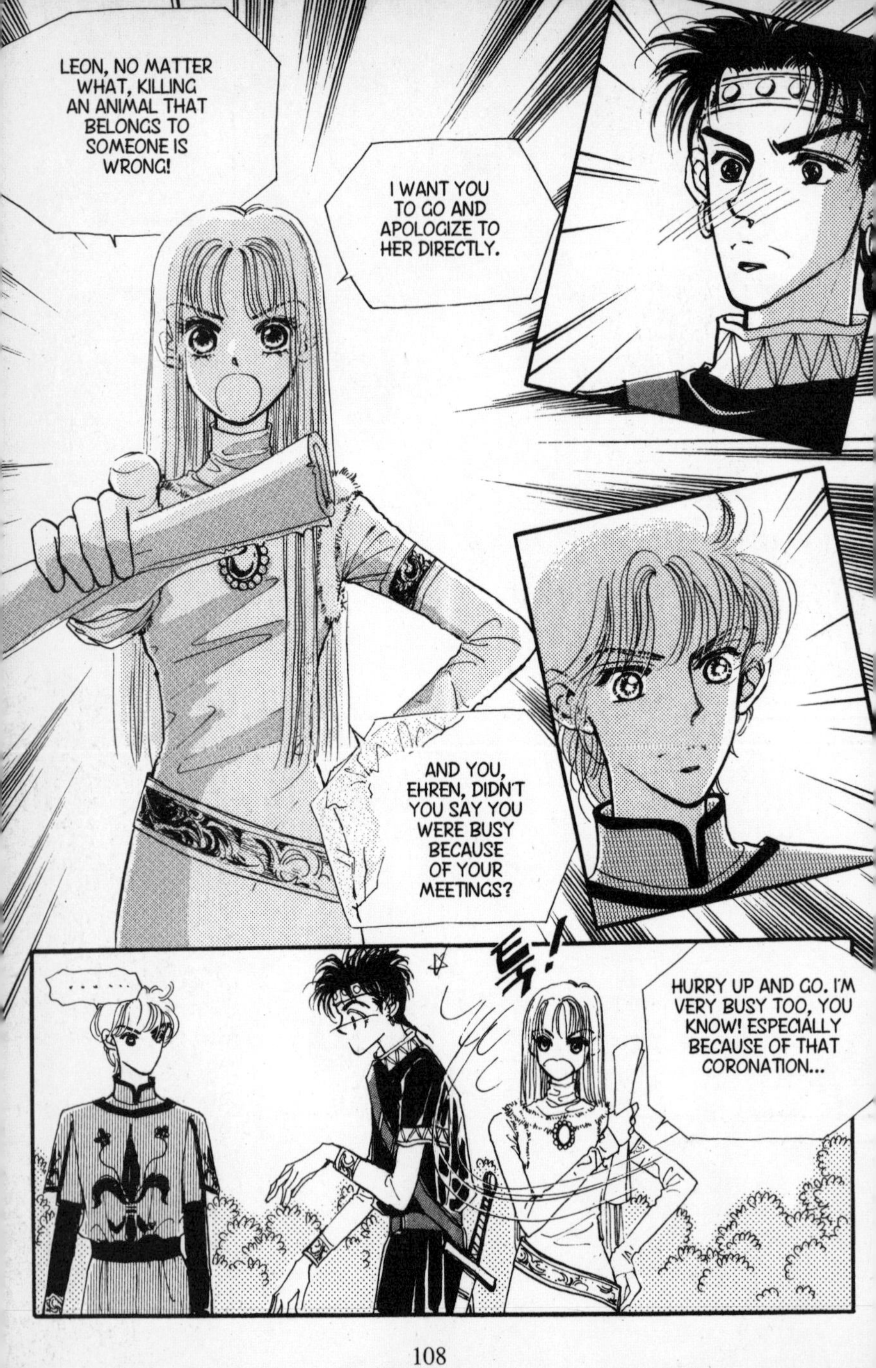
LEON, NO MATTER WHAT, KILLING AN ANIMAL THAT BELONGS TO SOMEONE IS WRONG!
I WANT YOU TO GO AND APOLOGIZE TO HER DIRECTLY.
AND YOU, EHREN, DIDN'T YOU SAY YOU WERE BUSY BECAUSE OF YOUR MEETINGS?
......
툭!
HURRY UP AND GO. I'M VERY BUSY TOO, YOU KNOW! ESPECIALLY BECAUSE OF THAT CORONATION...

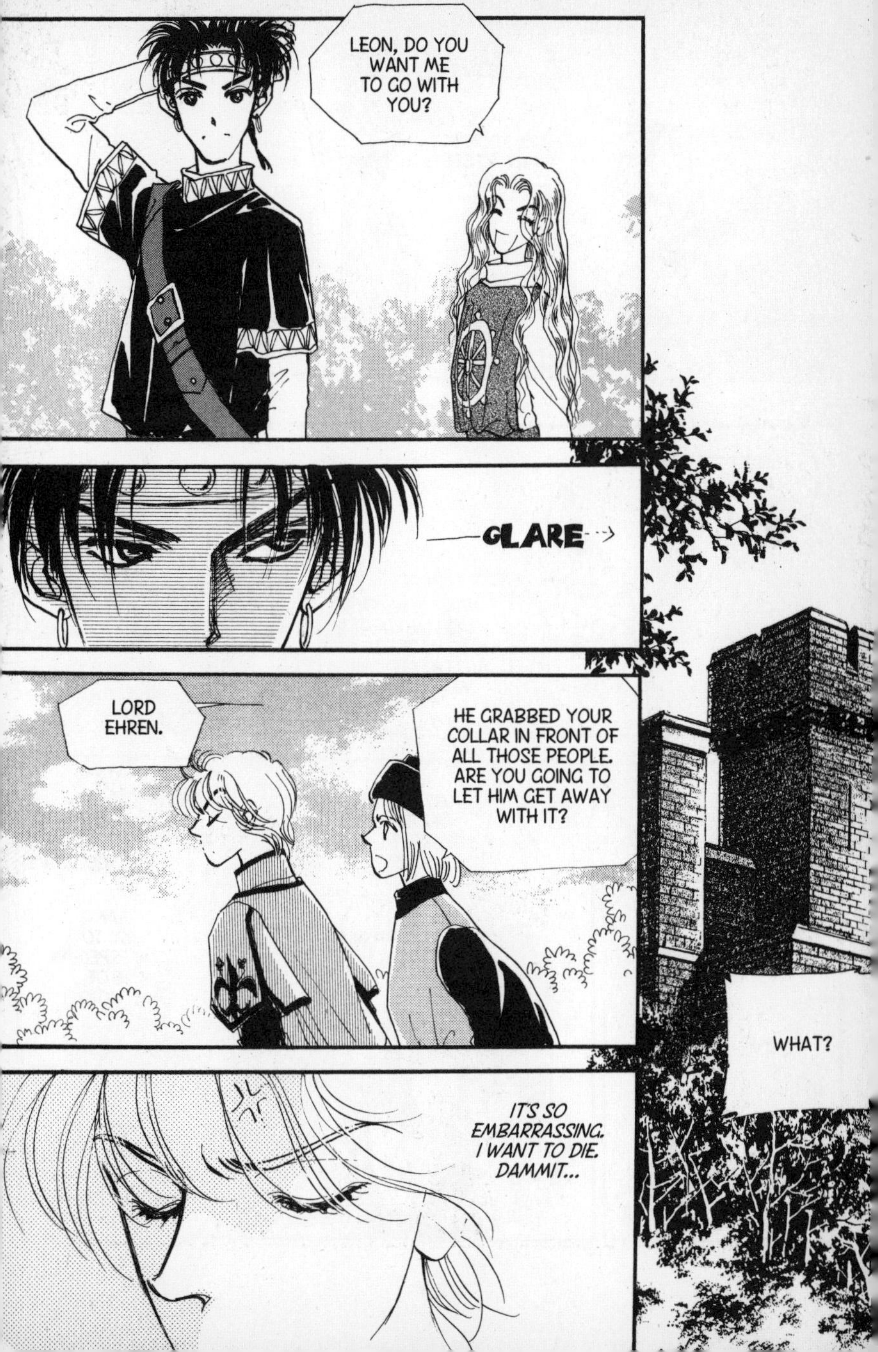
LEON, DO YOU WANT ME TO GO WITH YOU?
GLARE
LORD EHREN.
HE GRABBED YOUR COLLAR IN FRONT OF ALL THOSE PEOPLE. ARE YOU GOING TO LET HIM GET AWAY WITH IT?
IT'S SO EMBARRASSING. I WANT TO DIE. DAMMIT...
WHAT?

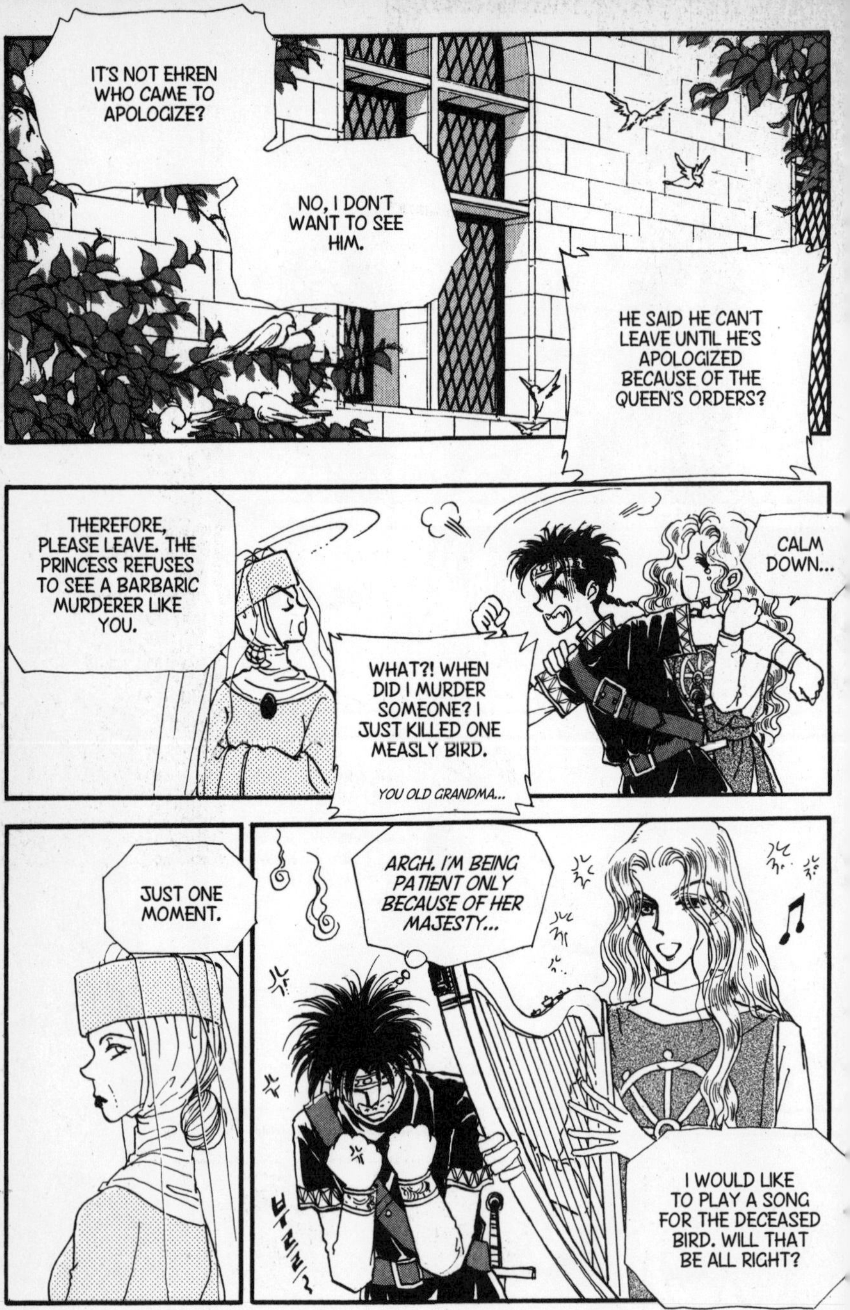
IT'S NOT EHREN WHO CAME TO APOLOGIZE?
NO, I DON'T WANT TO SEE HIM.
HE SAID HE CAN'T LEAVE UNTIL HE'S APOLOGIZED BECAUSE OF THE QUEEN'S ORDERS?
THEREFORE, PLEASE LEAVE. THE PRINCESS REFUSES TO SEE A BARBARIC MURDERER LIKE YOU.
WHAT?! WHEN DID I MURDER SOMEONE? I JUST KILLED ONE MEASLY BIRD.
YOU OLD GRANDMA...
CALM DOWN...
JUST ONE MOMENT.
ARGH. I'M BEING PATIENT ONLY BECAUSE OF HER MAJESTY...
I WOULD LIKE TO PLAY A SONG FOR THE DECEASED BIRD. WILL THAT BE ALL RIGHT?

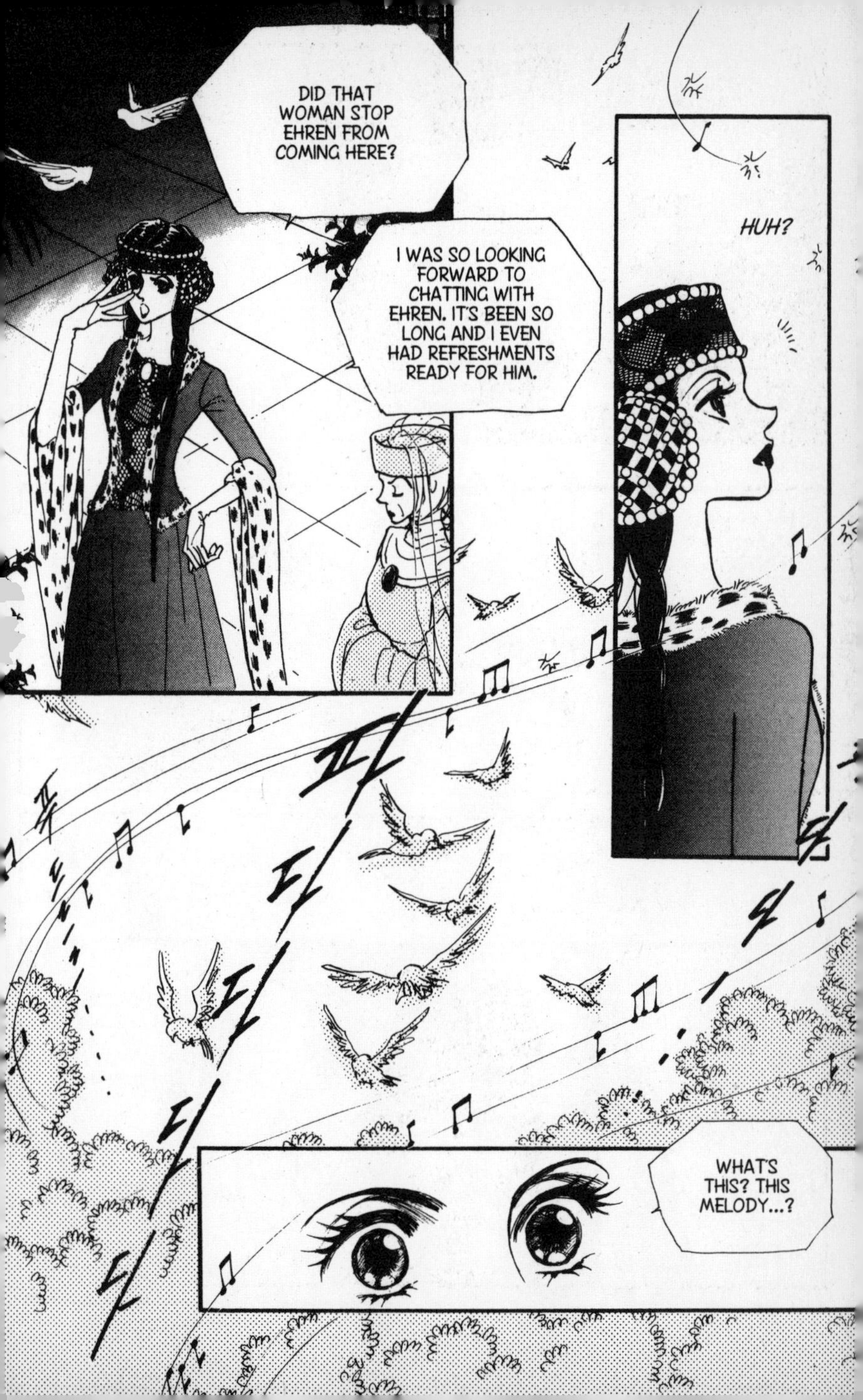
DID THAT WOMAN STOP EHREN FROM COMING HERE?
I WAS SO LOOKING FORWARD TO CHATTING WITH EHREN. IT'S BEEN SO LONG AND I EVEN HAD REFRESHMENTS READY FOR HIM.
HUH?
WHAT'S THIS? THIS MELODY...?

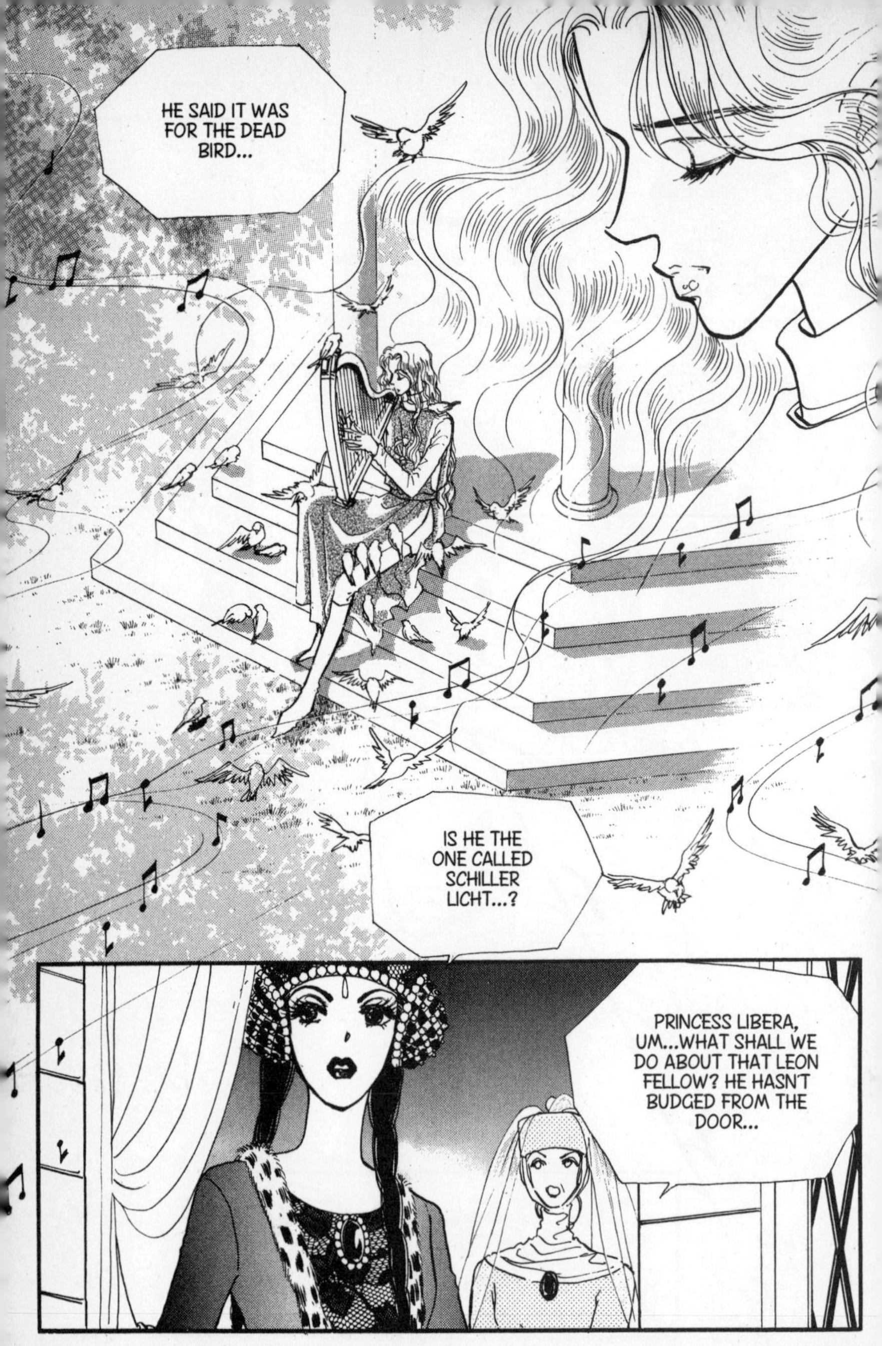
HE SAID IT WAS FOR THE DEAD BIRD...
IS HE THE ONE CALLED SCHILLER LICHT...?
PRINCESS LIBERA, UM...WHAT SHALL WE DO ABOUT THAT LEON FELLOW? HE HASN'T BUDGED FROM THE DOOR...

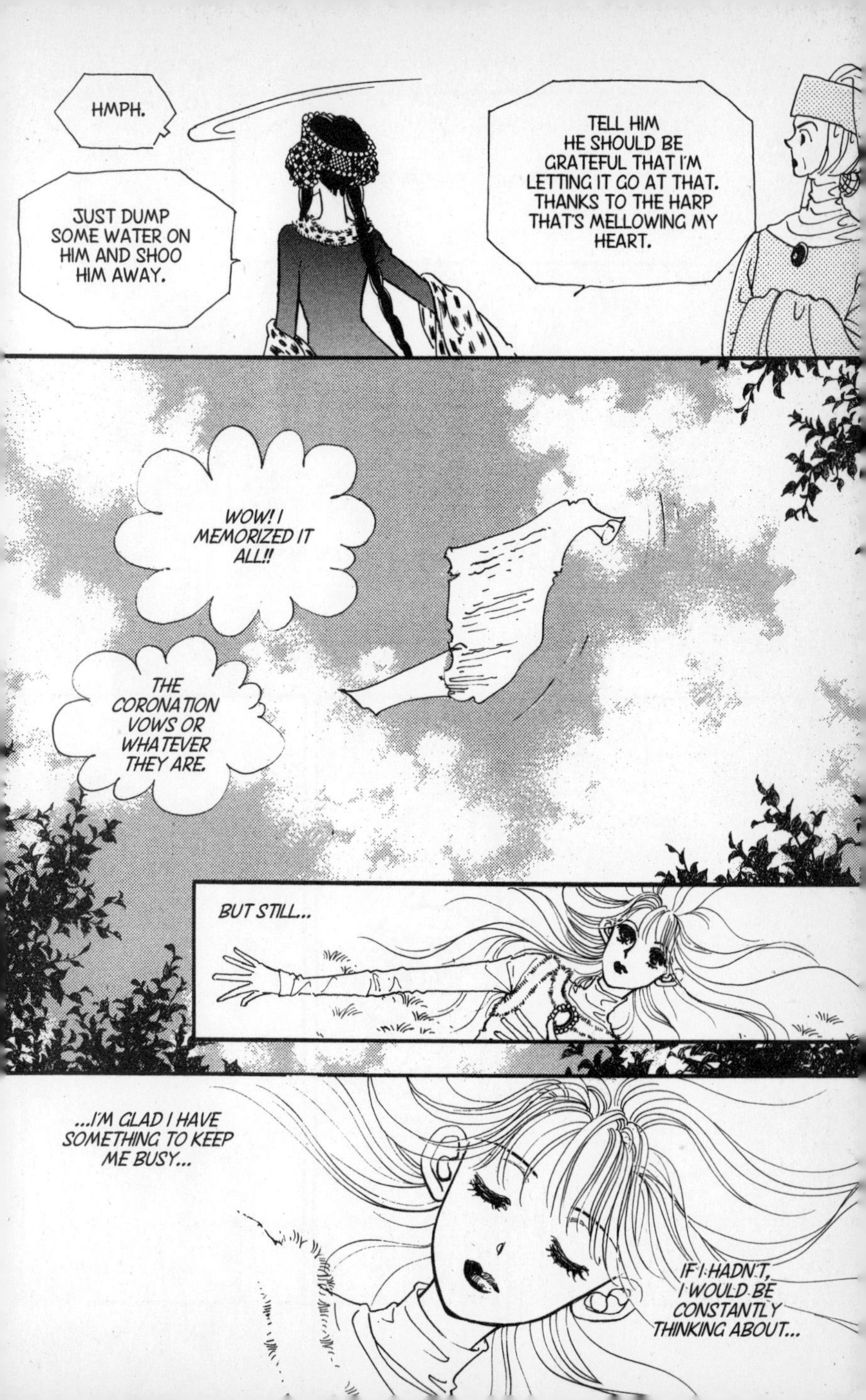
HMPH.
JUST DUMP SOME WATER ON HIM AND SHOO HIM AWAY.
TELL HIM HE SHOULD BE GRATEFUL THAT I'M LETTING IT GO AT THAT. THANKS TO THE HARP THAT'S MELLOWING MY HEART.
WOW! I MEMORIZED IT ALL!!
THE CORONATION VOWS OR WHATEVER THEY ARE.
BUT STILL...
...I'M GLAD I HAVE SOMETHING TO KEEP ME BUSY...
IF I HADN'T, I WOULD BE CONSTANTLY THINKING ABOUT...

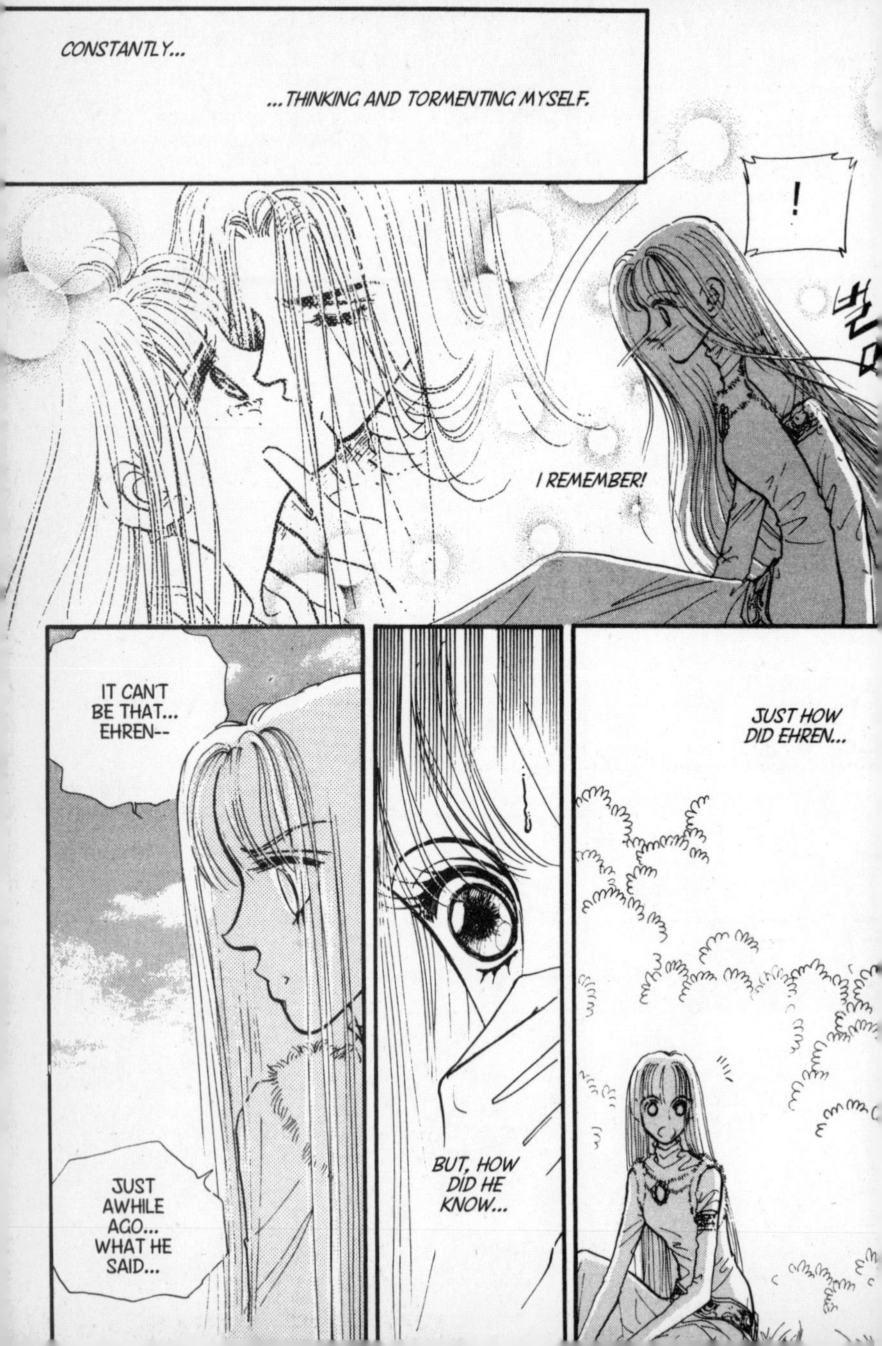
CONSTANTLY...
...THINKING AND TORMENTING MYSELF.
!
I REMEMBER!
IT CAN'T BE THAT... EHREN--
JUST AWHILE AGO... WHAT HE SAID...
BUT, HOW DID HE KNOW...
JUST HOW DID EHREN...

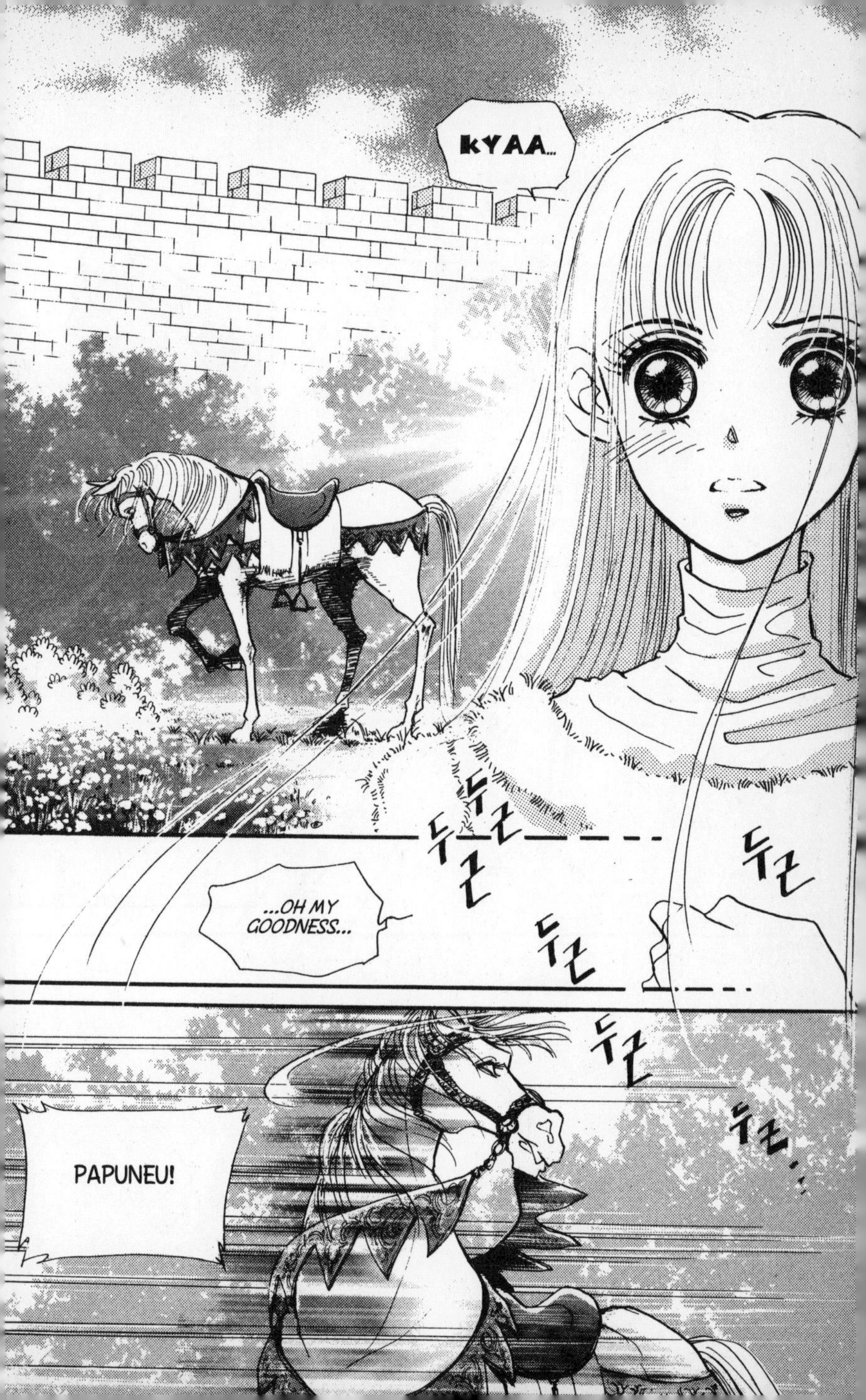
KYAA...
두근
두근
...OH MY GOODNESS...
두근
두근
두근
두근
PAPUNEU!

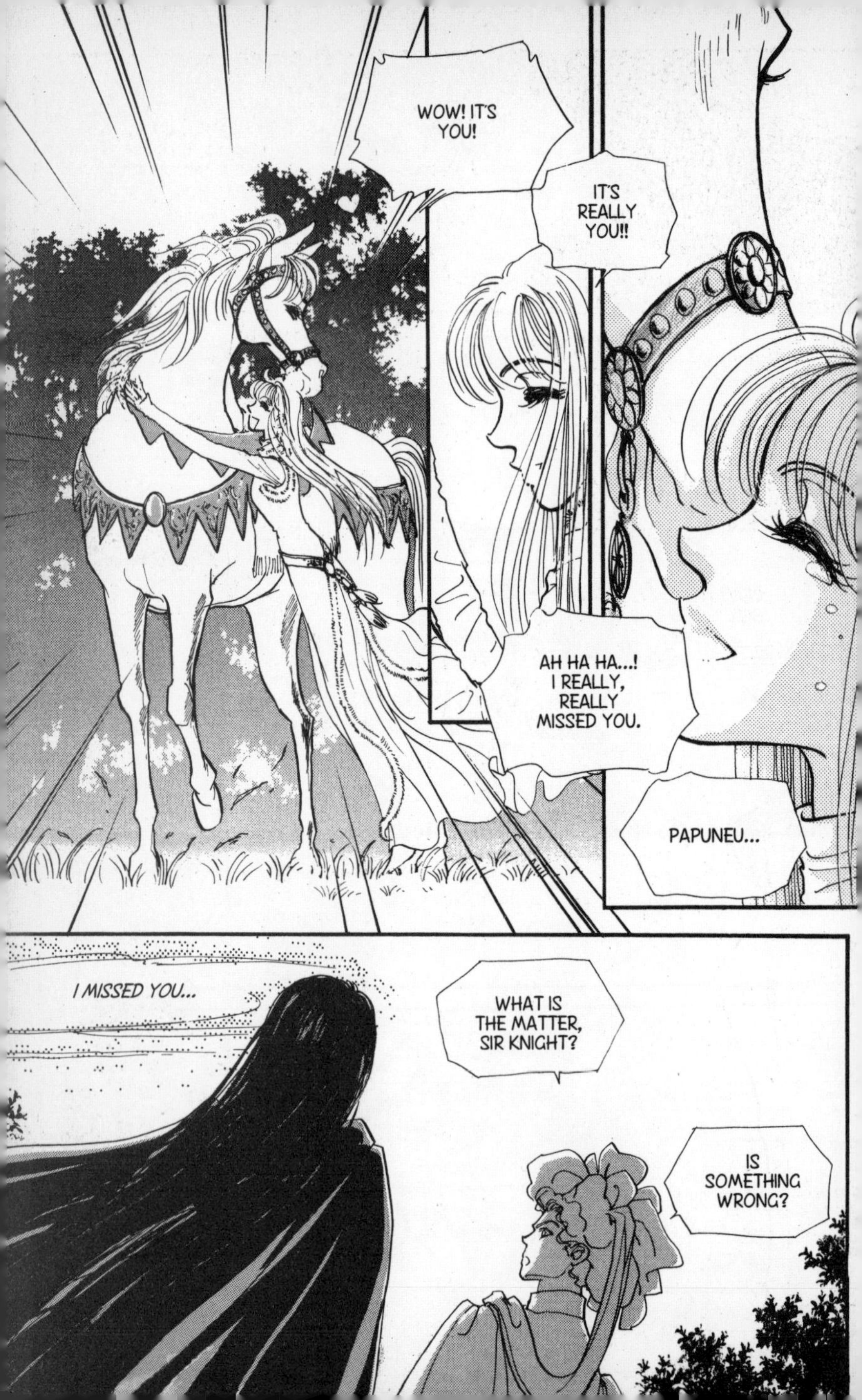
WOW! IT'S YOU!
IT'S REALLY YOU!!
AH HA HA...! I REALLY, REALLY MISSED YOU.
PAPUNEU...
I MISSED YOU...
WHAT IS THE MATTER, SIR KNIGHT?
IS SOMETHING WRONG?

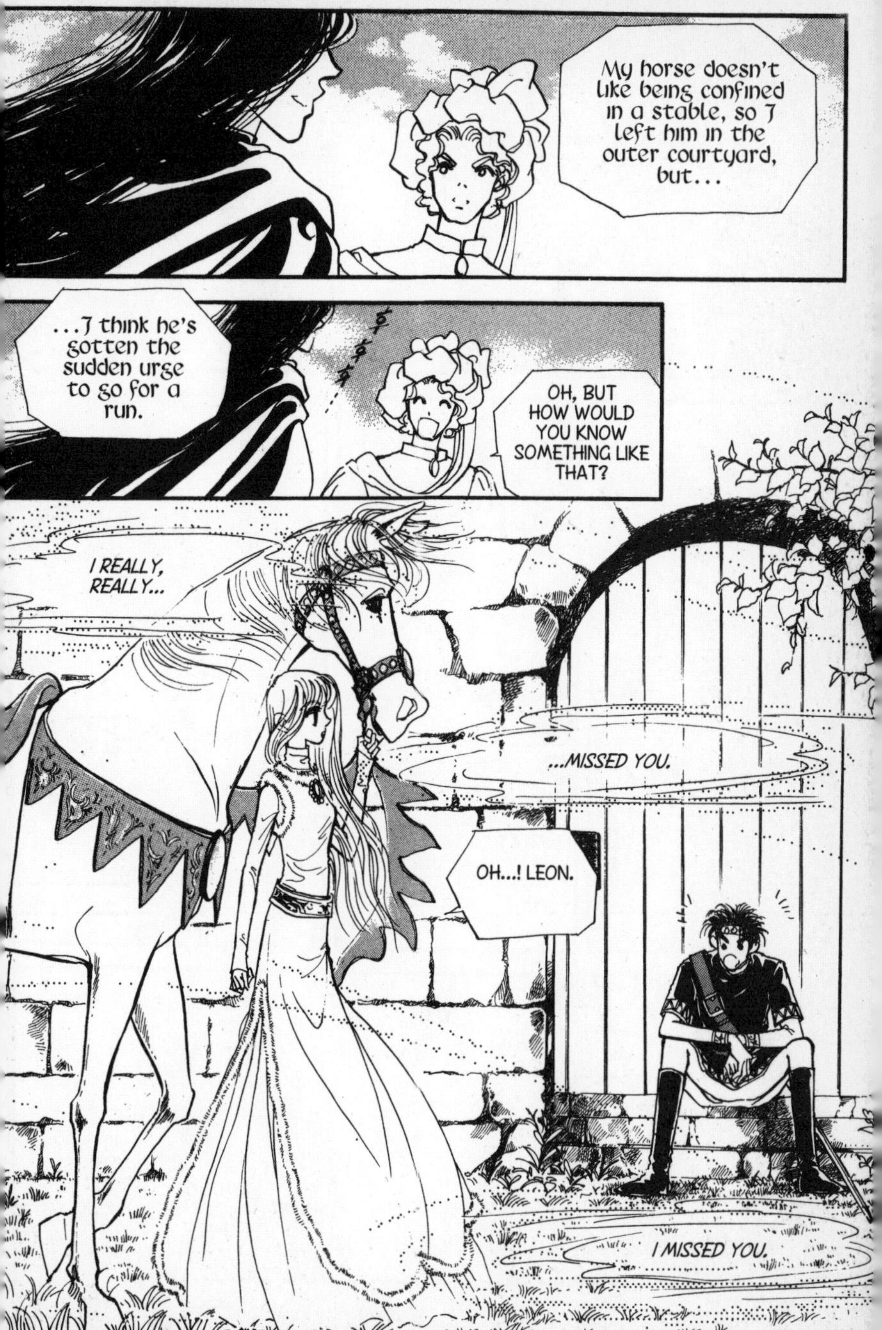

My horse doesn't like being confined in a stable, so I left him in the outer courtyard, but...
...I think he's gotten the sudden urge to go for a run.
OH, BUT HOW WOULD YOU KNOW SOMETHING LIKE THAT?
I REALLY, REALLY...
...MISSED YOU.
OH...! LEON.
I MISSED YOU.

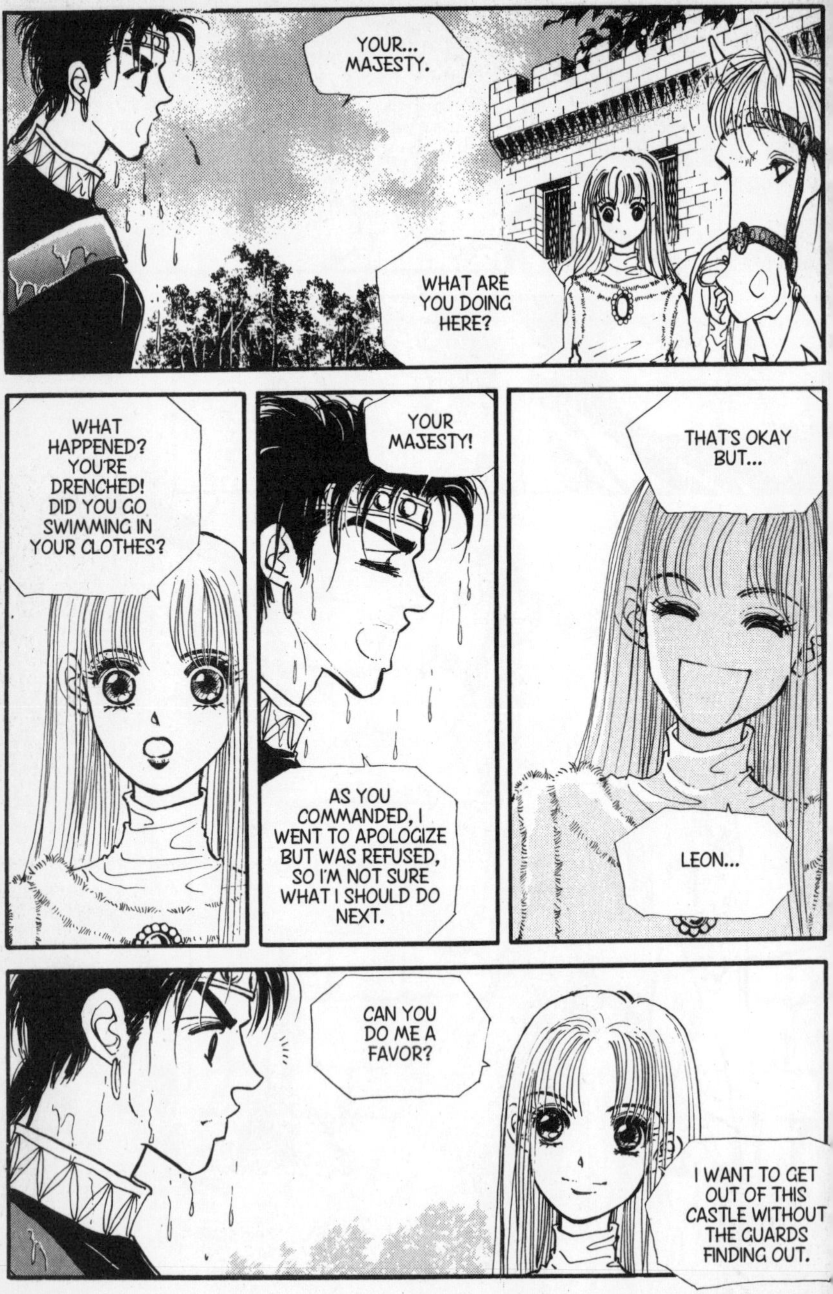
YOUR... MAJESTY.
WHAT ARE YOU DOING HERE?
WHAT HAPPENED? YOU'RE DRENCHED! DID YOU GO SWIMMING IN YOUR CLOTHES?
YOUR MAJESTY!
AS YOU COMMANDED, I WENT TO APOLOGIZE BUT WAS REFUSED, SO I'M NOT SURE WHAT I SHOULD DO NEXT.
THAT'S OKAY BUT...
LEON...
CAN YOU DO ME A FAVOR?
I WANT TO GET OUT OF THIS CASTLE WITHOUT THE GUARDS FINDING OUT.

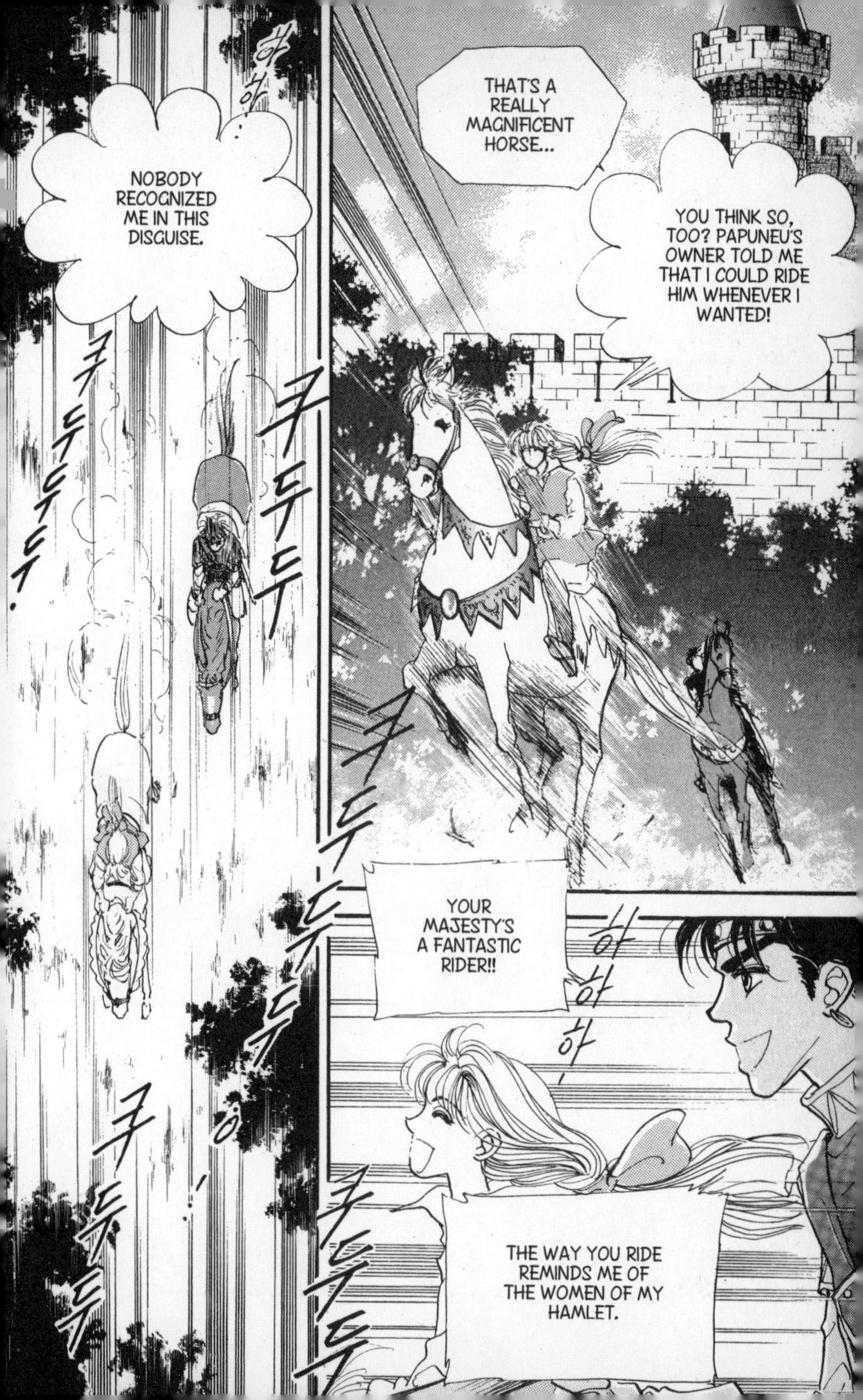
NOBODY RECOGNIZED ME IN THIS DISGUISE.
THAT'S A REALLY MAGNIFICENT HORSE...
YOU THINK SO, TOO? PAPUNEU'S OWNER TOLD ME THAT I COULD RIDE HIM WHENEVER I WANTED!
YOUR MAJESTY'S A FANTASTIC RIDER!!
THE WAY YOU RIDE REMINDS ME OF THE WOMEN OF MY HAMLET.

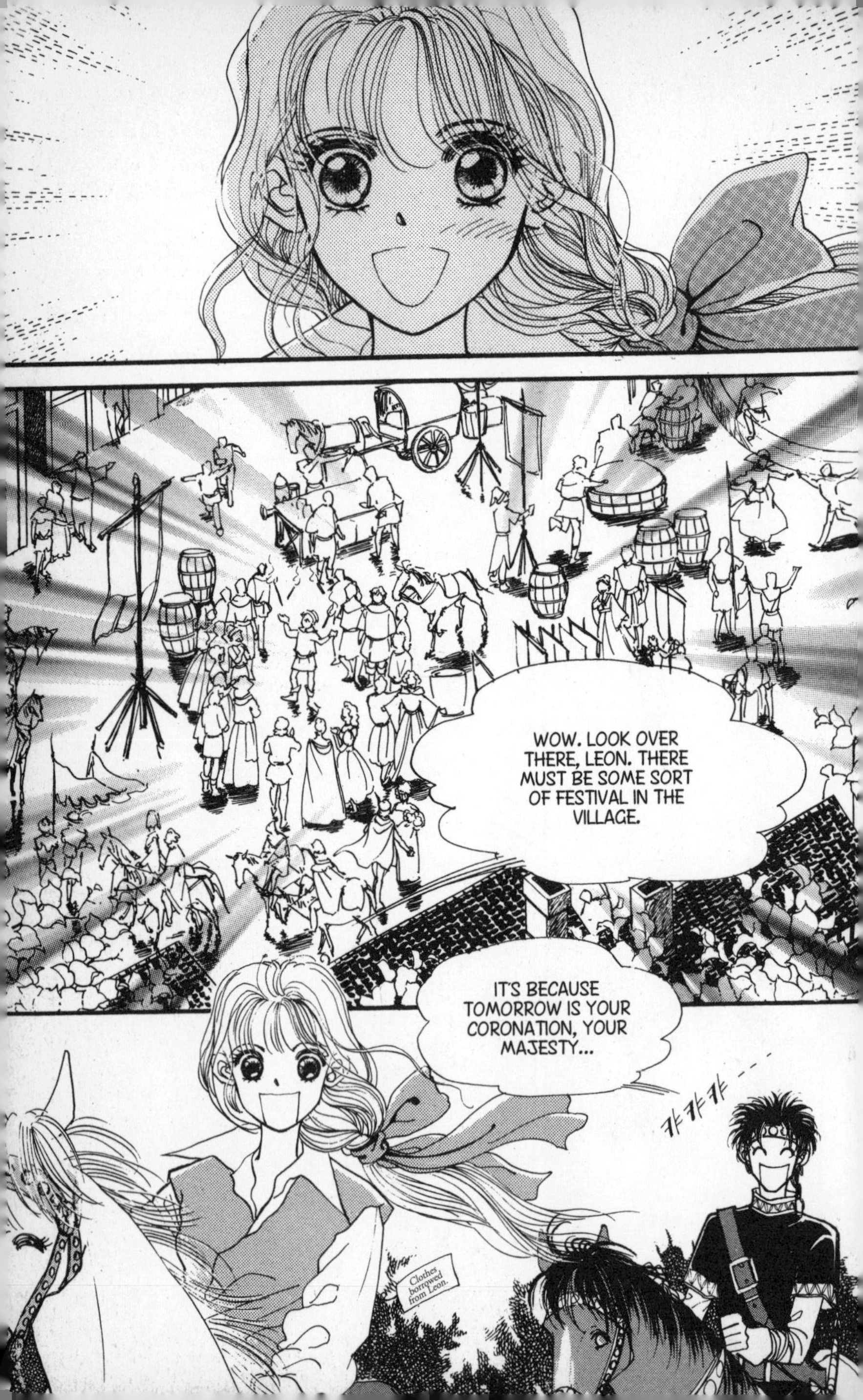
WOW. LOOK OVER THERE, LEON. THERE MUST BE SOME SORT OF FESTIVAL IN THE VILLAGE.
IT'S BECAUSE TOMORROW IS YOUR CORONATION, YOUR MAJESTY...
カカカ
Clothes borrowed from Leon.

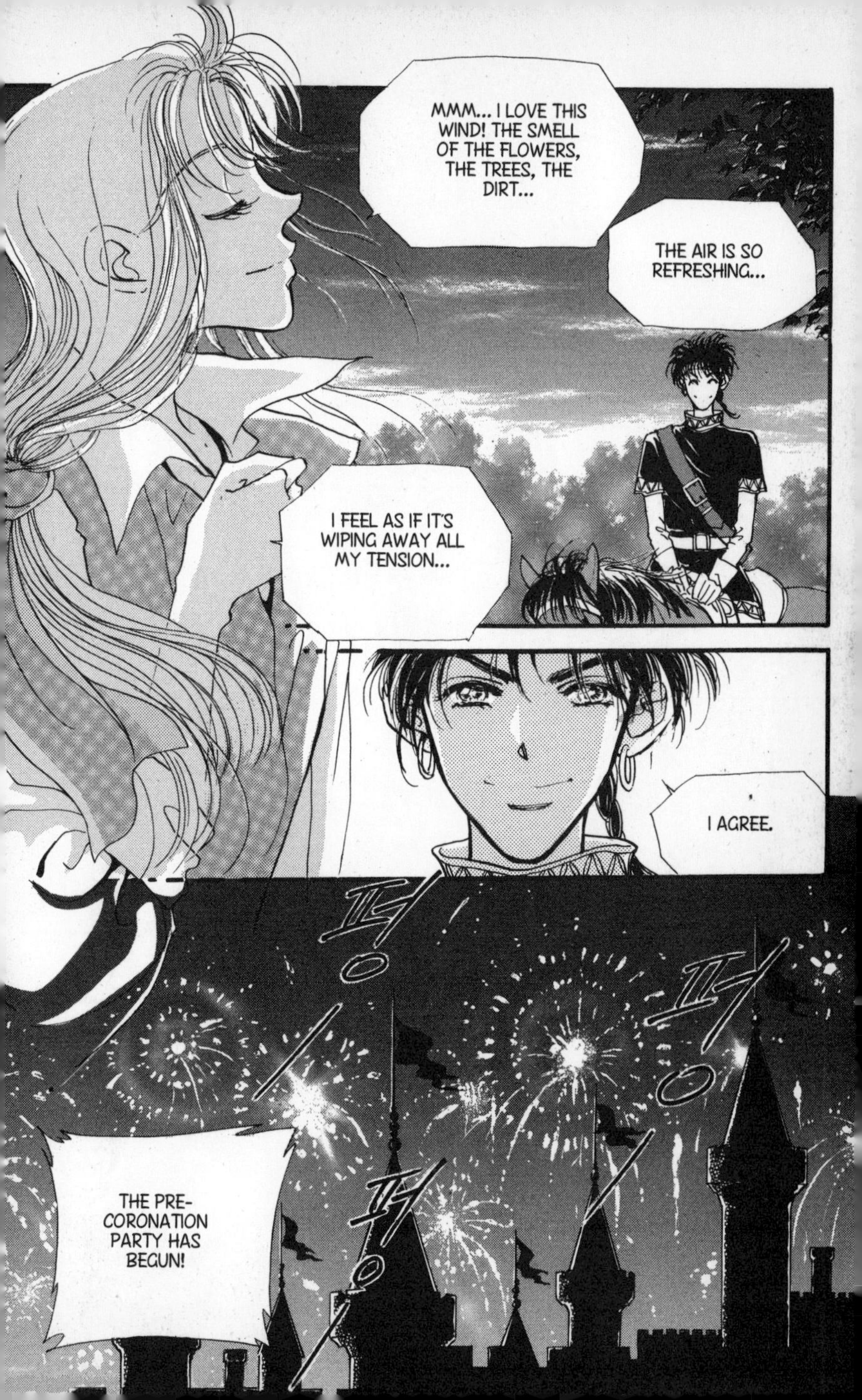
MMM... I LOVE THIS WIND! THE SMELL OF THE FLOWERS, THE TREES, THE DIRT...
THE AIR IS SO REFRESHING...
I FEEL AS IF IT'S WIPING AWAY ALL MY TENSION...
I AGREE.
THE PRE-CORONATION PARTY HAS BEGUN!

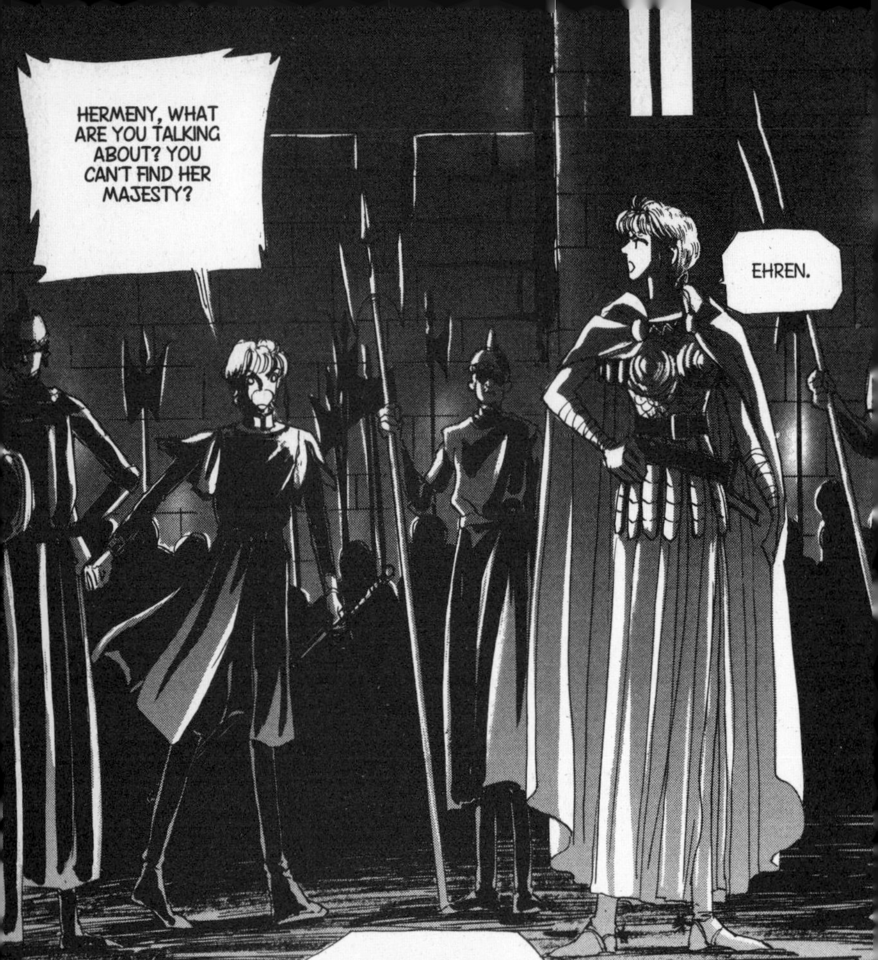
HERMENY, WHAT ARE YOU TALKING ABOUT? YOU CAN'T FIND HER MAJESTY?
EHREN.
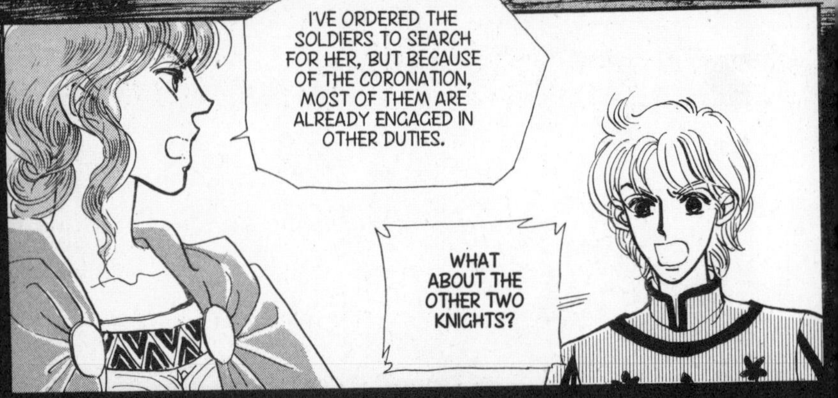
I'VE ORDERED THE SOLDIERS TO SEARCH FOR HER, BUT BECAUSE OF THE CORONATION, MOST OF THEM ARE ALREADY ENGAGED IN OTHER DUTIES.
WHAT ABOUT THE OTHER TWO KNIGHTS?

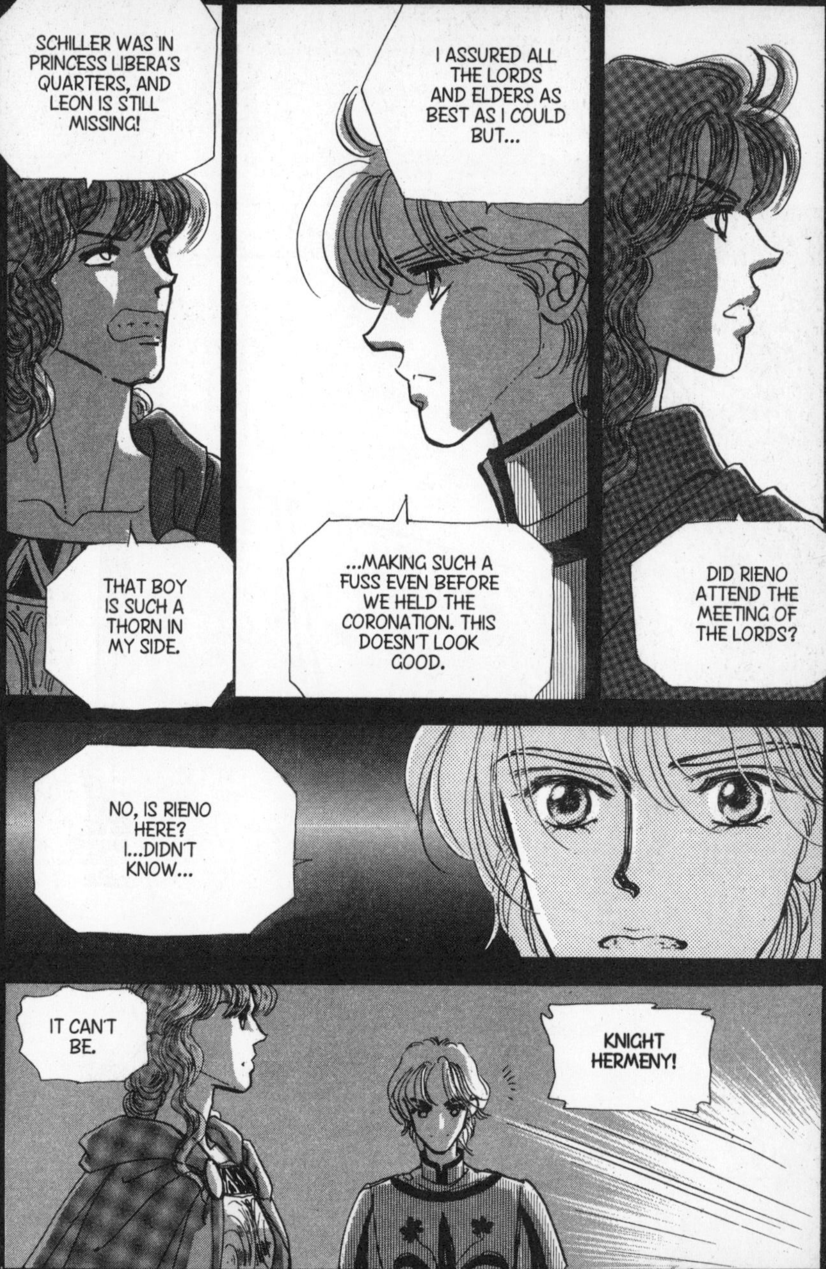
SCHILLER WAS IN PRINCESS LIBERA'S QUARTERS, AND LEON IS STILL MISSING!
THAT BOY IS SUCH A THORN IN MY SIDE.
I ASSURED ALL THE LORDS AND ELDERS AS BEST AS I COULD BUT...
...MAKING SUCH A FUSS EVEN BEFORE WE HELD THE CORONATION. THIS DOESN'T LOOK GOOD.
DID RIENO ATTEND THE MEETING OF THE LORDS?
NO, IS RIENO HERE? I...DIDN'T KNOW...
IT CAN'T BE.
KNIGHT HERMENY!

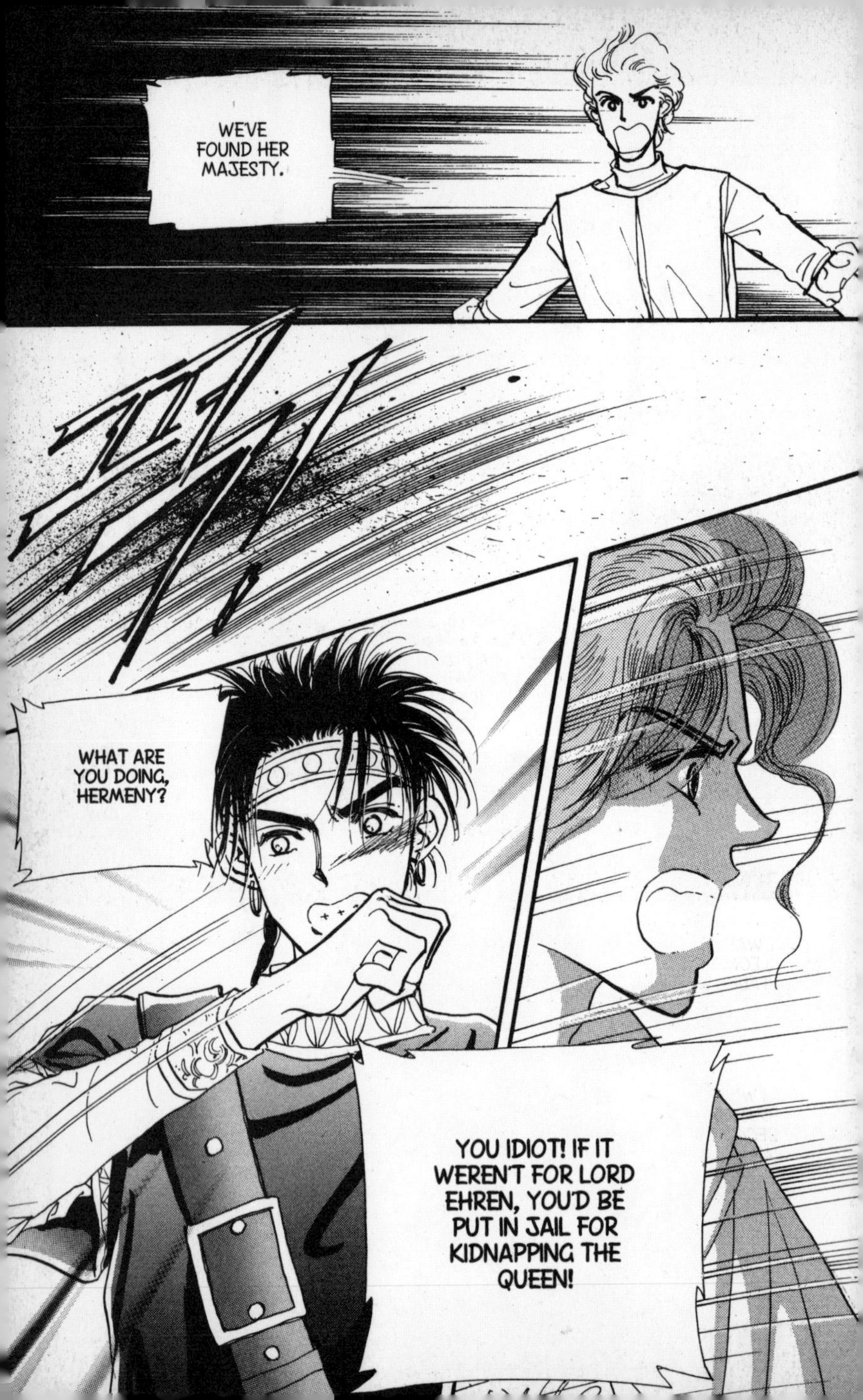
WE'VE FOUND HER MAJESTY.
WHAT ARE YOU DOING, HERMENY?
YOU IDIOT! IF IT WEREN'T FOR LORD EHREN, YOU'D BE PUT IN JAIL FOR KIDNAPPING THE QUEEN!

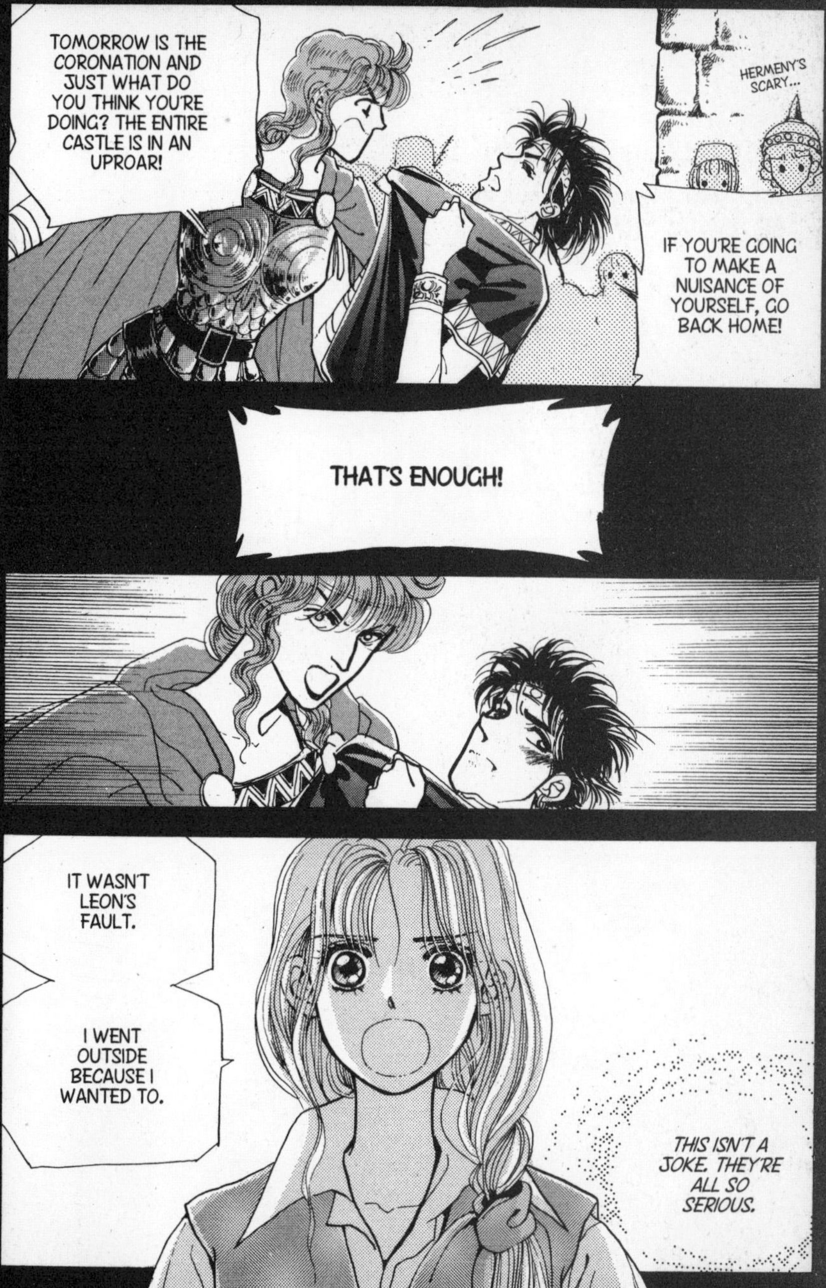
TOMORROW IS THE CORONATION AND JUST WHAT DO YOU THINK YOU'RE DOING? THE ENTIRE CASTLE IS IN AN UPROAR!
HERMENY'S SCARY...
IF YOU'RE GOING TO MAKE A NUISANCE OF YOURSELF, GO BACK HOME!
THAT'S ENOUGH!
IT WASN'T LEON'S FAULT.
I WENT OUTSIDE BECAUSE I WANTED TO.
THIS ISN'T A JOKE. THEY'RE ALL SO SERIOUS.

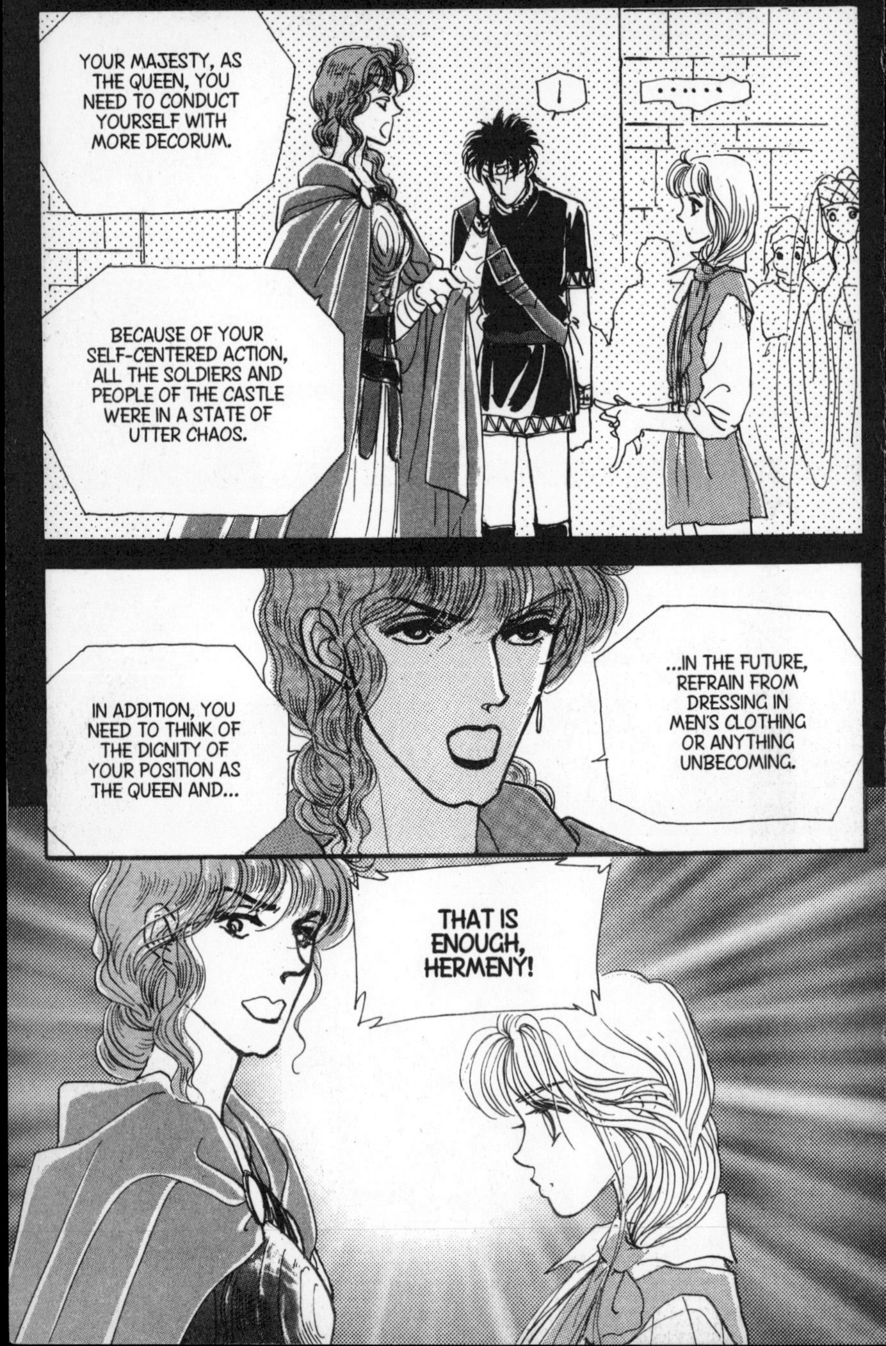
YOUR MAJESTY, AS THE QUEEN, YOU NEED TO CONDUCT YOURSELF WITH MORE DECORUM.
!
......
BECAUSE OF YOUR SELF-CENTERED ACTION, ALL THE SOLDIERS AND PEOPLE OF THE CASTLE WERE IN A STATE OF UTTER CHAOS.
IN ADDITION, YOU NEED TO THINK OF THE DIGNITY OF YOUR POSITION AS THE QUEEN AND...
...IN THE FUTURE, REFRAIN FROM DRESSING IN MEN'S CLOTHING OR ANYTHING UNBECOMING.
THAT IS ENOUGH, HERMENY!

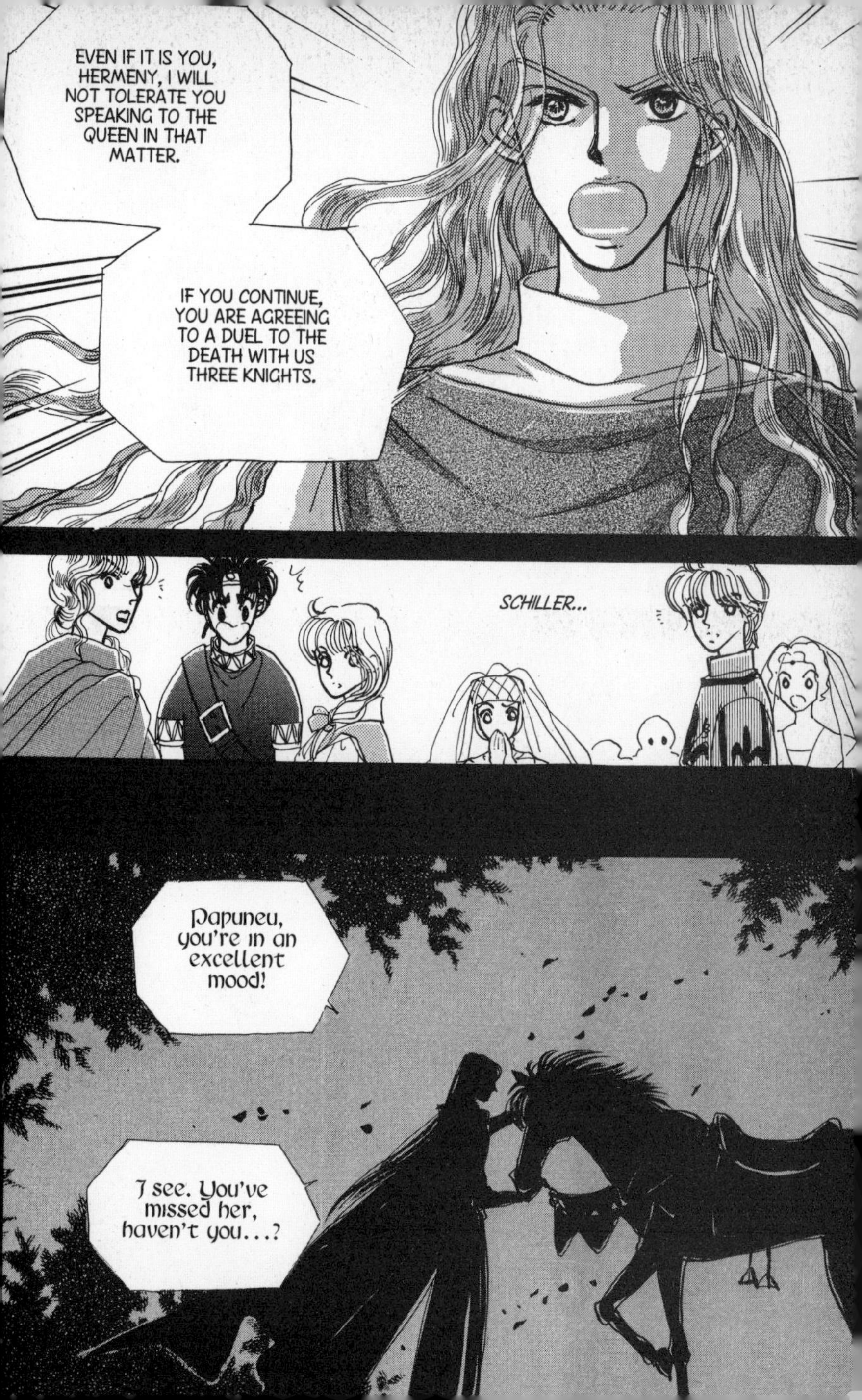
EVEN IF IT IS YOU, HERMENY, I WILL NOT TOLERATE YOU SPEAKING TO THE QUEEN IN THAT MATTER.
IF YOU CONTINUE, YOU ARE AGREEING TO A DUEL TO THE DEATH WITH US THREE KNIGHTS.
SCHILLER...
Papuneu, you're in an excellent mood!
I see. You've missed her, haven't you...?

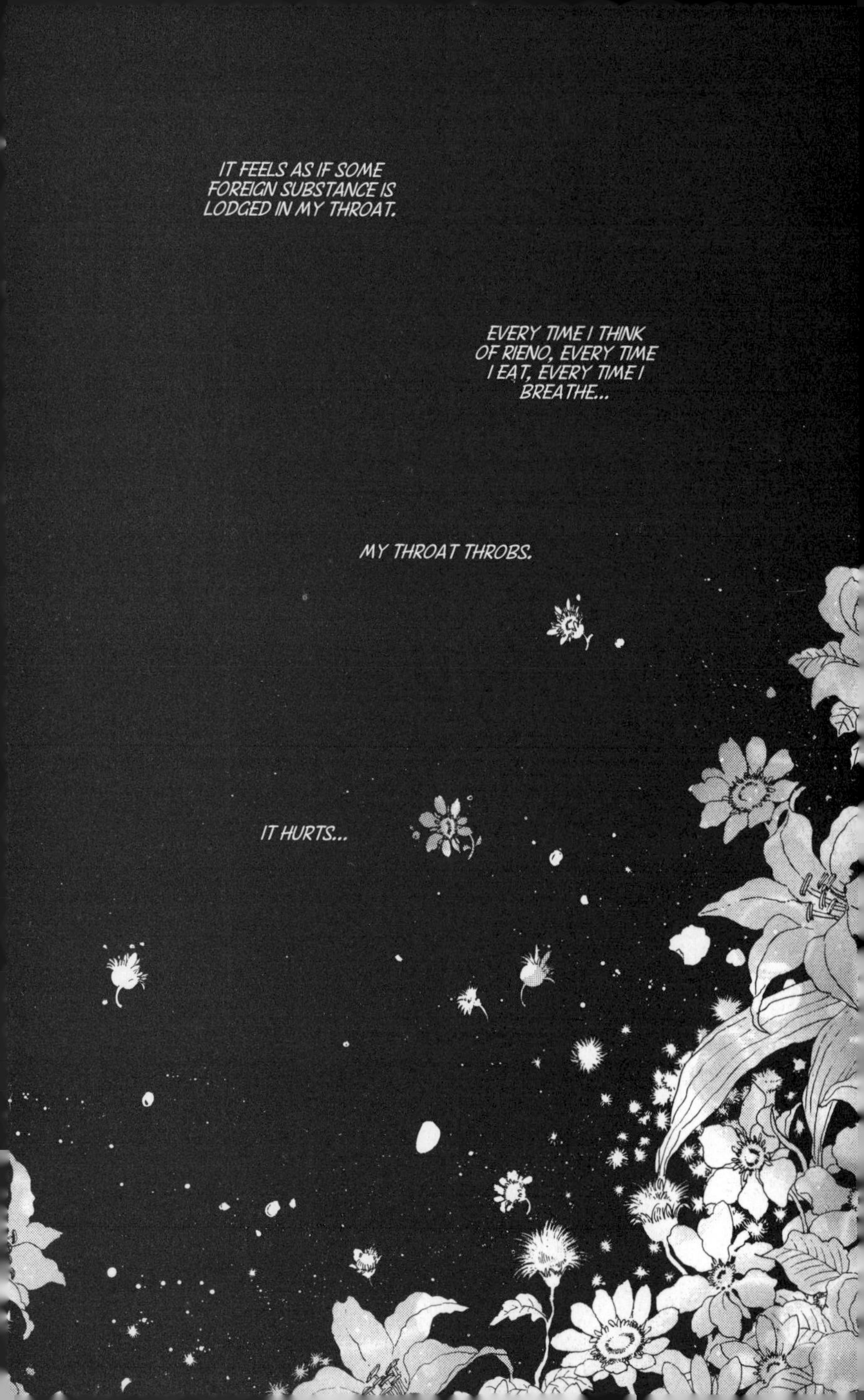
IT FEELS AS IF SOME FOREIGN SUBSTANCE IS LODGED IN MY THROAT.
EVERY TIME I THINK OF RIENO, EVERY TIME I EAT, EVERY TIME I BREATHE...
MY THROAT THROBS.
IT HURTS...

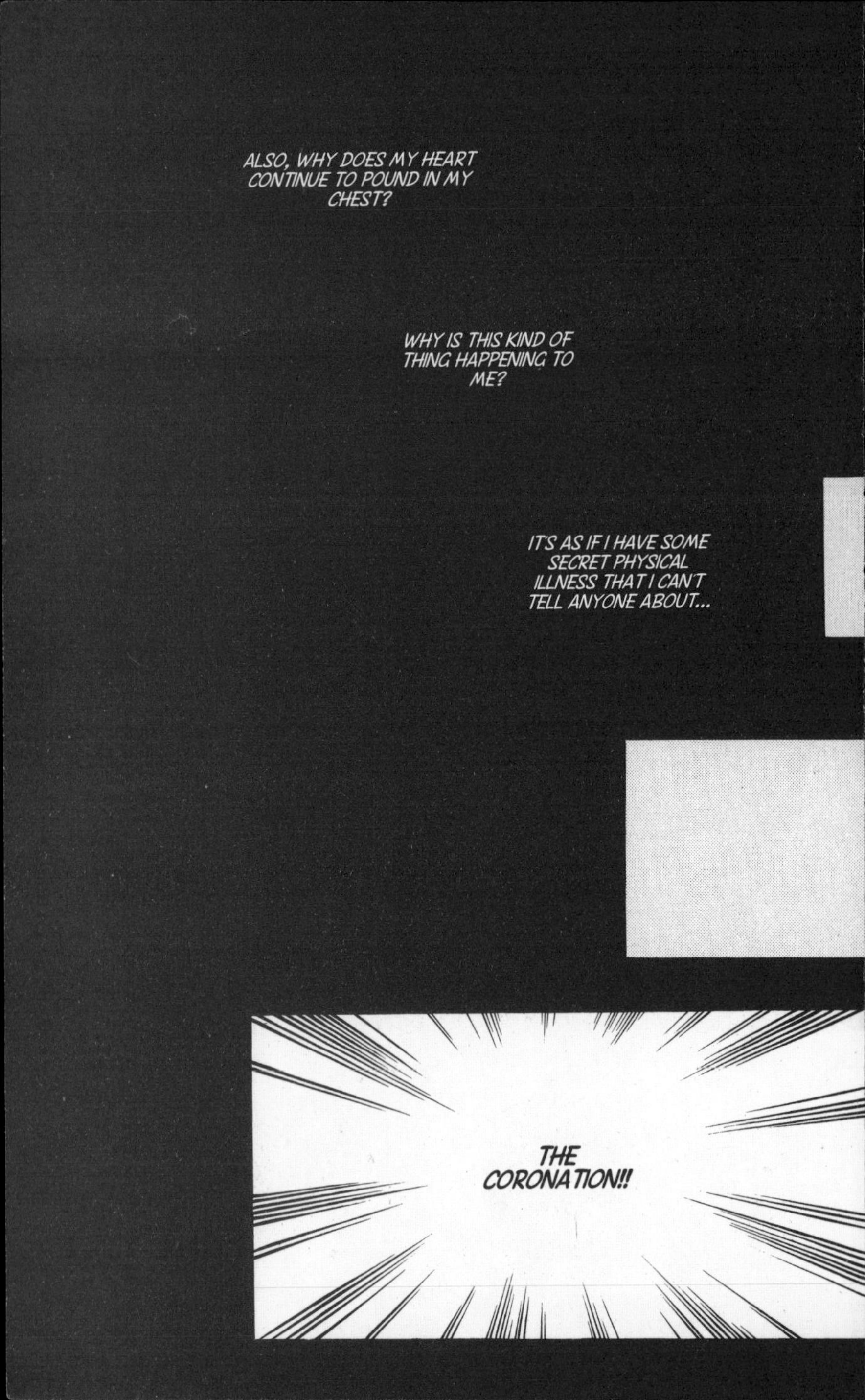
ALSO, WHY DOES MY HEART CONTINUE TO POUND IN MY CHEST?
WHY IS THIS KIND OF THING HAPPENING TO ME?
IT'S AS IF I HAVE SOME SECRET PHYSICAL ILLNESS THAT I CAN'T TELL ANYONE ABOUT...
THE CORONATION!!

AH...

....

ANYWAY...

......

......

....

RIGHT
NOW...

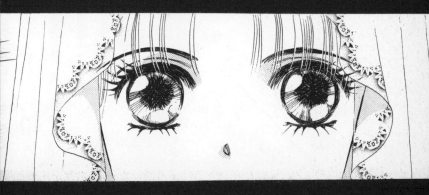

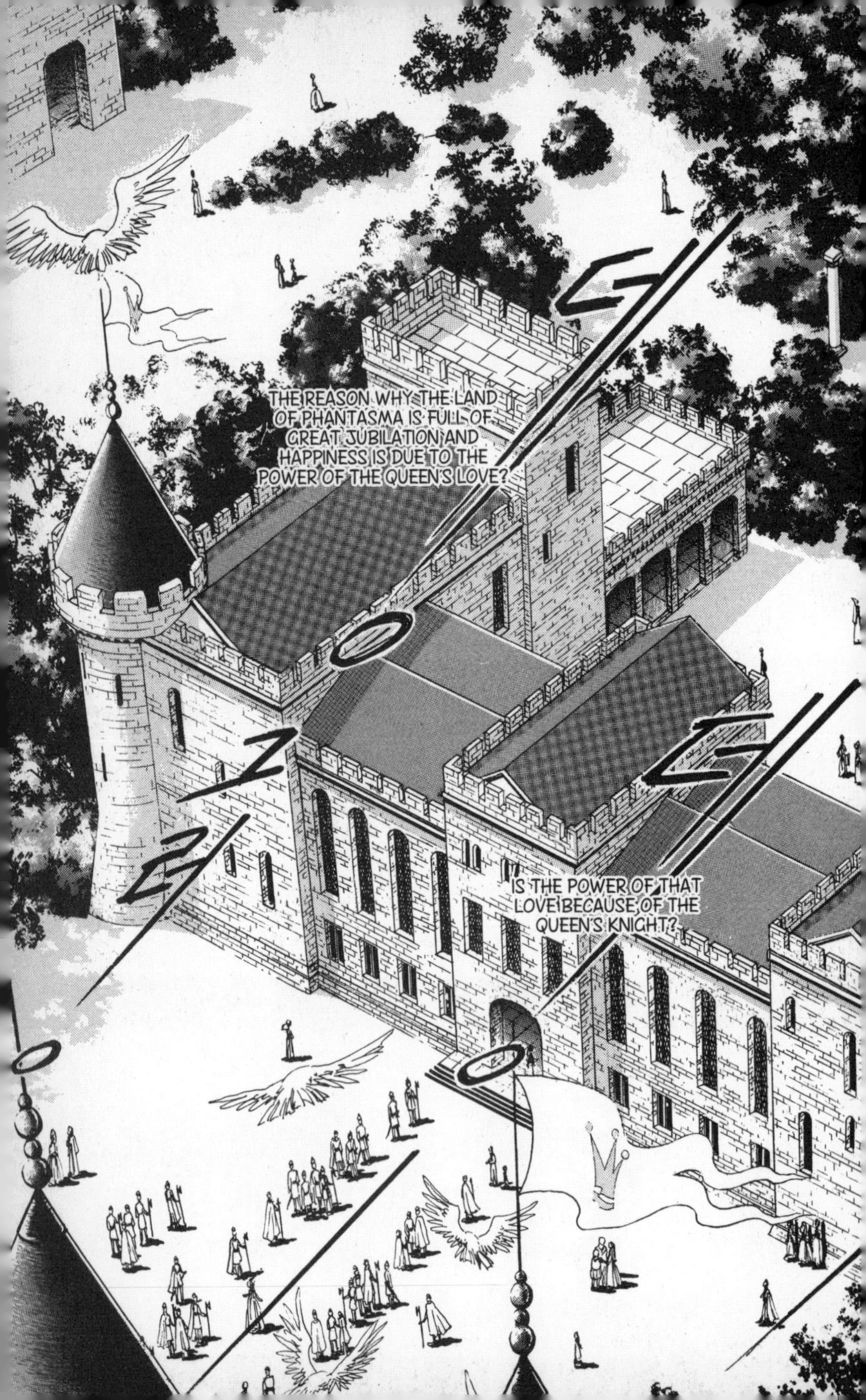
THE REASON WHY THE LAND OF PHANTASMA IS FULL OF GREAT JUBILATION AND HAPPINESS IS DUE TO THE POWER OF THE QUEEN'S LOVE?
IS THE POWER OF THAT LOVE BECAUSE OF THE QUEEN'S KNIGHT?

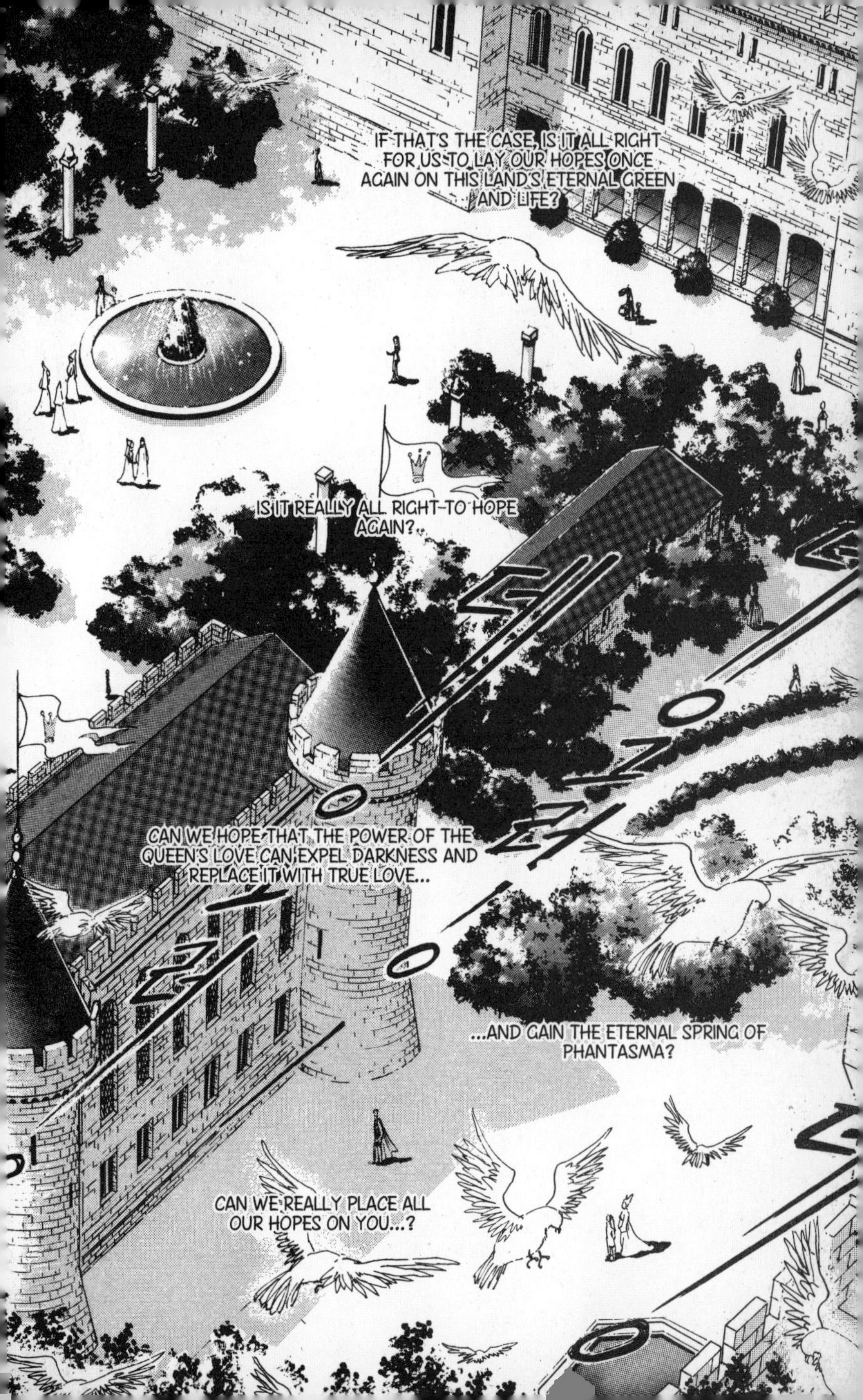
IF THAT'S THE CASE, IS IT ALL RIGHT FOR US TO LAY OUR HOPES ONCE AGAIN ON THIS LAND'S ETERNAL GREEN AND LIFE?
IS IT REALLY ALL RIGHT TO HOPE AGAIN?
CAN WE HOPE THAT THE POWER OF THE QUEEN'S LOVE CAN EXPEL DARKNESS AND REPLACE IT WITH TRUE LOVE...
...AND GAIN THE ETERNAL SPRING OF PHANTASMA?
CAN WE REALLY PLACE ALL OUR HOPES ON YOU...?

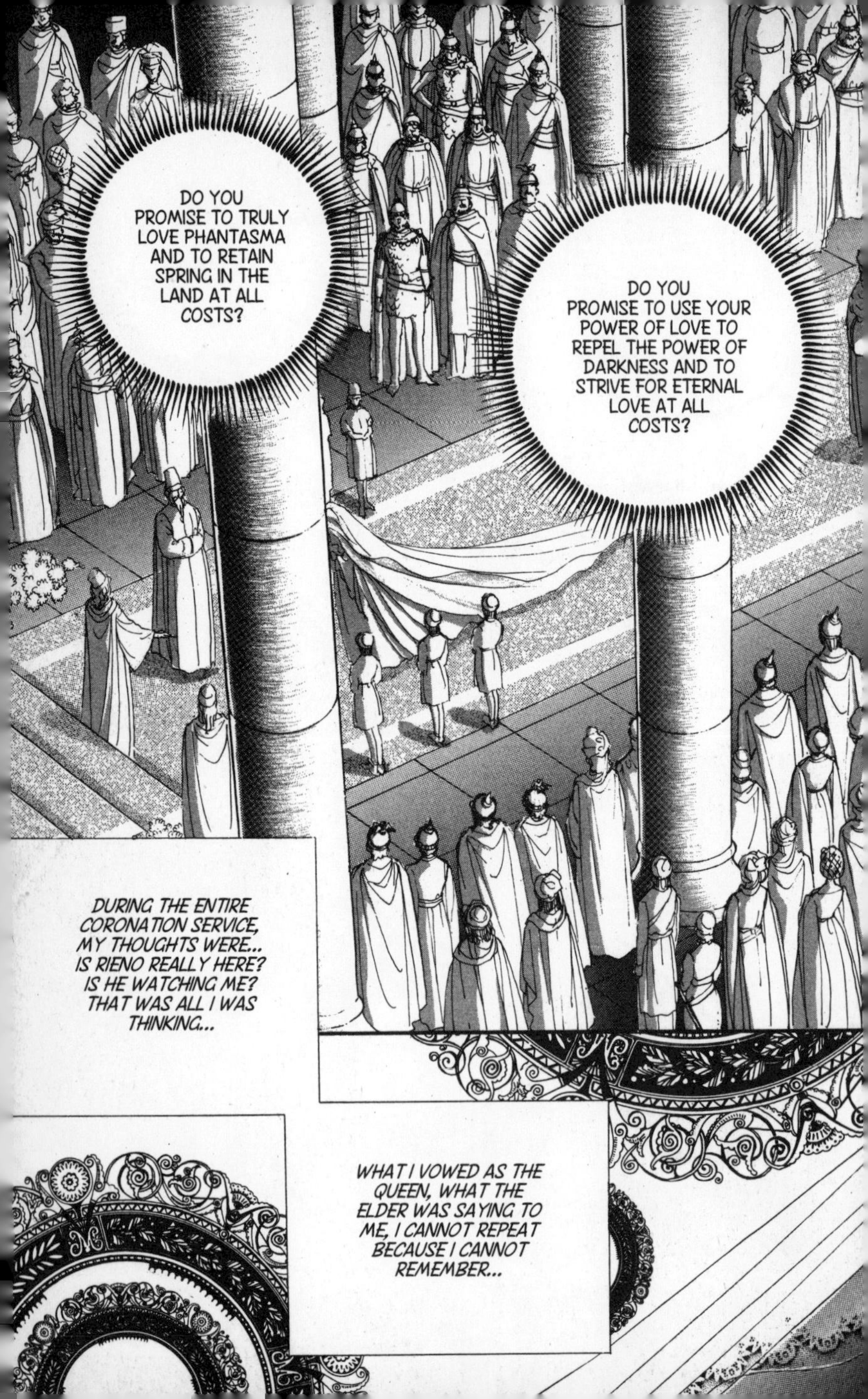
DO YOU PROMISE TO TRULY LOVE PHANTASMA AND TO RETAIN SPRING IN THE LAND AT ALL COSTS?
DO YOU PROMISE TO USE YOUR POWER OF LOVE TO REPEL THE POWER OF DARKNESS AND TO STRIVE FOR ETERNAL LOVE AT ALL COSTS?
DURING THE ENTIRE CORONATION SERVICE, MY THOUGHTS WERE... IS RIENO REALLY HERE? IS HE WATCHING ME? THAT WAS ALL I WAS THINKING...
WHAT I VOWED AS THE QUEEN, WHAT THE ELDER WAS SAYING TO ME, I CANNOT REPEAT BECAUSE I CANNOT REMEMBER...

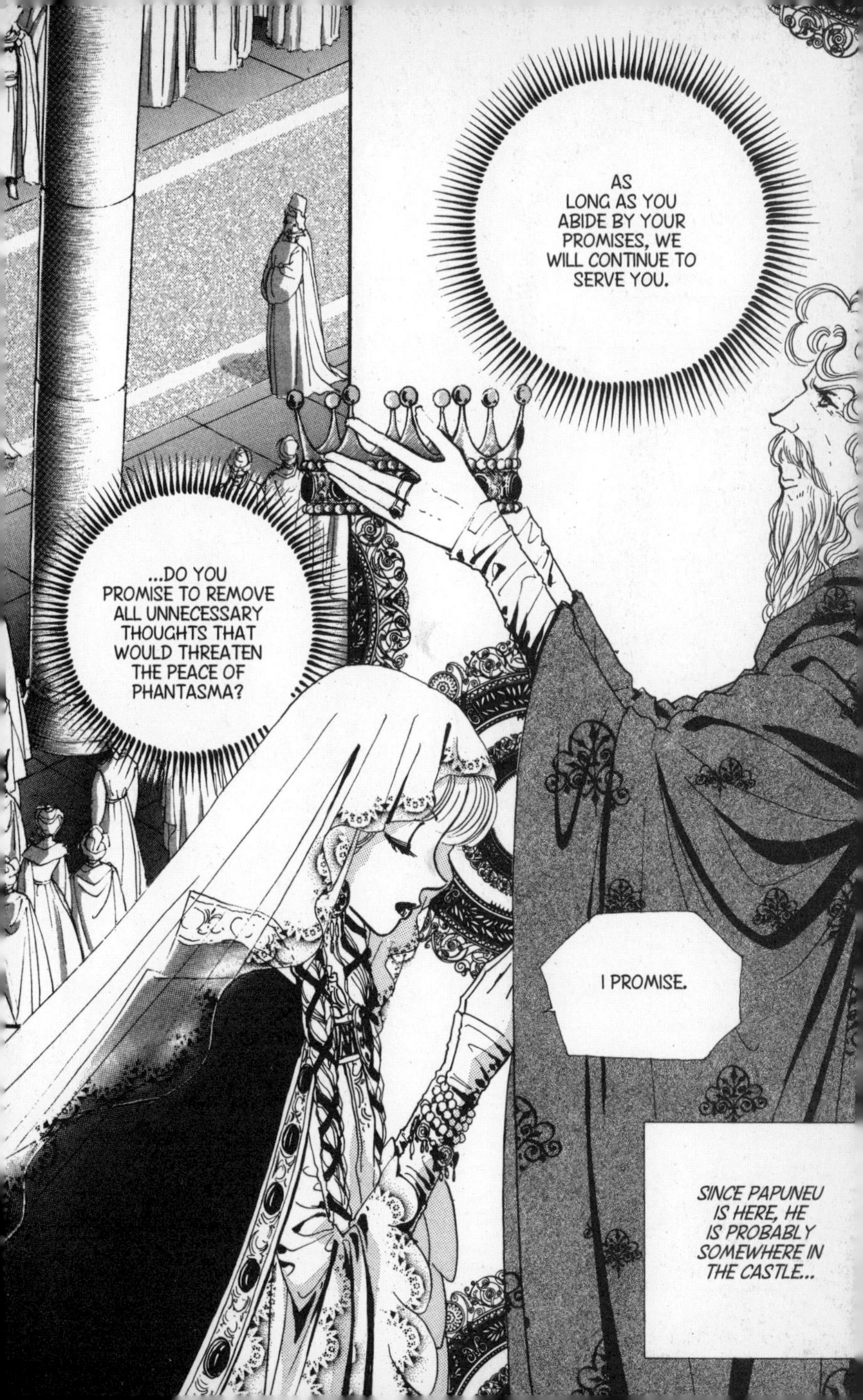
AS LONG AS YOU ABIDE BY YOUR PROMISES, WE WILL CONTINUE TO SERVE YOU.
...DO YOU PROMISE TO REMOVE ALL UNNECESSARY THOUGHTS THAT WOULD THREATEN THE PEACE OF PHANTASMA?
I PROMISE.
SINCE PAPUNEU IS HERE, HE IS PROBABLY SOMEWHERE IN THE CASTLE...

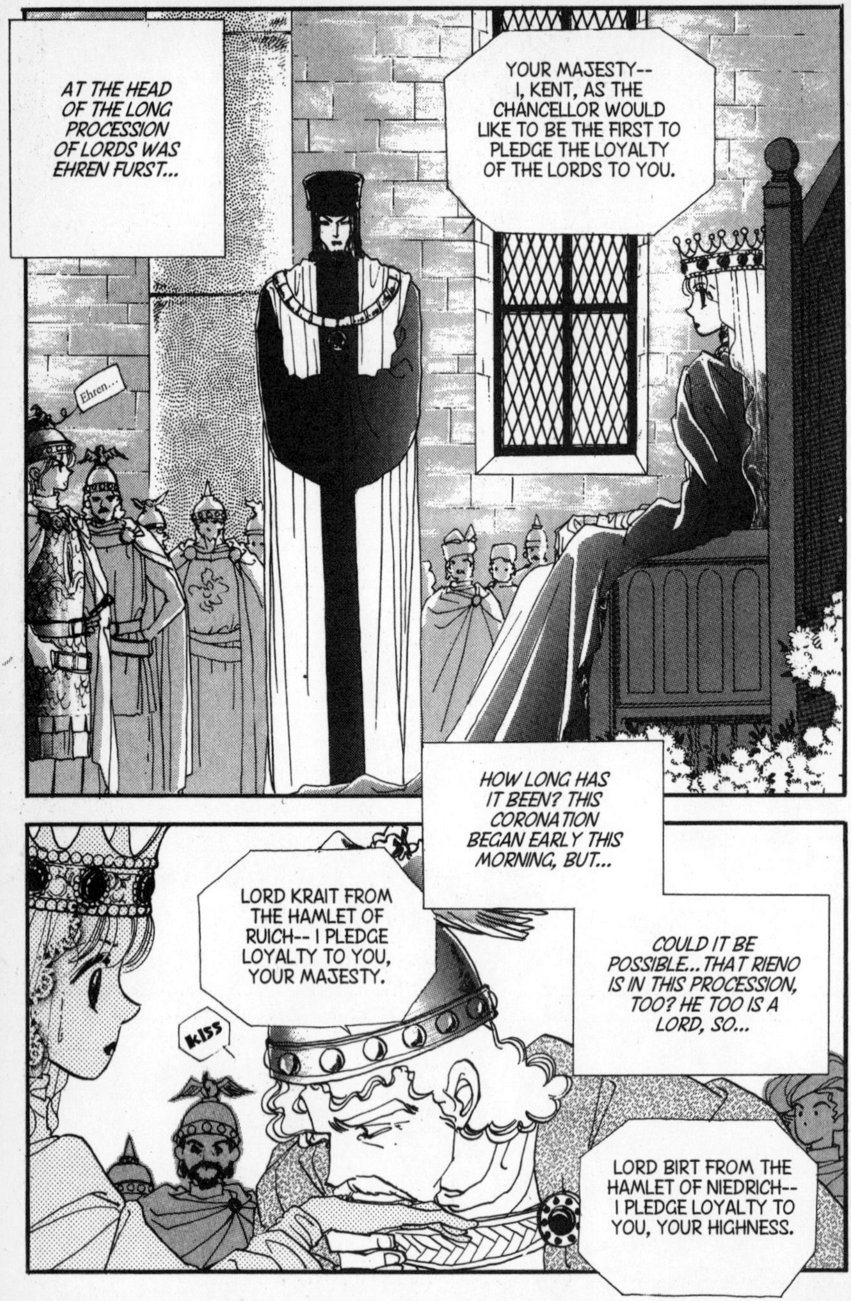
AT THE HEAD OF THE LONG PROCESSION OF LORDS WAS EHREN FURST...
YOUR MAJESTY-- I, KENT, AS THE CHANCELLOR WOULD LIKE TO BE THE FIRST TO PLEDGE THE LOYALTY OF THE LORDS TO YOU.
Ehren...
HOW LONG HAS IT BEEN? THIS CORONATION BEGAN EARLY THIS MORNING, BUT...
LORD KRAIT FROM THE HAMLET OF RUICH-- I PLEDGE LOYALTY TO YOU, YOUR MAJESTY.
COULD IT BE POSSIBLE...THAT RIENO IS IN THIS PROCESSION, TOO? HE TOO IS A LORD, SO...
KISS
LORD BIRT FROM THE HAMLET OF NIEDRICH-- I PLEDGE LOYALTY TO YOU, YOUR HIGHNESS.

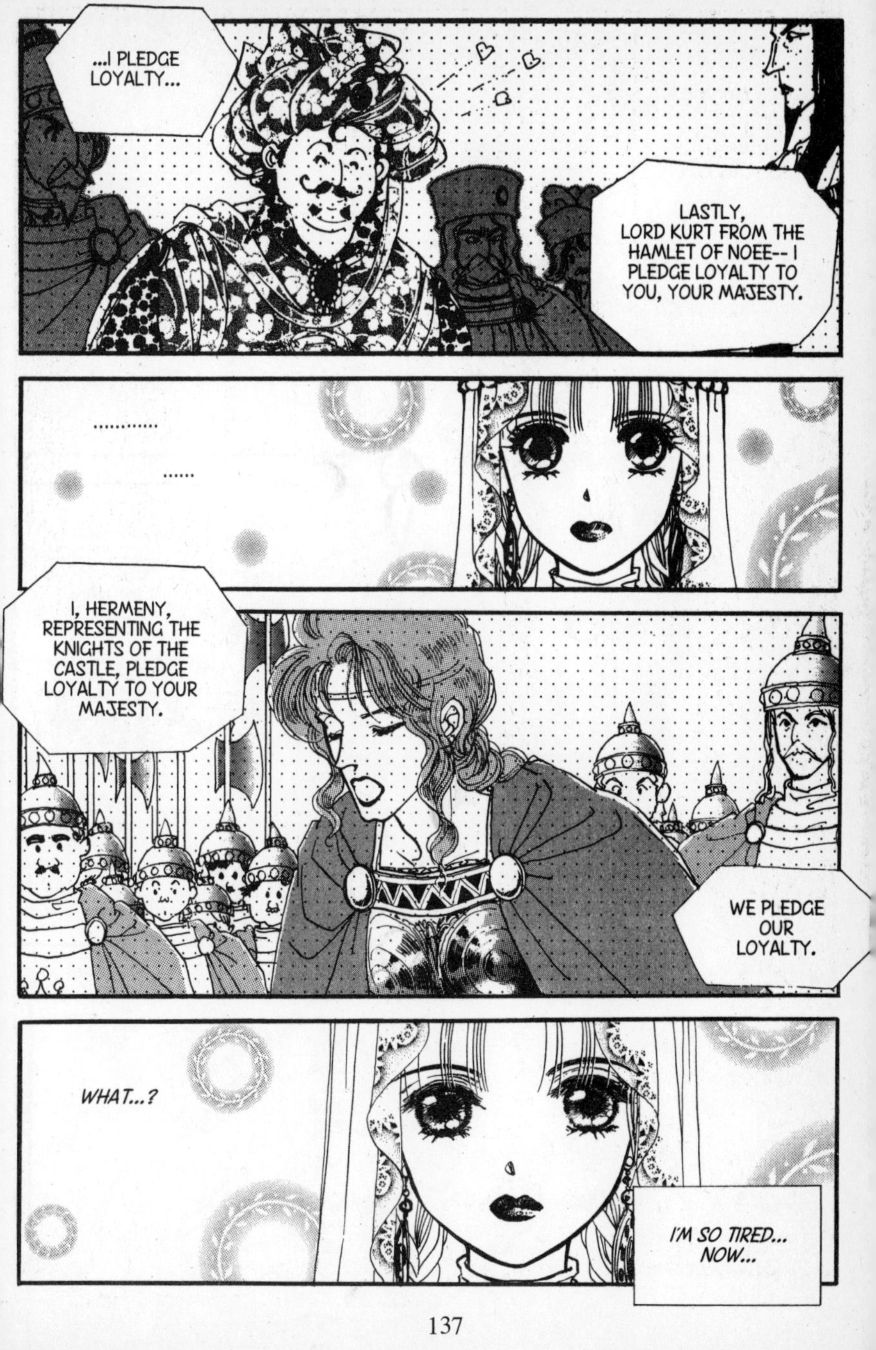
...I PLEDGE LOYALTY...
LASTLY, LORD KURT FROM THE HAMLET OF NOEE-- I PLEDGE LOYALTY TO YOU, YOUR MAJESTY.
....
......
I, HERMENY, REPRESENTING THE KNIGHTS OF THE CASTLE, PLEDGE LOYALTY TO YOUR MAJESTY.
WE PLEDGE OUR LOYALTY.
WHAT...?
I'M SO TIRED... NOW...

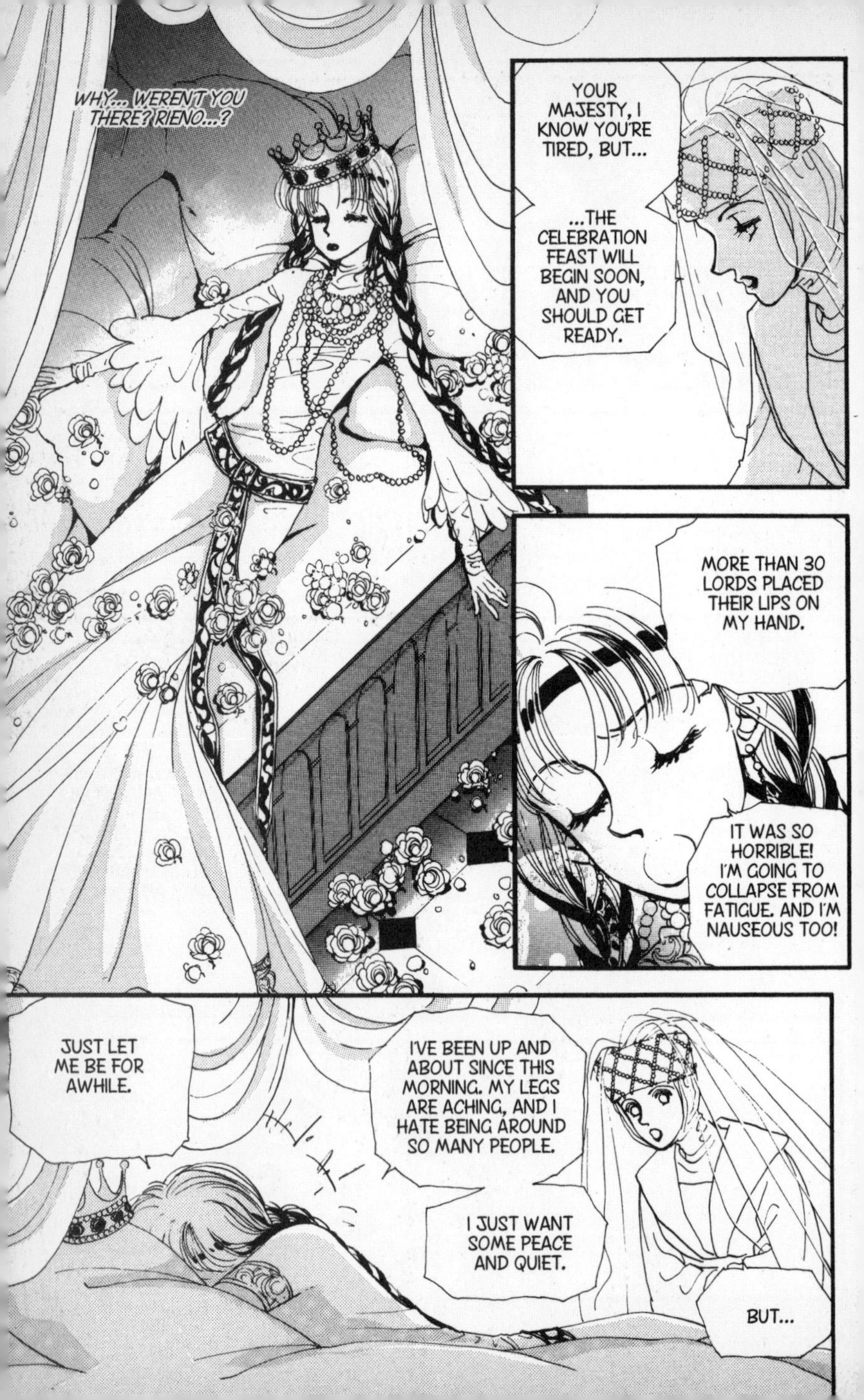
WHY... WEREN'T YOU THERE? RIENO...?
YOUR MAJESTY, I KNOW YOU'RE TIRED, BUT...
...THE CELEBRATION FEAST WILL BEGIN SOON, AND YOU SHOULD GET READY.
MORE THAN 30 LORDS PLACED THEIR LIPS ON MY HAND.
IT WAS SO HORRIBLE! I'M GOING TO COLLAPSE FROM FATIGUE. AND I'M NAUSEOUS TOO!
JUST LET ME BE FOR AWHILE.
I'VE BEEN UP AND ABOUT SINCE THIS MORNING. MY LEGS ARE ACHING, AND I HATE BEING AROUND SO MANY PEOPLE.
I JUST WANT SOME PEACE AND QUIET.
BUT...

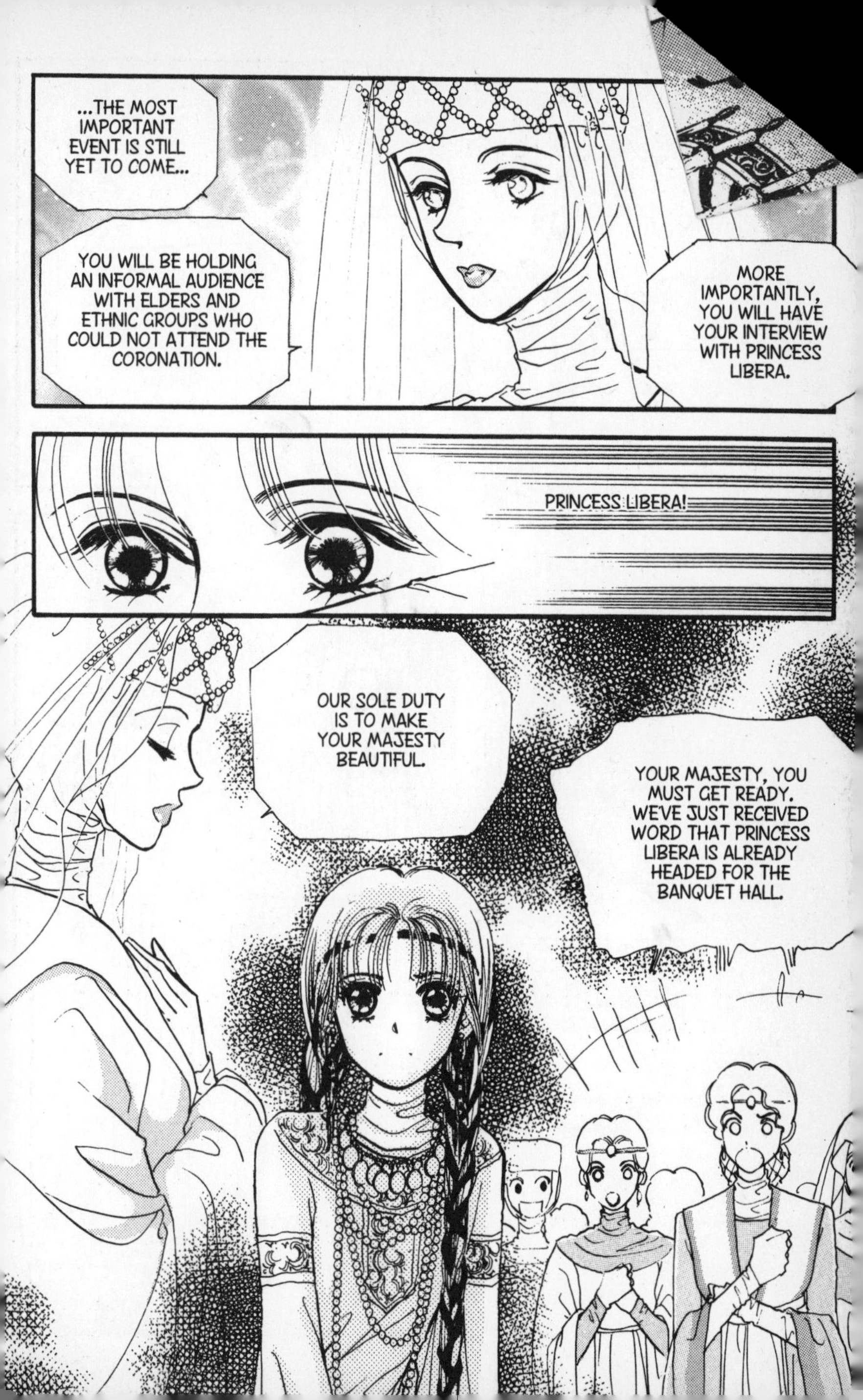
...THE MOST IMPORTANT EVENT IS STILL YET TO COME...
YOU WILL BE HOLDING AN INFORMAL AUDIENCE WITH ELDERS AND ETHNIC GROUPS WHO COULD NOT ATTEND THE CORONATION.
MORE IMPORTANTLY, YOU WILL HAVE YOUR INTERVIEW WITH PRINCESS LIBERA.
PRINCESS LIBERA!
OUR SOLE DUTY IS TO MAKE YOUR MAJESTY BEAUTIFUL.
YOUR MAJESTY, YOU MUST GET READY. WE'VE JUST RECEIVED WORD THAT PRINCESS LIBERA IS ALREADY HEADED FOR THE BANQUET HALL.

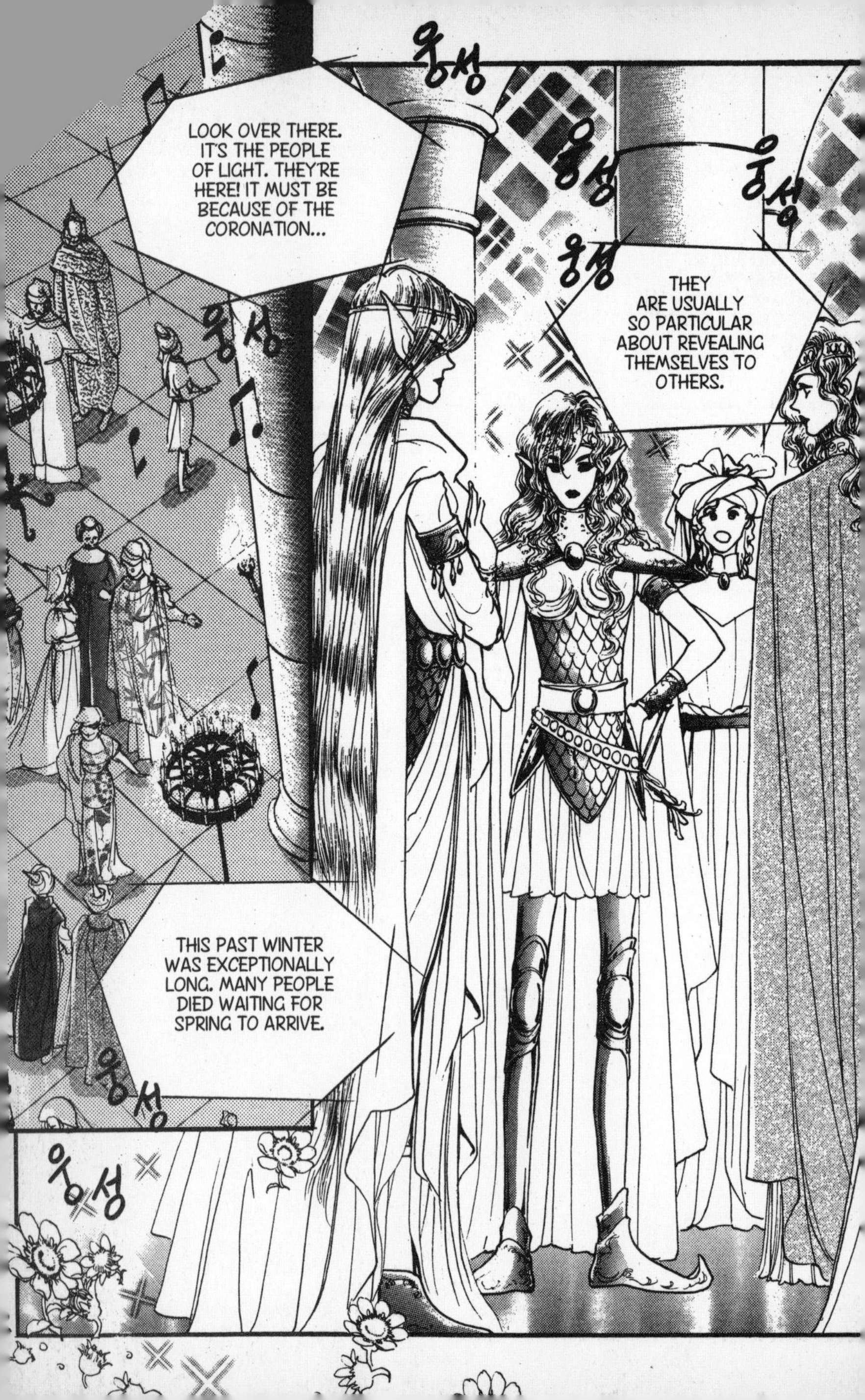
LOOK OVER THERE. IT'S THE PEOPLE OF LIGHT. THEY'RE HERE! IT MUST BE BECAUSE OF THE CORONATION...
웅성
웅성
웅성
웅성
웅성
THEY ARE USUALLY SO PARTICULAR ABOUT REVEALING THEMSELVES TO OTHERS.
THIS PAST WINTER WAS EXCEPTIONALLY LONG. MANY PEOPLE DIED WAITING FOR SPRING TO ARRIVE.
웅성
웅성

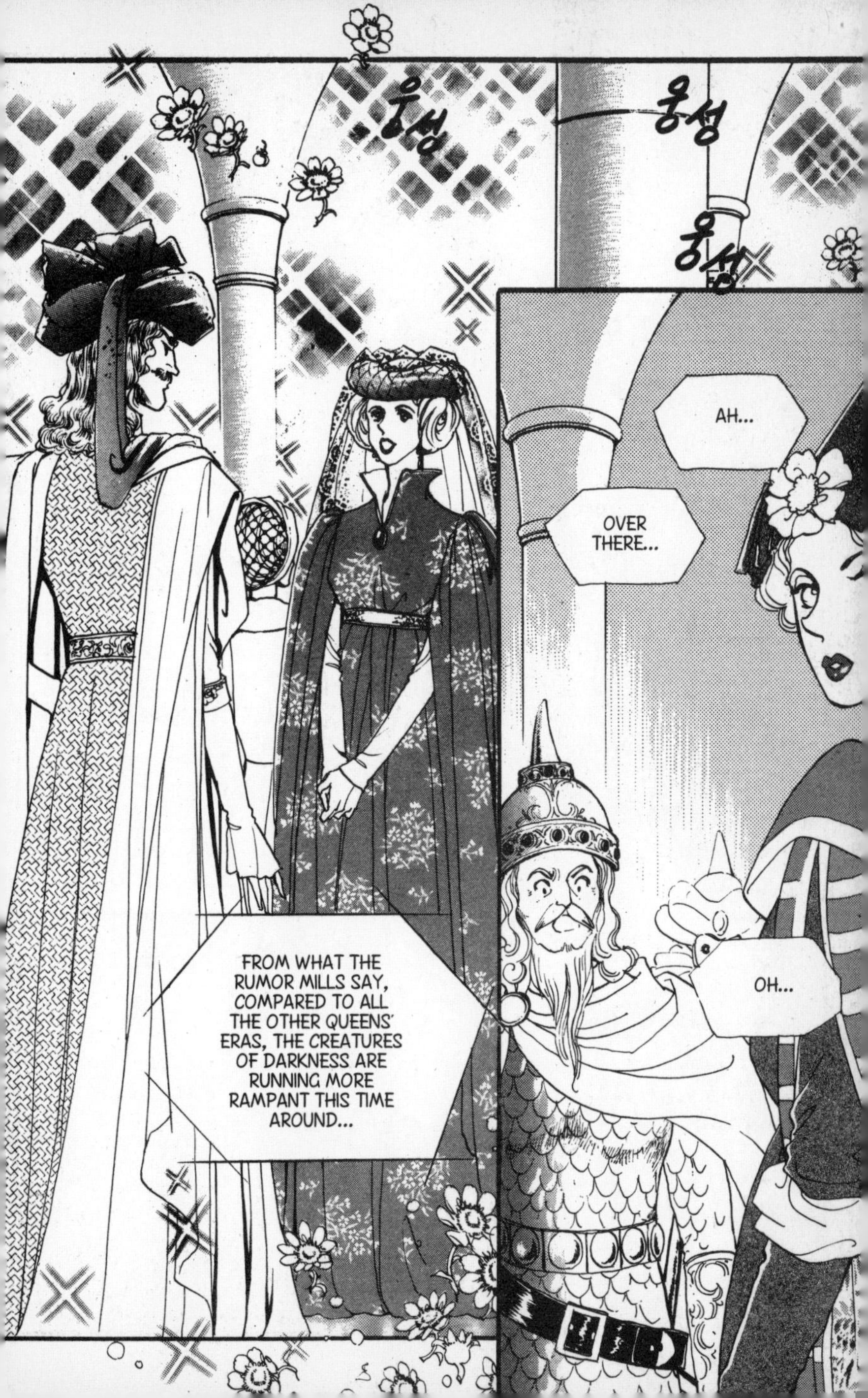
웅성
웅성
웅성
FROM WHAT THE RUMOR MILLS SAY, COMPARED TO ALL THE OTHER QUEENS' ERAS, THE CREATURES OF DARKNESS ARE RUNNING MORE RAMPANT THIS TIME AROUND...
AH...
OVER THERE...
OH...

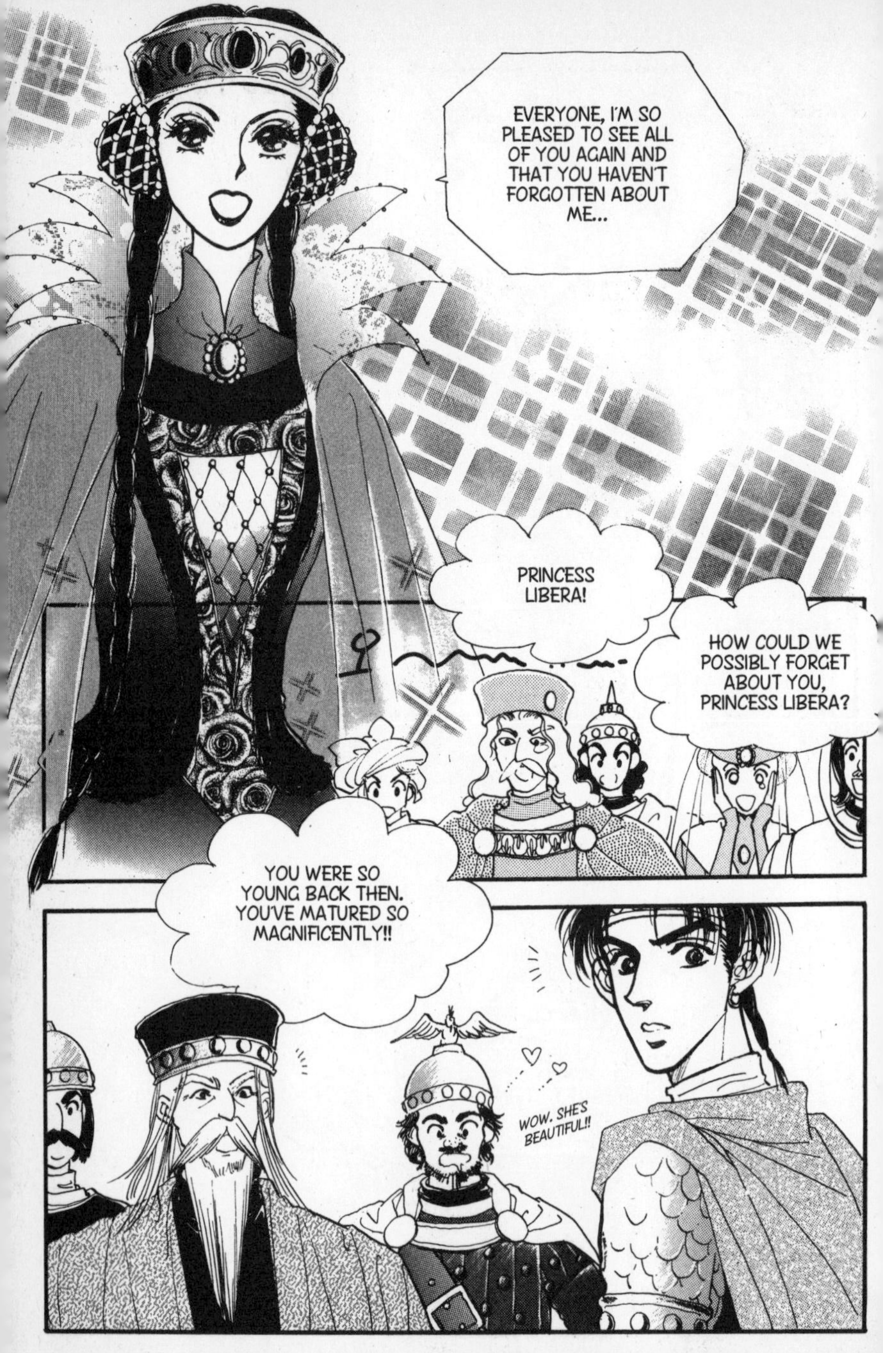
EVERYONE, I'M SO PLEASED TO SEE ALL OF YOU AGAIN AND THAT YOU HAVEN'T FORGOTTEN ABOUT ME...
PRINCESS LIBERA!
HOW COULD WE POSSIBLY FORGET ABOUT YOU, PRINCESS LIBERA?
YOU WERE SO YOUNG BACK THEN. YOU'VE MATURED SO MAGNIFICENTLY!!
WOW. SHE'S BEAUTIFUL!!

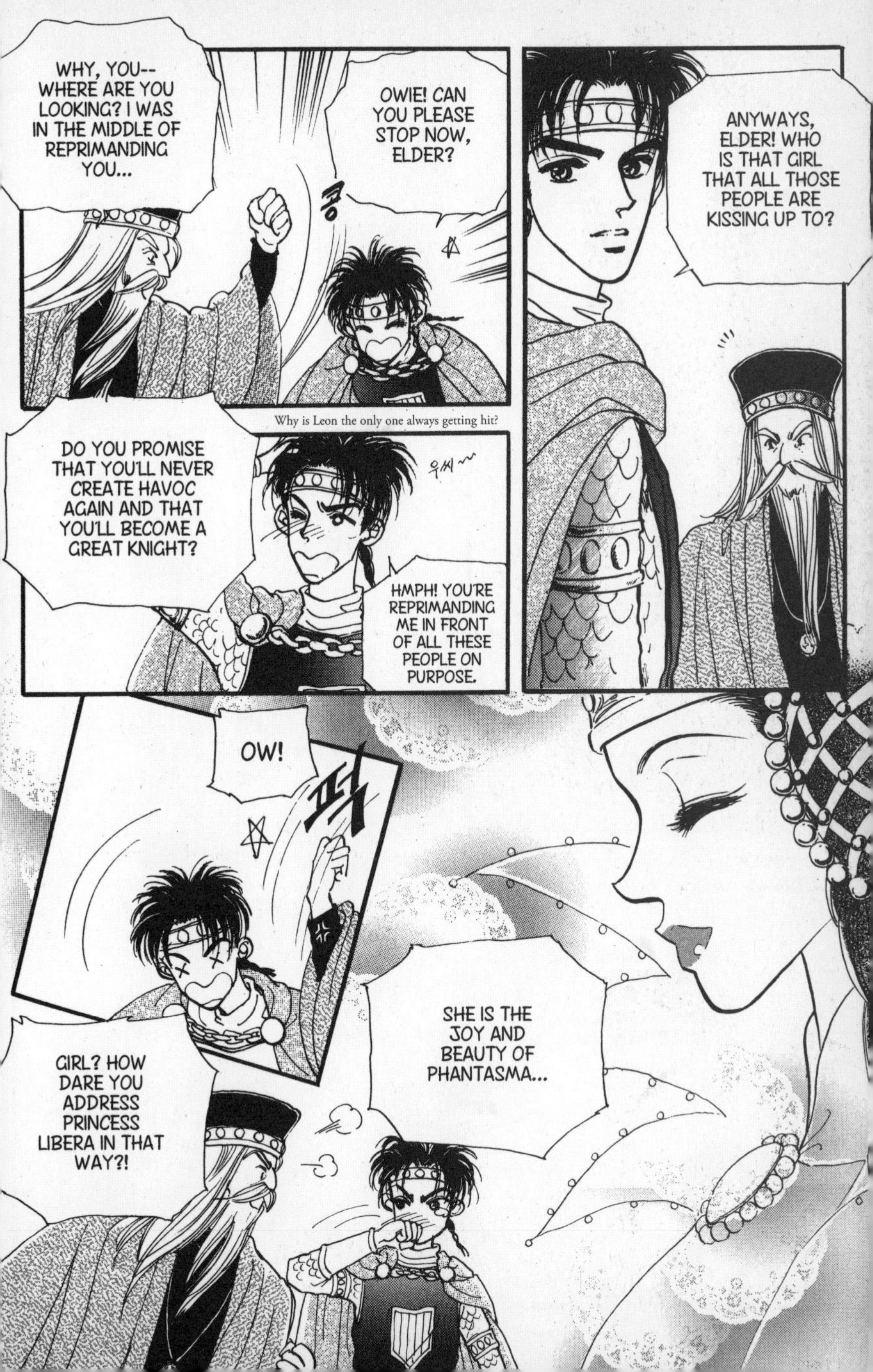
WHY, YOU-- WHERE ARE YOU LOOKING? I WAS IN THE MIDDLE OF REPRIMANDING YOU...
OWIE! CAN YOU PLEASE STOP NOW, ELDER?
쿵
Why is Leon the only one always getting hit?
DO YOU PROMISE THAT YOU'LL NEVER CREATE HAVOC AGAIN AND THAT YOU'LL BECOME A GREAT KNIGHT?
우씨~
HMPH! YOU'RE REPRIMANDING ME IN FRONT OF ALL THESE PEOPLE ON PURPOSE.
ANYWAYS, ELDER! WHO IS THAT GIRL THAT ALL THOSE PEOPLE ARE KISSING UP TO?
OW!
퍽
SHE IS THE JOY AND BEAUTY OF PHANTASMA...
GIRL? HOW DARE YOU ADDRESS PRINCESS LIBERA IN THAT WAY?!

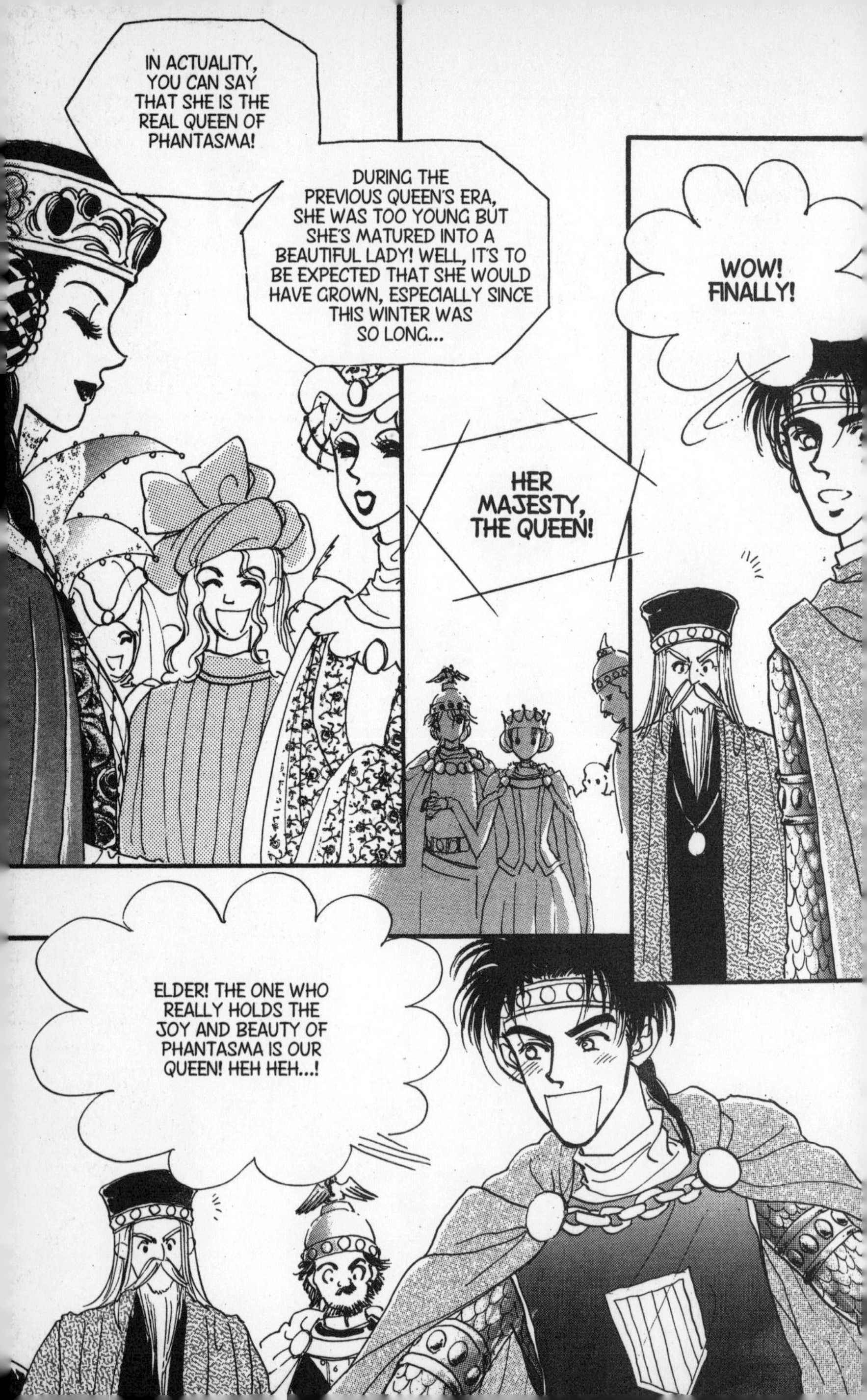
IN ACTUALITY, YOU CAN SAY THAT SHE IS THE REAL QUEEN OF PHANTASMA!
DURING THE PREVIOUS QUEEN'S ERA, SHE WAS TOO YOUNG BUT SHE'S MATURED INTO A BEAUTIFUL LADY! WELL, IT'S TO BE EXPECTED THAT SHE WOULD HAVE GROWN, ESPECIALLY SINCE THIS WINTER WAS SO LONG...
HER MAJESTY, THE QUEEN!
WOW! FINALLY!
ELDER! THE ONE WHO REALLY HOLDS THE JOY AND BEAUTY OF PHANTASMA IS OUR QUEEN! HEH HEH...!

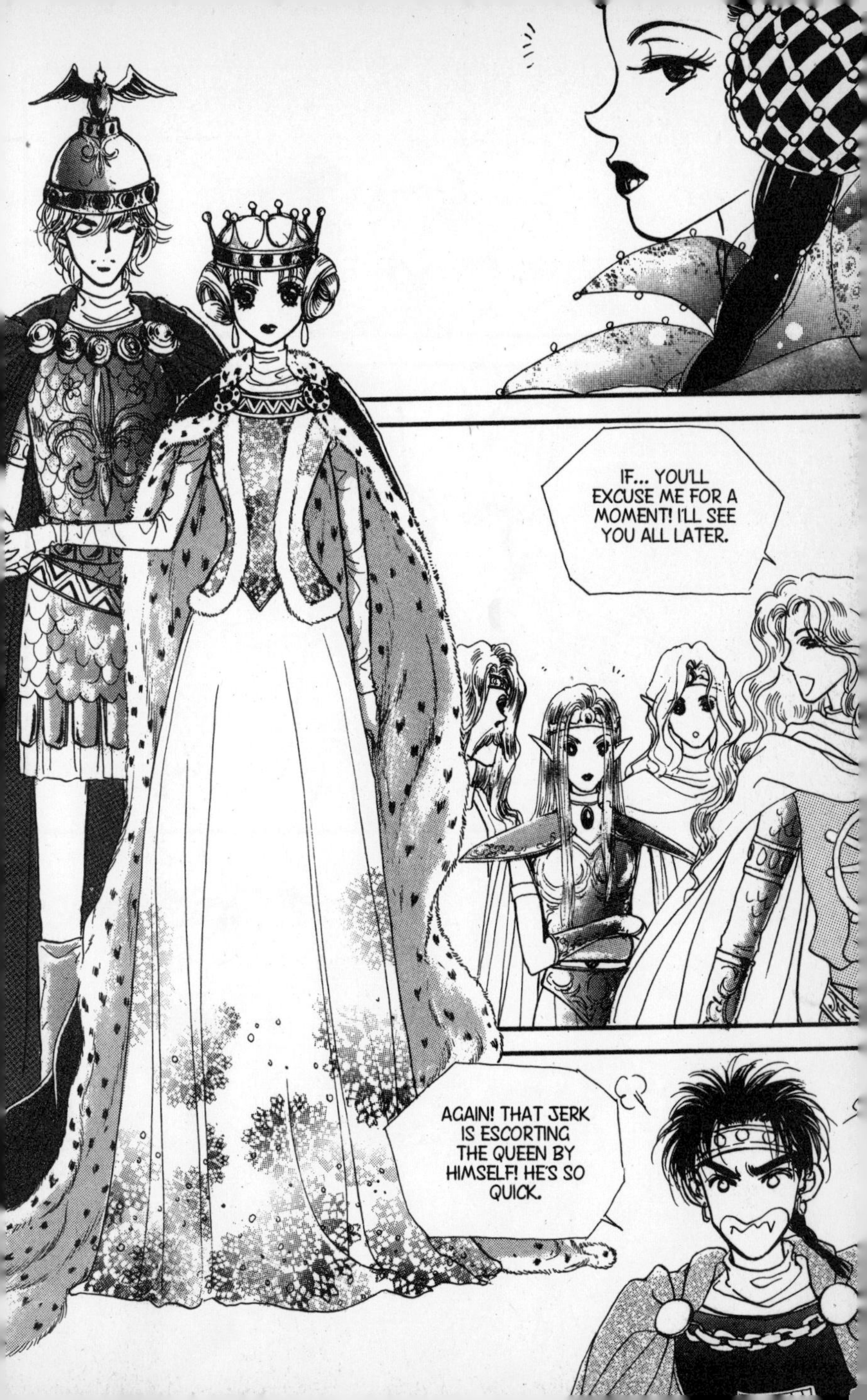
IF... YOU'LL EXCUSE ME FOR A MOMENT! I'LL SEE YOU ALL LATER.
AGAIN! THAT JERK IS ESCORTING THE QUEEN BY HIMSELF! HE'S SO QUICK.

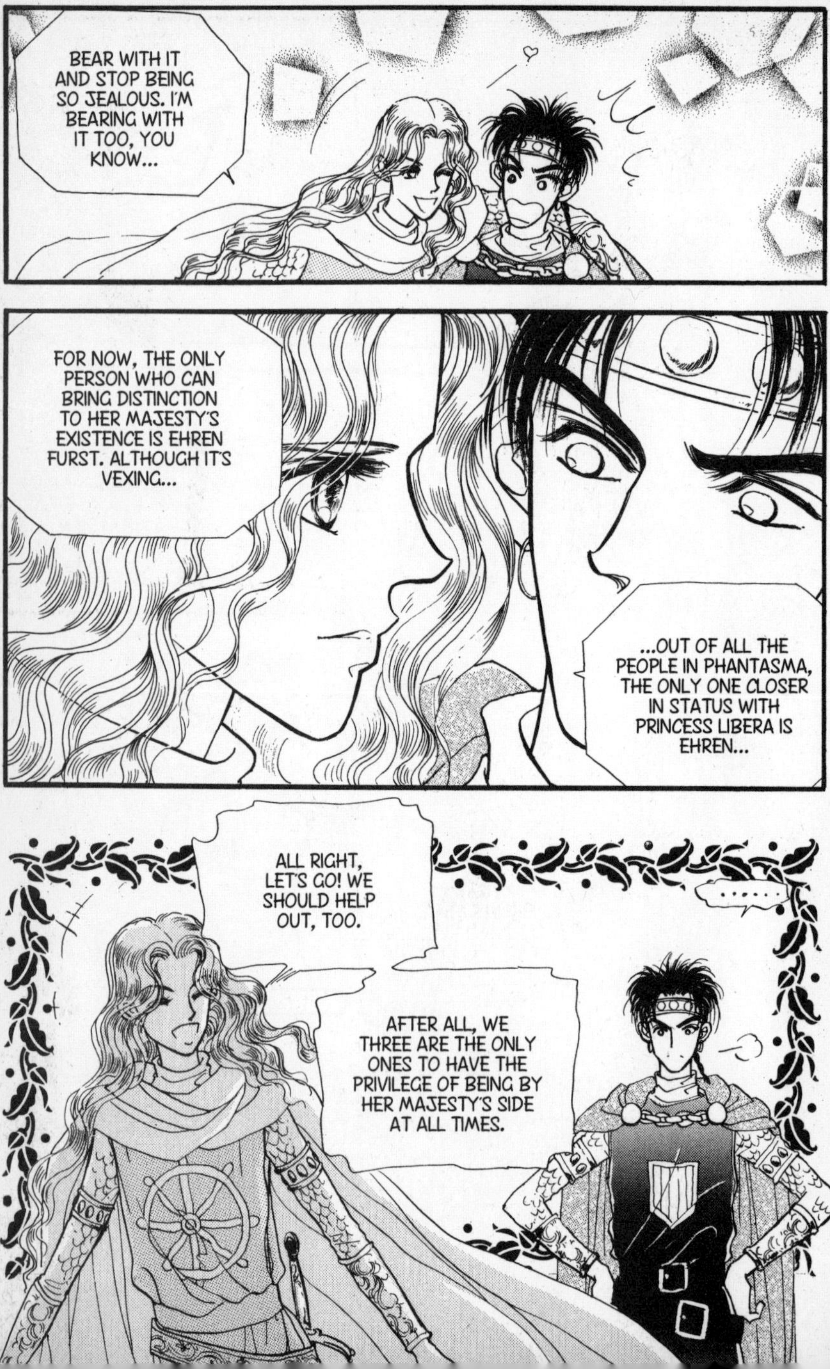
BEAR WITH IT AND STOP BEING SO JEALOUS. I'M BEARING WITH IT TOO, YOU KNOW...
FOR NOW, THE ONLY PERSON WHO CAN BRING DISTINCTION TO HER MAJESTY'S EXISTENCE IS EHREN FURST. ALTHOUGH IT'S VEXING...
...OUT OF ALL THE PEOPLE IN PHANTASMA, THE ONLY ONE CLOSER IN STATUS WITH PRINCESS LIBERA IS EHREN...
ALL RIGHT, LET'S GO! WE SHOULD HELP OUT, TOO.
AFTER ALL, WE THREE ARE THE ONLY ONES TO HAVE THE PRIVILEGE OF BEING BY HER MAJESTY'S SIDE AT ALL TIMES.
......

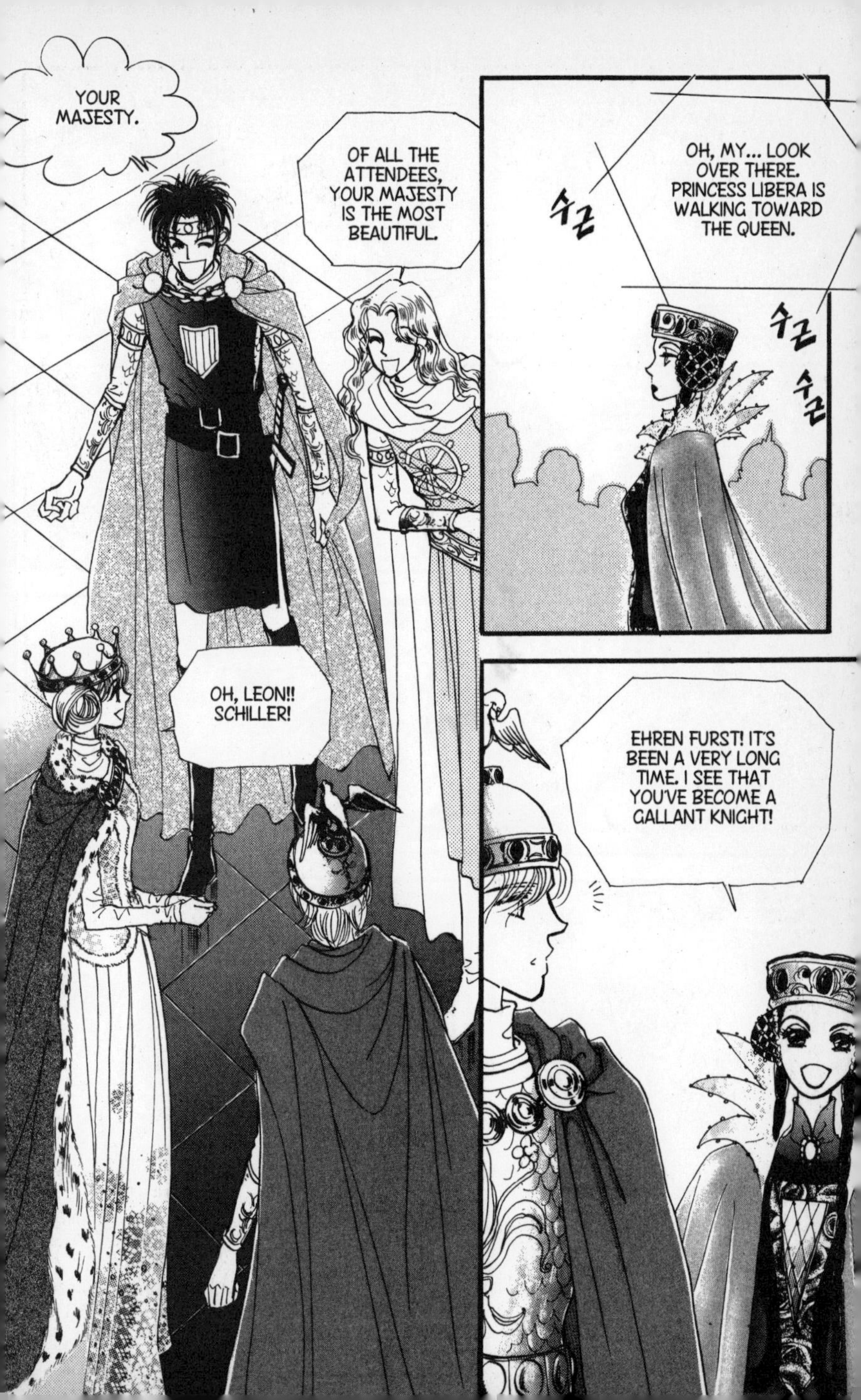
YOUR MAJESTY.
OF ALL THE ATTENDEES, YOUR MAJESTY IS THE MOST BEAUTIFUL.
OH, LEON!! SCHILLER!
수군
OH, MY... LOOK OVER THERE. PRINCESS LIBERA IS WALKING TOWARD THE QUEEN.
수군
수군
EHREN FURST! IT'S BEEN A VERY LONG TIME. I SEE THAT YOU'VE BECOME A GALLANT KNIGHT!

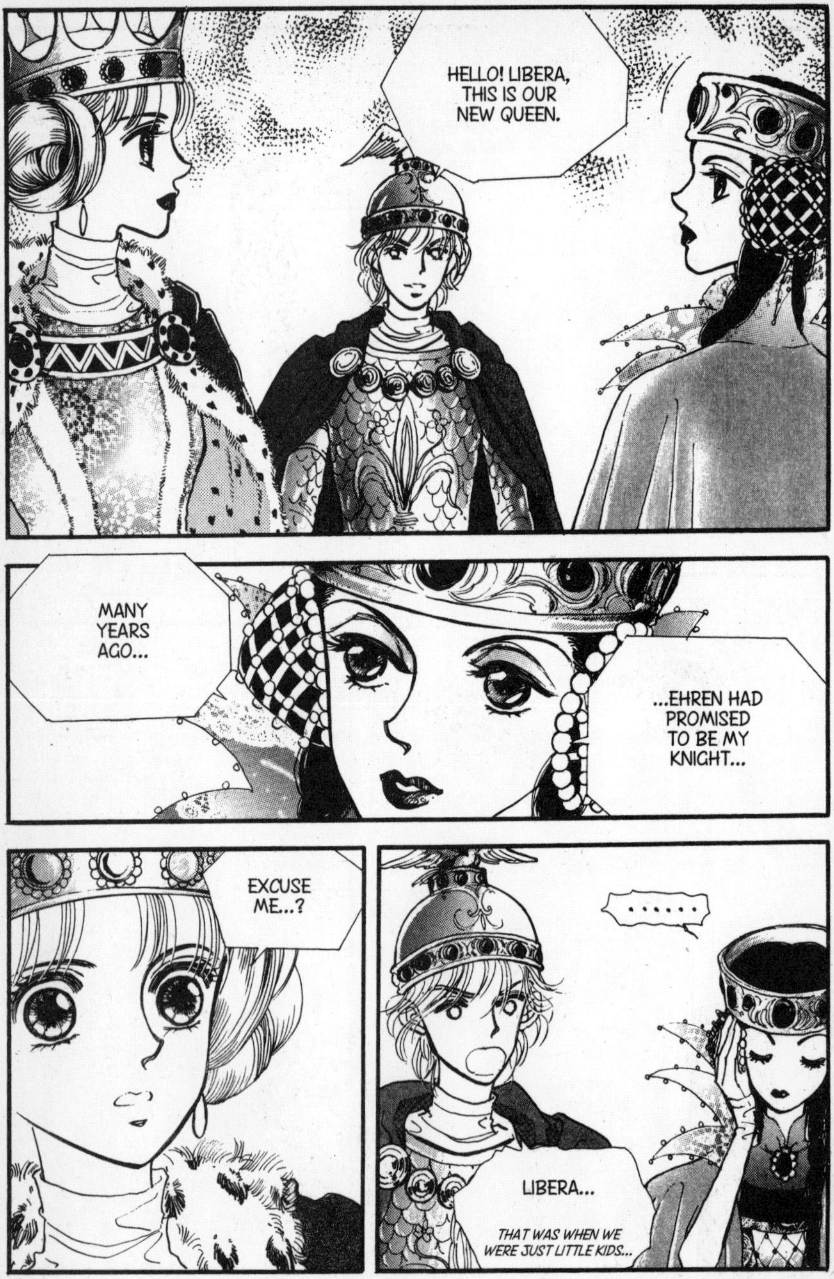

HELLO! LIBERA, THIS IS OUR NEW QUEEN.
MANY YEARS AGO...
...EHREN HAD PROMISED TO BE MY KNIGHT...
EXCUSE ME...?
......
LIBERA...
THAT WAS WHEN WE WERE JUST LITTLE KIDS...

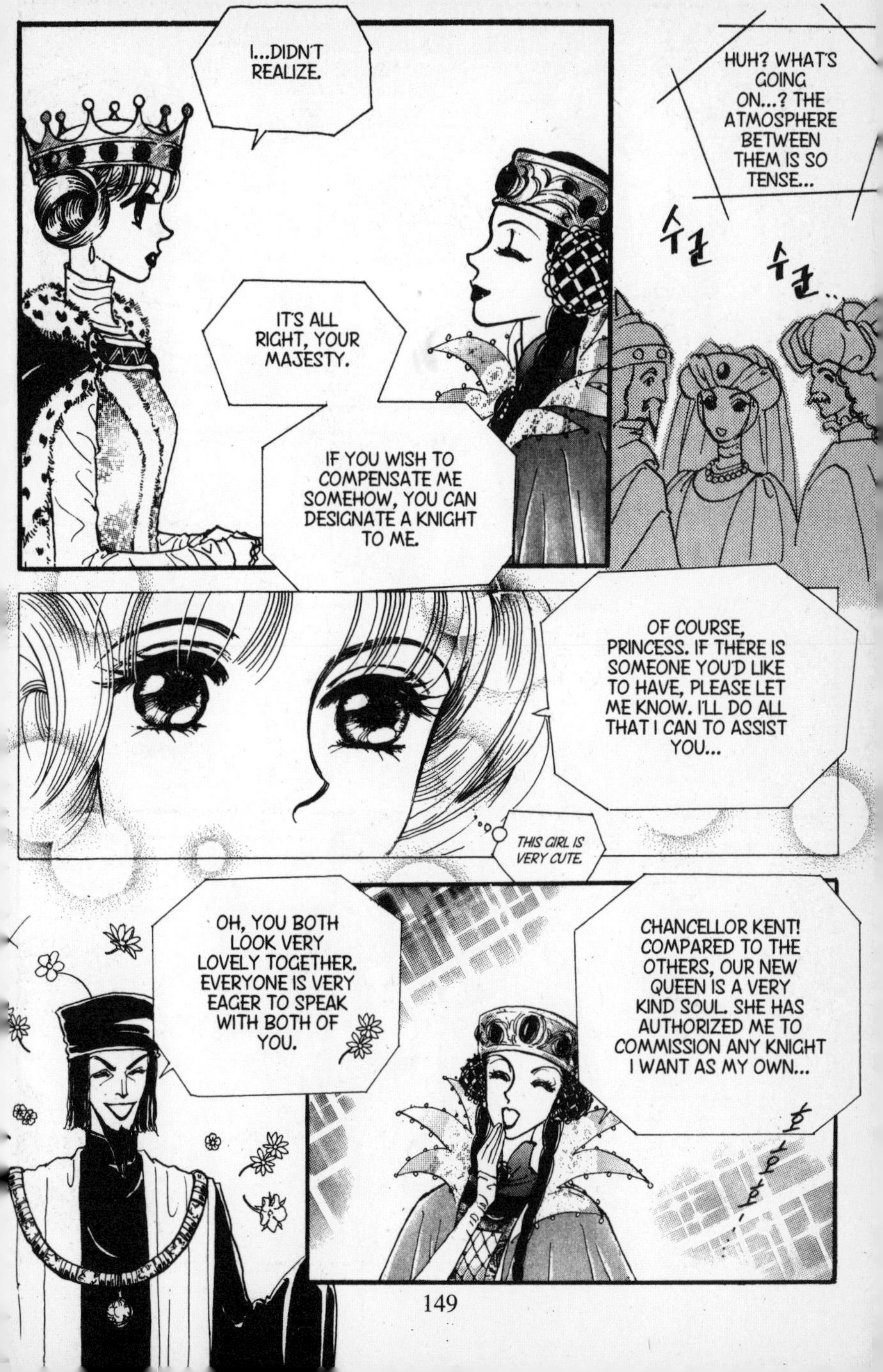
I...DIDN'T REALIZE.
IT'S ALL RIGHT, YOUR MAJESTY.
IF YOU WISH TO COMPENSATE ME SOMEHOW, YOU CAN DESIGNATE A KNIGHT TO ME.
HUH? WHAT'S GOING ON...? THE ATMOSPHERE BETWEEN THEM IS SO TENSE...
수군
수군...
OF COURSE, PRINCESS. IF THERE IS SOMEONE YOU'D LIKE TO HAVE, PLEASE LET ME KNOW. I'LL DO ALL THAT I CAN TO ASSIST YOU...
THIS GIRL IS VERY CUTE.
OH, YOU BOTH LOOK VERY LOVELY TOGETHER. EVERYONE IS VERY EAGER TO SPEAK WITH BOTH OF YOU.
CHANCELLOR KENT! COMPARED TO THE OTHERS, OUR NEW QUEEN IS A VERY KIND SOUL. SHE HAS AUTHORIZED ME TO COMMISSION ANY KNIGHT I WANT AS MY OWN...
호호호

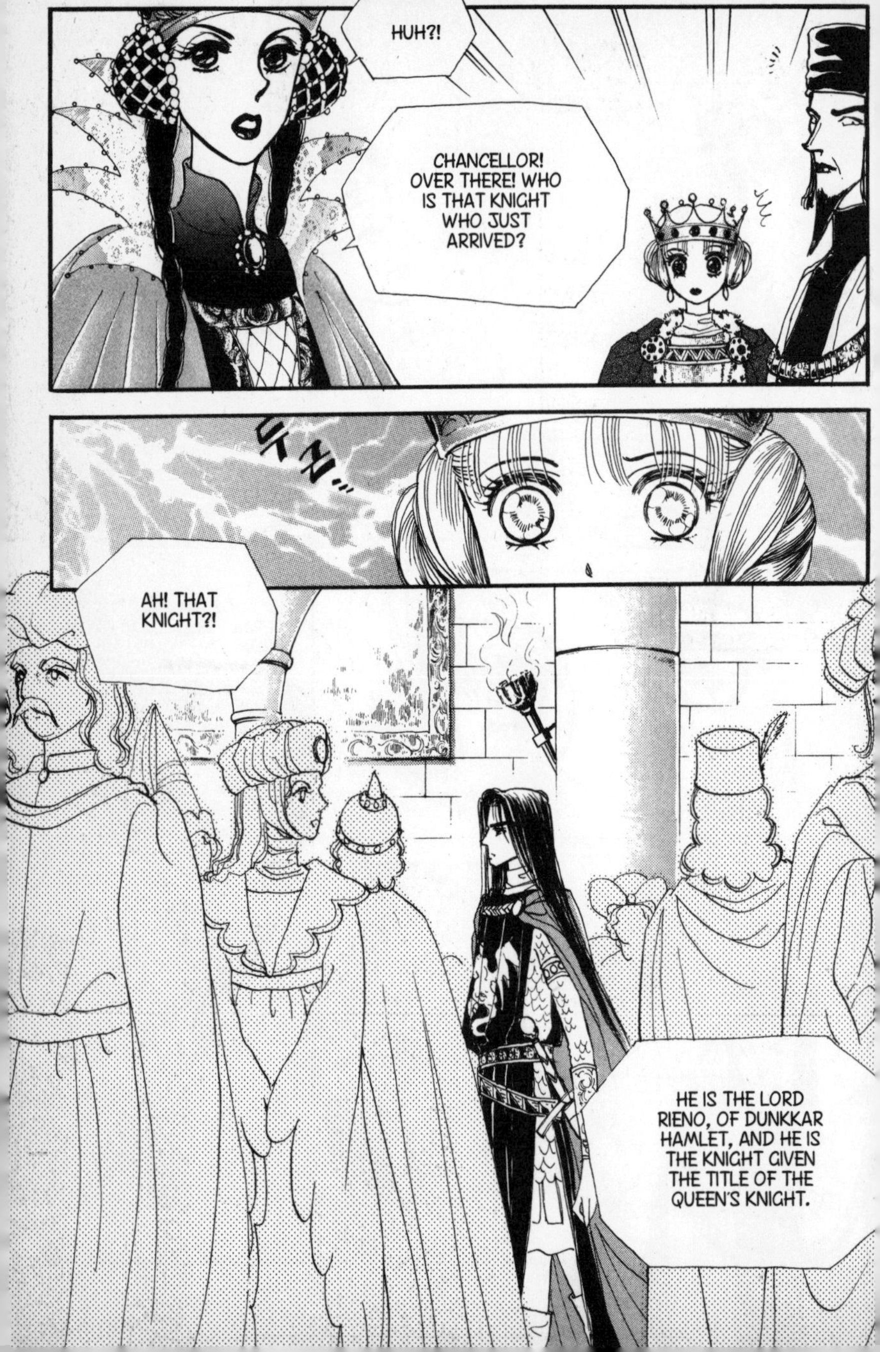
HUH?!
CHANCELLOR! OVER THERE! WHO IS THAT KNIGHT WHO JUST ARRIVED?
두근...
AH! THAT KNIGHT?!
HE IS THE LORD RIENO, OF DUNKKAR HAMLET, AND HE IS THE KNIGHT GIVEN THE TITLE OF THE QUEEN'S KNIGHT.

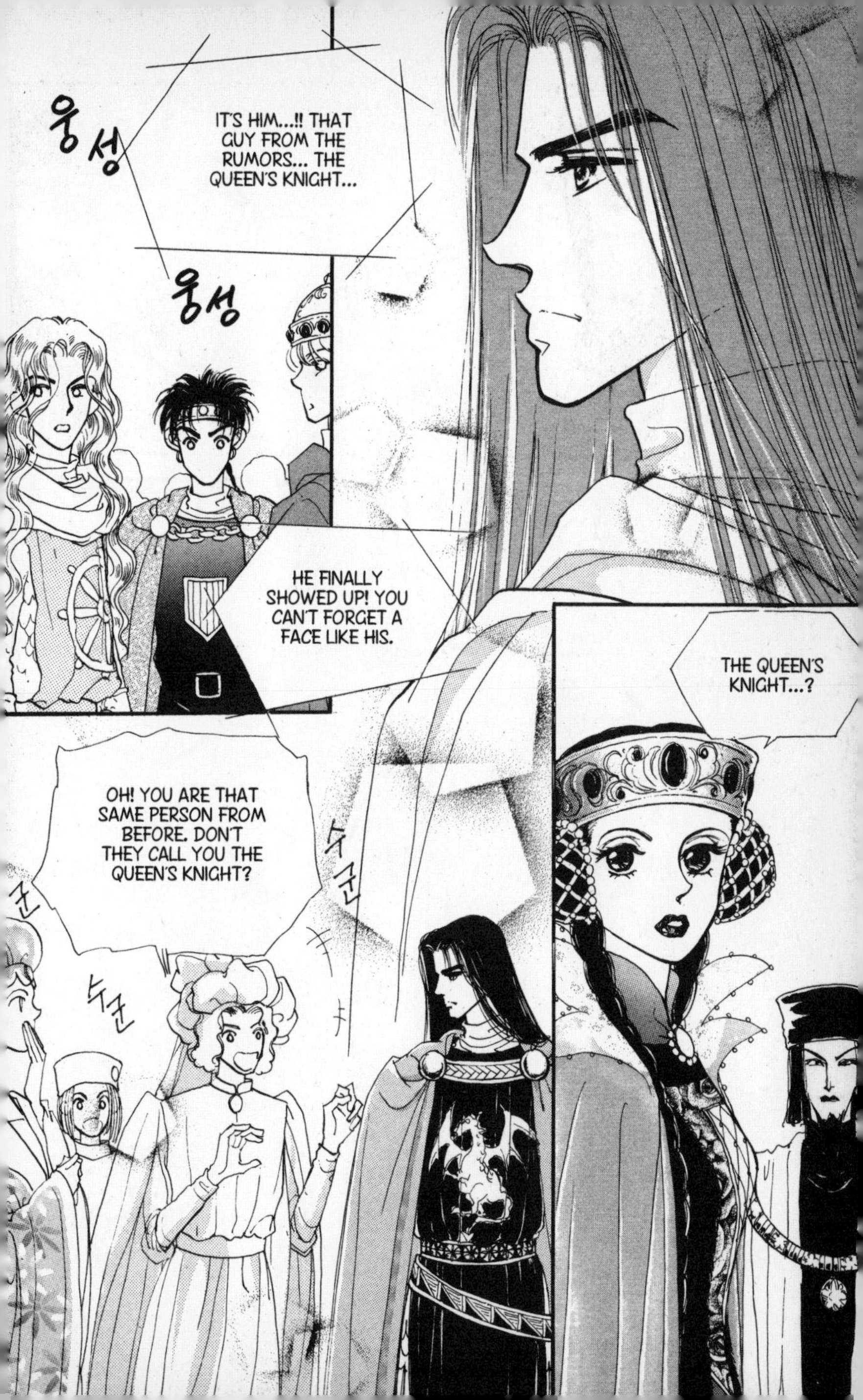
웅성
웅성
IT'S HIM...!! THAT GUY FROM THE RUMORS... THE QUEEN'S KNIGHT...
HE FINALLY SHOWED UP! YOU CAN'T FORGET A FACE LIKE HIS.
OH! YOU ARE THAT SAME PERSON FROM BEFORE. DON'T THEY CALL YOU THE QUEEN'S KNIGHT?
수군
수군
THE QUEEN'S KNIGHT...?

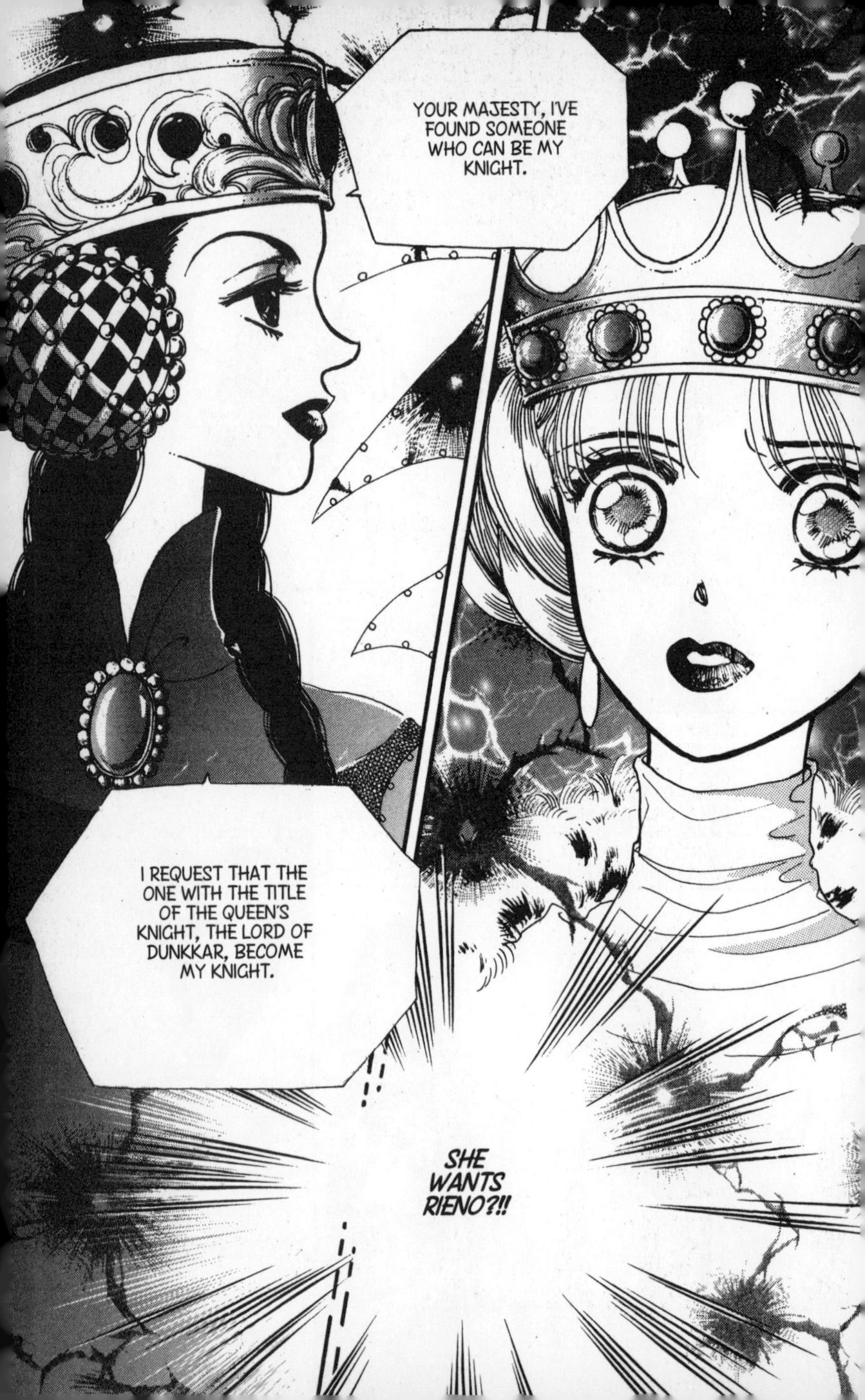
YOUR MAJESTY, I'VE FOUND SOMEONE WHO CAN BE MY KNIGHT.
I REQUEST THAT THE ONE WITH THE TITLE OF THE QUEEN'S KNIGHT, THE LORD OF DUNKKAR, BECOME MY KNIGHT.
SHE WANTS RIENO?!!

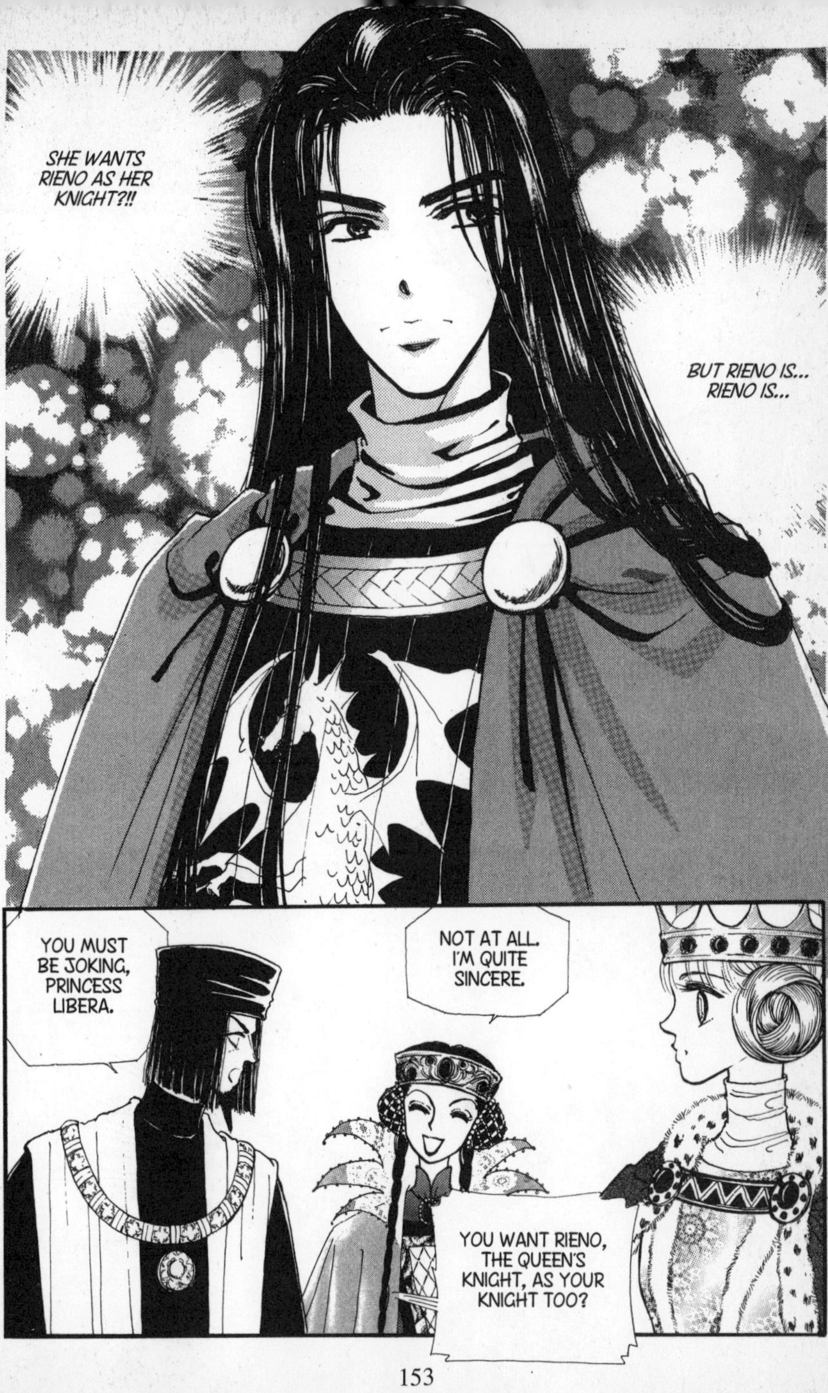
SHE WANTS RIENO AS HER KNIGHT?!!
BUT RIENO IS... RIENO IS...
YOU MUST BE JOKING, PRINCESS LIBERA.
NOT AT ALL. I'M QUITE SINCERE.
YOU WANT RIENO, THE QUEEN'S KNIGHT, AS YOUR KNIGHT TOO?

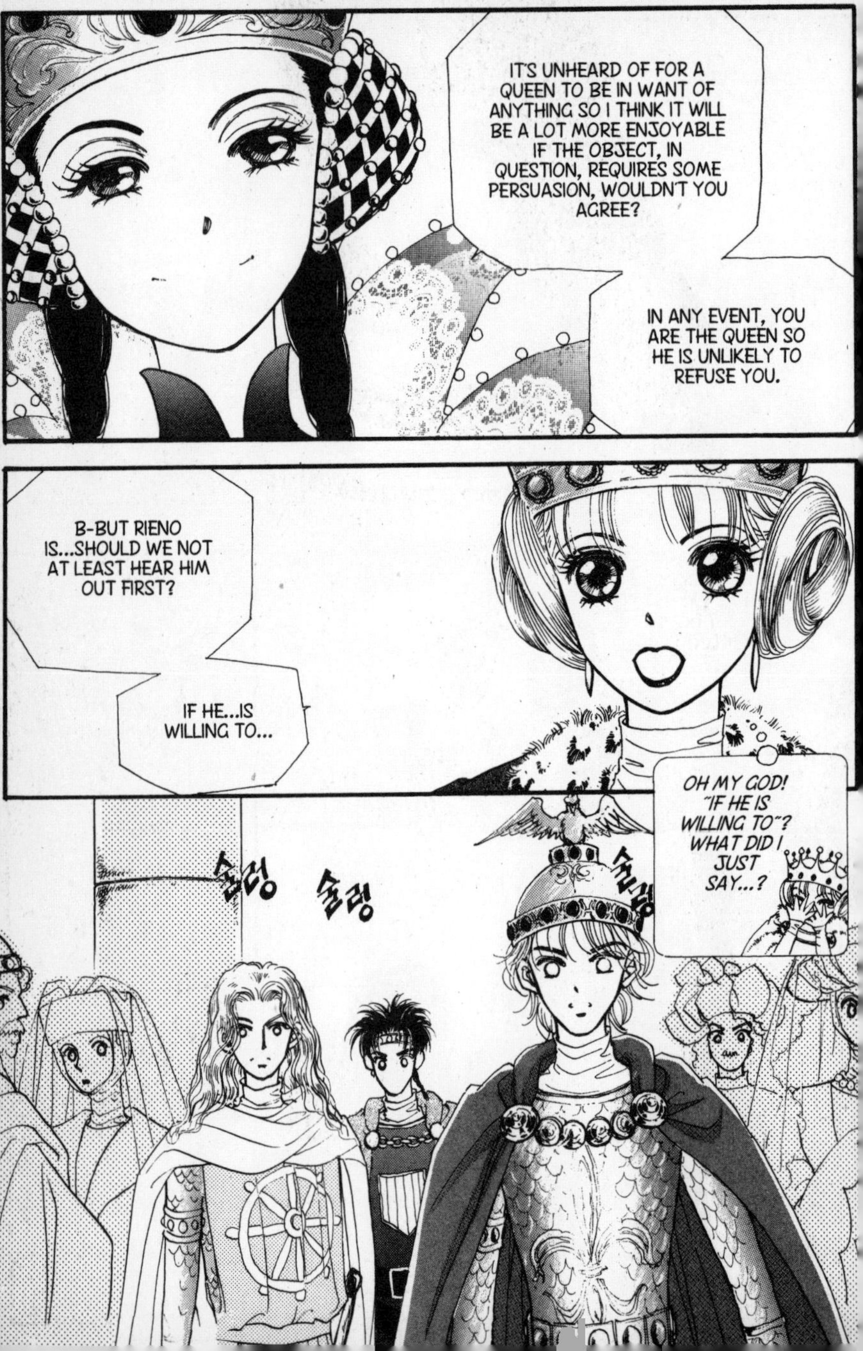
IT'S UNHEARD OF FOR A QUEEN TO BE IN WANT OF ANYTHING SO I THINK IT WILL BE A LOT MORE ENJOYABLE IF THE OBJECT, IN QUESTION, REQUIRES SOME PERSUASION, WOULDN'T YOU AGREE?
IN ANY EVENT, YOU ARE THE QUEEN SO HE IS UNLIKELY TO REFUSE YOU.
B-BUT RIENO IS...SHOULD WE NOT AT LEAST HEAR HIM OUT FIRST?
IF HE...IS WILLING TO...
술렁
술렁
술렁
OH MY GOD! "IF HE IS WILLING TO"? WHAT DID I JUST SAY...?

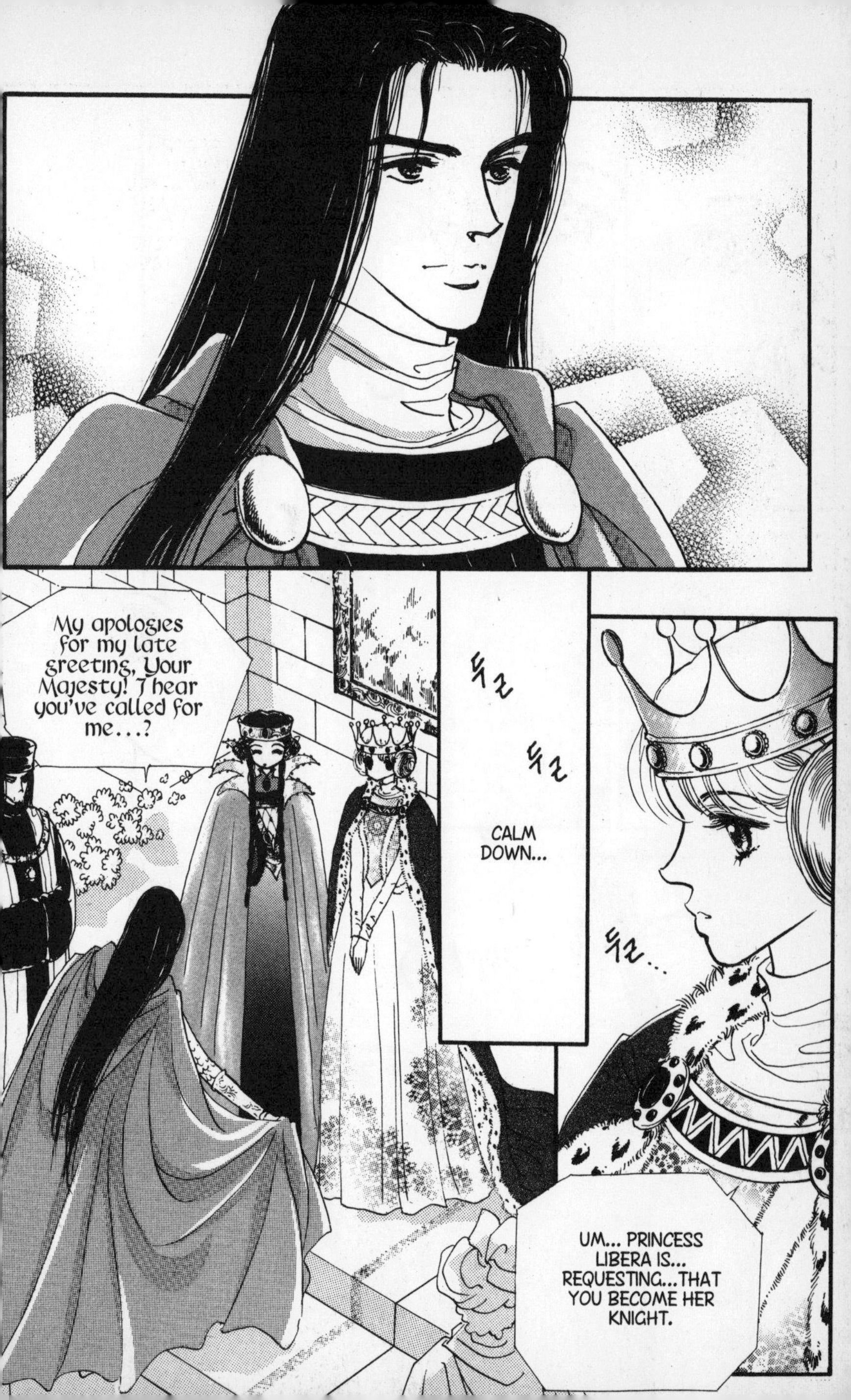
My apologies for my late greeting, Your Majesty! I hear you've called for me...?
두근
두근
CALM DOWN...
두근...
UM... PRINCESS LIBERA IS... REQUESTING...THAT YOU BECOME HER KNIGHT.

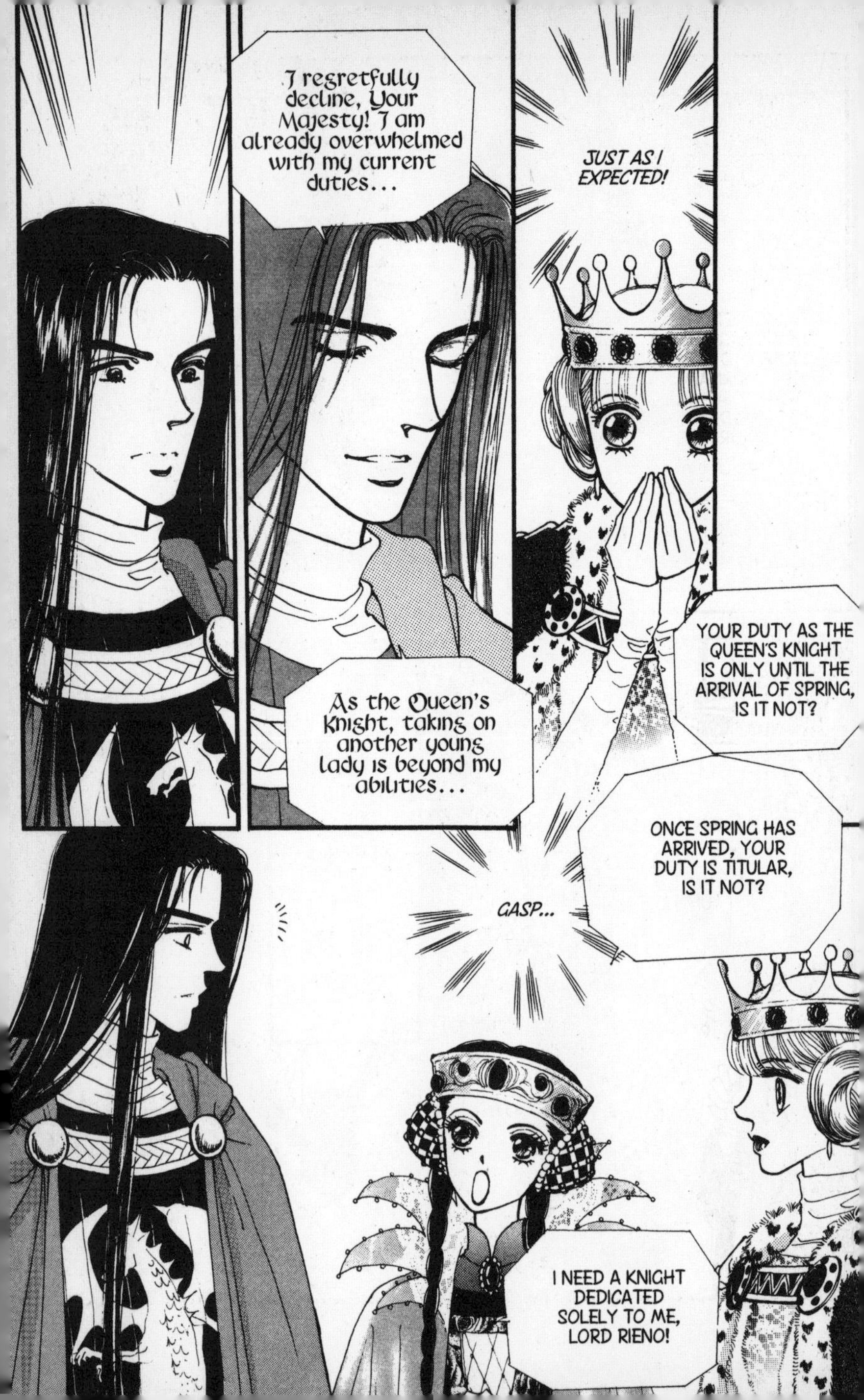

I regretfully decline, Your Majesty! I am already overwhelmed with my current duties...
As the Queen's Knight, taking on another young lady is beyond my abilities...
JUST AS I EXPECTED!
YOUR DUTY AS THE QUEEN'S KNIGHT IS ONLY UNTIL THE ARRIVAL OF SPRING, IS IT NOT?
GASP...
ONCE SPRING HAS ARRIVED, YOUR DUTY IS TITULAR, IS IT NOT?
I NEED A KNIGHT DEDICATED SOLELY TO ME, LORD RIENO!

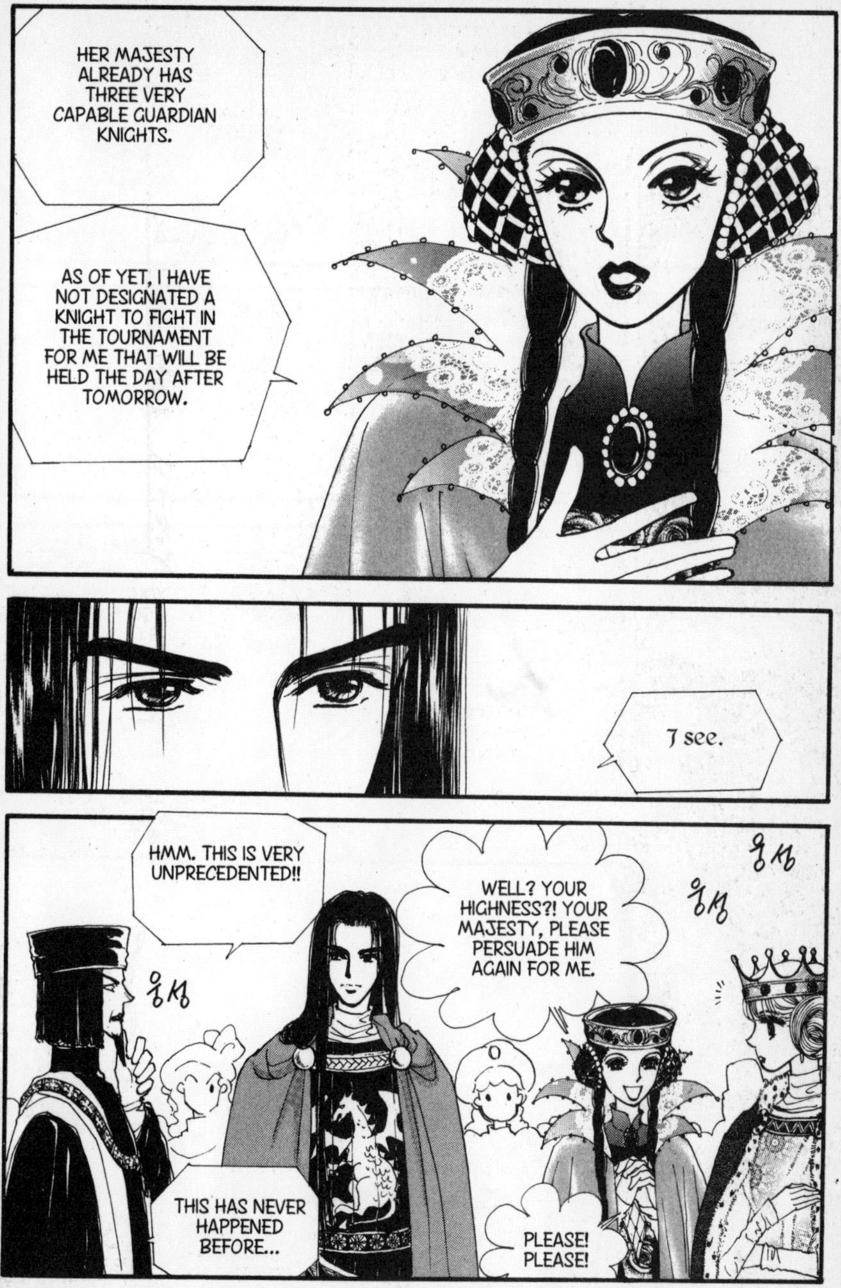
HER MAJESTY ALREADY HAS THREE VERY CAPABLE GUARDIAN KNIGHTS.
AS OF YET, I HAVE NOT DESIGNATED A KNIGHT TO FIGHT IN THE TOURNAMENT FOR ME THAT WILL BE HELD THE DAY AFTER TOMORROW.
I see.
HMM. THIS IS VERY UNPRECEDENTED!!
웅성
WELL? YOUR HIGHNESS?! YOUR MAJESTY, PLEASE PERSUADE HIM AGAIN FOR ME.
웅성
웅성
THIS HAS NEVER HAPPENED BEFORE...
PLEASE! PLEASE!

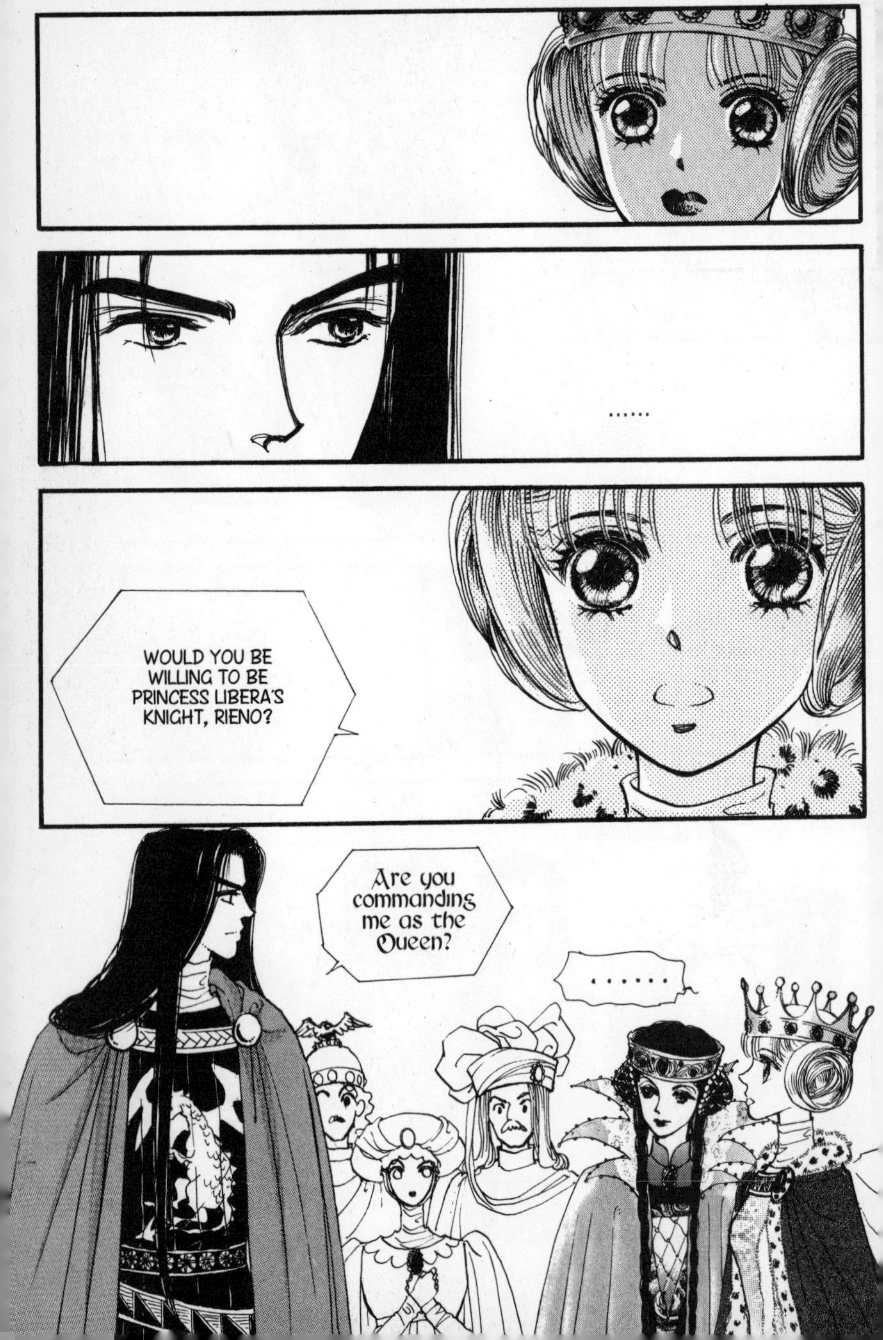
......
WOULD YOU BE WILLING TO BE PRINCESS LIBERA'S KNIGHT, RIENO?
Are you commanding me as the Queen?
......

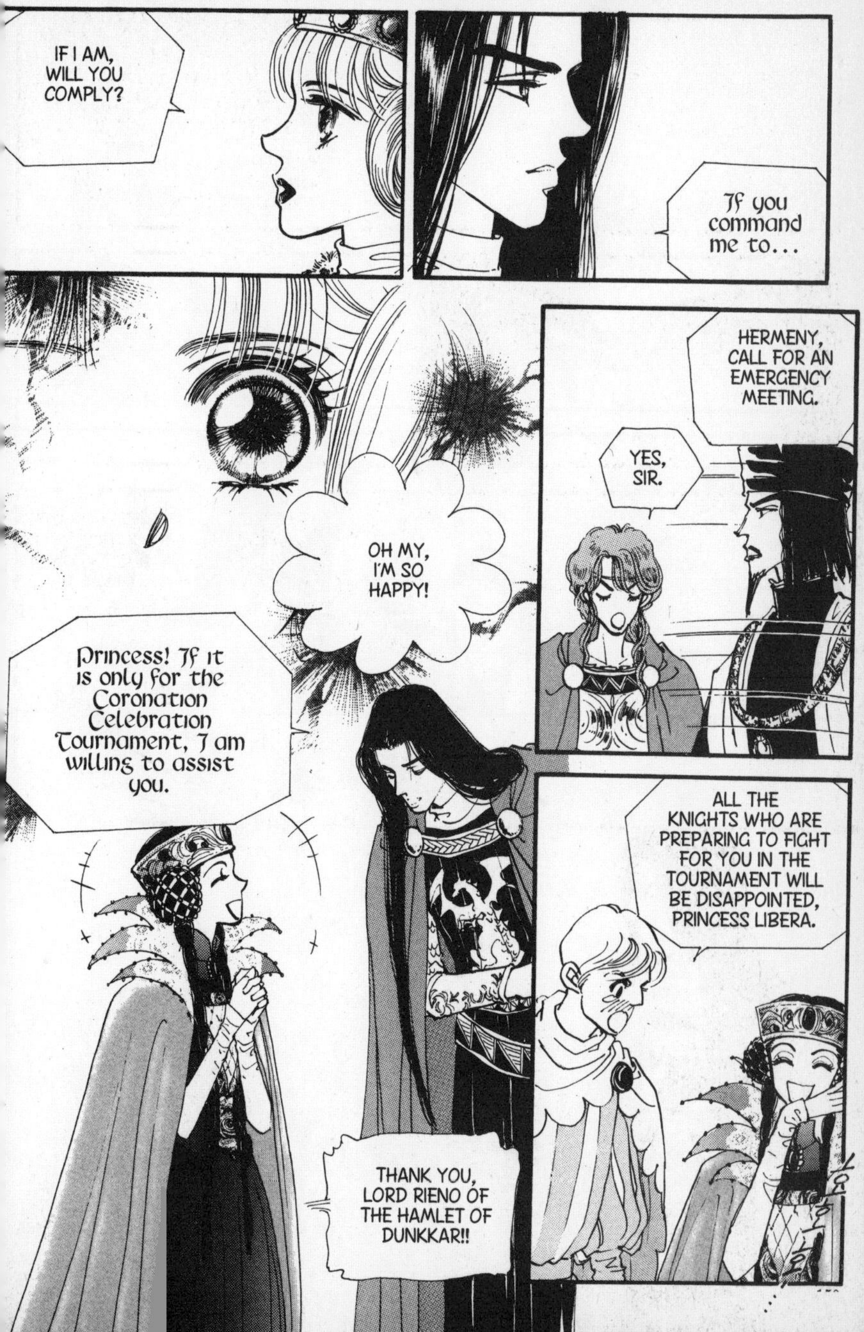
IF I AM, WILL YOU COMPLY?
If you command me to...
OH MY, I'M SO HAPPY!
Princess! If it is only for the Coronation Celebration Tournament, I am willing to assist you.
THANK YOU, LORD RIENO OF THE HAMLET OF DUNKKAR!!
HERMENY, CALL FOR AN EMERGENCY MEETING.
YES, SIR.
ALL THE KNIGHTS WHO ARE PREPARING TO FIGHT FOR YOU IN THE TOURNAMENT WILL BE DISAPPOINTED, PRINCESS LIBERA.

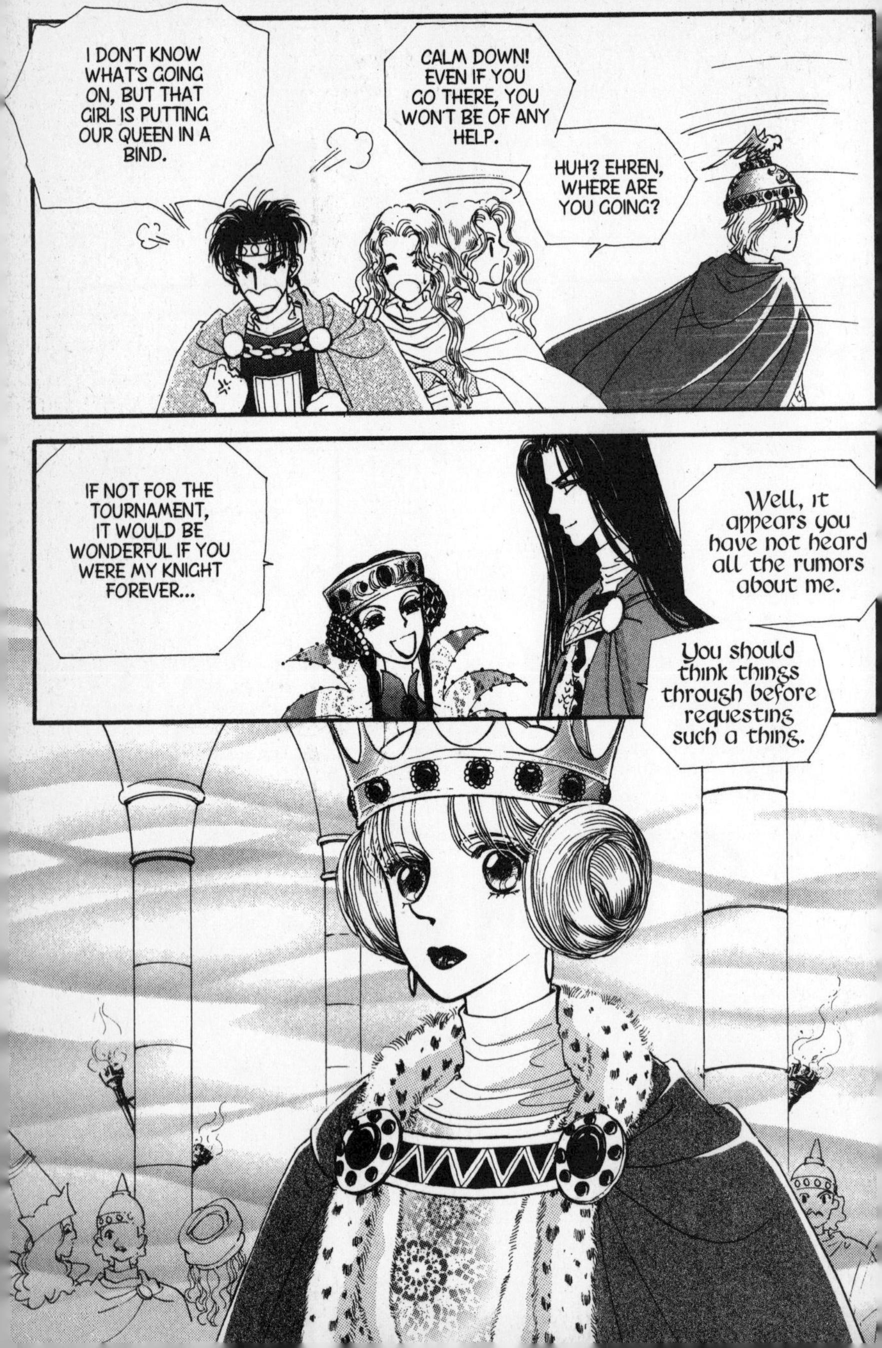
I DON'T KNOW WHAT'S GOING ON, BUT THAT GIRL IS PUTTING OUR QUEEN IN A BIND.
CALM DOWN! EVEN IF YOU GO THERE, YOU WON'T BE OF ANY HELP.
HUH? EHREN, WHERE ARE YOU GOING?
IF NOT FOR THE TOURNAMENT, IT WOULD BE WONDERFUL IF YOU WERE MY KNIGHT FOREVER...
Well, it appears you have not heard all the rumors about me.
You should think things through before requesting such a thing.

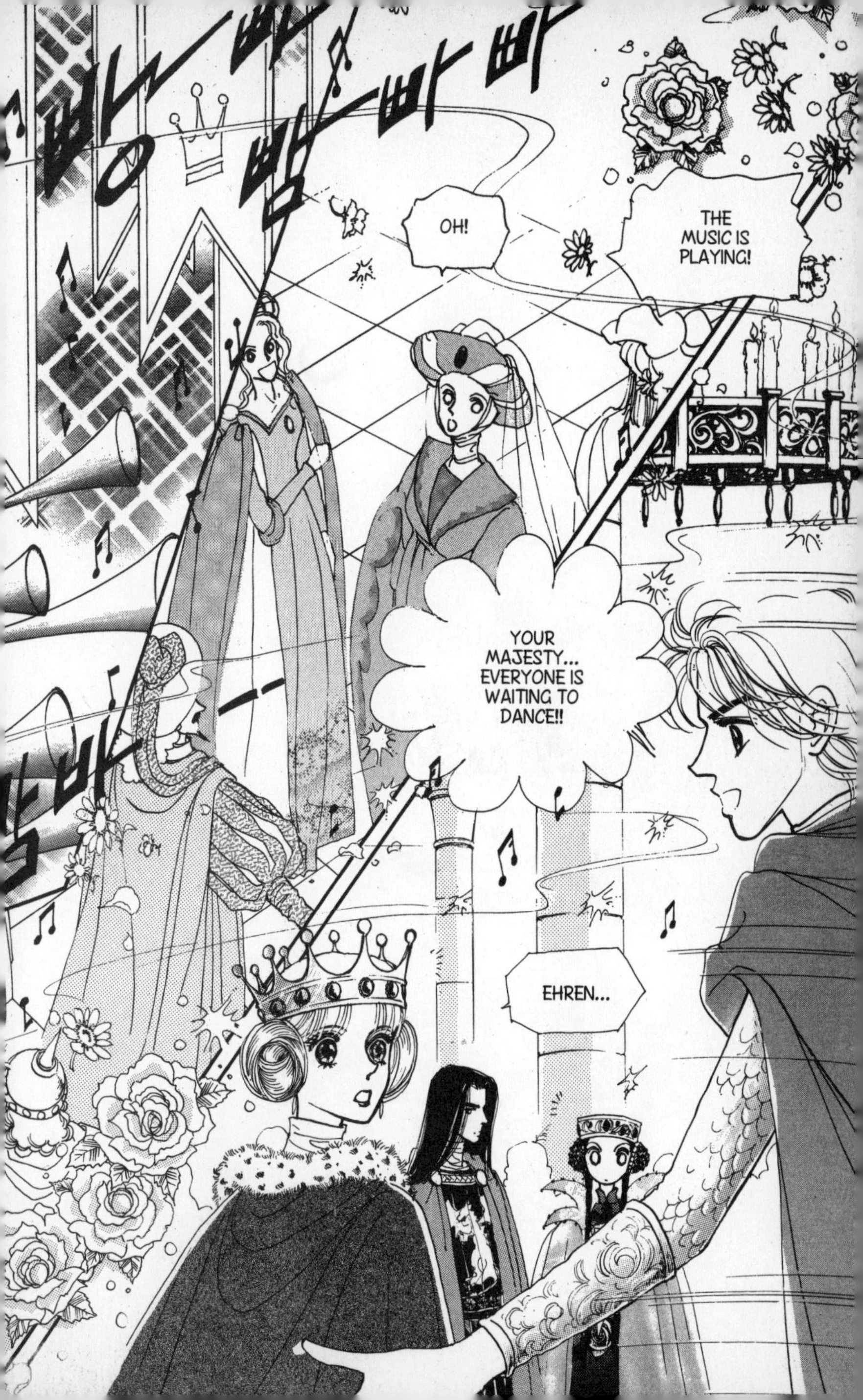
OH!
THE MUSIC IS PLAYING!
YOUR MAJESTY... EVERYONE IS WAITING TO DANCE!!
EHREN...

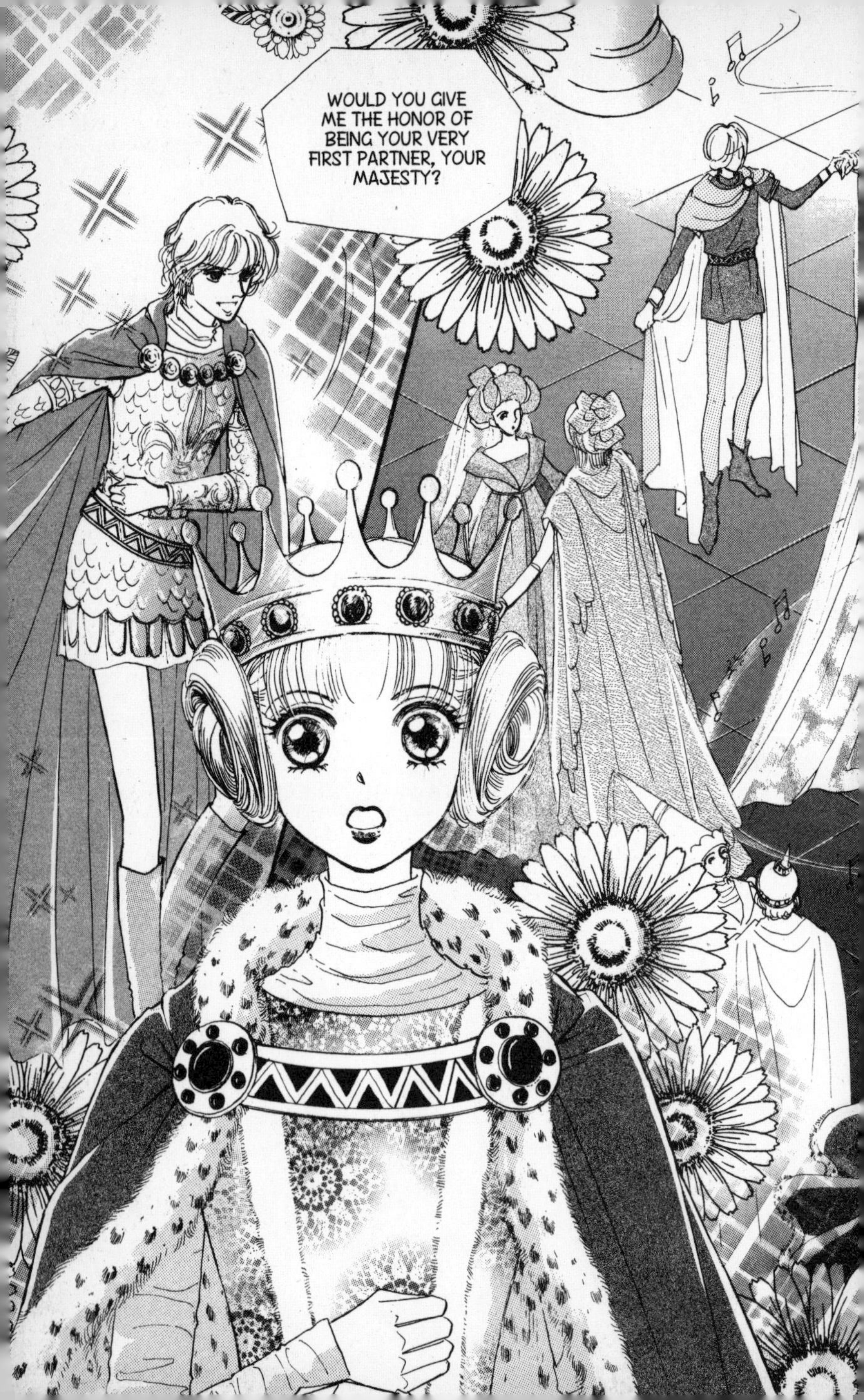
WOULD YOU GIVE ME THE HONOR OF BEING YOUR VERY FIRST PARTNER, YOUR MAJESTY?

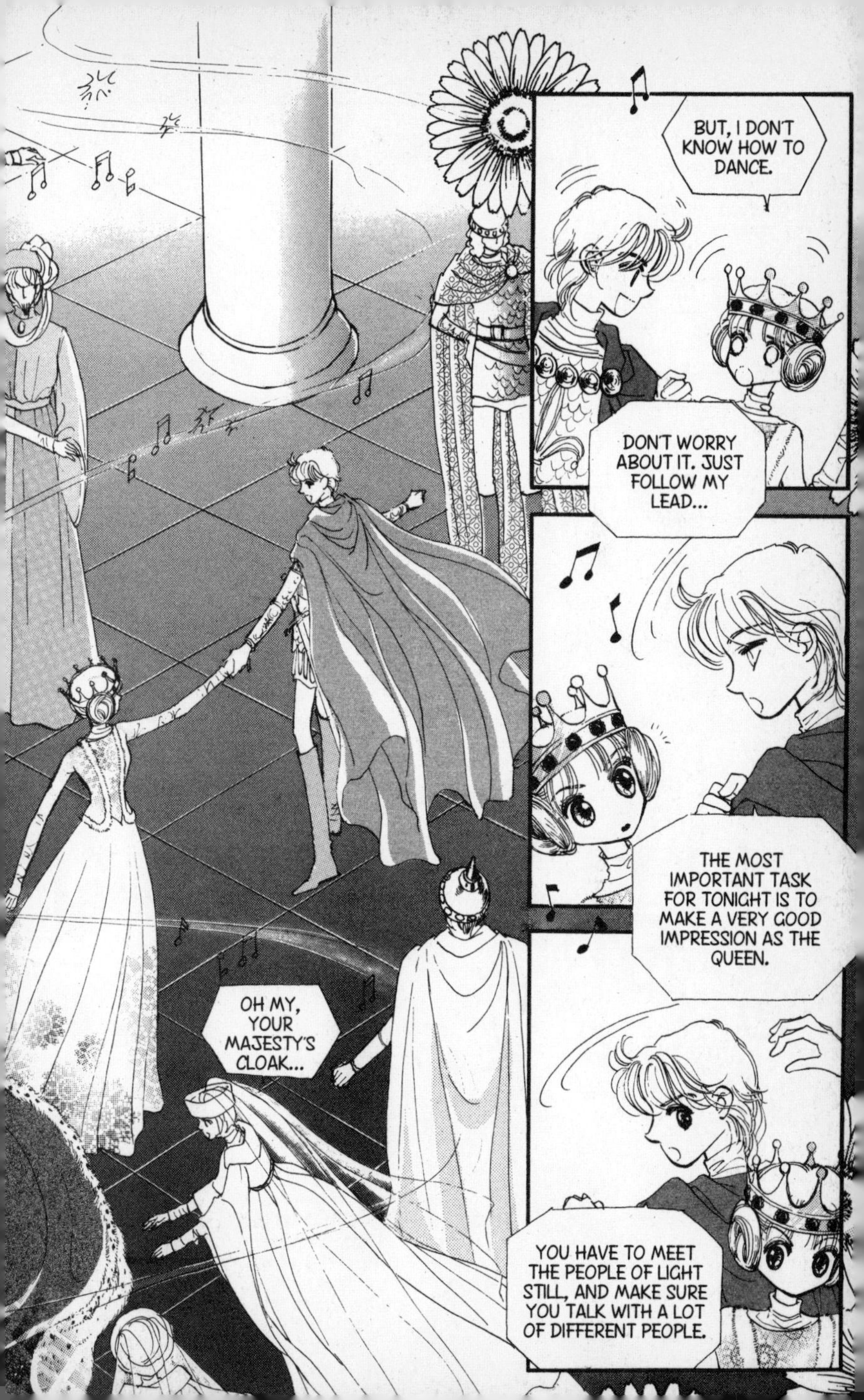
OH MY, YOUR MAJESTY'S CLOAK...
BUT, I DON'T KNOW HOW TO DANCE.
DON'T WORRY ABOUT IT. JUST FOLLOW MY LEAD...
THE MOST IMPORTANT TASK FOR TONIGHT IS TO MAKE A VERY GOOD IMPRESSION AS THE QUEEN.
YOU HAVE TO MEET THE PEOPLE OF LIGHT STILL, AND MAKE SURE YOU TALK WITH A LOT OF DIFFERENT PEOPLE.

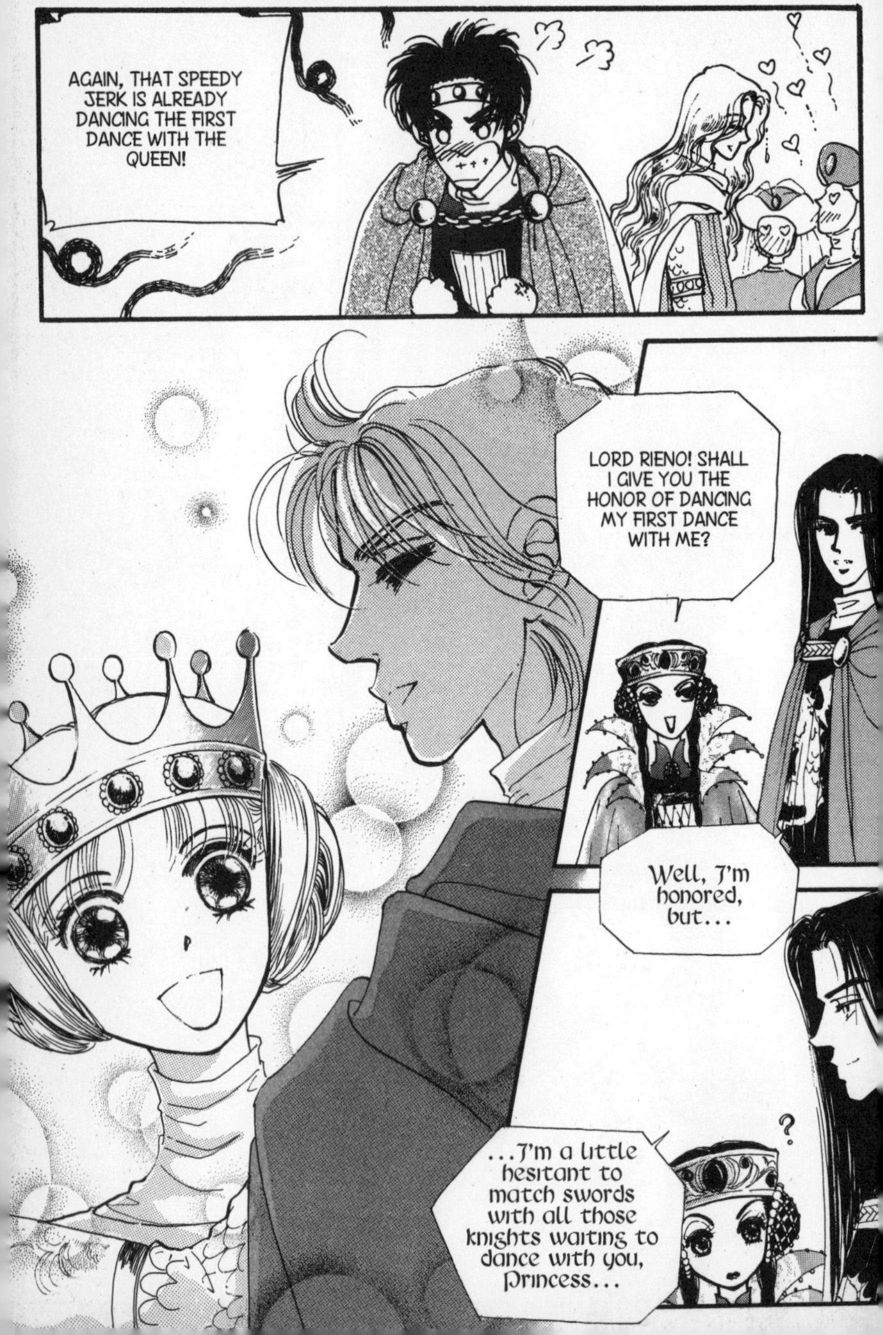
AGAIN, THAT SPEEDY JERK IS ALREADY DANCING THE FIRST DANCE WITH THE QUEEN!
LORD RIENO! SHALL I GIVE YOU THE HONOR OF DANCING MY FIRST DANCE WITH ME?
Well, I'm honored, but...
...I'm a little hesitant to match swords with all those knights waiting to dance with you, Princess...
?

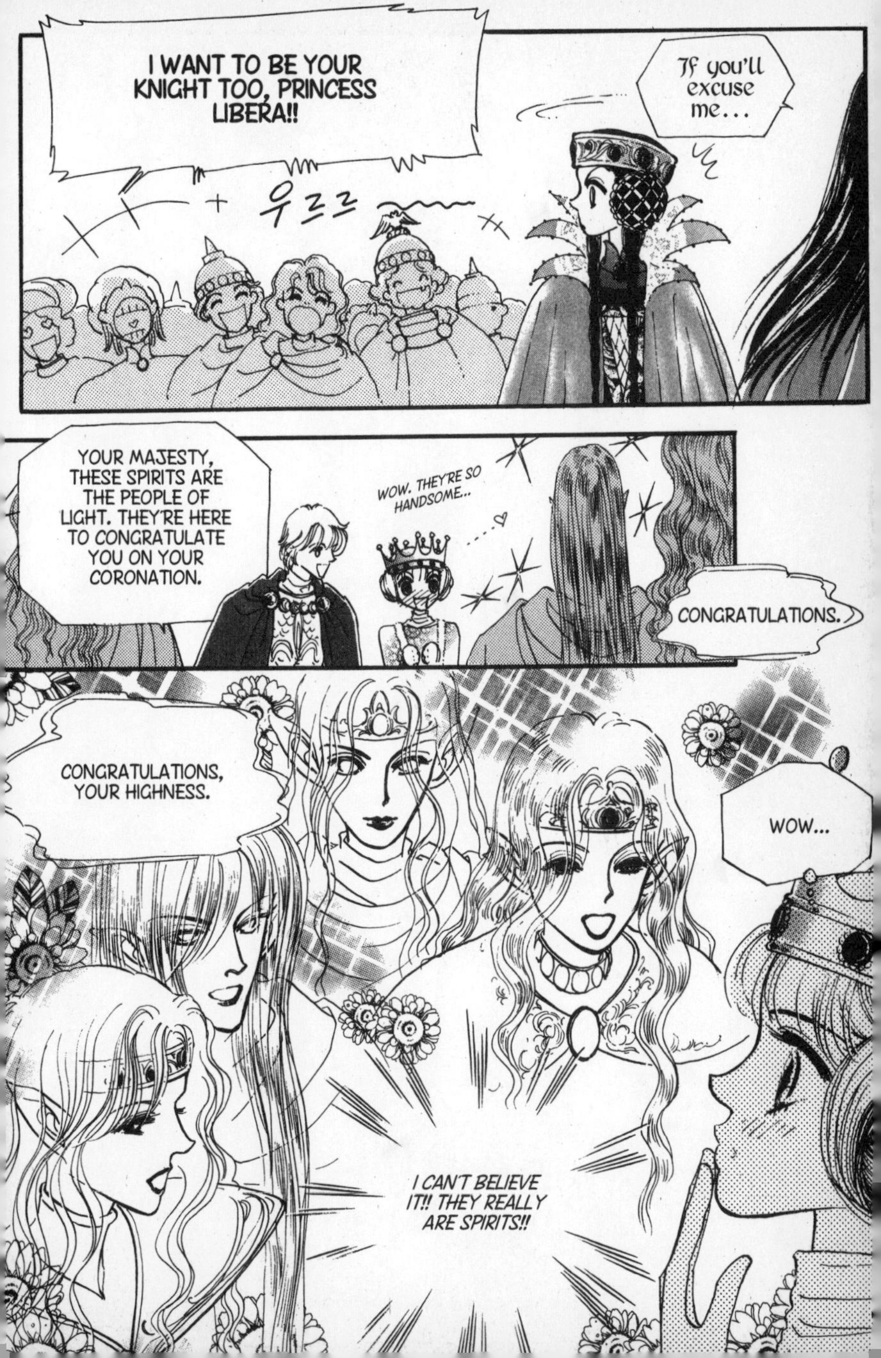
I WANT TO BE YOUR KNIGHT TOO, PRINCESS LIBERA!!
우르르
If you'll excuse me...
YOUR MAJESTY, THESE SPIRITS ARE THE PEOPLE OF LIGHT. THEY'RE HERE TO CONGRATULATE YOU ON YOUR CORONATION.
WOW. THEY'RE SO HANDSOME...
CONGRATULATIONS.
CONGRATULATIONS, YOUR HIGHNESS.
WOW...
I CAN'T BELIEVE IT!! THEY REALLY ARE SPIRITS!!

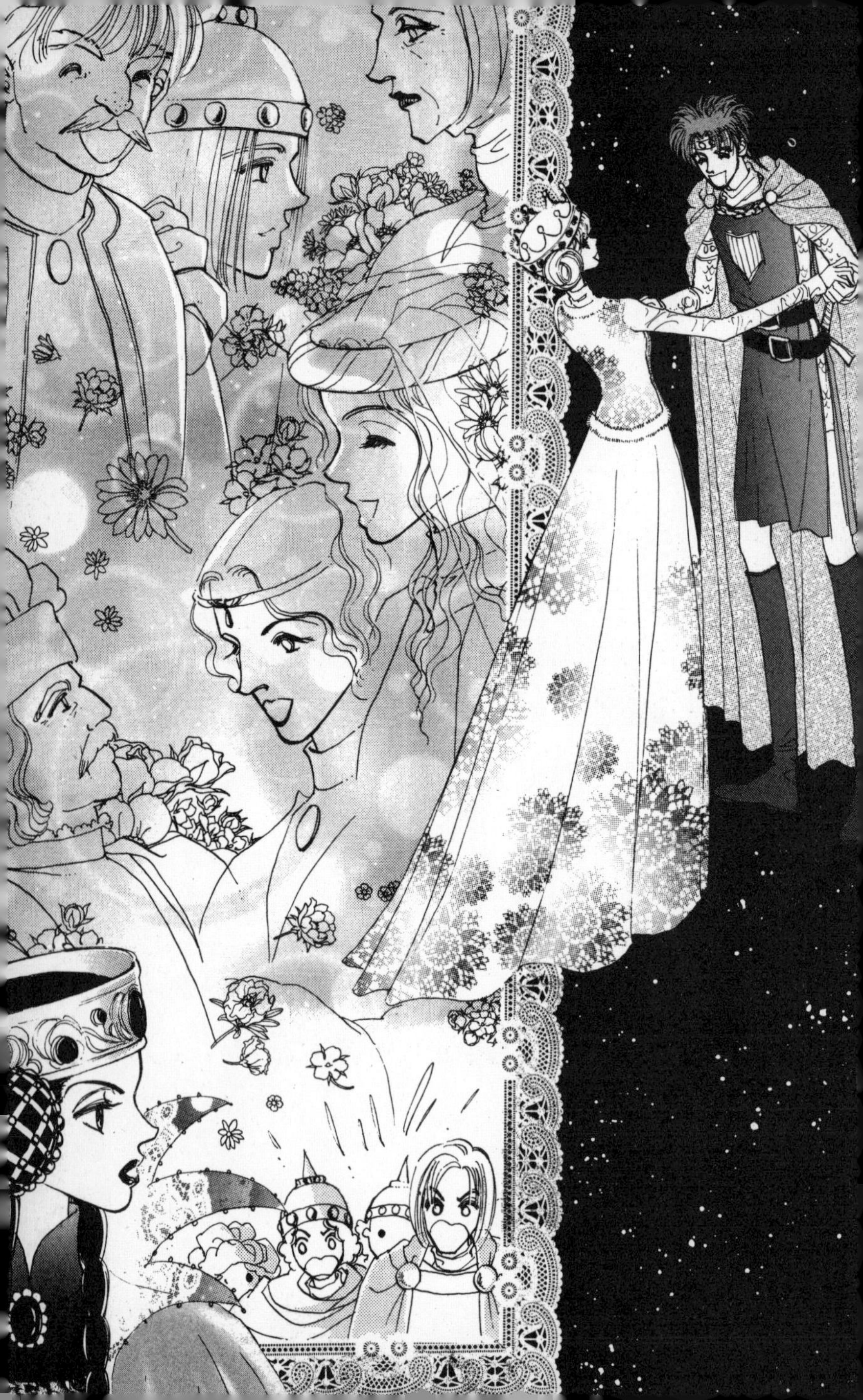

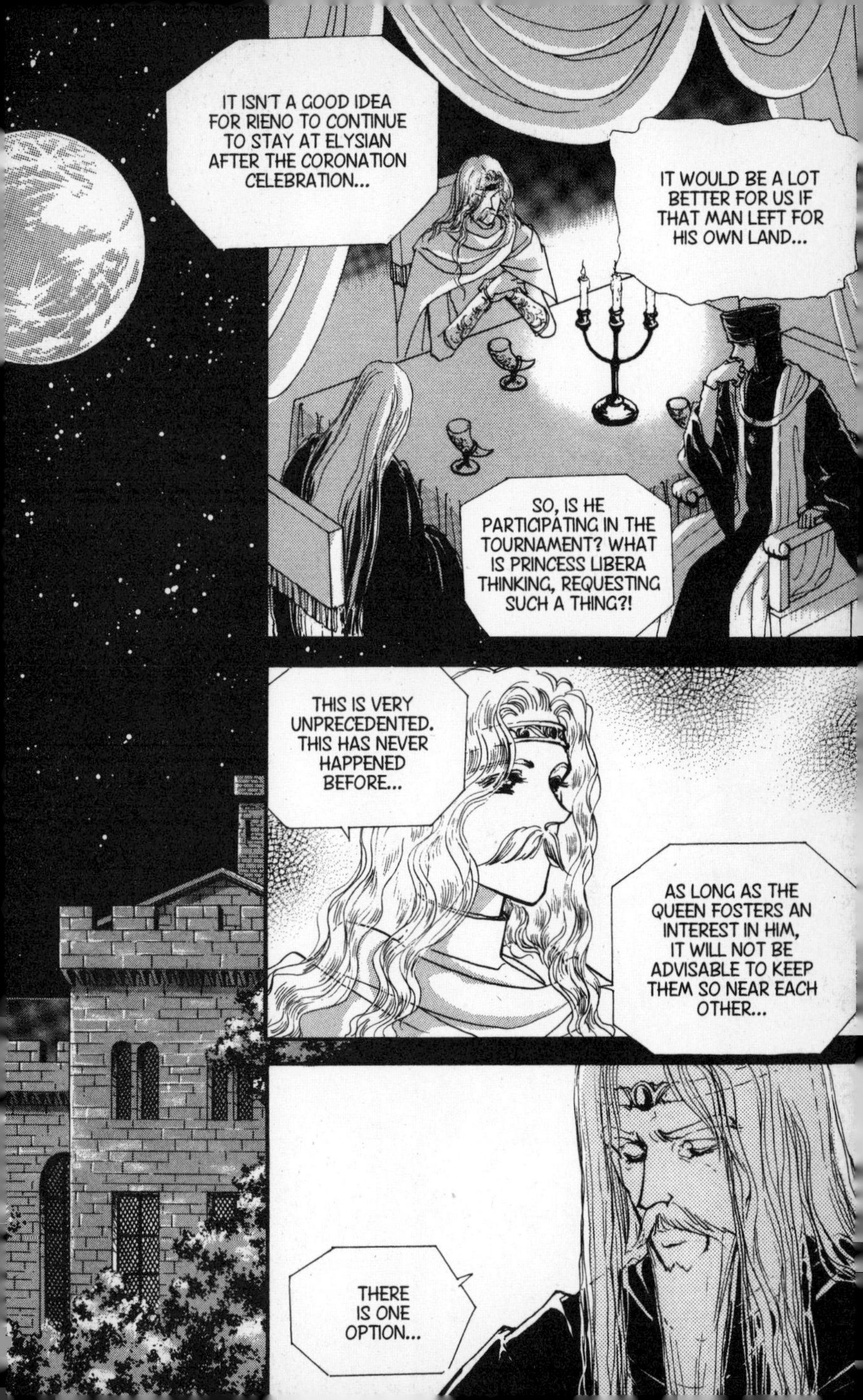
IT ISN'T A GOOD IDEA FOR RIENO TO CONTINUE TO STAY AT ELYSIAN AFTER THE CORONATION CELEBRATION...
IT WOULD BE A LOT BETTER FOR US IF THAT MAN LEFT FOR HIS OWN LAND...
SO, IS HE PARTICIPATING IN THE TOURNAMENT? WHAT IS PRINCESS LIBERA THINKING, REQUESTING SUCH A THING?!
THIS IS VERY UNPRECEDENTED. THIS HAS NEVER HAPPENED BEFORE...
AS LONG AS THE QUEEN FOSTERS AN INTEREST IN HIM, IT WILL NOT BE ADVISABLE TO KEEP THEM SO NEAR EACH OTHER...
THERE IS ONE OPTION...

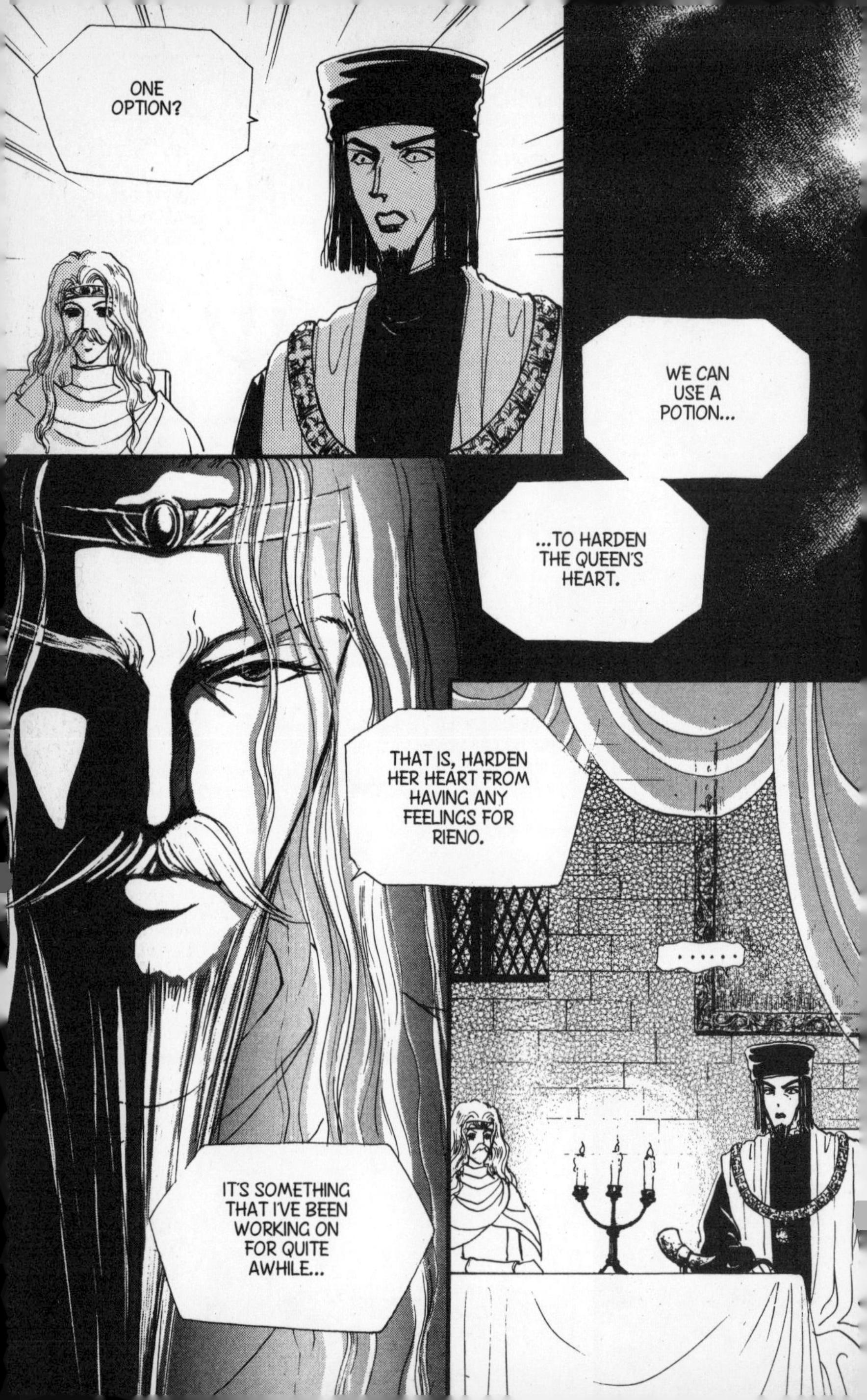
ONE OPTION?
WE CAN USE A POTION...
...TO HARDEN THE QUEEN'S HEART.
IT'S SOMETHING THAT I'VE BEEN WORKING ON FOR QUITE AWHILE...
THAT IS, HARDEN HER HEART FROM HAVING ANY FEELINGS FOR RIENO.
......

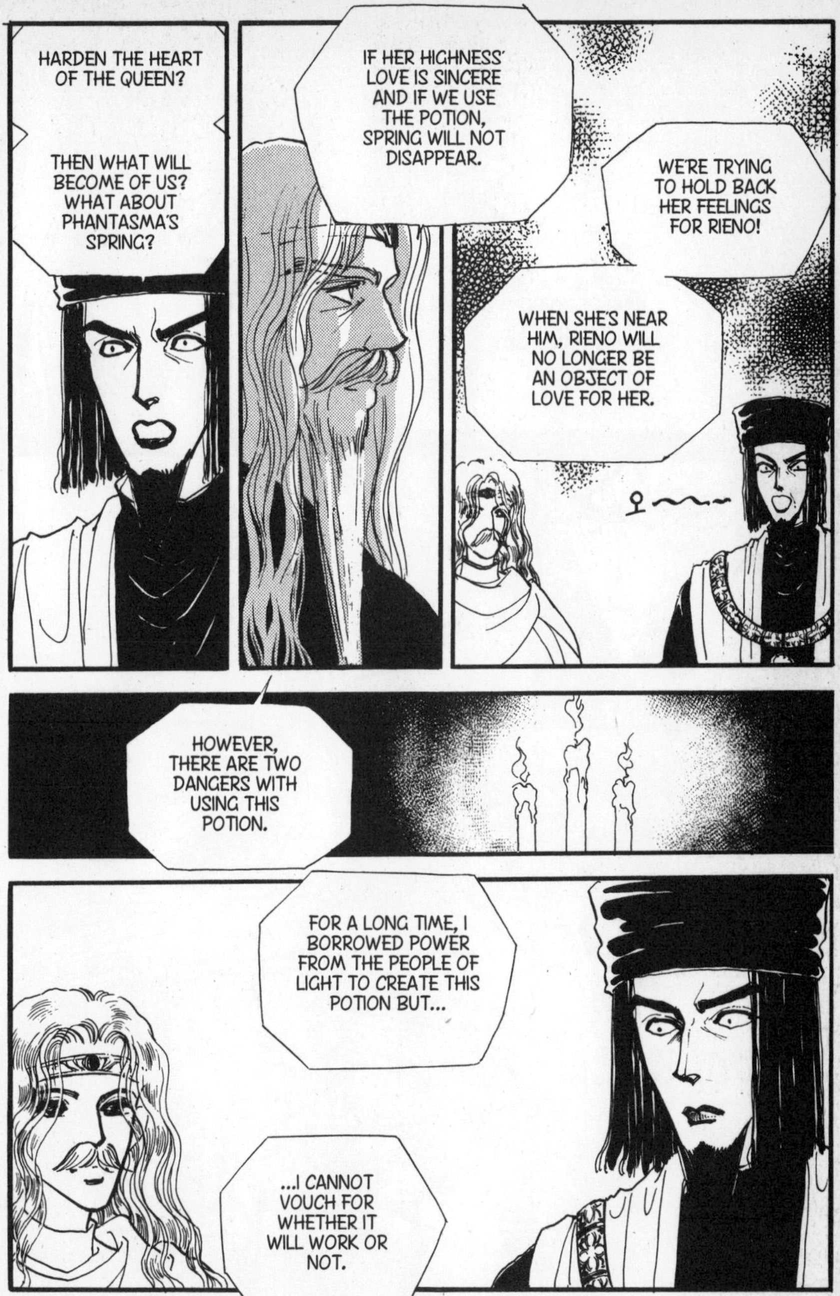
HARDEN THE HEART OF THE QUEEN?
THEN WHAT WILL BECOME OF US? WHAT ABOUT PHANTASMA'S SPRING?
IF HER HIGHNESS' LOVE IS SINCERE AND IF WE USE THE POTION, SPRING WILL NOT DISAPPEAR.
WE'RE TRYING TO HOLD BACK HER FEELINGS FOR RIENO!
WHEN SHE'S NEAR HIM, RIENO WILL NO LONGER BE AN OBJECT OF LOVE FOR HER.
HOWEVER, THERE ARE TWO DANGERS WITH USING THIS POTION.
FOR A LONG TIME, I BORROWED POWER FROM THE PEOPLE OF LIGHT TO CREATE THIS POTION BUT...
...I CANNOT VOUCH FOR WHETHER IT WILL WORK OR NOT.

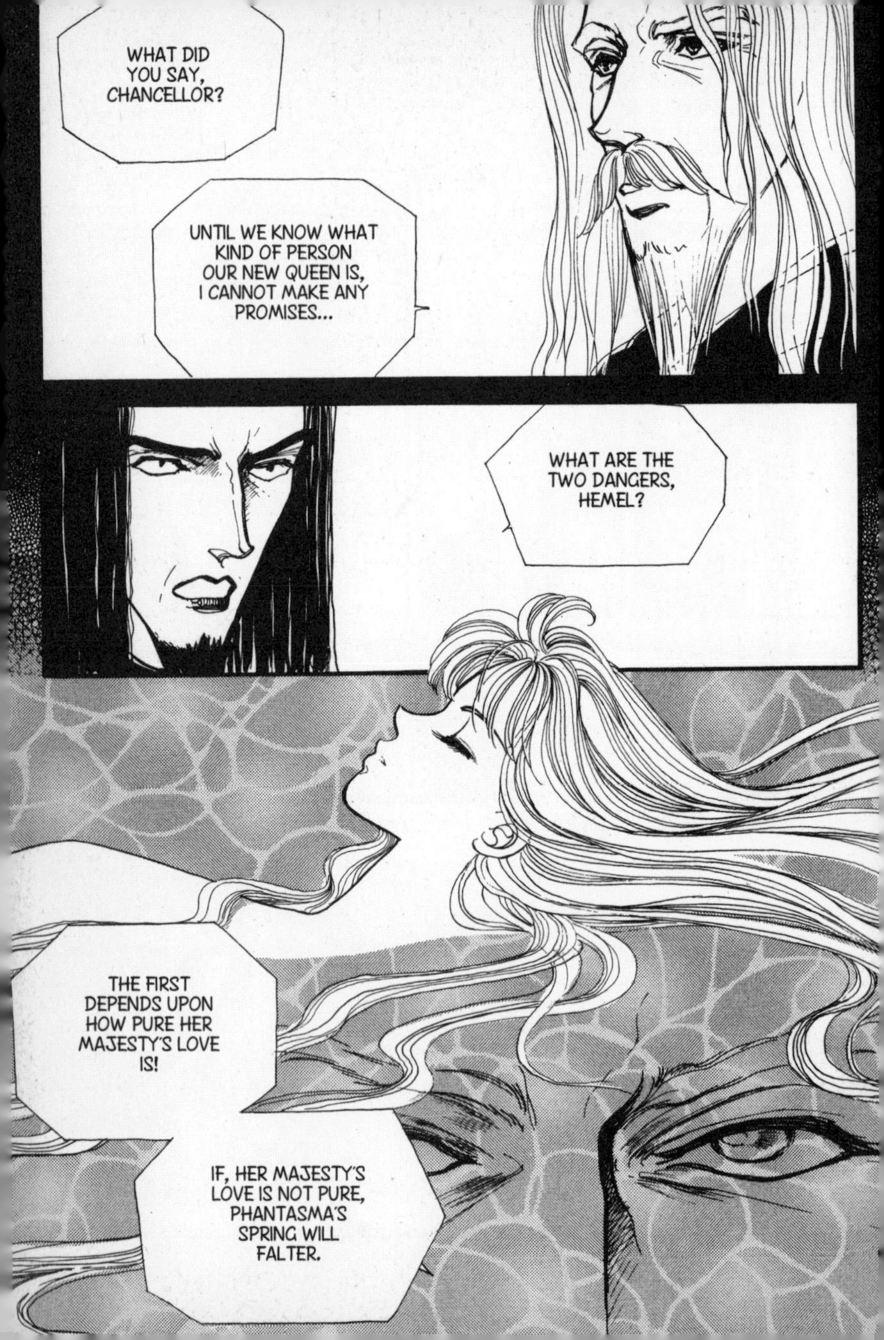
WHAT DID YOU SAY, CHANCELLOR?
UNTIL WE KNOW WHAT KIND OF PERSON OUR NEW QUEEN IS, I CANNOT MAKE ANY PROMISES...
WHAT ARE THE TWO DANGERS, HEMEL?
THE FIRST DEPENDS UPON HOW PURE HER MAJESTY'S LOVE IS!
IF, HER MAJESTY'S LOVE IS NOT PURE, PHANTASMA'S SPRING WILL FALTER.

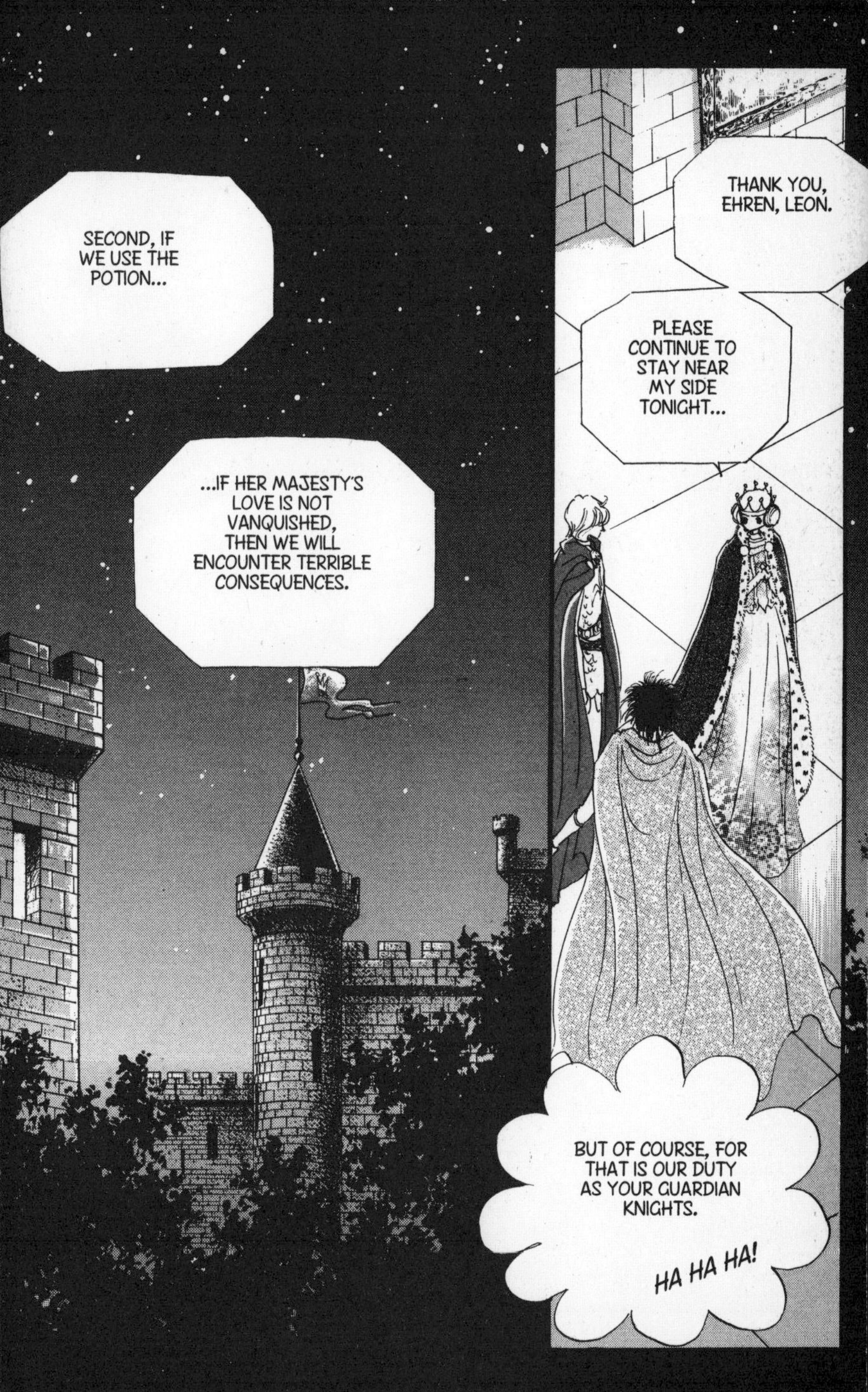
SECOND, IF WE USE THE POTION...
...IF HER MAJESTY'S LOVE IS NOT VANQUISHED, THEN WE WILL ENCOUNTER TERRIBLE CONSEQUENCES.
THANK YOU, EHREN, LEON.
PLEASE CONTINUE TO STAY NEAR MY SIDE TONIGHT...
BUT OF COURSE, FOR THAT IS OUR DUTY AS YOUR GUARDIAN KNIGHTS.
HA HA HA!

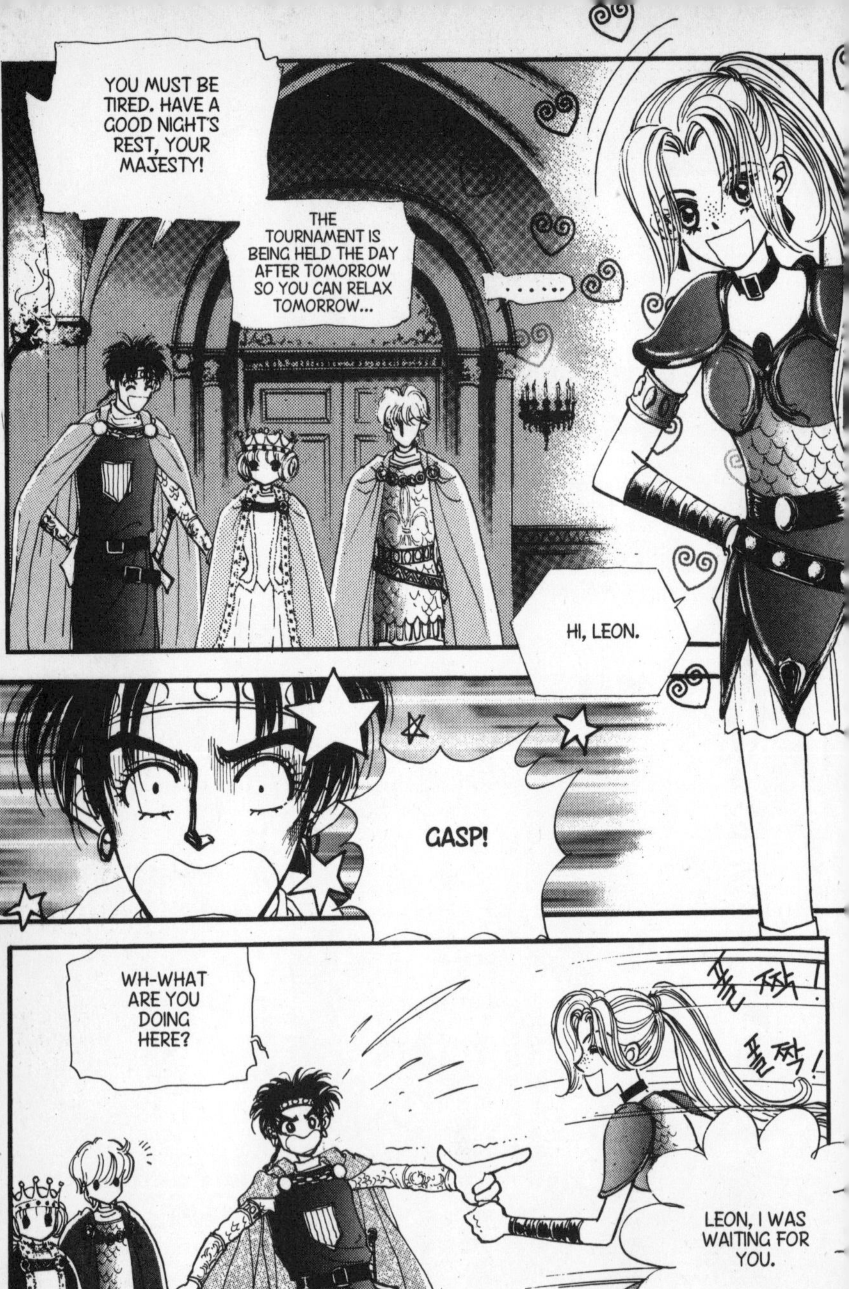
YOU MUST BE TIRED. HAVE A GOOD NIGHT'S REST, YOUR MAJESTY!
THE TOURNAMENT IS BEING HELD THE DAY AFTER TOMORROW SO YOU CAN RELAX TOMORROW...
......
HI, LEON.
GASP!
WH-WHAT ARE YOU DOING HERE?
LEON, I WAS WAITING FOR YOU.

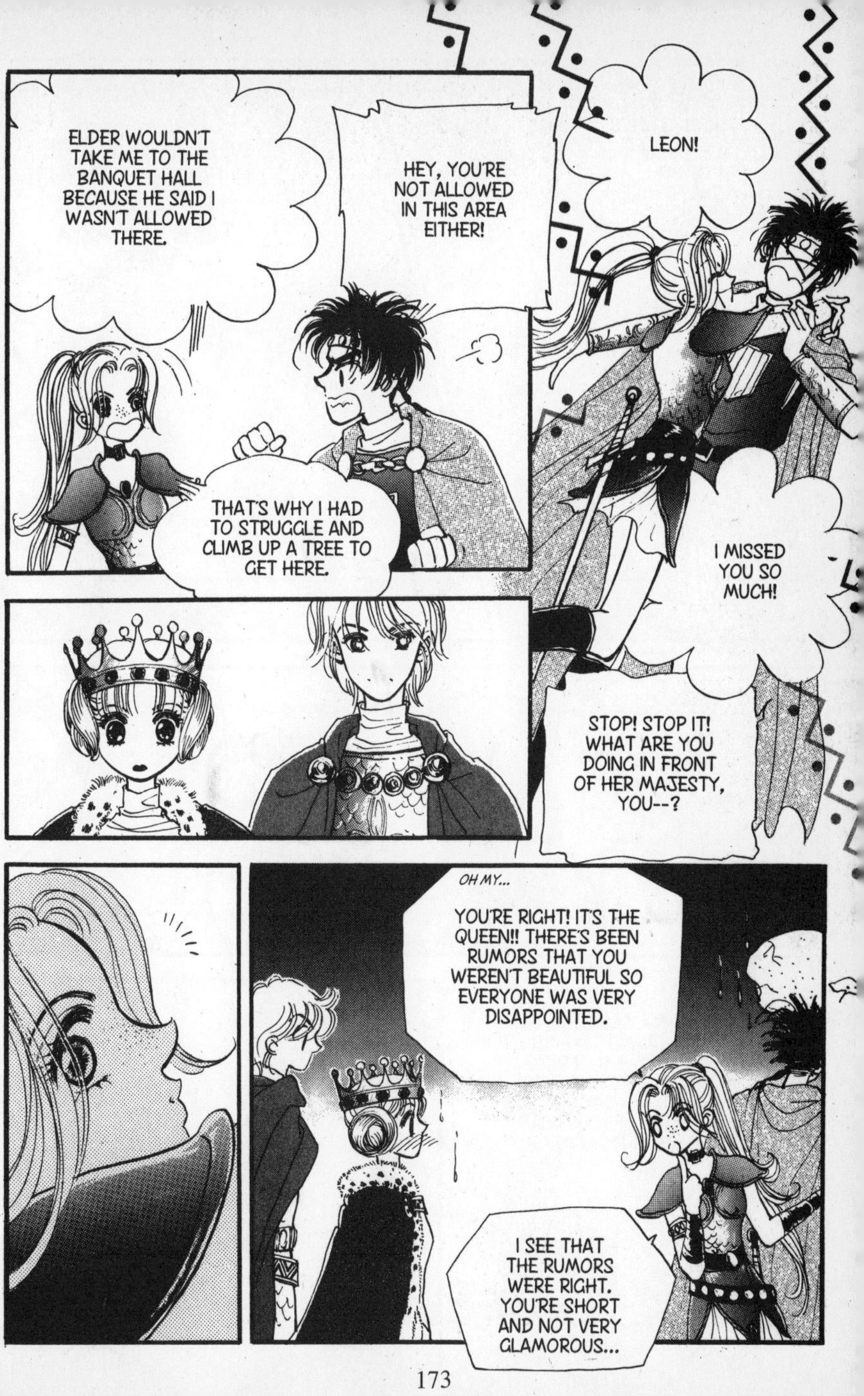

ELDER WOULDN'T TAKE ME TO THE BANQUET HALL BECAUSE HE SAID I WASN'T ALLOWED THERE.
HEY, YOU'RE NOT ALLOWED IN THIS AREA EITHER!
THAT'S WHY I HAD TO STRUGGLE AND CLIMB UP A TREE TO GET HERE.
LEON!
I MISSED YOU SO MUCH!
STOP! STOP IT! WHAT ARE YOU DOING IN FRONT OF HER MAJESTY, YOU--?
OH MY...
YOU'RE RIGHT! IT'S THE QUEEN!! THERE'S BEEN RUMORS THAT YOU WEREN'T BEAUTIFUL SO EVERYONE WAS VERY DISAPPOINTED.
I SEE THAT THE RUMORS WERE RIGHT. YOU'RE SHORT AND NOT VERY GLAMOROUS...

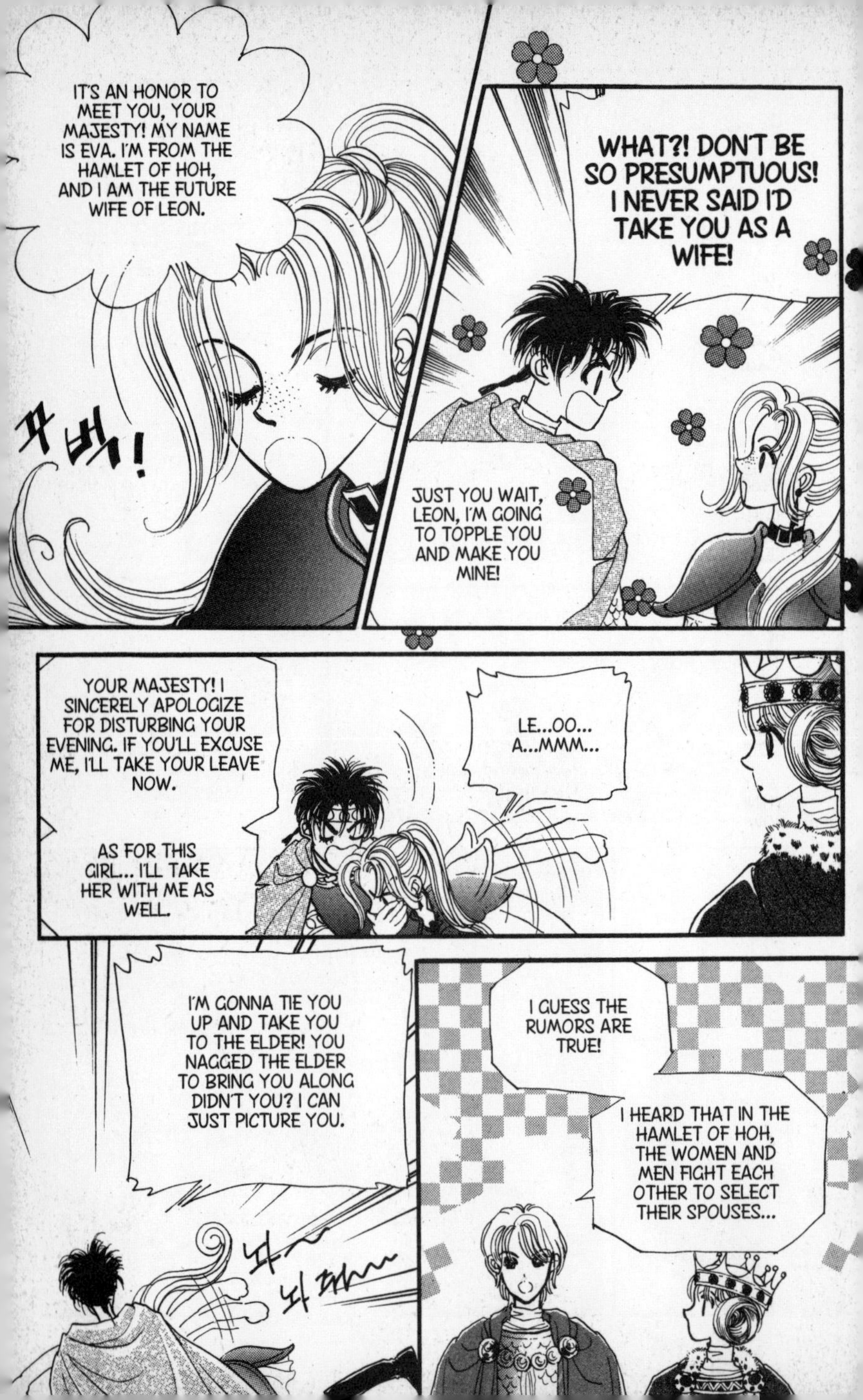
IT'S AN HONOR TO MEET YOU, YOUR MAJESTY! MY NAME IS EVA. I'M FROM THE HAMLET OF HOH, AND I AM THE FUTURE WIFE OF LEON.
WHAT?! DON'T BE SO PRESUMPTUOUS! I NEVER SAID I'D TAKE YOU AS A WIFE!
JUST YOU WAIT, LEON, I'M GOING TO TOPPLE YOU AND MAKE YOU MINE!
YOUR MAJESTY! I SINCERELY APOLOGIZE FOR DISTURBING YOUR EVENING. IF YOU'LL EXCUSE ME, I'LL TAKE YOUR LEAVE NOW.
AS FOR THIS GIRL... I'LL TAKE HER WITH ME AS WELL.
LE...OO... A...MMM...
I'M GONNA TIE YOU UP AND TAKE YOU TO THE ELDER! YOU NAGGED THE ELDER TO BRING YOU ALONG DIDN'T YOU? I CAN JUST PICTURE YOU.
I GUESS THE RUMORS ARE TRUE!
I HEARD THAT IN THE HAMLET OF HOH, THE WOMEN AND MEN FIGHT EACH OTHER TO SELECT THEIR SPOUSES...

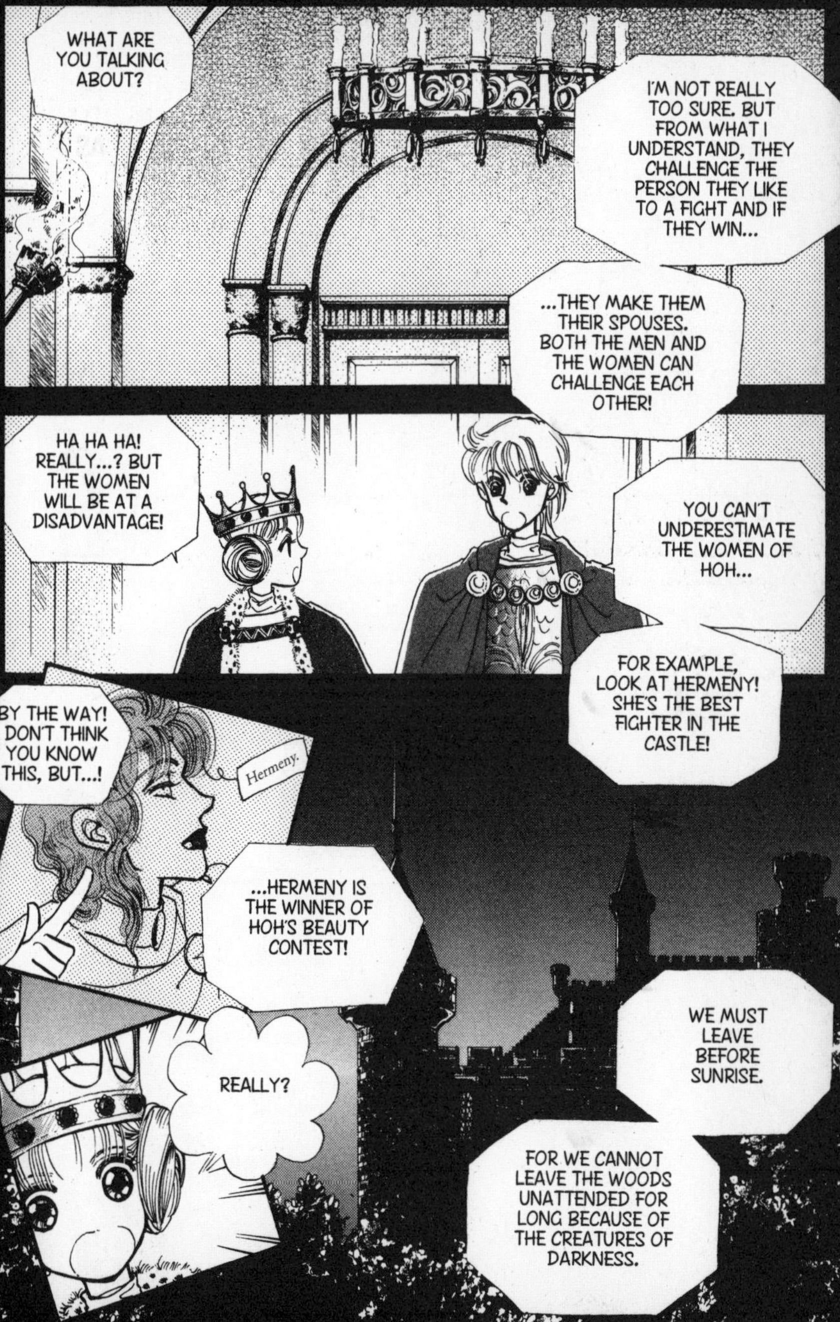
WHAT ARE YOU TALKING ABOUT?
I'M NOT REALLY TOO SURE. BUT FROM WHAT I UNDERSTAND, THEY CHALLENGE THE PERSON THEY LIKE TO A FIGHT AND IF THEY WIN...
...THEY MAKE THEM THEIR SPOUSES. BOTH THE MEN AND THE WOMEN CAN CHALLENGE EACH OTHER!
HA HA HA! REALLY...? BUT THE WOMEN WILL BE AT A DISADVANTAGE!
YOU CAN'T UNDERESTIMATE THE WOMEN OF HOH...
FOR EXAMPLE, LOOK AT HERMENY! SHE'S THE BEST FIGHTER IN THE CASTLE!
BY THE WAY! I DON'T THINK YOU KNOW THIS, BUT...!
Hermeny.
...HERMENY IS THE WINNER OF HOH'S BEAUTY CONTEST!
REALLY?
WE MUST LEAVE BEFORE SUNRISE.
FOR WE CANNOT LEAVE THE WOODS UNATTENDED FOR LONG BECAUSE OF THE CREATURES OF DARKNESS.

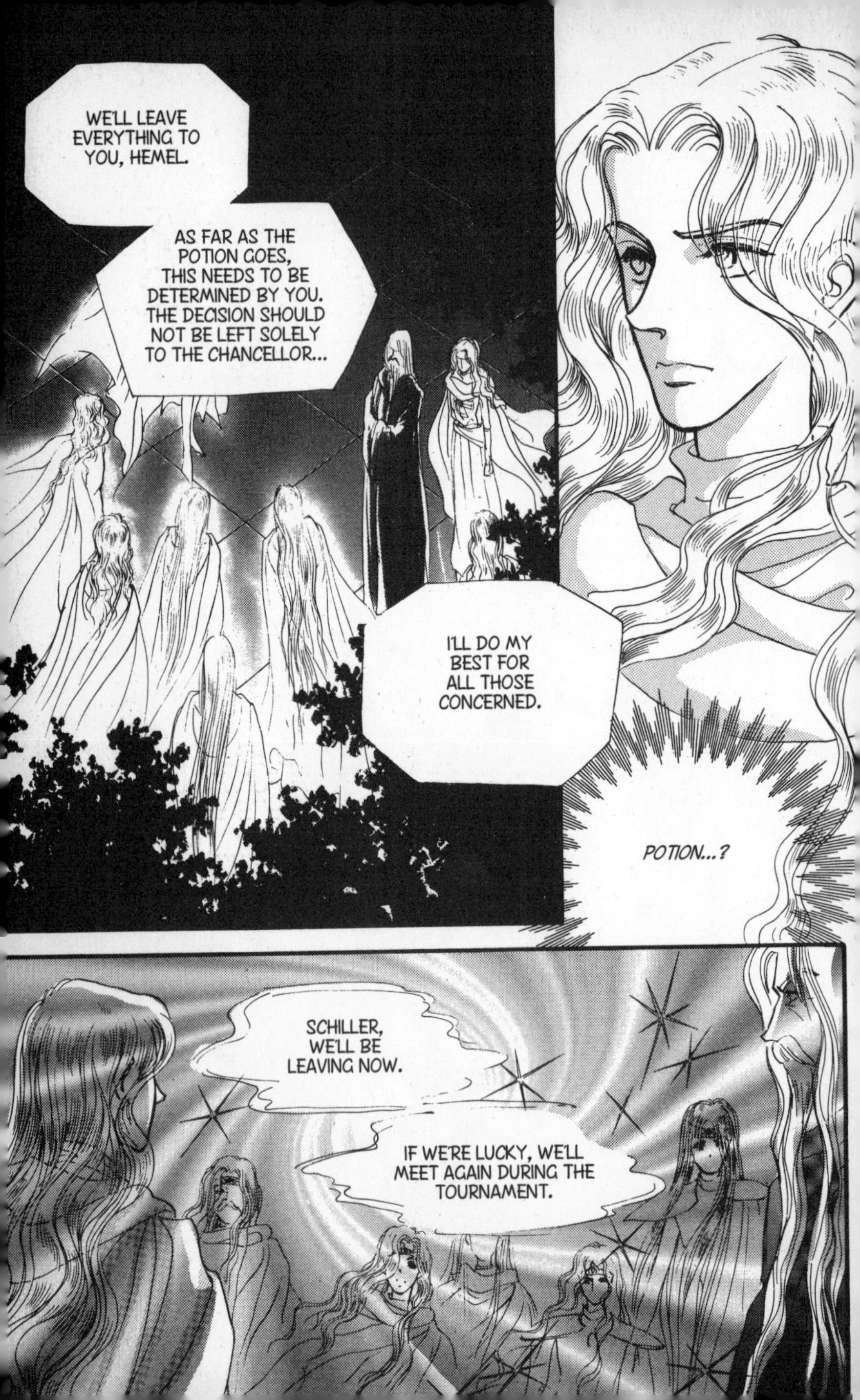
WE'LL LEAVE EVERYTHING TO YOU, HEMEL.
AS FAR AS THE POTION GOES, THIS NEEDS TO BE DETERMINED BY YOU. THE DECISION SHOULD NOT BE LEFT SOLELY TO THE CHANCELLOR...
I'LL DO MY BEST FOR ALL THOSE CONCERNED.
POTION...?
SCHILLER, WE'LL BE LEAVING NOW.
IF WE'RE LUCKY, WE'LL MEET AGAIN DURING THE TOURNAMENT.

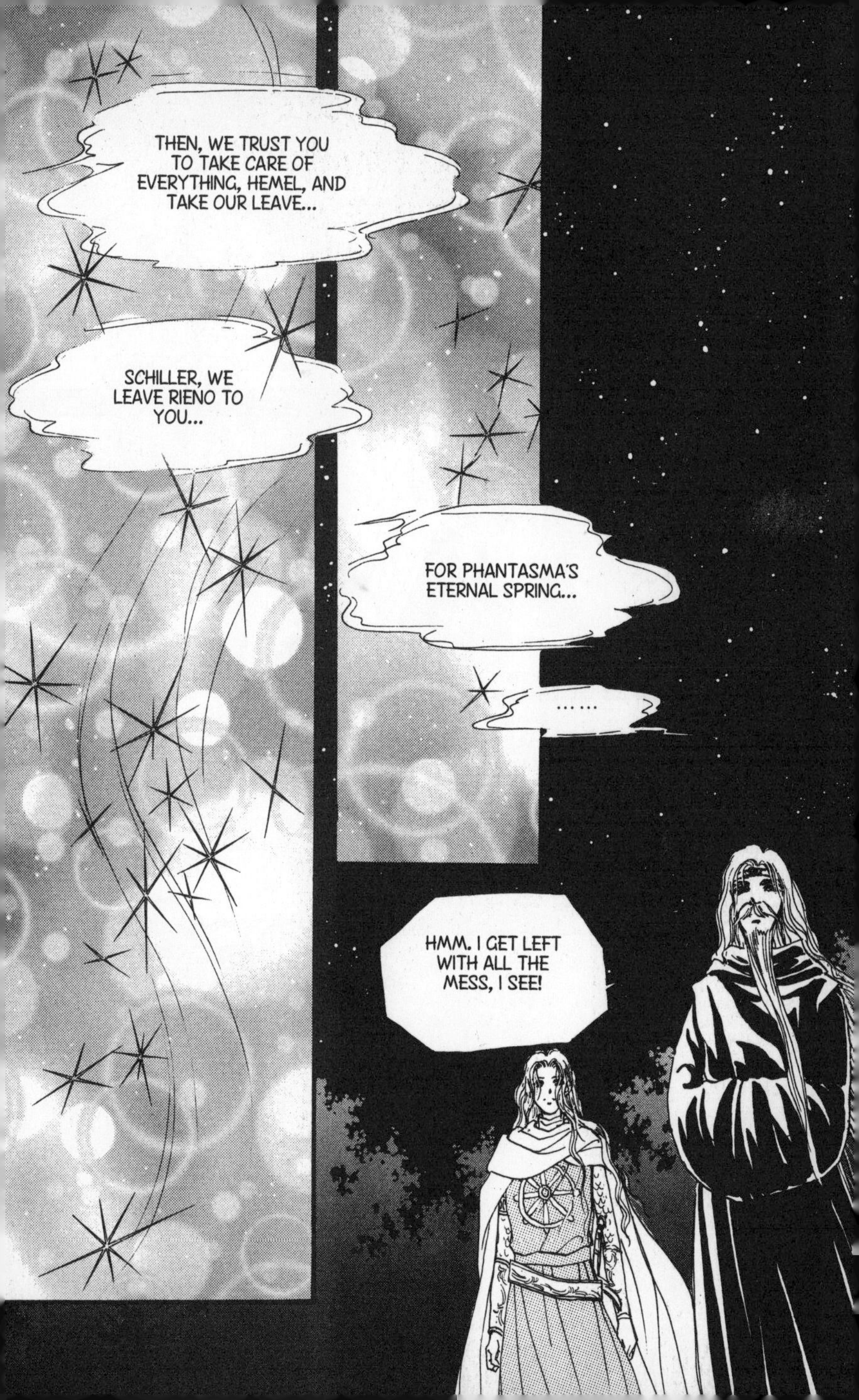
THEN, WE TRUST YOU TO TAKE CARE OF EVERYTHING, HEMEL, AND TAKE OUR LEAVE...
SCHILLER, WE LEAVE RIENO TO YOU...
FOR PHANTASMA'S ETERNAL SPRING...
......
HMM. I GET LEFT WITH ALL THE MESS, I SEE!

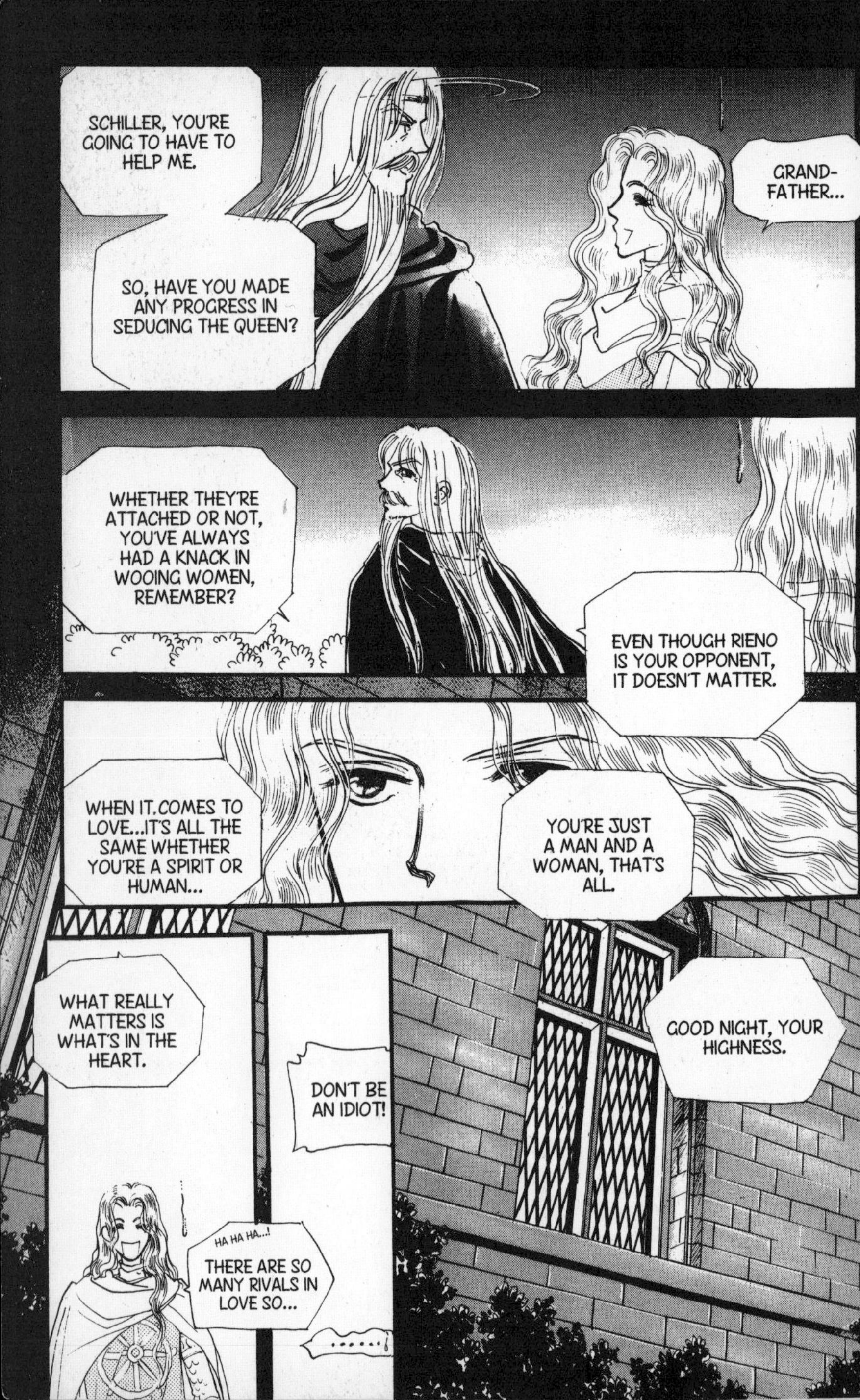
SCHILLER, YOU'RE GOING TO HAVE TO HELP ME.
SO, HAVE YOU MADE ANY PROGRESS IN SEDUCING THE QUEEN?
GRAND-FATHER...
WHETHER THEY'RE ATTACHED OR NOT, YOU'VE ALWAYS HAD A KNACK IN WOOING WOMEN, REMEMBER?
EVEN THOUGH RIENO IS YOUR OPPONENT, IT DOESN'T MATTER.
WHEN IT COMES TO LOVE...IT'S ALL THE SAME WHETHER YOU'RE A SPIRIT OR HUMAN...
YOU'RE JUST A MAN AND A WOMAN, THAT'S ALL.
WHAT REALLY MATTERS IS WHAT'S IN THE HEART.
DON'T BE AN IDIOT!
HA HA HA...!
THERE ARE SO MANY RIVALS IN LOVE SO...
......
GOOD NIGHT, YOUR HIGHNESS.

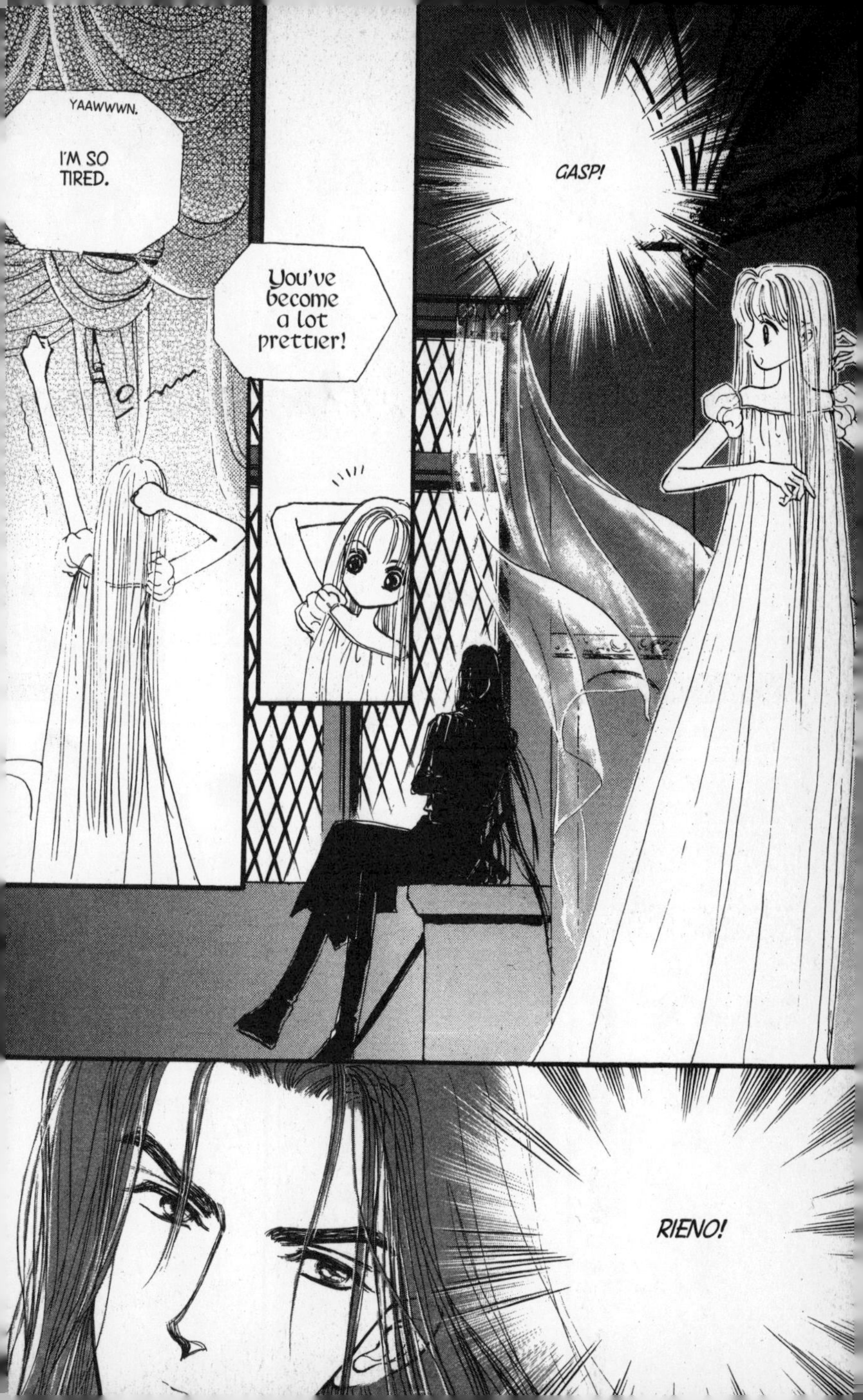
YAAWWWN.
I'M SO TIRED.
You've become a lot prettier!
GASP!
RIENO!

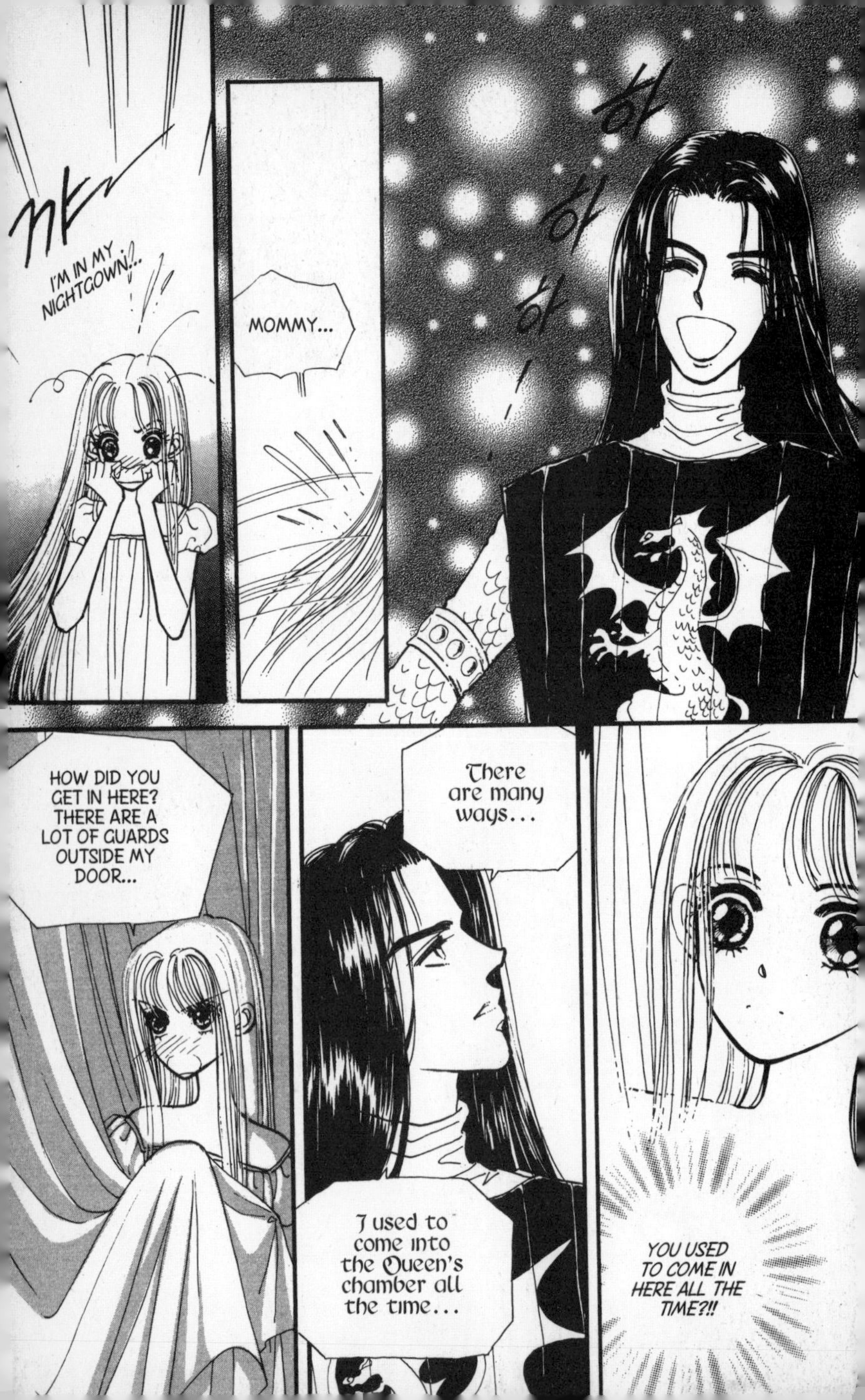

카~
I'M IN MY NIGHTGOWN!?..
MOMMY...
하하하하!
HOW DID YOU GET IN HERE? THERE ARE A LOT OF GUARDS OUTSIDE MY DOOR...
There are many ways...
I used to come into the Queen's chamber all the time...
YOU USED TO COME IN HERE ALL THE TIME?!!

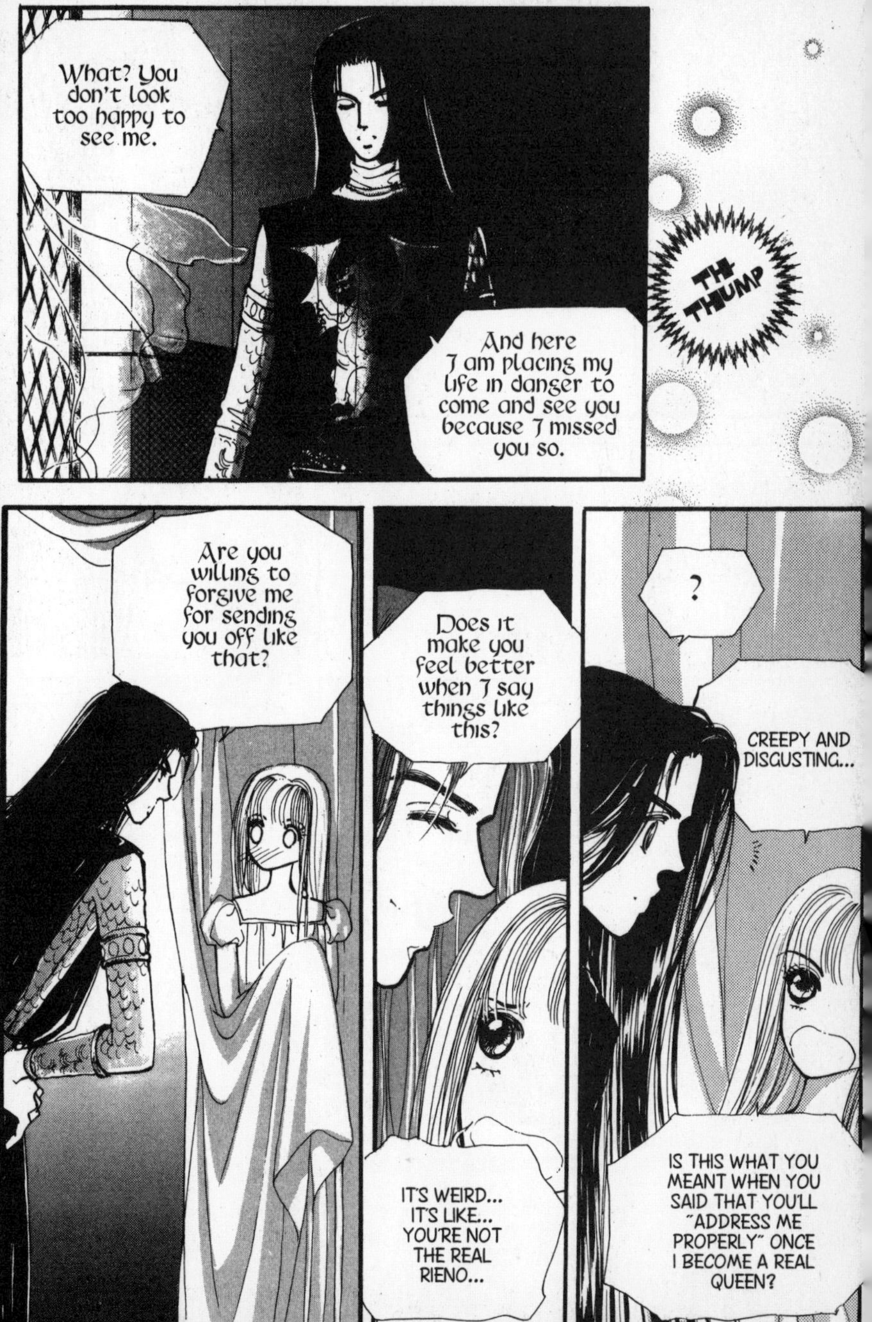
What? You don't look too happy to see me.
And here I am placing my life in danger to come and see you because I missed you so.
TH THUMP
Are you willing to forgive me for sending you off like that?
Does it make you feel better when I say things like this?
IT'S WEIRD... IT'S LIKE... YOU'RE NOT THE REAL RIENO...
?
CREEPY AND DISGUSTING...
IS THIS WHAT YOU MEANT WHEN YOU SAID THAT YOU'LL "ADDRESS ME PROPERLY" ONCE I BECOME A REAL QUEEN?

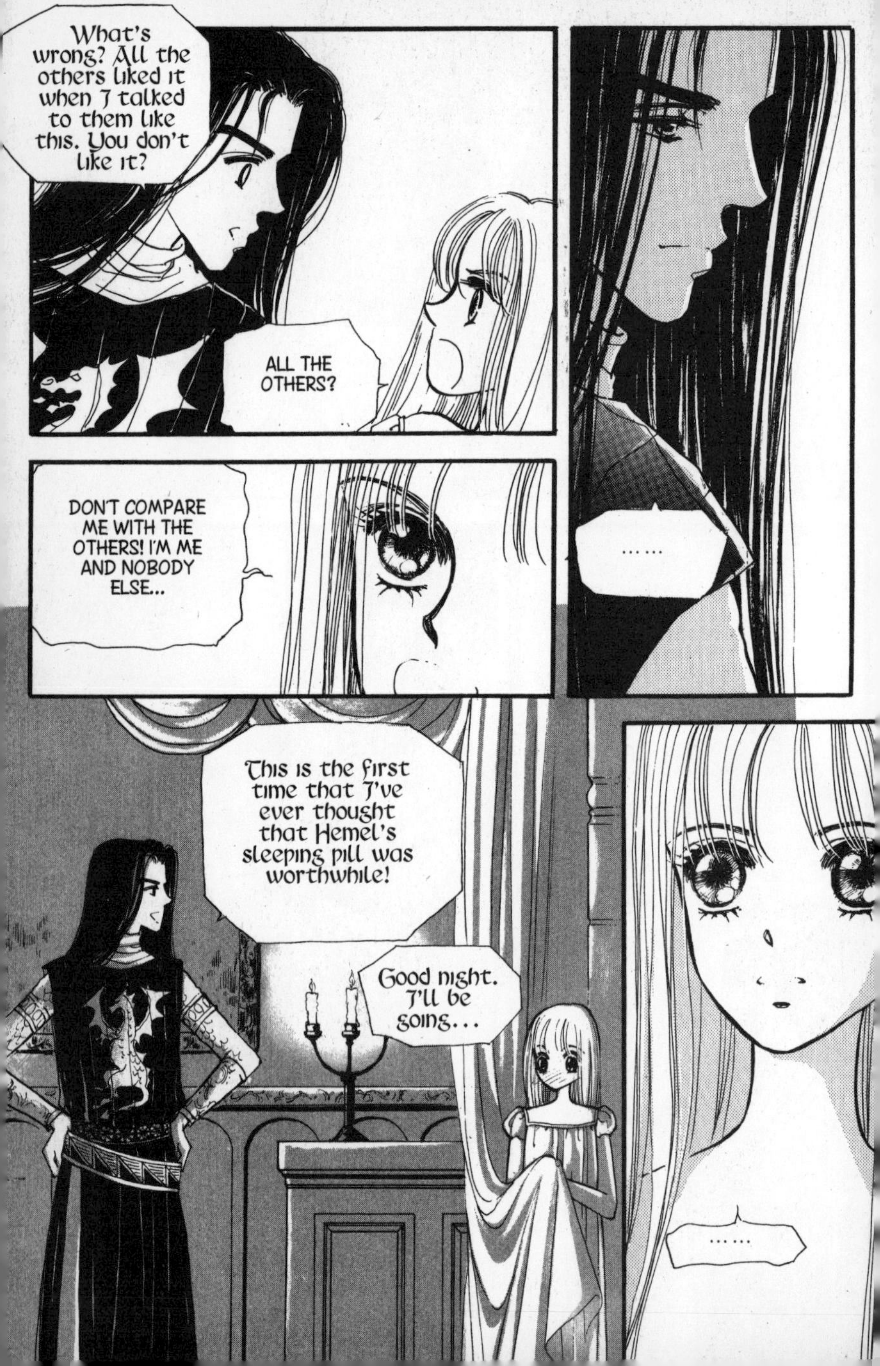
What's wrong? All the others liked it when I talked to them like this. You don't like it?
ALL THE OTHERS?
......
DON'T COMPARE ME WITH THE OTHERS! I'M ME AND NOBODY ELSE...
This is the first time that I've ever thought that Hemel's sleeping pill was worthwhile!
Good night. I'll be going...
......

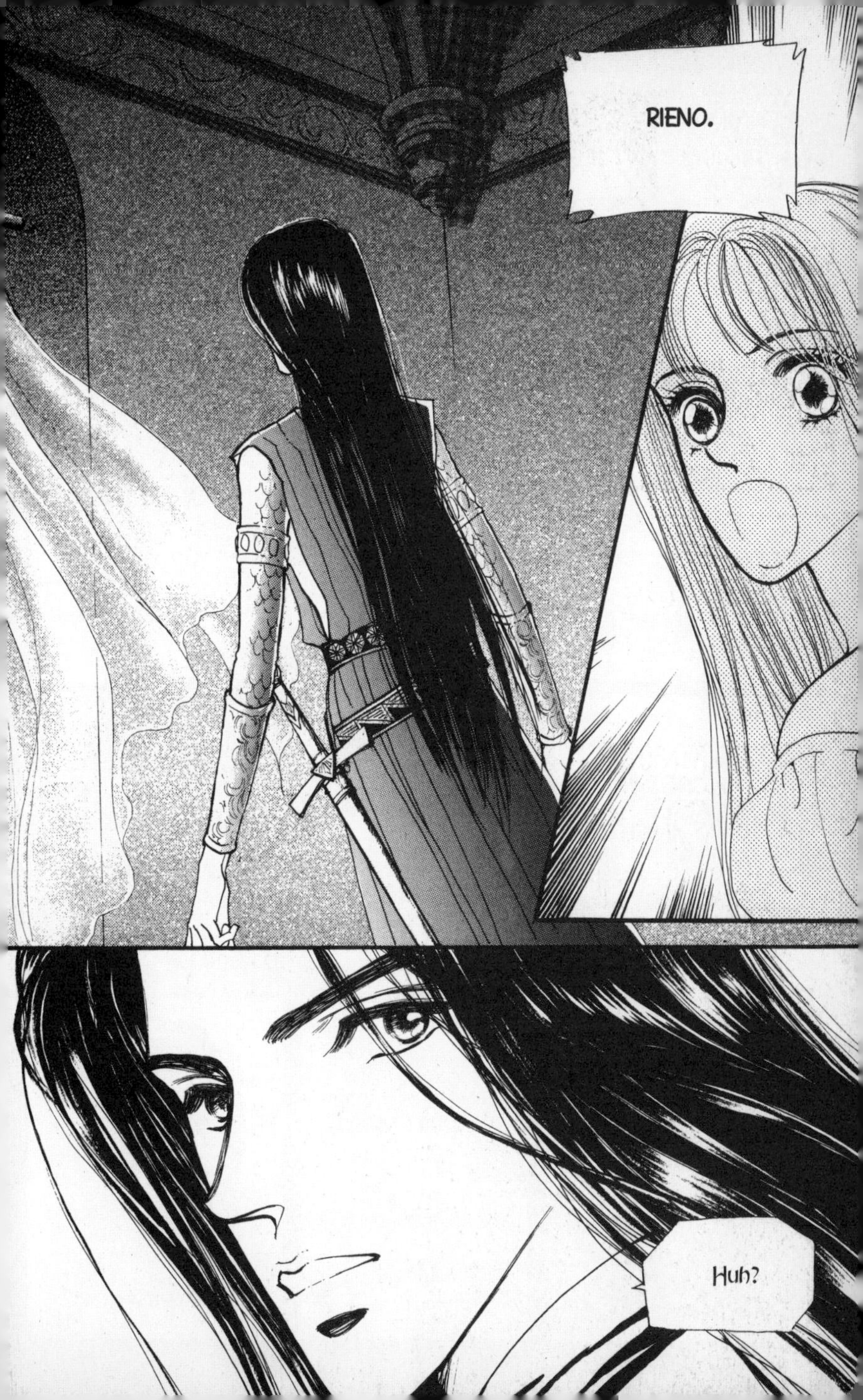
RIENO.
Huh?

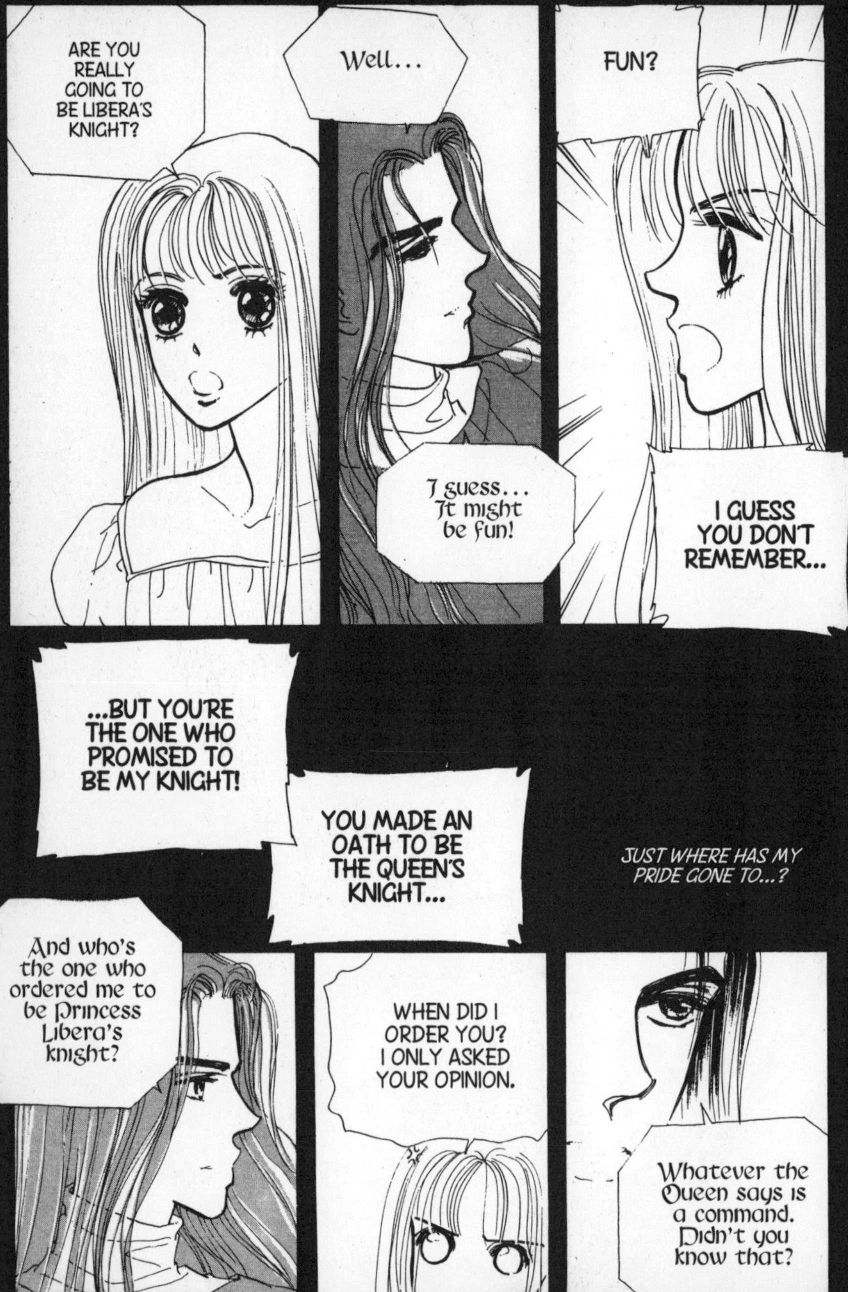
ARE YOU REALLY GOING TO BE LIBERA'S KNIGHT?
Well...
I guess... It might be fun!
FUN?
I GUESS YOU DON'T REMEMBER...
...BUT YOU'RE THE ONE WHO PROMISED TO BE MY KNIGHT!
YOU MADE AN OATH TO BE THE QUEEN'S KNIGHT...
JUST WHERE HAS MY PRIDE GONE TO...?
And who's the one who ordered me to be Princess Libera's knight?
WHEN DID I ORDER YOU? I ONLY ASKED YOUR OPINION.
Whatever the Queen says is a command. Didn't you know that?

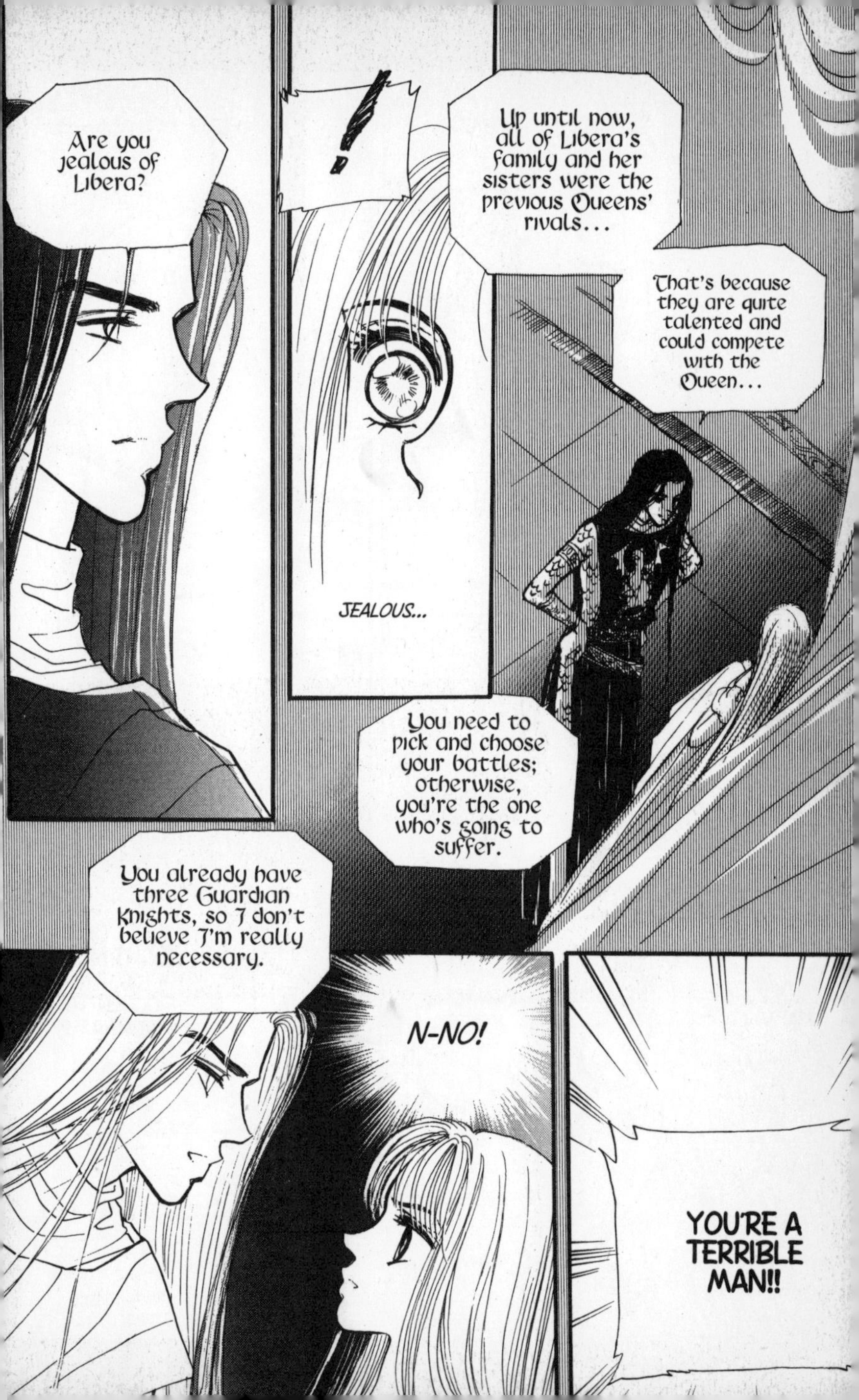
Are you jealous of Libera?
!
JEALOUS...
Up until now, all of Libera's family and her sisters were the previous Queens' rivals...
That's because they are quite talented and could compete with the Queen...
You need to pick and choose your battles; otherwise, you're the one who's going to suffer.
You already have three Guardian Knights, so I don't believe I'm really necessary.
N-NO!
YOU'RE A TERRIBLE MAN!!

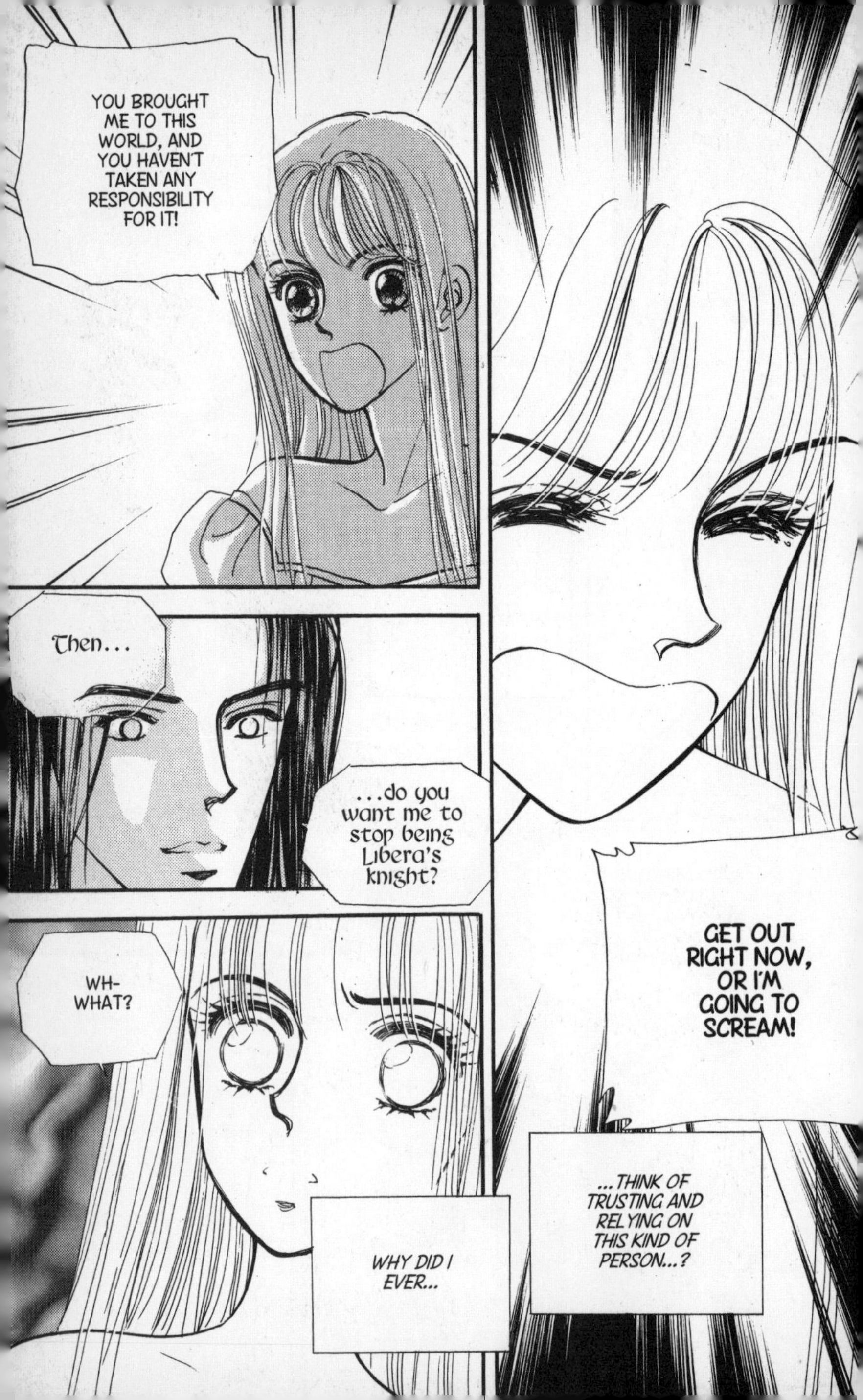
YOU BROUGHT ME TO THIS WORLD, AND YOU HAVEN'T TAKEN ANY RESPONSIBILITY FOR IT!
Then...
...do you want me to stop being Libera's knight?
WH-WHAT?
GET OUT RIGHT NOW, OR I'M GOING TO SCREAM!
WHY DID I EVER...
...THINK OF TRUSTING AND RELYING ON THIS KIND OF PERSON...?

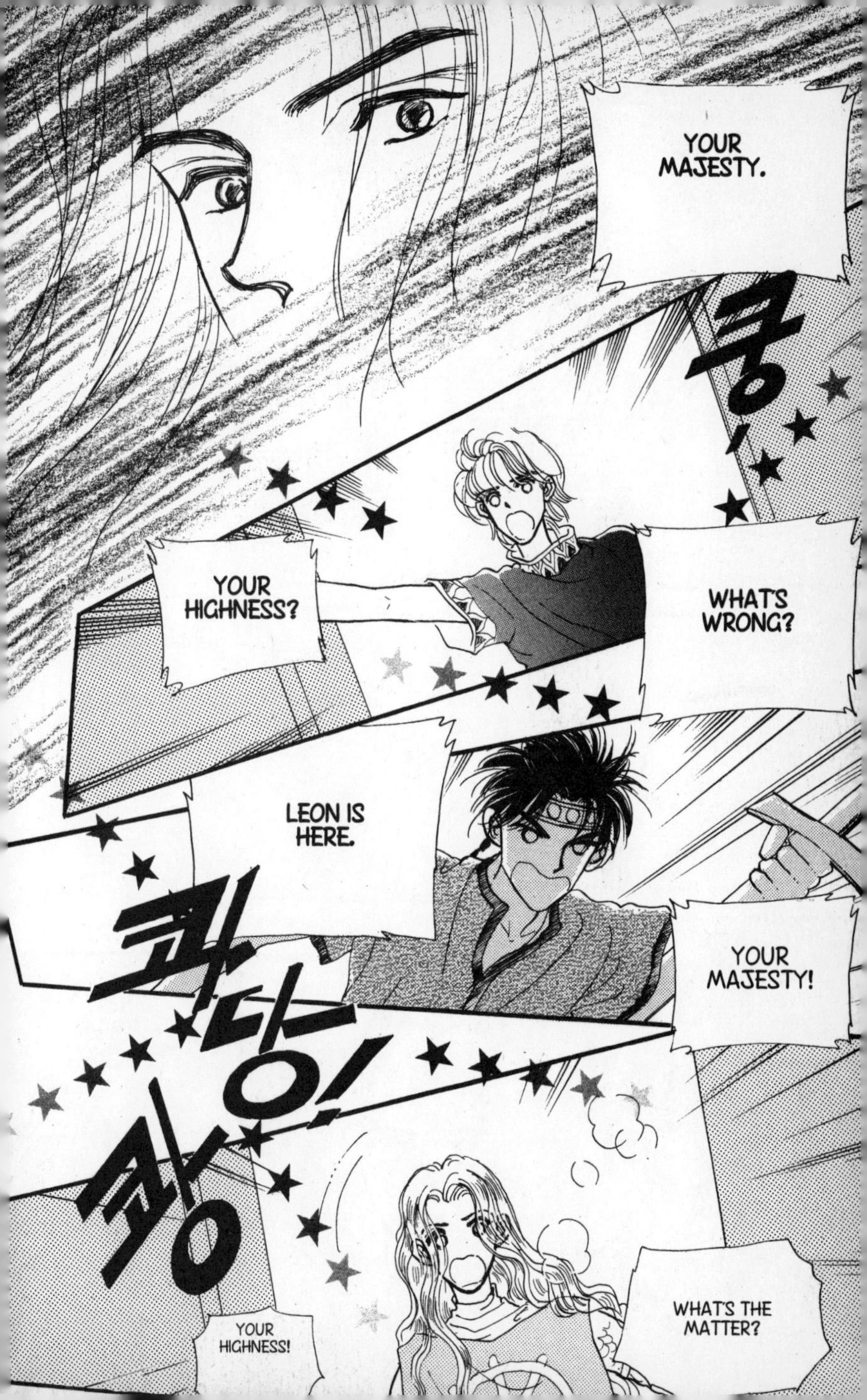
YOUR MAJESTY.
쿵!
YOUR HIGHNESS?
WHAT'S WRONG?
LEON IS HERE.
콰당!
쾅
YOUR MAJESTY!
YOUR HIGHNESS!
WHAT'S THE MATTER?

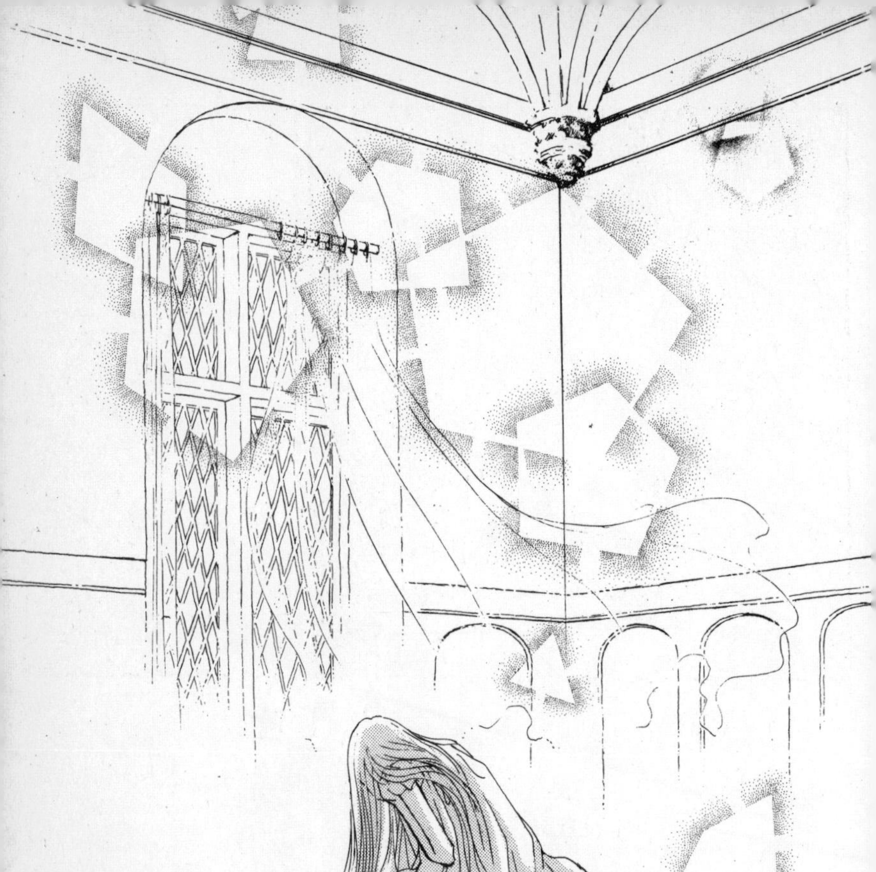

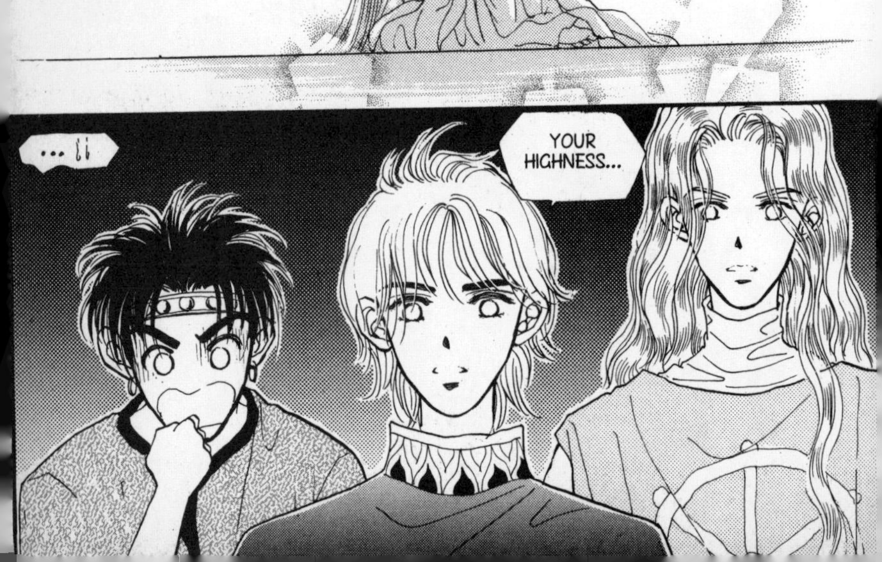
!!...
YOUR HIGHNESS...

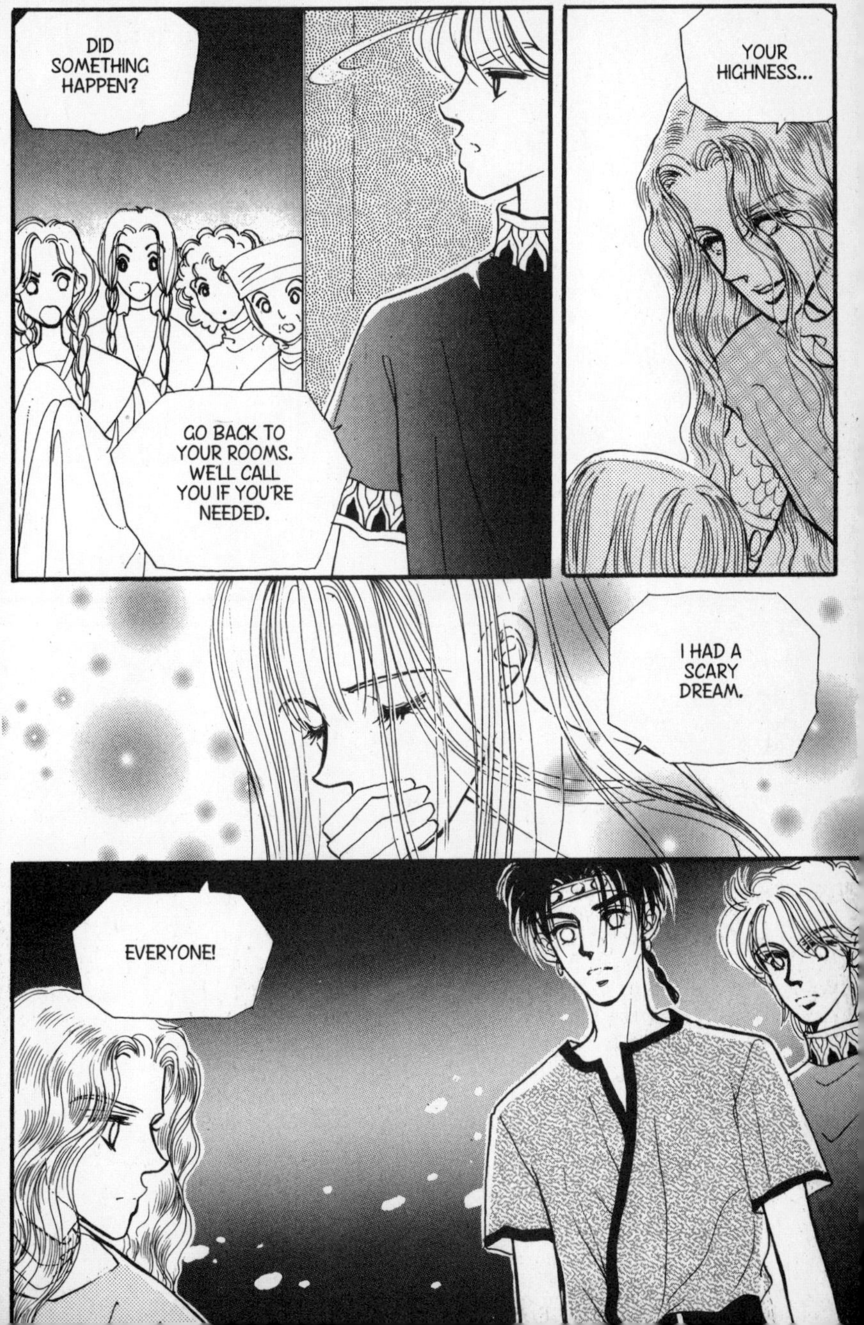
DID SOMETHING HAPPEN?
GO BACK TO YOUR ROOMS. WE'LL CALL YOU IF YOU'RE NEEDED.
YOUR HIGHNESS...
I HAD A SCARY DREAM.
EVERYONE!

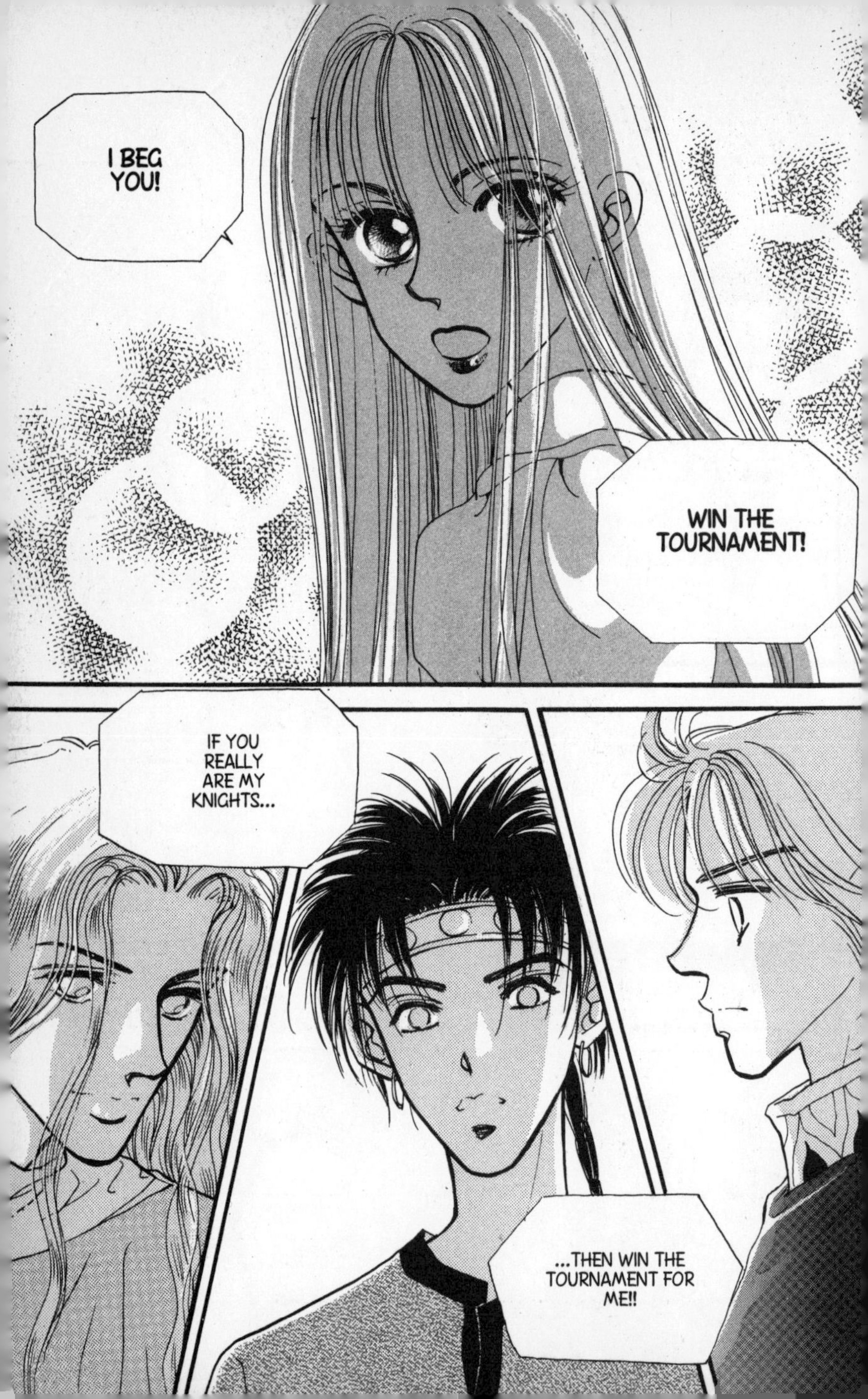
I BEG YOU!
WIN THE TOURNAMENT!
IF YOU REALLY ARE MY KNIGHTS...
...THEN WIN THE TOURNAMENT FOR ME!!

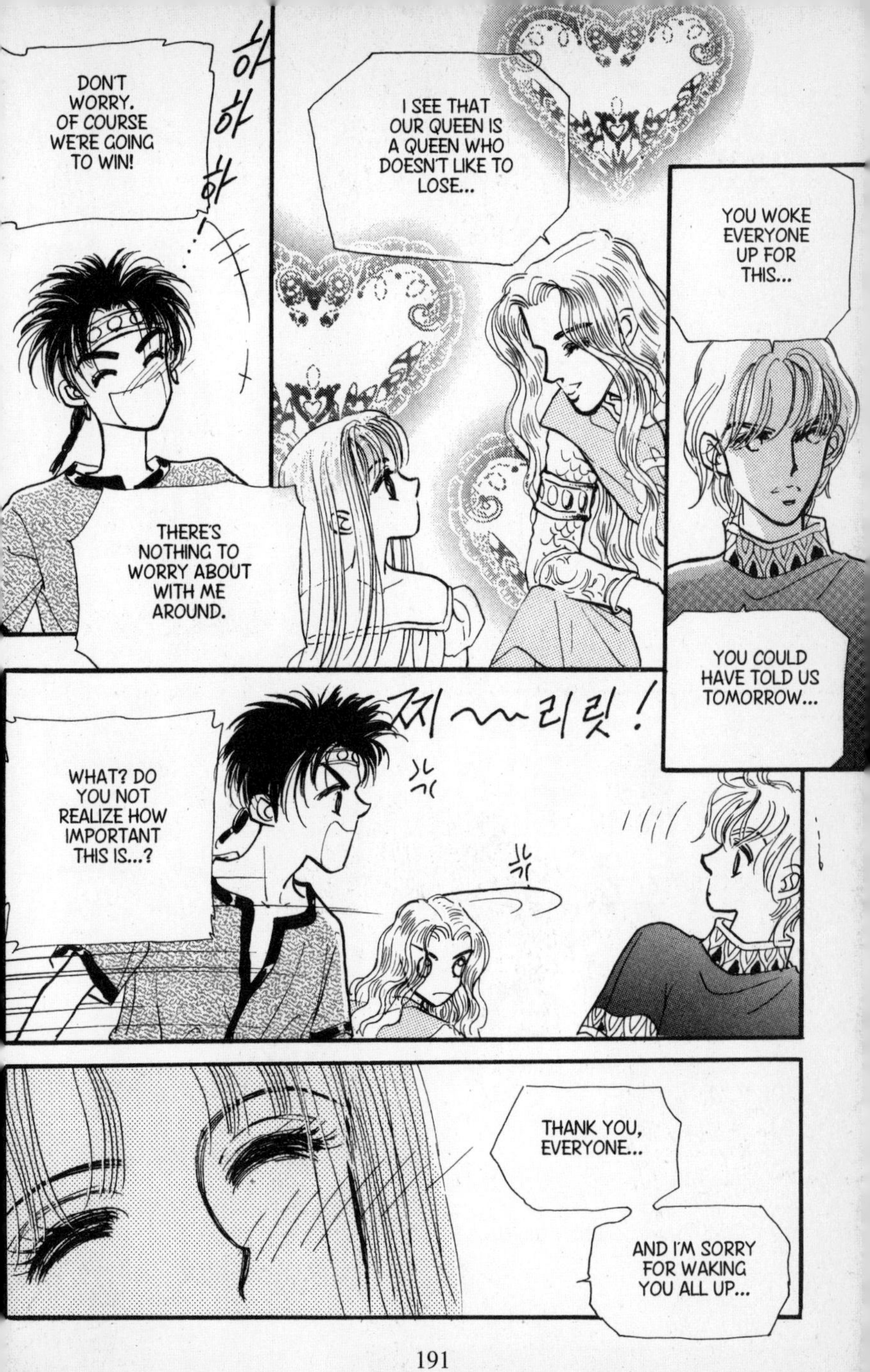
DON'T WORRY. OF COURSE WE'RE GOING TO WIN!
하하하
THERE'S NOTHING TO WORRY ABOUT WITH ME AROUND.
I SEE THAT OUR QUEEN IS A QUEEN WHO DOESN'T LIKE TO LOSE...
YOU WOKE EVERYONE UP FOR THIS...
YOU COULD HAVE TOLD US TOMORROW...
WHAT? DO YOU NOT REALIZE HOW IMPORTANT THIS IS...?
찌~~리릿!
THANK YOU, EVERYONE...
AND I'M SORRY FOR WAKING YOU ALL UP...

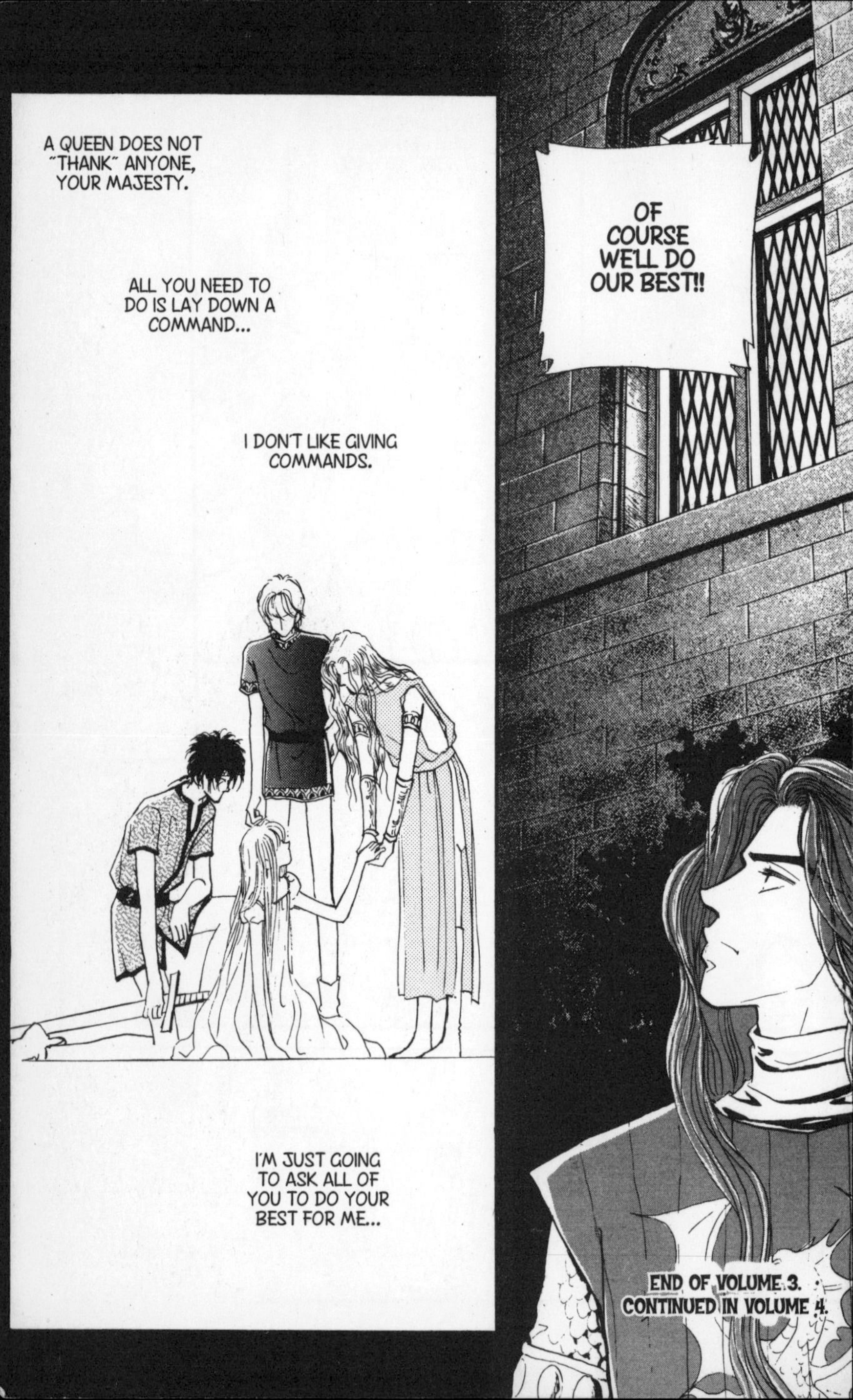
A QUEEN DOES NOT "THANK" ANYONE, YOUR MAJESTY.
ALL YOU NEED TO DO IS LAY DOWN A COMMAND...
I DON'T LIKE GIVING COMMANDS.
I'M JUST GOING TO ASK ALL OF YOU TO DO YOUR BEST FOR ME...
OF COURSE WE'LL DO OUR BEST!!
END OF VOLUME 3.
CONTINUED IN VOLUME 4.

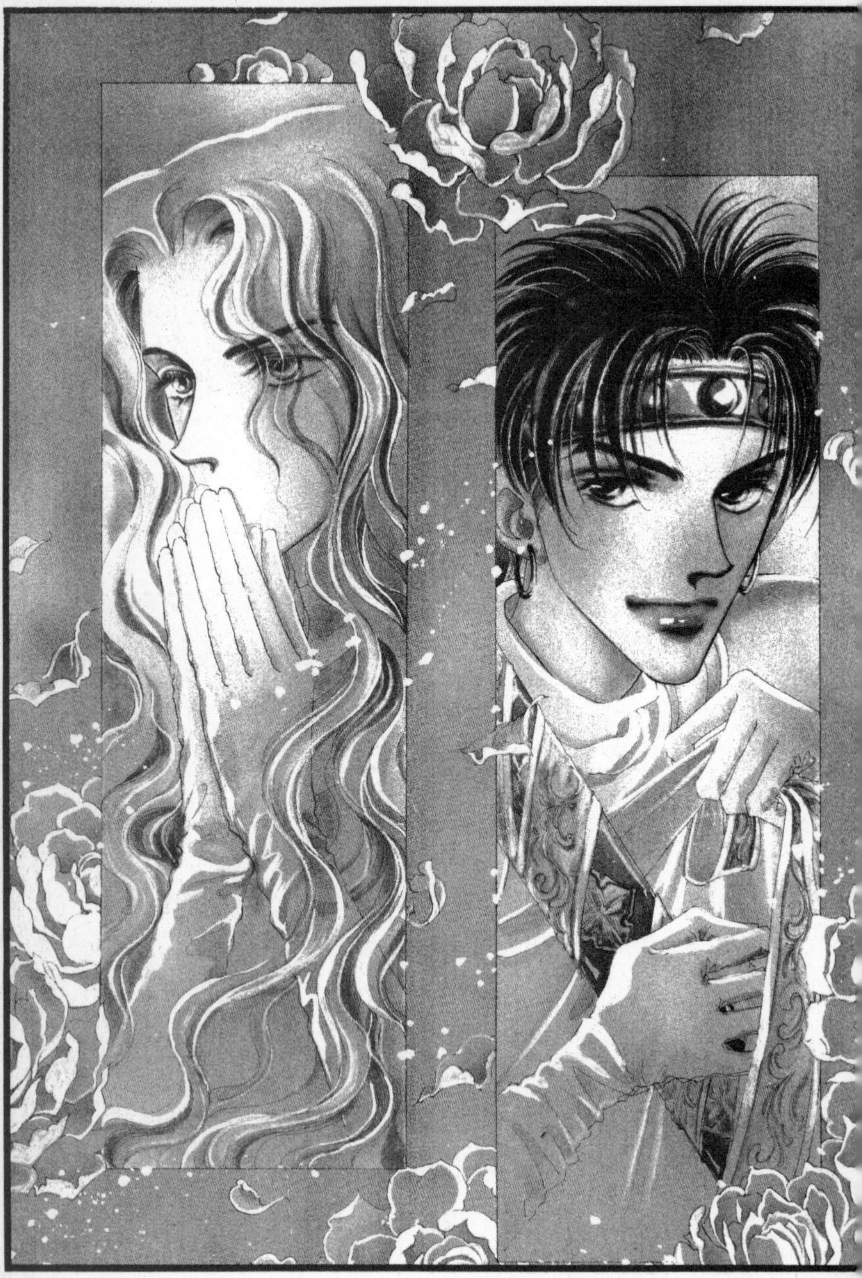

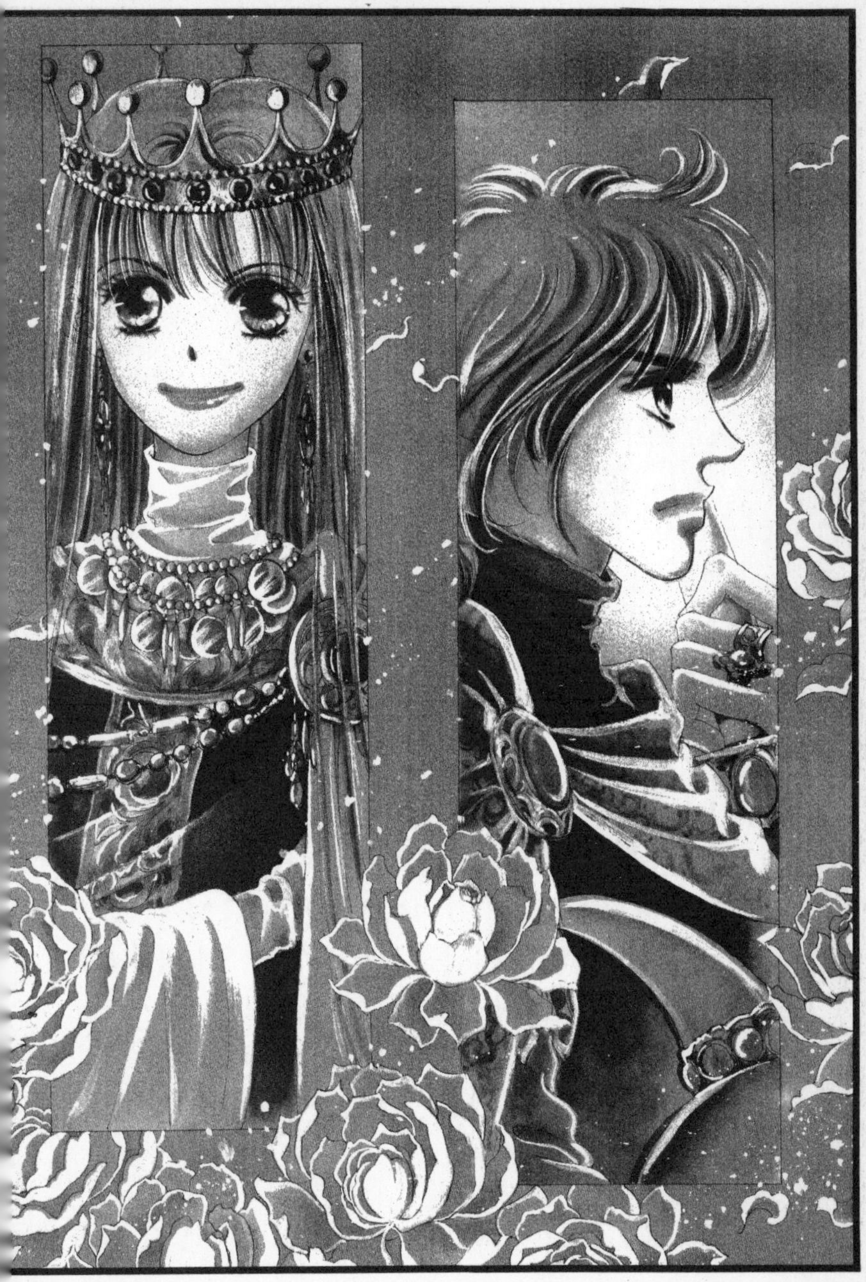

IN THE NEXT VOLUME OF...

THE QUEEN'S KNIGHT

AFTER YUNA'S CORONATION, A TOURNAMENT IS HELD IN CELEBRATION. THE WINNER OF THE TWO-DAY TOURNAMENT WILL BE AWARDED THE TITLE OF "THE KNIGHT OF CORONET" AND GIVEN A FLORAL CORONET. EVEN RIENO, WHO HAS NOT PARTICIPATED IN A TOURNAMENT SINCE THE PREVIOUS QUEEN OF PHANTASMA CALLED FORTH THE ORIGINAL ETERNAL WINTER, JOINS IN. HOWEVER, BEHIND THE SCENES YUNA AND LIBERA MAKE A WAGER ON THE TOURNAMENT-- AND RIENO IS THE PRIZE!

COMING SOON!

TOKYOPOP SHOP

WWW.TOKYOPOP.COM/SHOP

HOT NEWS!
Check out the
TOKYOPOP SHOP!
The world's best
collection of manga in
English is now available
online in one place!

WARCRAFT

SLAYERS MANGA NOVEL

THE TAROT CAFÉ

- LOOK FOR SPECIAL OFFERS
- PRE-ORDER UPCOMING RELEASES!
- COMPLETE YOUR COLLECTIONS

SOKORA REFUGEES

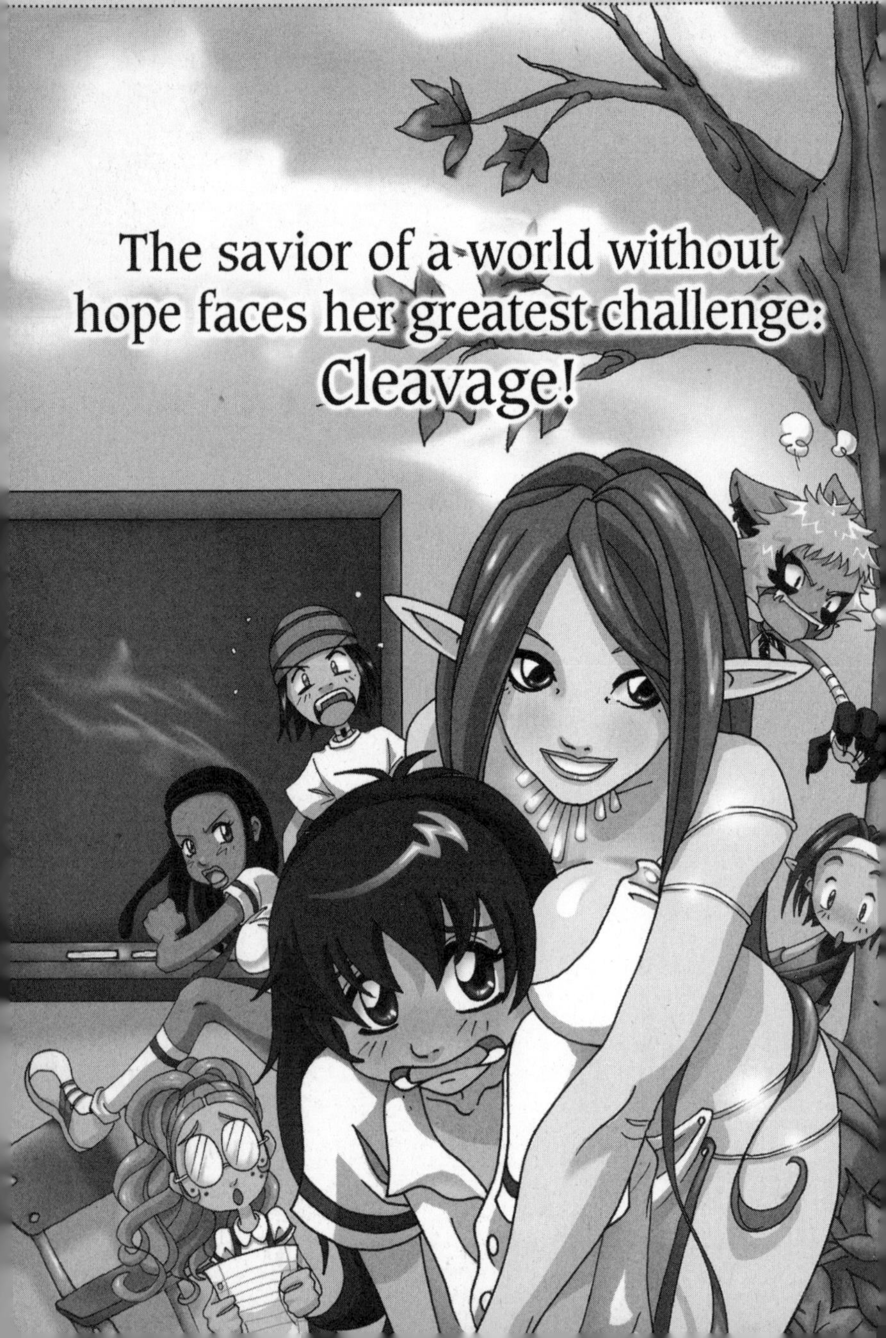
The savior of a world without hope faces her greatest challenge:
Cleavage!

SOKORA REFUGEES™

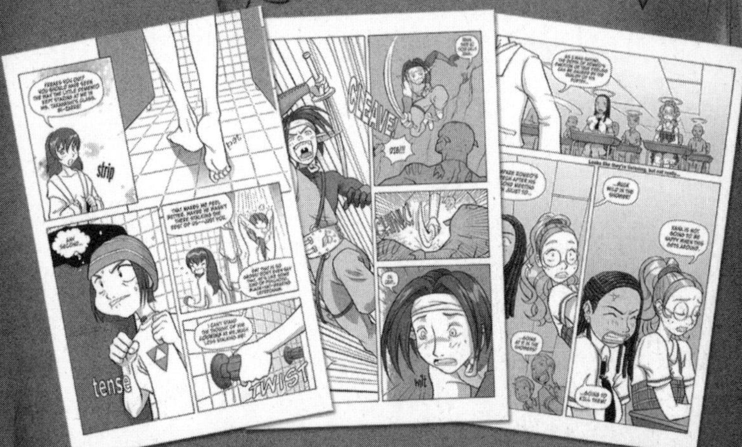
strip
pat
tense
TWIST
CLEAVE!
wet

Kana thought life couldn't get any worse—behind on her schoolwork and out of luck with boys, she is also the only one of her friends who hasn't "blossomed." When she falls through a magical portal in the girls' shower, she's transported to the enchanted world of Sokora—wearing nothing but a small robe! Now, on top of landing in this mysterious setting, she finds that her body is beginning to go through some tremendous changes.

Preview the manga at:
www.TOKYOPOP.com/sokora

T
TEEN
AGE 13+

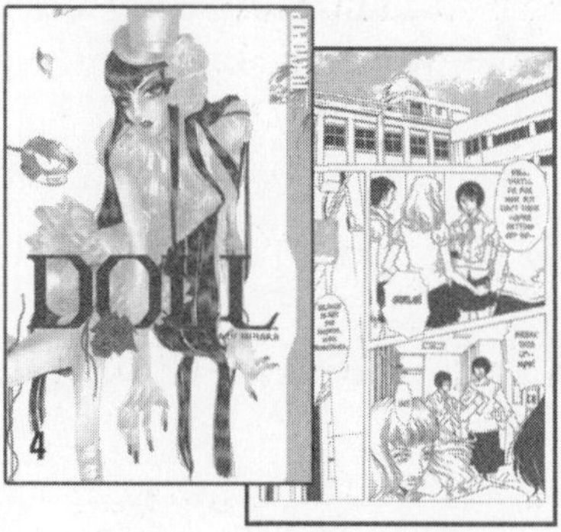
DOLL
4

BY MITSUKAZU MIHARA

DOLL

Mitsukazu Mihara's haunting *Doll* uses beautiful androids to examine what it means to be truly human. While the characters in *Doll* are draped in the chic Gothic-Lolita fashions that made Mihara-sensei famous, the themes explored are more universal—all emotions and walks of life have their day in *Doll*. *Doll* begins as a series of 'one-shot' stories and gradually dovetails into an epic of emotion and intrigue. It's like the *Twilight Zone* meets *Blade Runner!*

~Rob Tokar, Senior Editor

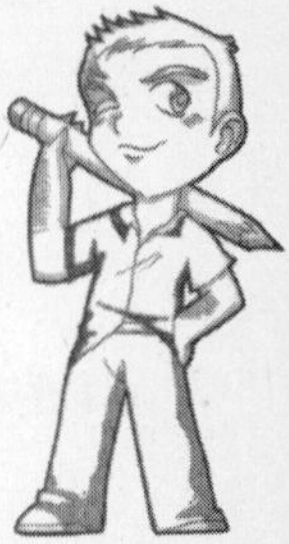

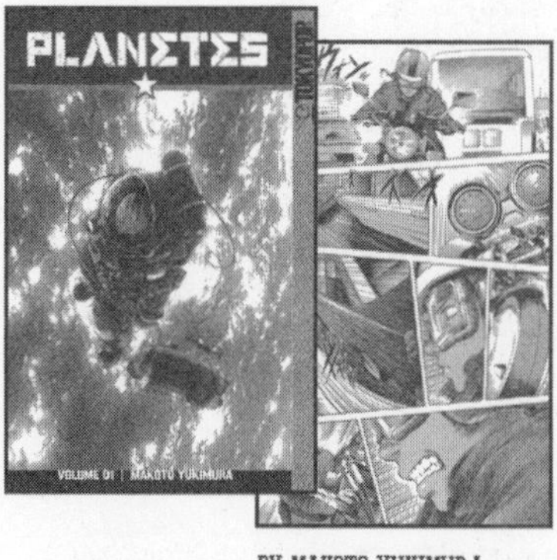
PLANETES
VOLUME 01 | MAKOTO YUKIMURA

BY MAKOTO YUKIMURA

PLANETES

Makoto Yukimura's profoundly moving and graphically arresting *Planetes* posits a near future where mankind's colonization of space has begun. Young Hachimaki yearns to join this exciting new frontier. Instead, he cleans the glut of orbital junk mankind's initial foray into space produced. He works with Fee, a nicotine-addict beauty with an abrasive edge, and Yuri, a veteran spaceman with a tragic past in search of inner peace. *Planetes* combines the scope of Jules Verne (*Around the World in Eighty Days*) and Robert Heinlein (*Starship Troopers*) with the philosophical wonder of *2001: A Space Odyssey.*

~Luis Reyes, Editor

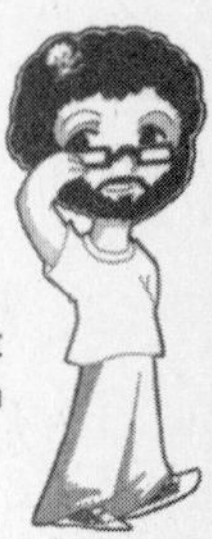

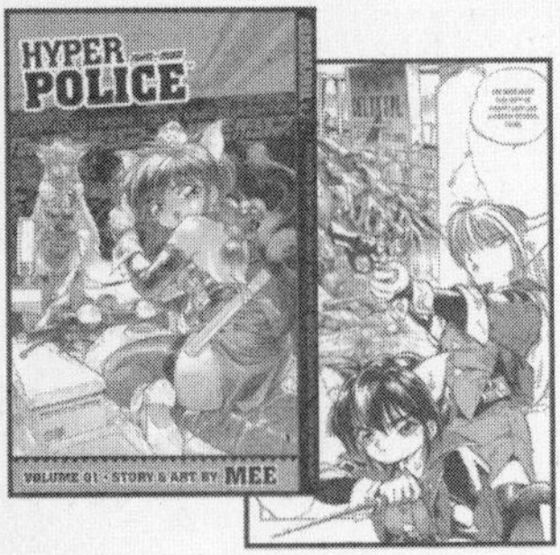
HYPER
POLICE
VOLUME 01 · STORY & ART BY MEE

HYPER POLICE

BY MEE

In a future rife with crime, humans are an endangered species—and monsters have taken over! Natsuki is a cat girl who uses magical powers to enforce the law. However, her greatest threat doesn't come from the criminals. Her partner Sakura, a "nine-tailed" fox, plots to eat Natsuki and gobble up her magic! In this dog-eat-dog world, Natsuki fights to stay on top!

OT
OLDER TEEN
AGE 16+

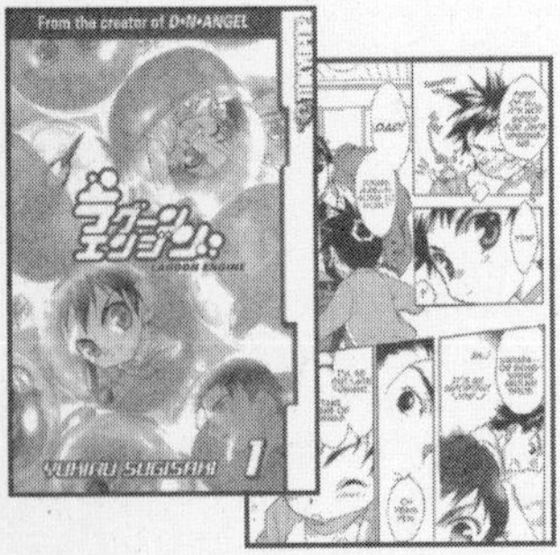
From the creator of D•N•ANGEL
YUKIRU SUGISAKI 1

LAGOON ENGINE

BY YUKIRU SUGISAKI

From the best-selling creator of *D·N·Angel!*

Yen and Jin are brothers in elementary school—and successors in the Ragun family craft. They are Gakushi, those who battle ghosts and evil spirits known as "Maga" by guessing their true name. As Yen and Jin train to join the family business, the two boys must keep their identities a secret...or risk death!

T
TEEN
AGE 13+

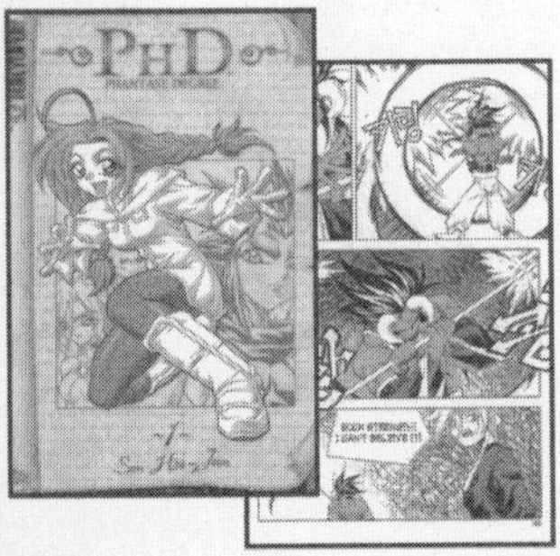
PHD

PHD: PHANTASY DEGREE

BY HEE-JOON SON

Sang is a fearlessly spunky young girl who is about to receive one hell of an education...at the Demon School Hades! She's on a mission to enroll into the monsters-only class. However, monster matriculation is not what is truly on her mind—she wants to acquire the fabled "King's Ring" from the fiancée of the chief commander of hell!

T
TEEN
AGE 13+

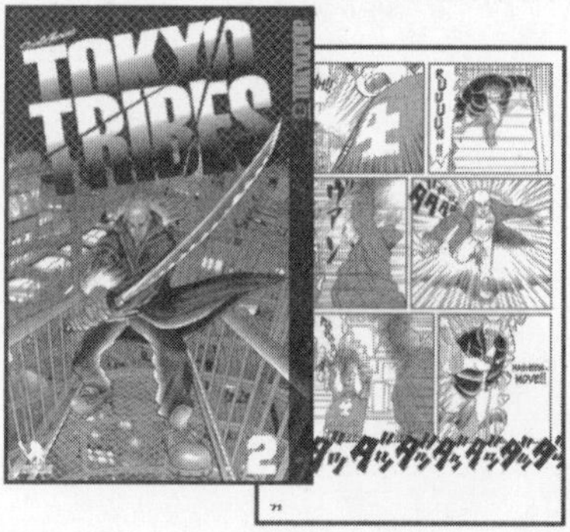
TOKYO TRIBES
2

BY SANTA INOUE

TOKYO TRIBES

Tokyo Tribes first hit Japanese audiences in the sleek pages of the ultra-hip skater fashion magazine *Boon*. Santa Inoue's hard-hitting tale of Tokyo street gangs battling it out in the concrete sprawl of Japan's capital raises the manga storytelling bar. Ornate with hip-hop trappings and packed with gangland grit, *Tokyo Tribes* paints a vivid, somewhat surreal vision of urban youth: rival gangs from various Tokyo barrios clash over turf, and when the heat between two of the tribes gets personal, a bitter rivalry explodes into all-out warfare.

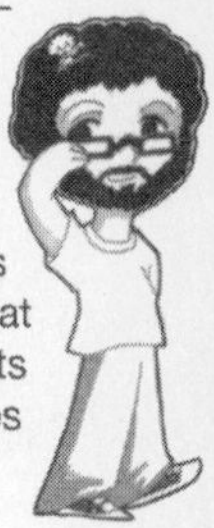

~Luis Reyes, Editor

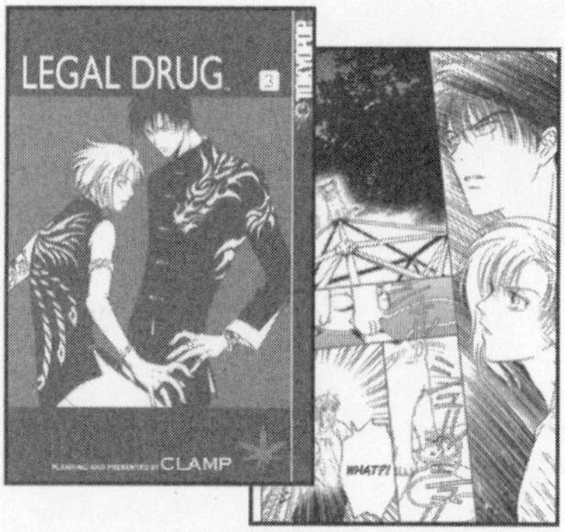
LEGAL DRUG
3
CLAMP
WHAT?!

BY CLAMP

LEGAL DRUG

CLAMP is the four-woman studio famous for creating much of the world's most popular manga. For the past 15 years they have produced such hits as the adorable *Cardcaptor Sakura,* the dark and brooding *Tokyo Babylon,* and the sci-fi romantic comedy *Chobits.* In *Legal Drug,* we meet Kazahaya and Rikuou, two ordinary pharmacists who moonlight as amateur sleuths for a mysterious boss. *Legal Drug* is a perfect dose of mystery, psychic powers and the kind of homoerotic tension for which CLAMP is renowned.

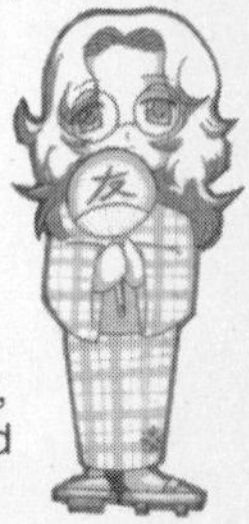

~Lillian Diaz-Przybyl, Jr. Editor

Dear Diary,
I'm starting to feel

When a young girl moves to the forgotten town of Bizenghast, she uncovers a terrifying collection of lost souls that leads her to the brink of insanity. One thing becomes painfully clear: The residents of Bizenghast are just dying to come home. © 2005 Mary Alice LeGrow. All Rights Reserved.

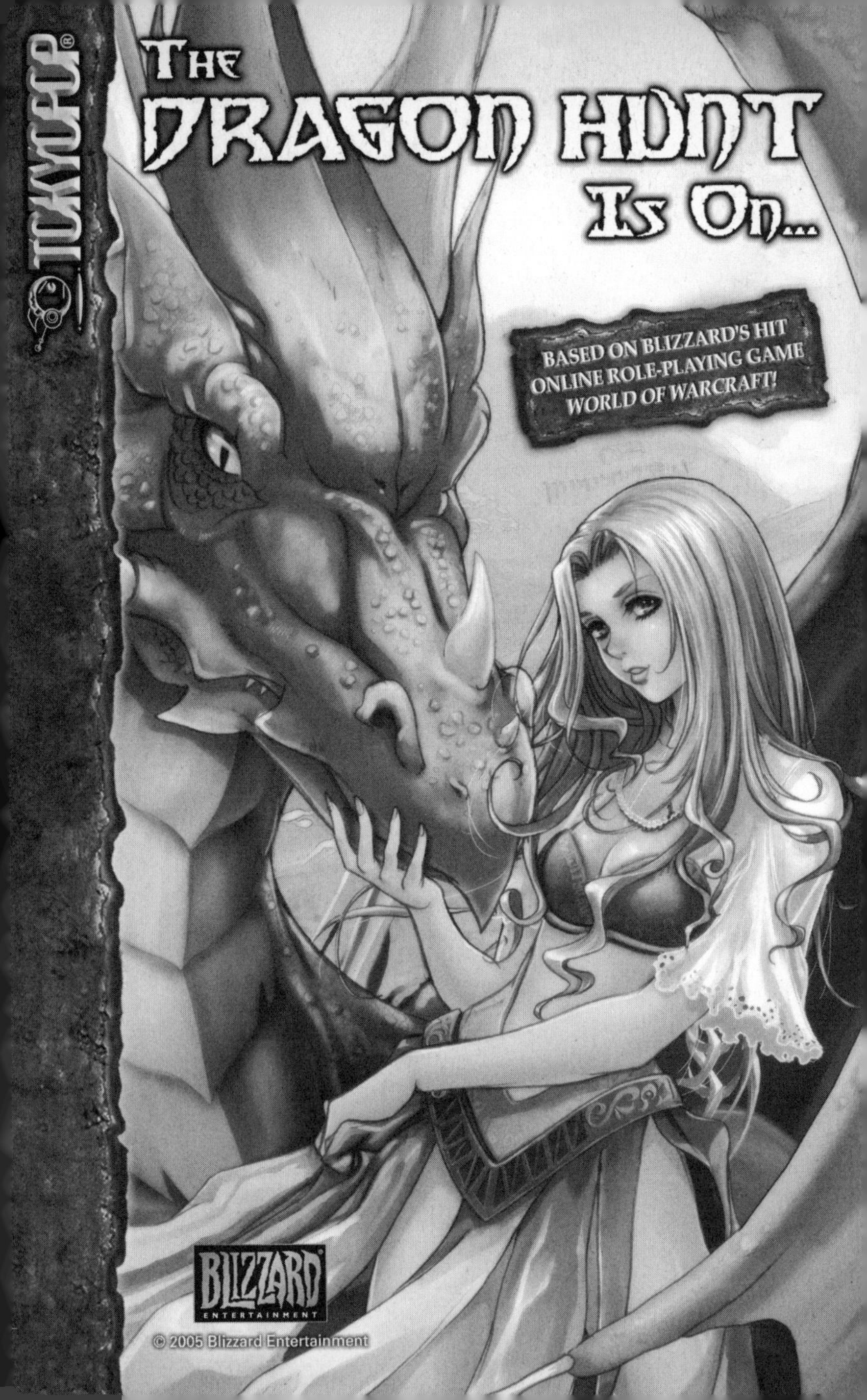
TOKYOPOP®
The Dragon Hunt Is On...
BASED ON BLIZZARD'S HIT ONLINE ROLE-PLAYING GAME WORLD OF WARCRAFT!
BLIZZARD® ENTERTAINMENT
© 2005 Blizzard Entertainment

WarCraft
THE SUNWELL TRILOGY

RICHARD A. KNAAK · KIM JAE-HWAN

From the artist of the
best-selling *King of Hell* series!

It's an epic quest to save the entire High Elven Kingdom from the forces of the Undead Scourge! Set in the mystical world of Azeroth, *Warcraft: The Sunwell Trilogy* chronicles the adventures of Kalec, a blue dragon who has taken human form to escape deadly forces, and Anveena, a beautiful young maiden with a mysterious power.

T
TEEN
AGE 13+

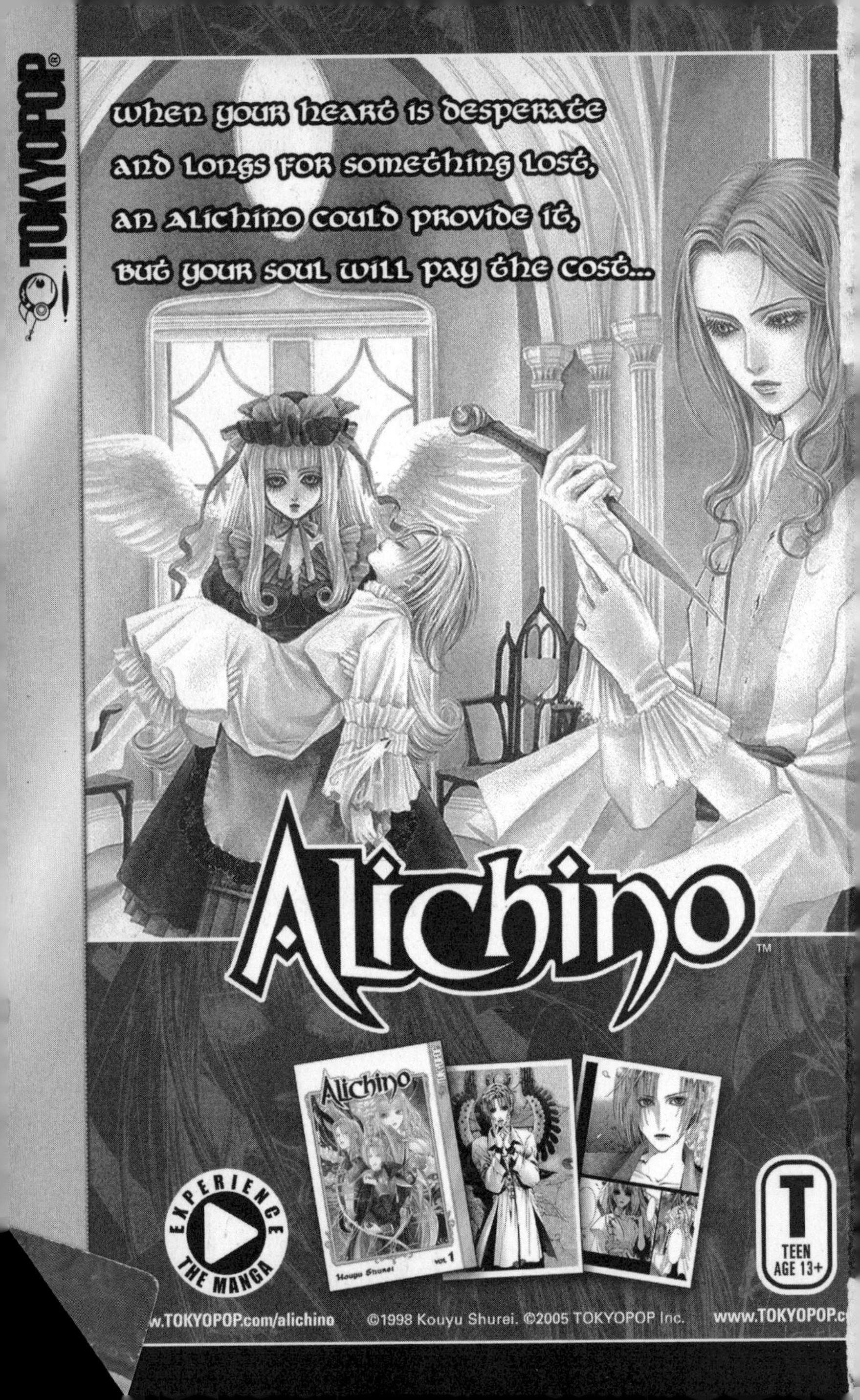
TOKYOPOP®
when your heart is desperate
and longs for something lost,
an alichino could provide it,
but your soul will pay the cost...
Alichino™
Alichino
Kouyu Shurei
VOL 1
EXPERIENCE THE MANGA
T
TEEN
AGE 13+
w.TOKYOPOP.com/alichino
©1998 Kouyu Shurei. ©2005 TOKYOPOP Inc.
www.TOKYOPOP.c